ON THE DOORPOSTS
OF YOUR HOUSE

על מזזות ביתך

Edited by Chaim Stern

with

Donna Berman
Edward Graham
H. Leonard Poller

Central Conference of American Rabbis
5755 New York 1994

CCAR Press, 355 Lexington Avenue, New York, NY 10017

Produced at Nostradamus Advertising by Wendy Wolf and Warren Wolfsohn.

06 05 04 03   10 9 8 7

Library of Congress Cataloging-in-Publication Data

['Al mezuzot betekha] = On the doorposts of your house : prayers and ceremonies
   for the Jewish home.
     p.   cm.
   Includes bibliographical references and index.
   ISBN 0-88123-043-X
   1. Reform Judaism—Prayer-books and devotions—English.   2. Reform
Judaism—Prayer-books and devotions—Hebrew.   I. Central Conference of American Rabbis.   II. Benedictions (Reform, Central Conference of American Rabbis).   1993.   III. Title: On the doorposts of your house.
BM665.C65 1993
296.4—dc20   93-24005
                                                  CIP

DESIGNED BY   *Barry Nostradamus Sher*

Dedicated to
Rabbi H. Leonard Poller

Publication of this book was made possible largely due to the generous contributions of admiring and grateful congregants and friends of Rabbi H. Leonard Poller of Larchmont Temple, Larchmont, New York: on the eve of his retirement after two decades as the beloved spiritual leader of the congregation and highly respected rabbi in the community.

This dedication is also a tribute by the Central Conference of American Rabbis in esteem and gratitude for his having served as Chairman of the Liturgy Committee of the Conference from 1986 to 1994. During that time, fourteen publications of a liturgical nature were produced, each one of which bears the imprint of Rabbi Poller's impeccable judgment and elegant style. He literally co-authored some, initiated others and broke down "writer's block" in yet others. A man of deep faith, he was a natural leader in such a prayerful enterprise. His concern for the well-being of the Conference was always paramount, while yet insisting unyieldingly on nothing less than excellence.

Contents

CONTENTS

Introduction

The Central Conference of American Rabbis presents *Al Mezuzot Beitecha, On the Doorposts of Your House: The Newly Revised Union Home Prayerbook.* Like its predecessor—*Shaarei Habayit, Gates of the House*—it carries forward our intention to provide for the Jewish community a liturgy for the individual and the family, as well as for the synagogue and the worshipping congregation.

This volume is, in part, a revision of *Gates of the House,* but it has been given a new name because it is more than that: it is an expansion that adds substance and a new outlook, so that 'Doorposts' is to a considerable degree a new creation.

The language of this volume is gender-sensitive. God is not referred to exclusively in masculine language.

Where it seemed necessary, we have revised the old; and we have added much that is new.

Included are prayers for pregnancy, for a Bar or Bat Mitzvah, and for some of the more painful events in life: times of anxiety, the death of a child, the termination of a pregnancy, and the like. We have, in addition, included all the main benedictions of the wedding service, the psalms that are generally read at a time of bereavement, prayers and meditations for the chronically ill, for the entire period of mourning *(Shiv'ah).* To the Weekday Services we have added one for the afternoon, and we have devised a cycle of daily worship for private prayer. We have greatly expanded the selections of readings for reflection and inspiration, adding passages from the Talmud, readings for reflection and study, selections from Pirkei Avot, and enlarging the selection of poems. For more detailed information, we refer the reader to the Notes.

We urge all who look into this book to consider the individual prayers, or many of them, at least, in a wider context: as part of rituals that they may want to establish in their own personal, family, and communal lives. Such rituals are coming into being even now; some may be ephemeral, but some may take root among our people and become part of our people's sacred times. Through our own observances, we can help discover which rituals may have a lasting value for us.

These words from the concluding paragraph of the Introduction to *Gates of the House* can, with little modification, serve us still. *On the Doorposts of Your House* 'expresses in contemporary terms the classic themes of Judaism. We pray that it will contribute to the further development of the spiritual life of the House of Israel. If our labors lead to a growing love of God, Israel, and Torah, we shall rejoice. May our homes always be miniature sanctuaries, enclaves of holiness where the distressed may find refuge, the weary find strength, and all who enter, peace.'

אם־יהוה לא יבנה בית, שוא עמלו בוניו בו.

CHAIM STERN

Chappaqua, New York
ערב שבת קדש 'וישב' תשנ'ג
23 Kislev 5753

A Note on Usage

This volume is intended primarily for the home, though it will be quite useful for travelers. It may also be used in the synagogue as a source of supplementary readings and prayers.

The typeface is intended to suggest how group worship might be conducted. In place of the conventional rubrics, 'Reader,' and 'All Reading,' we employ Roman type for 'Reader' and italics for 'All Reading' (and transliteration). Families and groups assembled for worship may of course choose to experiment with different patterns. We have chosen not to use a special typeface for 'Singing,' leaving it to individual and group decision.

The ° character indicates English texts that are not translations but variations on the theme of the Hebrew.

The ⟨ character indicates a *kamatz katan,* pronounced like the *o* in "often."

Prayers and Readings for Every Day

FOR EVERY DAY

Evening and morning prayers for children

Evening Prayer

Creator of day and night, thank You for this good world. Thank You for the day. I was so busy! Now I am tired, and I thank You for sleep.

Bless my family and friends, all those I love, all who love me. May my dreams be pleasant, and may I wake up with a smile, ready for the new day.

For all that I have learned this day, I thank and praise You. So each day I say:

שְׁמַע יִשְׂרָאֵל: יהוה אֱלֹהֵינוּ יהוה אֶחָד!

**Hear, O Israel: the Eternal One is our God,
the Eternal God alone!**

בָּרוּךְ שֵׁם כְּבוֹד מַלְכוּתוֹ לְעוֹלָם וָעֶד!

Blessed is God's glorious majesty for ever and ever!

❧ *Continue with V'ahavta on page 5.*

Morning Prayer

FOR BOYS

Mo-deh a-ni l'fa-neh-cha...   מוֹדֶה אֲנִי לְפָנֶיךָ...

FOR GIRLS

Mo-dah a-ni l'fa-neh-cha...   מוֹדָה אֲנִי לְפָנֶיךָ...

FOR BOTH

Thank You, God, for the new day. I hope it will be a day for learning, laughing, playing. Thank You for the love of my family and for the beautiful world which has awakened with me.

Today I hope to show my love for my parents and all my family, to be kind to my friends, and to be gentle with animals. For the power to grow, I give thanks. So each day I say:

שְׁמַע יִשְׂרָאֵל: יהוה אֱלֹהֵֽינוּ יהוה אֶחָד!

**Hear, O Israel: the Eternal One is our God,
the Eternal God alone!**

בָּרוּךְ שֵׁם כְּבוֹד מַלְכוּתוֹ לְעוֹלָם וָעֶד!

Blessed is God's glorious majesty for ever and ever!

❧ *Continue with V'ahavta on page 5.*

Evening and morning prayers for adults

Evening Prayer

God of the light and of the dark, You make my lids grow heavy; Your touch unseen brings sleep upon my eyes. Grant that I may lie down in peace, and let me rise up to life renewed. Let Your majesty and beauty be in my thought at the day's end, and at the moment of my awakening.

May angels' wings shelter me all through the night; be at my side, and let Your sheltering peace descend on me, on my dear ones, and on all Your children.

בְּיָדוֹ אַפְקִיד רוּחִי, בְּעֵת אִישַׁן וְאָעִֽירָה, וְעִם רוּחִי גְוִיָּתִי; יי לִי, וְלֹא אִירָא.

Into Your hands I commend my body and my spirit, both when I sleep and when I wake. In Your presence I cast off fear and lie down to rest and sleep.

שְׁמַע יִשְׂרָאֵל: יהוה אֱלֹהֵֽינוּ יהוה אֶחָד!

**Hear, O Israel: the Eternal One is our God,
the Eternal God alone!**

בָּרוּךְ שֵׁם כְּבוֹד מַלְכוּתוֹ לְעוֹלָם וָעֶד!

Blessed is God's glorious majesty for ever and ever!

❧ *V'ahavta, page 5, may be recited here.*

Morning Prayer

Praised be the Eternal God, who has awakened me to the new day, called me to be free, and formed me in the Divine Image. Blessed is the One who opens the eyes of the blind, who provides clothes for the naked, who brings freedom to the captive, and whose power lifts up the fallen.

Eternal One, Sovereign God of the universe: You remove sleep from the eyes, slumber from the eyelids. Help me to be awake this day to the wonders that surround me, alive to beauty and love and aware that all being is precious, that, wherever we go, we walk on holy ground.

שְׁמַע יִשְׂרָאֵל: יהוה אֱלֹהֵינוּ יהוה אֶחָד!

**Hear, O Israel: the Eternal One is our God,
the Eternal God alone!**

בָּרוּךְ שֵׁם כְּבוֹד מַלְכוּתוֹ לְעוֹלָם וָעֶד!

Blessed is God's glorious majesty for ever and ever!

V'AHAVTA

V'a-hav-ta et Adonai eh-lo-heh-cha	וְאָהַבְתָּ אֵת יהוה אֱלֹהֶיךָ
b'chol l'va-v'cha u-v'chol naf-sh'cha	בְּכָל־לְבָבְךָ וּבְכָל־נַפְשְׁךָ
u-v'chol m'o-deh-cha. V'ha-yu	וּבְכָל־מְאֹדֶךָ: וְהָיוּ
ha-d'va-rim ha-ei-leh a-sher a-no-chi	הַדְּבָרִים הָאֵלֶּה אֲשֶׁר אָנֹכִי
m'tza-v'cha ha-yom al l'va-veh-cha.	מְצַוְּךָ הַיּוֹם עַל־לְבָבֶךָ:
V'shi-nan-tam l'va-neh-cha	וְשִׁנַּנְתָּם לְבָנֶיךָ
v'di-bar-ta bam b'shiv-t'cha	וְדִבַּרְתָּ בָּם בְּשִׁבְתְּךָ
b'vei-teh-cha u-v'lech-t'cha	בְּבֵיתֶךָ וּבְלֶכְתְּךָ
va-deh-rech u-v'shoch-b'cha	בַדֶּרֶךְ וּבְשָׁכְבְּךָ
u-v'ku-meh-cha. U-k'shar-tam l'ot	וּבְקוּמֶךָ: וּקְשַׁרְתָּם לְאוֹת
al ya-deh-cha v'ha-yu l'to-ta-fot bein	עַל־יָדֶךָ וְהָיוּ לְטֹטָפֹת בֵּין
ei-neh-cha; u-ch'tav-tam al m'zu-zot	עֵינֶיךָ: וּכְתַבְתָּם עַל־מְזֻזֹת
bei-teh-cha u-vi-sh'a-reh-cha.	בֵּיתֶךָ וּבִשְׁעָרֶיךָ:

5

You shall love Your Eternal God with all your heart, with all your mind, with all your being. Set these words, which I command you this day, upon your heart. Teach them faithfully to your children; speak of them in your home and on your way, when you lie down and when you rise up. Bind them as a sign upon your hand; let them be a symbol before your eyes; inscribe them on the doorposts of your house, and on your gates.

L'ma-an tiz-k'ru va-a-si-tem	לְמַעַן תִּזְכְּרוּ וַעֲשִׂיתֶם
et kol mitz-vo-tai, vi-h'yi-tem	אֶת־כָּל־מִצְוֹתָי וִהְיִיתֶם
k'do-shim lei-lo-hei-chem. Ani	קְדֹשִׁים לֵאלֹהֵיכֶם: אֲנִי
Adonai Eh-lo-hei-chem a-sher	יהוה אֱלֹהֵיכֶם אֲשֶׁר
ho-tzei-ti et-chem mei-eh-retz	הוֹצֵאתִי אֶתְכֶם מֵאֶרֶץ
mitz-ra-yim li-h'yot la-chem	מִצְרַיִם לִהְיוֹת לָכֶם
lei-lo-him. Ani Adonai	לֵאלֹהִים. אֲנִי יהוה
Eh-lo-hei-chem.	אֱלֹהֵיכֶם:

Be mindful of all My Mitzvot, and do them: so shall you consecrate yourselves to your God. I am your Eternal God who led you out of Egypt to be your God; I am your Eternal God.

Blessings before eating

For bread

Ba-ruch a-ta A-do-nai,
Eh-lo-hei-nu meh-lech ha-o-lam,
ha-mo-tzi leh-chem
min ha-a-retz.

בָּרוּךְ אַתָּה יי
אֱלֹהֵינוּ מֶלֶךְ הָעוֹלָם,
הַמּוֹצִיא לֶחֶם
מִן הָאָרֶץ.

We praise You, Eternal One, Sovereign God of the universe,
You cause bread to come forth from the earth.

For the fruit of the vine

Ba-ruch a-ta A-do-nai,
Eh-lo-hei-nu meh-lech ha-o-lam,
bo-rei p'ri ha-ga-fen.

בָּרוּךְ אַתָּה יי
אֱלֹהֵינוּ מֶלֶךְ הָעוֹלָם,
בּוֹרֵא פְּרִי הַגָּפֶן.

We praise You, Eternal God, Sovereign of the universe,
Creator of the fruit of the vine.

For pastry

בָּרוּךְ אַתָּה יי אֱלֹהֵינוּ מֶלֶךְ הָעוֹלָם, בּוֹרֵא מִינֵי מְזוֹנוֹת.

We praise You, Eternal God, Sovereign of the universe,
Creator of many kinds of food.

For fruits that grow on trees

בָּרוּךְ אַתָּה יי אֱלֹהֵינוּ מֶלֶךְ הָעוֹלָם, בּוֹרֵא פְּרִי הָעֵץ.

We praise You, Eternal God, Sovereign of the universe,
Creator of the fruit of the tree.

For fruits and vegetables that grow in the soil

בָּרוּךְ אַתָּה יי אֱלֹהֵינוּ מֶלֶךְ הָעוֹלָם, בּוֹרֵא פְּרִי הָאֲדָמָה.

We praise You, Eternal God, Sovereign of the universe,
Creator of the fruit of the earth.

For all other food and drink

בָּרוּךְ אַתָּה יי אֱלֹהֵינוּ מֶלֶךְ הָעוֹלָם, שֶׁהַכֹּל נִהְיֶה בִּדְבָרוֹ.

We praise You, Eternal God, Sovereign of the universe,
by whose word all things come into being.

Thanksgiving for Food

בִּרְכַּת הַמָּזוֹן

ON SHABBAT AND YOM TOV

שִׁיר הַמַּעֲלוֹת

A PILGRIM SONG

When God restored the exiles to Zion, it seemed like a dream. Our mouths were filled with laughter, our tongues with joyful song. Then they said among the nations: God has done great things for them. Yes, God is doing great things for us, and we are joyful. Restore our fortunes, O God, as streams revive the desert. Then those who have sown in tears shall reap in joy. Those who go forth weeping, carrying bags of seeds, shall come home with shouts of joy, bearing their sheaves.

שִׁיר הַמַּעֲלוֹת בְּשׁוּב יהוה אֶת־שִׁיבַת צִיּוֹן, הָיִינוּ כְּחֹלְמִים. אָז יִמָּלֵא שְׂחוֹק פִּינוּ, וּלְשׁוֹנֵנוּ רִנָּה. אָז יֹאמְרוּ בַגּוֹיִם: הִגְדִּיל יהוה לַעֲשׂוֹת עִם־אֵלֶּה. הִגְדִּיל יהוה לַעֲשׂוֹת עִמָּנוּ, הָיִינוּ שְׂמֵחִים. שׁוּבָה יהוה אֶת־שְׁבִיתֵנוּ כַּאֲפִיקִים בַּנֶּגֶב. הַזֹּרְעִים בְּדִמְעָה בְּרִנָּה יִקְצֹרוּ. הָלוֹךְ יֵלֵךְ וּבָכֹה, נֹשֵׂא מֶשֶׁךְ־הַזָּרַע, בֹּא־יָבוֹא בְרִנָּה נֹשֵׂא אֲלֻמֹּתָיו.

[Psalm 126]

ON ALL OCCASIONS

LEADER

חֲבֵרִים וַחֲבֵרוֹת, נְבָרֵךְ.

Let us praise God.

GROUP

יְהִי שֵׁם יי מְבֹרָךְ מֵעַתָּה וְעַד עוֹלָם.

Praised be the name of God, now and for ever!

9

LEADER

יְהִי שֵׁם יי מְבֹרָךְ מֵעַתָּה וְעַד עוֹלָם.

Praised be the name of God, now and for ever!

בִּרְשׁוּת הַחֶבְרָה, נְבָרֵךְ אֱלֹהֵינוּ שֶׁאָכַלְנוּ מִשֶּׁלוֹ.

Praised be our God, of whose abundance we have eaten.

GROUP

בָּרוּךְ אֱלֹהֵינוּ שֶׁאָכַלְנוּ מִשֶּׁלוֹ, וּבְטוּבוֹ חָיִינוּ.

Praised be our God, of whose abundance we have eaten,
and by whose goodness we live.

LEADER

בָּרוּךְ אֱלֹהֵינוּ שֶׁאָכַלְנוּ מִשֶּׁלוֹ, וּבְטוּבוֹ חָיִינוּ.

Praised be our God, of whose abundance we have eaten,
and by whose goodness we live.

GROUP

בָּרוּךְ הוּא וּבָרוּךְ שְׁמוֹ.

Praised be the Eternal God!

TOGETHER

בָּרוּךְ אַתָּה יי אֱלֹהֵינוּ מֶלֶךְ הָעוֹלָם, הַזָּן אֶת־הָעוֹלָם כֻּלוֹ בְּטוּבוֹ, בְּחֵן בְּחֶסֶד וּבְרַחֲמִים. הוּא נוֹתֵן לֶחֶם לְכָל־בָּשָׂר, כִּי לְעוֹלָם חַסְדוֹ. וּבְטוּבוֹ הַגָּדוֹל תָּמִיד לֹא חָסַר לָנוּ, וְאַל יֶחְסַר לָנוּ, מָזוֹן לְעוֹלָם וָעֶד, בַּעֲבוּר שְׁמוֹ הַגָּדוֹל. כִּי הוּא אֵל זָן וּמְפַרְנֵס לַכֹּל, וּמֵטִיב לַכֹּל וּמֵכִין מָזוֹן לְכָל־בְּרִיּוֹתָיו אֲשֶׁר בָּרָא. בָּרוּךְ אַתָּה יי הַזָּן אֶת־הַכֹּל.

Sovereign God of the universe, we praise You: Your goodness sustains the world. You are the God of grace, love, and compassion, the source of bread for all who live—for Your love is everlasting. In Your great goodness we need never lack for food; You provide food enough for all.

We praise You, O God, Source of food for all who live.

10

נוֹדֶה לְךָ, יְיָ אֱלֹהֵינוּ, עַל שֶׁהִנְחַלְתָּ לַאֲבוֹתֵינוּ וּלְאִמּוֹתֵינוּ אֶרֶץ חֶמְדָּה טוֹבָה וּרְחָבָה; וְעַל שֶׁהוֹצֵאתָנוּ מֵאֶרֶץ מִצְרָיִם; וּפְדִיתָנוּ מִבֵּית עֲבָדִים; וְעַל בְּרִיתְךָ שֶׁחָתַמְתָּ בְּלִבֵּנוּ; וְעַל תּוֹרָתְךָ שֶׁלִּמַּדְתָּנוּ, וְעַל חֻקֶּיךָ שֶׁהוֹדַעְתָּנוּ, וְעַל חַיִּים חֵן וָחֶסֶד שֶׁחוֹנַנְתָּנוּ, וְעַל אֲכִילַת מָזוֹן שָׁאַתָּה זָן וּמְפַרְנֵס אוֹתָנוּ תָּמִיד, בְּכָל־יוֹם וּבְכָל־עֵת וּבְכָל־שָׁעָה.

For this good earth that you have entrusted to our mothers and fathers, and to us; for our deliverance from bondage; for the covenant You have sealed into our hearts; for Your life-giving love and grace; for Torah, our way of life, and for the food that sustains us day by day, we give You thanks.

ON CHANUKAH

עַל הַנִּסִּים וְעַל הַפֻּרְקָן וְעַל הַגְּבוּרוֹת וְעַל הַתְּשׁוּעוֹת וְעַל הַנֶּחָמוֹת שֶׁעָשִׂיתָ לַאֲבוֹתֵינוּ וּלְאִמּוֹתֵינוּ בַּיָּמִים הָהֵם וּבַזְּמַן הַזֶּה. בִּימֵי מַתִּתְיָהוּ בֶּן־יוֹחָנָן כֹּהֵן גָּדוֹל, חַשְׁמוֹנַאי וּבָנָיו, כְּשֶׁעָמְדָה מַלְכוּת יָוָן הָרְשָׁעָה עַל עַמְּךָ יִשְׂרָאֵל, לְהַשְׁכִּיחָם תּוֹרָתֶךָ וּלְהַעֲבִירָם מֵחֻקֵּי רְצוֹנֶךָ. וְאַתָּה בְּרַחֲמֶיךָ הָרַבִּים עָמַדְתָּ לָהֶם בְּעֵת צָרָתָם, רַבְתָּ אֶת־רִיבָם, דַּנְתָּ אֶת־דִּינָם, מָסַרְתָּ גִבּוֹרִים בְּיַד חַלָּשִׁים, וְרַבִּים בְּיַד מְעַטִּים, וּטְמֵאִים בְּיַד טְהוֹרִים, וּרְשָׁעִים בְּיַד צַדִּיקִים, וְזֵדִים בְּיַד עוֹסְקֵי תוֹרָתֶךָ. וּלְךָ עָשִׂיתָ שֵׁם גָּדוֹל וְקָדוֹשׁ בְּעוֹלָמֶךָ, וּלְעַמְּךָ יִשְׂרָאֵל עָשִׂיתָ תְּשׁוּעָה גְדוֹלָה וּפֻרְקָן כְּהַיּוֹם הַזֶּה, וְאַחַר כֵּן בָּאוּ בָנֶיךָ לִדְבִיר בֵּיתֶךָ, וּפִנּוּ אֶת־הֵיכָלֶךָ, וְטִהֲרוּ אֶת־מִקְדָּשֶׁךָ, וְהִדְלִיקוּ נֵרוֹת בְּחַצְרוֹת קָדְשֶׁךָ, וְקָבְעוּ שְׁמוֹנַת יְמֵי חֲנֻכָּה אֵלּוּ, לְהוֹדוֹת וּלְהַלֵּל לְשִׁמְךָ הַגָּדוֹל.

In days of old at this season You saved our people by wonders and mighty deeds. In the days of Mattathias the Hasmonean, the tyrannic Empire sought to destroy our people Israel by making them forget their Torah, and by forcing them to abandon their ancient way of life.

Through the power of Your spirit the weak defeated the strong, the few prevailed over the many, and the righteous were victorious. Then Your children returned to Your House to purify the

11

sanctuary and to kindle its lights. And they dedicated these days to give thanks and praise to Your majestic glory.

ON PURIM

עַל הַנִּסִּים וְעַל הַפֻּרְקָן וְעַל הַגְּבוּרוֹת וְעַל הַתְּשׁוּעוֹת וְעַל הַנֶּחָמוֹת שֶׁעָשִׂיתָ לַאֲבוֹתֵינוּ וּלְאִמּוֹתֵינוּ בַּיָּמִים הָהֵם וּבַזְּמַן הַזֶּה. בִּימֵי מָרְדְּכַי וְאֶסְתֵּר בְּשׁוּשַׁן הַבִּירָה, כְּשֶׁעָמַד עֲלֵיהֶם הָמָן הָרָשָׁע, בִּקֵּשׁ לְהַשְׁמִיד לַהֲרוֹג וּלְאַבֵּד אֶת־כָּל־הַיְּהוּדִים, מִנַּעַר וְעַד־זָקֵן, טַף וְנָשִׁים, בְּיוֹם אֶחָד, בִּשְׁלֹשָׁה עָשָׂר לְחֹדֶשׁ שְׁנֵים־עָשָׂר, הוּא־חֹדֶשׁ אֲדָר, וּשְׁלָלָם לָבוֹז. וְאַתָּה בְּרַחֲמֶיךָ הָרַבִּים הֵפַרְתָּ אֶת־עֲצָתוֹ וְקִלְקַלְתָּ אֶת־מַחֲשַׁבְתּוֹ.

In days of old at this season You saved our people by wonders and mighty deeds.

In the days of Mordechai and Esther, the wicked Haman arose in Persia, plotting the destruction of all the Jews, young and old alike. He planned to destroy them in a single day, the thirteenth of Adar, and to plunder their possessions.

But through Your great mercy his plan was thwarted, his scheme frustrated. We therefore thank and bless You, the great and gracious God!

ON ALL OCCASIONS

וְעַל הַכֹּל, יי אֱלֹהֵינוּ, אֲנַחְנוּ מוֹדִים לָךְ וּמְבָרְכִים אוֹתָךְ. יִתְבָּרַךְ שִׁמְךָ בְּפִי כָל־חַי תָּמִיד לְעוֹלָם וָעֶד, כַּכָּתוּב: וְאָכַלְתָּ וְשָׂבָעְתָּ, וּבֵרַכְתָּ אֶת־ יהוה אֱלֹהֶיךָ עַל־הָאָרֶץ הַטֹּבָה אֲשֶׁר נָתַן־לָךְ. בָּרוּךְ אַתָּה יי עַל־הָאָרֶץ וְעַל־הַמָּזוֹן.

For all this we thank You. Let Your praise ever be on the lips of all who live, as it is written: 'When you have eaten and are satisfied, give praise to your God who has given you this good earth.'

We praise You, O God, for the earth, and for its sustenance. Amen.

רַחֵם, יי אֱלֹהֵינוּ, עַל יִשְׂרָאֵל עַמֶּךָ, וְעַל יְרוּשָׁלַיִם עִירֶךָ, וְעַל צִיּוֹן מִשְׁכַּן כְּבוֹדֶךָ. אֱלֹהֵינוּ אָבִינוּ, רְעֵנוּ זוּנֵנוּ, פַּרְנְסֵנוּ וְכַלְכְּלֵנוּ וְהַרְוִיחֵנוּ, וְהַרְוַח לָנוּ,

יי אֱלֹהֵינוּ, מְהֵרָה מִכָּל־צָרוֹתֵינוּ. וְנָא אַל תַּצְרִיכֵנוּ, יי אֱלֹהֵינוּ, לֹא לִידֵי מַתְּנַת בָּשָׂר וָדָם וְלֹא לִידֵי הַלְוָאָתָם, כִּי אִם לְיָדְךָ הַמְּלֵאָה הַפְּתוּחָה הַגְּדוּשָׁה וְהָרְחָבָה, שֶׁלֹּא נֵבוֹשׁ וְלֹא נִכָּלֵם לְעוֹלָם וָעֶד.

Eternal God, Source of our being, show compassion for Israel Your peo-ple, Jerusalem Your city, and Zion, the ancient dwelling-place of Your glory. Guide and sustain us in all our habitations, and be a help to us in all our troubles. May we ever be able to help ourselves and one another, even as we rely on Your open and generous bounty.

ON SHABBAT

רְצֵה וְהַחֲלִיצֵנוּ, יי אֱלֹהֵינוּ, בְּמִצְוֹתֶיךָ וּבְמִצְוַת יוֹם הַשְּׁבִיעִי הַשַּׁבָּת הַגָּדוֹל וְהַקָּדוֹשׁ הַזֶּה, כִּי יוֹם זֶה גָּדוֹל וְקָדוֹשׁ הוּא לְפָנֶיךָ, לִשְׁבָּת־בּוֹ וְלָנוּחַ בּוֹ בְּאַהֲבָה כְּמִצְוַת רְצוֹנֶךָ. וּבִרְצוֹנְךָ הָנַח לָנוּ, יי אֱלֹהֵינוּ, שֶׁלֹּא תְהֵא צָרָה וְיָגוֹן וַאֲנָחָה בְּיוֹם מְנוּחָתֵנוּ. וְהַרְאֵנוּ, יי אֱלֹהֵינוּ, בְּנֶחָמַת צִיּוֹן עִירֶךָ וּבְבִנְיַן יְרוּשָׁלַיִם עִיר קָדְשֶׁךָ, כִּי אַתָּה הוּא בַּעַל הַיְשׁוּעוֹת וּבַעַל הַנֶּחָמוֹת.

Eternal God, strengthen our resolve to live by Your Mitzvot, and especially the Mitzvah of the seventh day, the great and holy Sabbath, the day of rest and serenity, of loving reflection upon Your will. Source of deliverance and of consolation, give us this day rest from sorrow, anguish, and pain, and renew our vision of a more beautiful world.

ON ROSH CHODESH AND YOM TOV

אֱלֹהֵינוּ וֵאלֹהֵי אֲבוֹתֵינוּ וְאִמּוֹתֵינוּ, יַעֲלֶה וְיָבֹא וְיִזָּכֵר זִכְרוֹנֵנוּ וְזִכְרוֹן כָּל־עַמְּךָ בֵּית יִשְׂרָאֵל לְפָנֶיךָ לְטוֹבָה וְלִבְרָכָה לְחַיִּים וּלְשָׁלוֹם בְּיוֹם . . .

◆ רֹאשׁ הַחֹדֶשׁ הַזֶּה,

◆ חַג הַמַּצּוֹת הַזֶּה,

◆ הָעַצְמָאוּת הַזֶּה,

◆ חַג הַשָּׁבֻעוֹת הַזֶּה,

◆ הַזִּכָּרוֹן הַזֶּה,

◆ חַג הַסֻּכּוֹת הַזֶּה,

◆ הַשְּׁמִינִי חַג הָעֲצֶרֶת הַזֶּה,

זָכְרֵנוּ, יי אֱלֹהֵינוּ, בּוֹ לְטוֹבָה. אָמֵן.
וּפָקְדֵנוּ בוֹ לִבְרָכָה. אָמֵן.
וְהוֹשִׁיעֵנוּ בוֹ לְחַיִּים. אָמֵן.

Our God and God of all ages, be mindful of us and of all Your people of the House of Israel. Grant us well-being and blessing, life and peace, on this . . .

◆ First day of the new month,

◆ Festival of Pesach,

◆ Day of Independence,

◆ Festival of Shavuot,

◆ Day of Remembrance,

◆ Festival of Sukkot,

◆ Festival of Sh'mini Atzeret–Simchat Torah,

Remember us this day for well-being.
Bless us this day with Your presence.
Help us this day to lead a full life.

ON ALL OCCASIONS

וּבְנֵה יְרוּשָׁלַיִם עִיר הַקֹּדֶשׁ בִּמְהֵרָה בְיָמֵינוּ. בָּרוּךְ אַתָּה יי בּוֹנֵה בְרַחֲמָיו
יְרוּשָׁלָיִם. אָמֵן.

Let Jerusalem, the holy city, be renewed in our time. We praise You, O God; in compassion You rebuild Jerusalem. Amen.

בָּרוּךְ אַתָּה יי אֱלֹהֵינוּ מֶלֶךְ הָעוֹלָם, הָאֵל אָבִינוּ מַלְכֵּנוּ, אַדִּירֵנוּ,
בּוֹרְאֵנוּ, גּוֹאֲלֵנוּ, יוֹצְרֵנוּ, קְדוֹשֵׁנוּ, קְדוֹשׁ יַעֲקֹב, רוֹעֵנוּ רוֹעֵה יִשְׂרָאֵל,
הַמֶּלֶךְ הַטּוֹב וְהַמֵּטִיב לַכֹּל, שֶׁבְּכָל־יוֹם וָיוֹם הוּא הֵטִיב, הוּא מֵטִיב, הוּא
יֵיטִיב לָנוּ. הוּא גְמָלָנוּ, הוּא גוֹמְלֵנוּ, הוּא יִגְמְלֵנוּ לָעַד, לְחֵן לְחֶסֶד
וּלְרַחֲמִים וּלְרֶוַח, הַצָּלָה וְהַצְלָחָה, בְּרָכָה וִישׁוּעָה, נֶחָמָה, פַּרְנָסָה וְכַלְכָּלָה,
וְרַחֲמִים וְחַיִּים וְשָׁלוֹם, וְכָל־טוֹב, וּמִכָּל־טוּב אַל־יְחַסְּרֵנוּ.

We praise You, divine Parent of Israel, Source of liberating power and vision, of all that is holy and good. You have shown us love and kindness always; day by day You grant us grace and compassion, deliverance and freedom, prosperity and blessing, life and peace.

הָרַחֲמָן, הוּא יִמְלוֹךְ עָלֵינוּ לְעוֹלָם וָעֶד.

Merciful One, be our God for ever.

הָרַחֲמָן, הוּא יִתְבָּרַךְ בַּשָּׁמַיִם וּבָאָרֶץ.

Merciful One, heaven and earth alike are blessed by Your presence.

הָרַחֲמָן, הוּא יִשְׁתַּבַּח לְדוֹר דּוֹרִים, וְיִתְפָּאַר בָּנוּ לָנֶצַח נְצָחִים,
וְיִתְהַדַּר בָּנוּ לָעַד וּלְעוֹלְמֵי עוֹלָמִים.

Merciful One, let all the generations proclaim Your glory.

הָרַחֲמָן, הוּא יְפַרְנְסֵנוּ בְּכָבוֹד.

Merciful One, help us to sustain ourselves in honor.

הָרַחֲמָן, הוּא יִשְׁבּוֹר עֻלֵנוּ מֵעַל צַוָּארֵנוּ.

Merciful One, help us break the yoke of oppression from off our necks.

הָרַחֲמָן, הוּא יִשְׁלַח בְּרָכָה מְרֻבָּה בַּבַּיִת הַזֶּה
וְעַל שֻׁלְחָן זֶה שֶׁאָכַלְנוּ עָלָיו.

Merciful One, bless this house, this table at which we have eaten.

הָרַחֲמָן, הוּא יִשְׁלַח לָנוּ אֶת־אֵלִיָּהוּ הַנָּבִיא, זָכוּר לַטּוֹב,
וִיבַשֶּׂר־לָנוּ בְּשׂוֹרוֹת טוֹבוֹת, יְשׁוּעוֹת וְנֶחָמוֹת.

Merciful One, send us Elijah-tidings, glimpses of good to come, of redemption and consolation.

הָרַחֲמָן, הוּא יְזַכֵּנוּ לִימוֹת הַגְּאוּלָה וּלְחַיֵּי הָעוֹלָם הַבָּא.

Merciful One, find us worthy of witnessing a time of redemption and of attaining eternal life.

ONE OR MORE OF THE FOLLOWING MAY BE ADDED HERE

הָרַחֲמָן, הוּא קֶרֶן לְעַמּוֹ יָרִים.

Merciful One, give strength to Your people.

הָרַחֲמָן, הוּא יִשְׁלַח בְּרָכָה וְהַצְלָחָה בְּכָל־מַעֲשֵׂי יָדֵינוּ.

Merciful One, bless and prosper the work of our hands.

הָרַחֲמָן, הוּא יִרְפָּאֵנוּ רְפוּאָה שְׁלֵמָה,
רְפוּאַת הַנֶּפֶשׁ וּרְפוּאַת הַגּוּף.

Merciful One, grant us health of body and spirit.

הָרַחֲמָן, הוּא יִפְרֹשׂ עָלֵינוּ סֻכַּת שְׁלוֹמוֹ.

Merciful One, spread over us the shelter of Your peace.

הָרַחֲמָן, הוּא יִטַּע תּוֹרָתוֹ וְאַהֲבָתוֹ בְּלִבֵּנוּ
וְיָאִיר עֵינֵינוּ בִּמְאוֹר תּוֹרָתוֹ.

Merciful One, implant Your teaching and Your love in our hearts and illumine our eyes with the light of Torah.

הָרַחֲמָן, הוּא יְמַלֵּא מִשְׁאֲלוֹת לִבֵּנוּ לְטוֹבָה.

Merciful One, fulfill for good the desires of our hearts.

הָרַחֲמָן, הוּא יְבָרֵךְ אוֹתָנוּ וְאֶת־כָּל־אֲשֶׁר לָנוּ, כְּמוֹ שֶׁנִּתְבָּרְכוּ אֲבוֹתֵינוּ אַבְרָהָם, יִצְחָק, וְיַעֲקֹב, וְאִמּוֹתֵינוּ שָׂרָה, רִבְקָה, לֵאָה וְרָחֵל, בַּכֹּל מִכֹּל כֹּל, כֵּן יְבָרֵךְ אוֹתָנוּ כֻּלָּנוּ יַחַד, בִּבְרָכָה שְׁלֵמָה, וְנֹאמַר: אָמֵן.

Merciful One, bless us and all our dear ones; as You blessed our ancestors Abraham, Isaac, and Jacob; Sarah, Rebekah, Leah, and Rachel, so bless us, one and all; and let us say: Amen.

בַּמָּרוֹם יְלַמְּדוּ עָלֵינוּ זְכוּת שֶׁתְּהֵא לְמִשְׁמֶרֶת שָׁלוֹם; וְנִשָּׂא בְרָכָה מֵאֵת יי וּצְדָקָה מֵאֱלֹהֵי יִשְׁעֵנוּ, וְנִמְצָא חֵן וְשֵׂכֶל טוֹב בְּעֵינֵי אֱלֹהִים וְאָדָם.

May we receive blessings from the Eternal One, kindness from God our help, and may we all find divine and human grace and favor.

ON SHABBAT

הָרַחֲמָן, הוּא יַנְחִילֵנוּ יוֹם שֶׁכֻּלוֹ שַׁבָּת.

Merciful One, help us to see the coming of a time that is all Shabbat.

ON ROSH CHODESH

הָרַחֲמָן, הוּא יְחַדֵּשׁ עָלֵינוּ אֶת־הַחֹדֶשׁ הַזֶּה לְטוֹבָה וְלִבְרָכָה.

Merciful One, bring us a month of renewed good and blessing.

ON YOM TOV

הָרַחֲמָן, הוּא יַנְחִילֵנוּ יוֹם שֶׁכֻּלוֹ טוֹב.

Merciful One, help us to see the coming of a time that is all good.

ON YOM HA-ATZMA-UT

הָרַחֲמָן, הוּא יָאִיר אוֹר חָדָשׁ עַל צִיּוֹן וְנִזְכֶּה כֻלָּנוּ לְאוֹרוֹ.

Merciful One, shed a new light upon Zion, and may it be our blessing to see its splendor.

ON ROSH HASHANAH

הָרַחֲמָן, הוּא יְחַדֵּשׁ עָלֵינוּ אֶת־הַשָּׁנָה הַזֹּאת לְטוֹבָה וְלִבְרָכָה.

Merciful One, bring us a year of renewed good and blessing.

ON ALL OCCASIONS

עֹשֶׂה שָׁלוֹם בִּמְרוֹמָיו, הוּא יַעֲשֶׂה שָׁלוֹם עָלֵינוּ וְעַל־כָּל־יִשְׂרָאֵל וְאִמְרוּ אָמֵן.

May the Source of perfect peace grant peace to us, to all Israel, and to all the world.

הוֹדוּ לַיהוה כִּי־טוֹב, כִּי לְעוֹלָם חַסְדּוֹ. פּוֹתֵחַ אֶת־יָדֶךָ, וּמַשְׂבִּיעַ לְכָל־חַי רָצוֹן. בָּרוּךְ הַגֶּבֶר אֲשֶׁר יִבְטַח בַּיהוה וְהָיָה יהוה מִבְטַחוֹ. יהוה עֹז לְעַמּוֹ יִתֵּן, יהוה יְבָרֵךְ אֶת־עַמּוֹ בַשָּׁלוֹם.

17

Give thanks to God, who is good, whose love is everlasting, whose hand is open to feed all that lives.

Blessed are you who trust in God, who make God Your stronghold.

Eternal God: give strength to Your people; Eternal God: bless Your people with peace.

Thanksgiving for Food—Short Form

בִּרְכַּת הַמָּזוֹן בִּקְצָרָה

ON SHABBAT AND YOM TOV

A PILGRIM SONG

שִׁיר הַמַּעֲלוֹת

When God restored the exiles to Zion, it seemed like a dream. Our mouths were filled with laughter, our tongues with joyful song. Then they said among the nations: God has done great things for them. Yes, God is doing great things for us, and we are joyful. Restore our fortunes, O God, as streams revive the desert. Then those who have sown in tears shall reap in joy. Those who go forth weeping, carrying bags of seeds, shall come home with shouts of joy, bearing their sheaves.

שִׁיר הַמַּעֲלוֹת בְּשׁוּב יְהוה אֶת־שִׁיבַת צִיּוֹן, הָיִינוּ כְּחֹלְמִים. אָז יִמָּלֵא שְׂחוֹק פִּינוּ, וּלְשׁוֹנֵנוּ רִנָּה. אָז יֹאמְרוּ בַגּוֹיִם: הִגְדִּיל יְהוה לַעֲשׂוֹת עִם־אֵלֶּה. הִגְדִּיל יְהוה לַעֲשׂוֹת עִמָּנוּ, הָיִינוּ שְׂמֵחִים. שׁוּבָה יְהוה אֶת־שְׁבִיתֵנוּ כַּאֲפִיקִים בַּנֶּגֶב. הַזֹּרְעִים בְּדִמְעָה בְּרִנָּה יִקְצֹרוּ. הָלוֹךְ יֵלֵךְ וּבָכֹה, נֹשֵׂא מֶשֶׁךְ־הַזָּרַע, בֹּא־יָבוֹא בְרִנָּה נֹשֵׂא אֲלֻמֹּתָיו.

[*Psalm 126*]

ON ALL OCCASIONS

LEADER

Let us praise God.

חֲבֵרִים וַחֲבֵרוֹת, נְבָרֵךְ.

GROUP

יְהִי שֵׁם יי מְבֹרָךְ מֵעַתָּה וְעַד עוֹלָם.

Praised be the name of God, now and for ever!

LEADER

יְהִי שֵׁם יי מְבֹרָךְ מֵעַתָּה וְעַד עוֹלָם.

Praised be the name of God, now and for ever!

בִּרְשׁוּת הַחֶבְרָה, נְבָרֵךְ אֱלֹהֵינוּ שֶׁאָכַלְנוּ מִשֶּׁלוֹ.

Praised be our God, of whose abundance we have eaten.

GROUP

בָּרוּךְ אֱלֹהֵינוּ שֶׁאָכַלְנוּ מִשֶּׁלוֹ, וּבְטוּבוֹ חָיִינוּ.

Praised be our God, of whose abundance we have eaten,
and by whose goodness we live.

LEADER

בָּרוּךְ אֱלֹהֵינוּ שֶׁאָכַלְנוּ מִשֶּׁלוֹ, וּבְטוּבוֹ חָיִינוּ.

Praised be our God, of whose abundance we have eaten,
and by whose goodness we live.

GROUP

בָּרוּךְ הוּא וּבָרוּךְ שְׁמוֹ.

Praised be the Eternal God!

TOGETHER

בָּרוּךְ אַתָּה יי אֱלֹהֵינוּ מֶלֶךְ הָעוֹלָם, הַזָּן אֶת־הָעוֹלָם כֻּלּוֹ בְּטוּבוֹ, בְּחֵן בְּחֶסֶד וּבְרַחֲמִים. הוּא נוֹתֵן לֶחֶם לְכָל־בָּשָׂר, כִּי לְעוֹלָם חַסְדּוֹ. וּבְטוּבוֹ הַגָּדוֹל תָּמִיד לֹא חָסַר לָנוּ, וְאַל יֶחְסַר לָנוּ, מָזוֹן לְעוֹלָם וָעֶד, בַּעֲבוּר שְׁמוֹ הַגָּדוֹל. כִּי הוּא אֵל זָן וּמְפַרְנֵס לַכֹּל, וּמֵטִיב לַכֹּל וּמֵכִין מָזוֹן לְכָל־בְּרִיּוֹתָיו אֲשֶׁר בָּרָא. בָּרוּךְ אַתָּה יי הַזָּן אֶת־הַכֹּל.

Sovereign God of the universe, we praise You: Your goodness sustains the world. You are the God of grace, love, and compassion, the source of bread for all who live—for Your love is everlasting. In Your great goodness we need never lack for food; You provide food enough for all.

We praise You, O God, Source of food for all who live.

וְעַל הַכֹּל, יי אֱלֹהֵינוּ, אֲנַחְנוּ מוֹדִים לָךְ וּמְבָרְכִים אוֹתָךְ. יִתְבָּרַךְ שִׁמְךָ בְּפִי כָל־חַי תָּמִיד לְעוֹלָם וָעֶד, כַּכָּתוּב: וְאָכַלְתָּ וְשָׂבָעְתָּ, וּבֵרַכְתָּ אֶת־

20

יהוה אֱלֹהֶיךָ עַל־הָאָרֶץ הַטֹּבָה אֲשֶׁר נָתַן־לָךְ. בָּרוּךְ אַתָּה יי עַל־הָאָרֶץ וְעַל־הַמָּזוֹן.

For all this we thank You. Let Your praise ever be on the lips of all who live, as it is written: 'When you have eaten and are satisfied, give praise to your God who has given you this good earth.'

We praise You, O God, for the earth, and for its sustenance. Amen.

נוֹדֶה לְךָ, יי אֱלֹהֵינוּ, עַל שֶׁהִנְחַלְתָּ לַאֲבוֹתֵינוּ וּלְאִמּוֹתֵינוּ אֶרֶץ חֶמְדָּה טוֹבָה וּרְחָבָה, וְעַל אֲכִילַת מָזוֹן שָׁאַתָּה זָן וּמְפַרְנֵס אוֹתָנוּ תָּמִיד, בְּכָל־יוֹם וּבְכָל־עֵת וּבְכָל־שָׁעָה.

For this good earth that you have entrusted to our mothers and fathers, and to us, and for the food that sustains us day by day, we give You thanks.

וּבְנֵה יְרוּשָׁלַיִם עִיר הַקֹּדֶשׁ בִּמְהֵרָה בְיָמֵינוּ. בָּרוּךְ אַתָּה יי בּוֹנֶה בְּרַחֲמָיו יְרוּשָׁלָיִם. אָמֵן.

Let Jerusalem, the holy city, be renewed in our time. We praise You, O God; in compassion You rebuild Jerusalem. Amen.

הָרַחֲמָן, הוּא יְבָרֵךְ אוֹתָנוּ וְאֶת־כָּל־אֲשֶׁר לָנוּ, כְּמוֹ שֶׁנִּתְבָּרְכוּ אֲבוֹתֵינוּ אַבְרָהָם, יִצְחָק, וְיַעֲקֹב, וְאִמּוֹתֵינוּ שָׂרָה, רִבְקָה, לֵאָה וְרָחֵל, בַּכֹּל מִכֹּל כֹּל, כֵּן יְבָרֵךְ אוֹתָנוּ כֻּלָּנוּ יַחַד, בִּבְרָכָה שְׁלֵמָה, וְנֹאמַר: אָמֵן.

Merciful One, bless us and all our dear ones; as You blessed our ancestors Abraham, Isaac, and Jacob; Sarah, Rebekah, Leah, and Rachel, so bless us, one and all; and let us say: Amen.

ON SHABBAT

הָרַחֲמָן, הוּא יַנְחִילֵנוּ יוֹם שֶׁכֻּלּוֹ שַׁבָּת.

Merciful One, help us to see the coming of a time that is all Shabbat.

ON YOM TOV

הָרַחֲמָן, הוּא יַנְחִילֵנוּ יוֹם שֶׁכֻּלּוֹ טוֹב.

Merciful One, help us to see the coming of a time that is all good.

ON ROSH HASHANAH

הָרַחֲמָן, הוּא יְחַדֵּשׁ עָלֵינוּ אֶת־הַשָּׁנָה הַזֹּאת לְטוֹבָה וְלִבְרָכָה.

Merciful One, bring us a year of renewed good and blessing.

ON ALL OCCASIONS

עֹשֶׂה שָׁלוֹם בִּמְרוֹמָיו, הוּא יַעֲשֶׂה שָׁלוֹם עָלֵינוּ וְעַל־כָּל־יִשְׂרָאֵל וְאִמְרוּ אָמֵן.

May the Source of perfect peace grant peace to us, to all Israel, and to all the world.

Eternal God: give strength to Your people; Eternal God: bless Your people with peace.

יהוה עֹז לְעַמּוֹ יִתֵּן, יהוה יְבָרֵךְ אֶת־עַמּוֹ בַשָּׁלוֹם.

Transliteration of the Thanksgiving for food—Short form

LEADER

Cha-vei-rim va-cha-vei-rot n'va-reich.

GROUP

Y'hi sheim A-do-nai m'vo-rach mei-a-ta v'ad o-lam!

LEADER

Y'hi sheim A-do-nai m'vo-rach mei-a-ta v'ad o-lam!

Bi-r'shut ha-chev-rah, n'va-reich Eh-lo-hei-nu sheh-a-chal-nu mi-sheh-lo.

GROUP

Ba-ruch Eh-lo-hei-nu sheh-a-chal-nu mi-sheh-lo, u-v'tu-vo cha-yi-nu.

LEADER

Ba-ruch Eh-lo-hei-nu sheh-a-chal-nu mi-sheh-lo, u-v'tu-vo cha-yi-nu.

GROUP

Ba-ruch hu u-va-ruch sh'mo.

TOGETHER

Ba-ruch a-ta Adonai, Eh-lo-hei-nu meh-lech ha-o-lam, ha-zan et ha-o-lam ku-lo b'tu-vo. B'chein, b'cheh-sed, u-v'ra-cha-mim hu no-tein leh-chem l'chol ba-sar, ki l'o-lam chas-do. U-v'tu-vo ha-ga-dol ta-mid lo cha-sar la-nu, v'al yech-sar la-nu ma-zon l'o-lam va-ed, ba-a-vur sh'mo ha-ga-dol. Ki hu Eil zan u-m'far-neis la-kol u-mei-chin ma-zon l'chol b'ri-yo-tav a-sher ba-ra. Ba-ruch a-ta Adonai, ha-zan et ha-kol.

V'al ha-kol, Adonai Eh-lo-hei-nu, A-nach-nu mo-dim lach u-m'var-chim o-tach. Yit-ba-rach shim'cha b'fi kol chai ta-mid l'o-lam va-ed. Ka-ka-tuv: 'V'a-chal-ta v'sa-va-ta, u-vei-rach-ta et Adonai Eh-lo-heh-cha al ha-a-retz ha-to-vah asher na-tan lach.' Ba-ruch a-ta Adonai, al ha-a-retz v'al ha-ma-zon.

No-deh l'cha, Adonai Eh-lo-hei-nu, al sheh-hin-chal-ta la-a-vo-tei-nu u-l'i-mo-tei-nu eh-retz chem-dah to-vah u-r'cha-vah, v'al a-chi-lat ma-zon sheh-a-tah zan u-m'far-neis o-ta-nu b'chol yom u-v'chol eit u-v'chol sha-ah. U-v'nei Y'ru-sha-la-yim ir ha-ko-desh bi-m'hei-ra b'ya-mei-nu. Ba-ruch a-ta Adonai, bo-neh b'ra-cha-mav Y'ru-sha-la-yim, A-mein.

Ha-ra-cha-man hu y'va-reich o-ta-nu v'et kol a-sher la-nu, k'mo sheh-nit-ba-r'chu a-vo-tei-nu Av-ra-ham, Yitz-chak v'Ya-a-kov, v'i-mo-tei-nu Sa-rah, Riv-kah, Lei-ah, v'Ra-cheil ba-kol mi-kol kol, kein y'va-reich o-ta-nu ku-la-nu ya-chad bi-v'ra-cha sh'lei-ma, v'no-mar: A-mein.

ON SHABBAT

Ha-ra-cha-man, hu yan-chi-lei-nu yom sheh-ku-lo sha-bat.

ON YOM TOV

Ha-ra-cha-man, hu yan-chi-lei-nu yom sheh-ku-lo tov.

ON ROSH HASHANAH

Ha-ra-cha-man, hu y'cha-deish a-lei-nu et ha-sha-nah ha-zot l'to-vah v'li-v'ra-chah.

ON ALL OCCASIONS

O-seh sha-lom bi-m'ro-mav, hu ya-a-seh sha-lom a-lei-nu, v'al kol Yis-ra-eil, v'i-m'ru, A-mein.

Adonai oz l'a-mo yi-tein, Adonai y'va-reich et a-mo va-sha-lom.

Thanksgiving for Certain Fruits and Grains

בְּרָכָה מֵעֵין שָׁלֹשׁ

❧ *Whenever bread has not been eaten, the following blessing is said after eating certain foods. These are: a) the fruits of the vine and tree: grapes, olives, figs, dates, and pomegranates—the five varieties mentioned in the Torah as characteristic of the land of Israel; and b) the fruits of the soil: wheat, rye, barley, oats, and spelt—the five grains mentioned in the Torah as characteristic of the land of Israel. After all other food and drink, when bread has not been eaten, the general blessing 'Birkat Borei N'fashot' [see page 26] is used.*

בָּרוּךְ אַתָּה יי אֱלֹהֵינוּ מֶלֶךְ הָעוֹלָם,

AFTER WINE

עַל הַגֶּפֶן וְעַל פְּרִי הַגֶּפֶן.

AFTER FRUIT

עַל הָעֵץ וְעַל פְּרִי הָעֵץ.

AFTER GRAINS

עַל הַמִּחְיָה וְעַל הַכַּלְכָּלָה.

AFTER ALL OF THEM TOGETHER

עַל הַמִּחְיָה וְעַל הַכַּלְכָּלָה, וְעַל הַגֶּפֶן וְעַל פְּרִי הַגֶּפֶן.

וְעַל תְּנוּבַת הַשָּׂדֶה, וְעַל אֶרֶץ חֶמְדָּה טוֹבָה וּרְחָבָה שֶׁרָצִיתָ וְהִנְחַלְתָּ לַאֲבוֹתֵינוּ וּלְאִמּוֹתֵינוּ, לֶאֱכֹל מִפִּרְיָה וְלִשְׂבֹּעַ מִטּוּבָהּ. רַחֶם נָא, יי אֱלֹהֵינוּ, עַל יִשְׂרָאֵל עַמֶּךָ, וְעַל יְרוּשָׁלַיִם עִירֶךָ, וְעַל צִיּוֹן מִשְׁכַּן כְּבוֹדֶךָ. וּבְנֵה יְרוּשָׁלַיִם, עִיר הַקֹּדֶשׁ, בִּמְהֵרָה בְיָמֵינוּ וְשַׂמְּחֵנוּ בְּבִנְיָנָהּ וְנֹאכַל מִפִּרְיָהּ וְנִשְׂבַּע מִטּוּבָהּ וּנְבָרֶכְךָ עָלֶיהָ בִּקְדֻשָּׁה וּבְטָהֳרָה.

We thank You for earth's bounty, and for the good and pleasant earth You have given us, to eat its fruit and enjoy its goodness.

24

Eternal God, show compassion for Israel Your people, and for Zion, the ancient dwelling-place of Your glory. Let Jerusalem, the holy city, be renewed in our time. Enable us to rejoice there in its renewal, eating its fruit, enjoying its goodness, and with hearts renewed singing Your praise.

ON SHABBAT

וּרְצֵה וְהַחֲלִיצֵנוּ בְּיוֹם הַשַּׁבָּת הַזֶּה.

Give us well-being on this Sabbath day.

ON ROSH CHODESH

וְזָכְרֵנוּ לְטוֹבָה בְּיוֹם רֹאשׁ הַחֹדֶשׁ הַזֶּה.

Remember us for good in this new month.

ON YOM TOV

Give us joy on this . . .	. . . וְשַׂמְּחֵנוּ בְּיוֹם
◆ Festival of Pesach.	◆ חַג הַמַּצּוֹת הַזֶּה.
◆ Day of Independence.	◆ הָעַצְמָאוּת הַזֶּה.
◆ Festival of Shavuot.	◆ חַג הַשָּׁבֻעוֹת הַזֶּה.
◆ Festival of Sukkot.	◆ חַג הַסֻּכּוֹת הַזֶּה.
◆ Festival of Sh'mini Atzeret–Simchat Torah.	◆ הַשְּׁמִינִי חַג הָעֲצֶרֶת הַזֶּה.

ON ROSH HASHANAH

וְזָכְרֵנוּ לְטוֹבָה בְּיוֹם הַזִּכָּרוֹן הַזֶּה.

Remember us for good on this Day of Remembrance.

ON ALL OCCASIONS

כִּי אַתָּה יי טוֹב וּמֵטִיב לַכֹּל וְנוֹדֶה לְךָ עַל הָאָרֶץ וְעַל הַמִּחְיָה. בָּרוּךְ אַתָּה יי עַל הָאָרֶץ וְעַל הַמִּחְיָה וְעַל פְּרִי הַגֶּפֶן וְעַל הַפֵּרוֹת.

Source of good, we thank You for the good earth and its fruit, and the gift of life. Amen.

Short Thanksgiving for Other Foods

בִּרְכַּת בּוֹרֵא נְפָשׁוֹת

❧ *When no bread has been eaten—after eating or drinking foods not included in the Birkat Hamazon (page 19) or the B'racha Mei-ein Shalosh (page 24).*

בָּרוּךְ אַתָּה יי אֱלֹהֵינוּ מֶלֶךְ הָעוֹלָם, בּוֹרֵא נְפָשׁוֹת רַבּוֹת וְחֶסְרוֹנָן עַל
כָּל־מַה שֶּׁבָּרֵאתָ לְהַחֲיוֹת בָּהֶם נֶפֶשׁ כָּל־חָי. בָּרוּךְ חֵי הָעוֹלָמִים.

We praise You, Eternal God, Sovereign of the universe, Creator of the living and their needs. Life of all life, we thank You for the food that keeps us alive.

Benedictions of praise and thanksgiving

❦ *For blessings before eating, see p. 7.*

On a joyous occasion

Ba-ruch a-ta A-do-nai,
Eh-lo-hei-nu meh-lech ha-o-lam,
sheh-he-che-ya-nu, v'ki-y'ma-nu,
v'hi-gi-a-nu la-z'man ha-zeh.

בָּרוּךְ אַתָּה יי
אֱלֹהֵינוּ מֶלֶךְ הָעוֹלָם,
שֶׁהֶחֱיָנוּ וְקִיְּמָנוּ
וְהִגִּיעָנוּ לִזְמַן הַזֶּה.

We praise You, Eternal God, Sovereign of the universe, for giving us
life, for sustaining us, and for enabling us to reach this season.

For lightning or other natural wonders

בָּרוּךְ אַתָּה יי אֱלֹהֵינוּ מֶלֶךְ הָעוֹלָם, עֹשֶׂה מַעֲשֵׂה בְרֵאשִׁית.

We praise You, Eternal God, Sovereign of the universe,
Source of creation and its wonders.

For thunder

בָּרוּךְ אַתָּה יי אֱלֹהֵינוּ מֶלֶךְ הָעוֹלָם, שֶׁכֹּחוֹ וּגְבוּרָתוֹ מָלֵא עוֹלָם.

We praise You, Eternal God, Sovereign of the universe,
whose power and might pervade the world.

For natural beauty

בָּרוּךְ אַתָּה יי אֱלֹהֵינוּ מֶלֶךְ הָעוֹלָם, שֶׁכָּכָה לוֹ בְּעוֹלָמוֹ.

We praise You, Eternal God, Sovereign of the universe,
whose world is filled with beauty.

For a rainbow

בָּרוּךְ אַתָּה יי אֱלֹהֵינוּ מֶלֶךְ הָעוֹלָם, זוֹכֵר הַבְּרִית וְנֶאֱמָן בִּבְרִיתוֹ
וְקַיָּם בְּמַאֲמָרוֹ.

We praise You, Eternal God, Sovereign of the universe:
true to Your word, You remember Your covenant with creation.

For the ocean

בָּרוּךְ אַתָּה יי אֱלֹהֵינוּ מֶלֶךְ הָעוֹלָם, שֶׁעָשָׂה אֶת־הַיָּם הַגָּדוֹל.

We praise You, Eternal God, Sovereign of the universe,
for the life-giving waters of the sea.

For flowers and herbs

בָּרוּךְ אַתָּה יי אֱלֹהֵינוּ מֶלֶךְ הָעוֹלָם, בּוֹרֵא עִשְׂבֵי בְשָׂמִים.

We praise You, Eternal God, Sovereign of the universe,
for fragrant flowers and herbs.

For shrubs, bushes, and trees

בָּרוּךְ אַתָּה יי אֱלֹהֵינוּ מֶלֶךְ הָעוֹלָם, בּוֹרֵא עֲצֵי בְשָׂמִים.

We praise You, Eternal God, Sovereign of the universe,
for trees and their fragrance.

For edible fruits and nuts

בָּרוּךְ אַתָּה יי אֱלֹהֵינוּ מֶלֶךְ הָעוֹלָם, הַנּוֹתֵן רֵיחַ טוֹב בַּפֵּרוֹת.

We praise You, Eternal God, Sovereign of the universe,
for giving fruits their goodly aroma.

On seeing trees in blossom for the first time in the year

בָּרוּךְ אַתָּה יי אֱלֹהֵינוּ מֶלֶךְ הָעוֹלָם, אֲשֶׁר בָּרָא בְּעוֹלָמוֹ בְּרִיּוֹת טוֹבוֹת
וְאִילָנוֹת טוֹבִים, לְהָנוֹת בָּהֶם בְּנֵי אָדָם.

We praise You, Eternal God, Sovereign of the universe:
You have created goodly creatures and lovely trees that fill the eye
and win the heart.

For perfumes or spices

בָּרוּךְ אַתָּה יי אֱלֹהֵינוּ מֶלֶךְ הָעוֹלָם, בּוֹרֵא מִינֵי בְשָׂמִים.

We praise You, Eternal God, Sovereign of the universe,
for all the world's spices.

28

Upon doing or benefitting from an action that improves the world around us

בָּרוּךְ אַתָּה יי אֱלֹהֵינוּ מֶלֶךְ הָעוֹלָם, אֲשֶׁר קִדְּשָׁנוּ בְּמִצְוֹתָיו וְצִוָּנוּ לַעֲשׂוֹת מַעֲקֶה.

We praise You, Eternal God, Sovereign of the universe: You call us to holiness. We give thanks for all whose labor benefits the world.

Upon experiencing a wonder, an exceptional joy, or a deliverance

בָּרוּךְ אַתָּה יי אֱלֹהֵינוּ מֶלֶךְ הָעוֹלָם, שֶׁעָשָׂה לִי נֵס בַּמָּקוֹם הַזֶּה.

Sovereign God of the universe, for the wonder I have experienced in this place, I give thanks.

On seeing a Torah scholar

בָּרוּךְ אַתָּה יי אֱלֹהֵינוּ מֶלֶךְ הָעוֹלָם, שֶׁחָלַק מֵחָכְמָתוֹ לִירֵאָיו.

We praise You, Eternal God, Sovereign of the universe:
You share Your wisdom with those who revere You.

On seeing a secular scholar

בָּרוּךְ אַתָּה יי אֱלֹהֵינוּ מֶלֶךְ הָעוֹלָם, שֶׁנָּתַן מֵחָכְמָתוֹ לְבָשָׂר וָדָם.

We praise You, Eternal God, Sovereign of the universe:
You give of Your wisdom to flesh and blood.

On seeing a head of state

בָּרוּךְ אַתָּה יי אֱלֹהֵינוּ מֶלֶךְ הָעוֹלָם, שֶׁנָּתַן מִכְּבוֹדוֹ לְבָשָׂר וָדָם.

We praise You, Eternal God, Sovereign of the universe:
You give of Your glory to flesh and blood.

To acknowledge events that are experienced as sublime and/or mysterious

בָּרוּךְ אַתָּה יי אֱלֹהֵינוּ מֶלֶךְ הָעוֹלָם, חֲכַם הָרָזִים.

We praise You, Eternal God, Sovereign of the universe:
You see what is hidden from our sight.

Upon recovery from serious illness or upon escape from danger

❧ *See also page 158.*

לְךָ־אֶזְבַּח זֶבַח תּוֹדָה וּבְשֵׁם יהוה אֶקְרָא.

To You, Eternal One, I offer my thanksgiving, and glorify Your name.

בָּרוּךְ אַתָּה יי אֱלֹהֵינוּ מֶלֶךְ הָעוֹלָם, שֶׁגְּמָלַנִי כָּל־טוֹב.

I praise You, Eternal God, Sovereign of the universe:
You bestow great goodness upon me.

*If this prayer is recited at a public service,
the assembly responds:*

מִי שֶׁגְּמָלְךָ כָּל־טוֹב, הוּא יִגְמָלְךָ כָּל־טוֹב סֶלָה.

*May the One who has been gracious to you continue to
favor you with all that is good.*

בָּרוּךְ אַתָּה יי אֱלֹהֵינוּ מֶלֶךְ הָעוֹלָם, שֶׁהֶחֱיָנוּ וְקִיְּמָנוּ וְהִגִּיעָנוּ
לַזְּמַן הַזֶּה.

*We praise You, Eternal God, Sovereign of the universe, for
giving us life, for sustaining us, and for enabling us to
reach this season.*

On hearing good tidings

בָּרוּךְ אַתָּה יי אֱלֹהֵינוּ מֶלֶךְ הָעוֹלָם, הַטּוֹב וְהַמֵּטִיב.

We praise You, Eternal God, Sovereign of the universe:
You are the Source of all good.

New benedictions of praise

For a spouse or other loved one,
on a significant anniversary or birthday

FOR A MALE

בָּרוּךְ אַתָּה יי אֱלֹהֵינוּ מֶלֶךְ הָעוֹלָם, הַמְאַפְשֵׁר לִי לַחֲלוֹק חַיַּי
עִם רֵעַ אָהוּב וְאוֹהֵב.

FOR A FEMALE

בָּרוּךְ אַתָּה יי אֱלֹהֵינוּ מֶלֶךְ הָעוֹלָם, הַמְאַפְשֵׁר לִי לַחֲלוֹק
חַיַּי עִם רֵעָה אָהוּבָה וְאוֹהֶבֶת.

*We praise You, Eternal God, Sovereign of the universe: You
enable us to share life with a beloved and loving friend.*

❦ *See also related prayers in 'The Path of Life,' pages 123, 136–7.*

For a parent, on a significant anniversary or birthday

We give thanks that we are able to fulfill the Mitzvah of honoring
parents.

בָּרוּךְ אַתָּה יי אֱלֹהֵינוּ מֶלֶךְ הָעוֹלָם, שֶׁנָּתַן לָנוּ הוֹרִים אוֹהֲבִים
לִשְׂמֹחַ בָּהֶם.

We praise You, Eternal God, Sovereign of the universe:
You give us loving parents in whom we rejoice.

Response:

בָּרוּךְ שֶׁנָּתַן־לָנוּ בָּנִים יְקָרִים וּבָנוֹת יְקָרוֹת לִשְׂמֹחַ בָּהֶם.

*Praised be the One who gives us precious children in whom
we rejoice.*

❦ *See also related prayers in 'The Path of Life,' pages 123, 136–7.*

For a child, on a significant occasion or birthday

We give thanks for the gift of children.

בָּרוּךְ אַתָּה יי אֱלֹהֵינוּ מֶלֶךְ הָעוֹלָם, שֶׁנָּתַן־לָנוּ בָּנִים יְקָרִים וּבָנוֹת יְקָרוֹת לִשְׂמֹחַ בָּהֶם.

We praise You, Eternal God, Sovereign of the universe:
You give us precious children in whom we rejoice.

Response:

בָּרוּךְ שֶׁנָּתַן לָנוּ הוֹרִים אוֹהֲבִים לִשְׂמֹחַ בָּהֶם.

Praised be the One who gives us loving parents in whom we rejoice.

❧ *See also related prayers in 'The Path of Life,' pages 123–6.*

On fashioning or experiencing a work of art or craft

בָּרוּךְ הַנּוֹתֵן לָנוּ כִּשָּׁרוֹן לִיצוֹר יְפִי וְלֵהָנוֹת מִמֶּנּוּ.

Praised be the One who makes us able to create and to enjoy works of beauty.

Before participating in a physical activity such as a sport, or before physical exercise

בָּרוּךְ יוֹצֵר הַגּוּף וְכִשְׁרוֹנוֹ, שֶׁנָּטַע בְּתוֹכֵנוּ שִׂמְחַת הַמִּשְׂחָק.

Praised be the Creator of the body and its skills, who has implanted within us the joy of play.

On recovering from a significant loss

בָּרוּךְ הָעוֹזֵר לָנוּ לְהַשְׁלִים עִם אָבְדָן, וּמְלַמְּדֵנוּ לִגְבּוֹר עַל מְרִירוּת וְיֵאוּשׁ, וּמוֹרֵנוּ לִחְיוֹת חַיִּים טוֹבִים עַל אַף הַכֹּל.

Praised be the One who helps us to accept loss, teaching us to overcome bitterness and despair, guiding us—in the face of adversity—to live lives that count for good.

❧ *See also related prayers in 'The Path of Life,' pages 146–150.*

New benedictions for the fulfillment of mitzvot

**On performing an act to benefit others,
such as donating blood or signing an intention
to be an organ transplant donor**

בָּרוּךְ אֱלֹהֵינוּ אֲשֶׁר נָתַן לָנוּ מֵחָכְמָתוֹ וְהִשְׁפִּיעַ עָלֵינוּ לַעֲזוֹר לִבְנֵי אָדָם בְּאֹרַח חַיֵּינוּ וְאַף בְּמוֹתֵנוּ.

Praised be our God who imparts wisdom to us and influences us to help others by our way of living, and in our dying.

**On reaching the age of civic responsibility (such as voting) or
before performing a civic duty**

בָּרוּךְ שֶׁקְּרָאָנוּ לְרוֹמֵם־גּוֹי בִּצְדָקָה, כַּכָּתוּב: וְדִרְשׁוּ אֶת־שְׁלוֹם הָעִיר . . . וְהִתְפַּלְלוּ בַעֲדָהּ אֶל־יהוה, כִּי בִשְׁלוֹמָהּ יִהְיֶה לָכֶם שָׁלוֹם.

Praised be the One who has called us to exalt our nation with righteousness, and taught us: 'Seek the welfare of your community and pray on its behalf, so that all may share in its well-being.'

[Proverbs 14:34; Jeremiah 29:7]

Prayers and Readings for Shabbat, Festivals and Special Days

SHABBAT, FESTIVALS
AND SPECIAL DAYS

Welcoming Shabbat
קַבָּלַת שַׁבָּת

🍎 *It is customary, before the beginning of Shabbat, for each member of the household to put money aside for some worthy cause.*

Happy are those who consider the poor.

[Psalm 41:2]

We hereby vow to fulfill the Mitzvah of Tzedakah as we begin the Sabbath day. We remember the words of Your prophet, who called us to share our bread with the hungry, to clothe the naked, and never to hide ourselves from our own kin.

May we, together with the whole House of Israel, be mindful of the needs of others, sharing with them the fruits of our labor and helping to sustain them, so that the promise may be fulfilled:

Then your light shall blaze forth like the dawn, and your wounds shall quickly heal; your righteousness shall walk before you, the glory of the Eternal One shall follow you.

שָׁלוֹם עֲלֵיכֶם, מַלְאֲכֵי הַשָּׁרֵת, מַלְאֲכֵי עֶלְיוֹן,

מִמֶּלֶךְ מַלְכֵי הַמְּלָכִים, הַקָּדוֹשׁ בָּרוּךְ הוּא.

בּוֹאֲכֶם לְשָׁלוֹם, מַלְאֲכֵי הַשָּׁלוֹם, מַלְאֲכֵי עֶלְיוֹן,

מִמֶּלֶךְ מַלְכֵי הַמְּלָכִים, הַקָּדוֹשׁ בָּרוּךְ הוּא.

בָּרְכוּנִי לְשָׁלוֹם, מַלְאֲכֵי הַשָּׁלוֹם, מַלְאֲכֵי עֶלְיוֹן,

מִמֶּלֶךְ מַלְכֵי הַמְּלָכִים, הַקָּדוֹשׁ בָּרוּךְ הוּא.

צֵאתְכֶם לְשָׁלוֹם, מַלְאֲכֵי הַשָּׁלוֹם, מַלְאֲכֵי עֶלְיוֹן,

מִמֶּלֶךְ מַלְכֵי הַמְּלָכִים, הַקָּדוֹשׁ בָּרוּךְ הוּא.

🍎 *For transliteration, see page 45.*

Peace be to you, ministering angels, messengers of the Most High, of the supreme Sovereign, the Holy One, ever to be praised.

Enter in peace, O messengers of the Most High, of the supreme Sovereign, the Holy One, ever to be praised.

Bless us with peace, O messengers of the Most High, of the supreme Sovereign, the Holy One, ever to be praised.

Depart in peace, O messengers of the Most High, of the supreme Sovereign, the Holy One, ever to be praised.

הַדְלָקַת הַנֵּרוֹת

O God, You are the light by which we see the ones we love. As we kindle these lights, we begin a holy time. May we and all Israel find in it refreshment of body and spirit, and the sense that You are near to us at all times.

Ba-ruch a-ta Adonai, Eh-lo-hei-nu　　　בָּרוּךְ אַתָּה יי אֱלֹהֵינוּ
meh-lech ha-o-lam a-sher　　　　　　מֶלֶךְ הָעוֹלָם, אֲשֶׁר
ki-d'sha-nu b'mitz-vo-tav v'tzi-va-nu　　קִדְּשָׁנוּ בְּמִצְוֹתָיו וְצִוָּנוּ
l'had-lik ner shel Shabbat.　　　　　לְהַדְלִיק נֵר שֶׁל שַׁבָּת.

We praise You, Eternal God, Sovereign of the universe: You hallow us with Mitzvot, and command us to kindle the lights of Shabbat.

May we be blessed with Shabbat joy.

May we be blessed with Shabbat peace.

May we be blessed with Shabbat light.

Our ancestors hallowed the Sabbath day. In dark times it was a refuge for them, and in times of prosperity it gave them rest and joy. Steadfast in their faith, they bequeathed it to us.

We give thanks, therefore, for our home, where we find rest from the day's work, and refuge from cares. May it be warm with love and companionship; may our joys be heightened and our sorrows softened by the love we give and receive.

❧ *The following may be said in praise of a wife, mother, grandmother and/or any other adult woman of the household:*

A woman of valor—seek her out; she is to be valued above rubies.

She opens her hand to those in need, and offers her help to the poor.

Adorned with strength and dignity, she looks to the future with
　　cheerful trust.

Her speech is wise, and the law of kindness is on her lips.

Those who love her rise up with praise, and call her blessed:

38

Many women have done well, but you surpass them all.

Charm is deceptive and beauty short-lived, but a woman loyal to God has truly earned praise.

Honor her for her work; her life proclaims her praise.

[*From Proverbs 31*]

❦ *The following may be said in praise of a husband, father, grandfather and/or any other adult man of the household:*

Blessed is the man loyal to God, who greatly delights in the Eternal One's commandments!

His descendants will be honored in the land: the generation of the upright will be blessed.

His household prospers, and his righteousness endures forever.

Light dawns in the darkness for the upright; for the man who is gracious, merciful, and just.

He is not afraid of evil tidings; his mind is firm, trusting in the Eternal One.

His heart is steady, he is not afraid.

He has been generous, has given freely to the poor; his righteousness endures for ever; his life is exalted in honor.

[*From Psalm 112*]

THE PARENTS BLESS THE CHILDREN

Blessed is the parent, and blessed the child, when their hearts are turned to one another. Blessed is the home filled with gladness and light, the spirit of Shabbat. May God bless you and guide you. Seek truth always, be charitable in your words, just and loving in your deeds. A noble heritage has been entrusted to you; guard it well.

FOR A BOY

יְשִׂמְךָ אֱלֹהִים כְּאֶפְרַיִם וְכִמְנַשֶּׁה.

May God inspire you to live in the tradition of Ephraim and Menasheh, who carried forward the life of our people.

FOR A GIRL

יְשִׂמֵךְ אֱלֹהִים כְּשָׂרָה, רִבְקָה, לֵאָה וְרָחֵל.

May God inspire you to live in the tradition of Sarah, Rebekah, Leah, and Rachel, who carried forward the life of our people.

FOR BOTH

Y'va-reh-ch'cha Adonai v'yish-m'reh-cha.   יְבָרֶכְךָ יהוה וְיִשְׁמְרֶךָ.

Ya-eir Adonai pa-nav ei-leh-cha   יָאֵר יהוה פָּנָיו אֵלֶיךָ

vi-chu-neh-ka.   וִיחֻנֶּךָ.

Yi-sa Adonai pa-nav ei-leh-cha   יִשָּׂא יהוה פָּנָיו אֵלֶיךָ

v'ya-seim l'cha sha-lom.   וְיָשֵׂם לְךָ שָׁלוֹם.

May God bless you and keep you. May God look kindly upon you, and be gracious to you. May God reach out to You in tenderness, and give you peace.

❧ *There may now be a moment of silence, in which all present think of one another with blessing.*

Kiddush for Shabbat Evening

🍇 *Wine and grape juice are equally "fruit of the vine."*

WE HOLD THE CUP AND SAY:

'Six days shall you labor and do all your work, but the seventh day is consecrated to the Eternal One, your God.' With the fruit of the vine, our symbol of joy, we celebrate this sacred day, on which cares and sorrows fade from our minds. We give thanks for life and its blessings, for work and rest, for home and love and friendship. On Shabbat, eternal sign of creation, we rejoice that we are created in the Image of God.

Va-y'chu-lu ha-sha-ma-yim v'ha-a-retz	וַיְכֻלּוּ הַשָּׁמַיִם וְהָאָרֶץ
v'chol tz'va-am, va-y'chal Eh-lo-him	וְכָל־צְבָאָם: וַיְכַל אֱלֹהִים
ba-yom ha-sh'vi-i m'lach-to	בַּיּוֹם הַשְּׁבִיעִי מְלַאכְתּוֹ
a-sher a-sa, va-yish-bot ba-yom	אֲשֶׁר עָשָׂה וַיִּשְׁבֹּת בַּיּוֹם
ha-sh'vi-i mi-kol m'lach-to a-sher	הַשְּׁבִיעִי מִכָּל־מְלַאכְתּוֹ אֲשֶׁר
a-sa. Va-y'va-rech Eh-lo-him et yom	עָשָׂה: וַיְבָרֶךְ אֱלֹהִים אֶת־יוֹם
ha-sh'vi-i va-y'ka-deish o-to, ki vo	הַשְּׁבִיעִי וַיְקַדֵּשׁ אֹתוֹ כִּי בוֹ
sha-vat mi-kol m'lach-to a-sher	שָׁבַת מִכָּל־מְלַאכְתּוֹ אֲשֶׁר־
ba-ra Eh-lo-him la-a-sot.	בָּרָא אֱלֹהִים לַעֲשׂוֹת:

Now the whole universe—sky, earth, and all their array—was completed. With the seventh day God ended the work of creation, resting on the seventh day, with all the work completed. Then God blessed the seventh day and sanctified it, this day having completed the work of creation.

Ba-ruch a-ta Adonai, Eh-lo-hei-nu	בָּרוּךְ אַתָּה יי אֱלֹהֵינוּ
meh-lech ha-o-lam, bo-rei	מֶלֶךְ הָעוֹלָם, בּוֹרֵא
p'ri ha-ga-fen.	פְּרִי הַגָּפֶן.

Ba-ruch a-ta A-do-nai, Eh-lo-hei-nu	בָּרוּךְ אַתָּה יי אֱלֹהֵינוּ
meh-lech ha-o-lam, a-sher ki-d'sha-nu	מֶלֶךְ הָעוֹלָם, אֲשֶׁר קִדְּשָׁנוּ
b'mitz-vo-tav v'ra-tza va-nu, v'shabbat	בְּמִצְוֹתָיו וְרָצָה בָנוּ, וְשַׁבָּת
ko-d'sho b'a-ha-va u-v'ra-tzon	קָדְשׁוֹ בְּאַהֲבָה וּבְרָצוֹן
hin-chi-la-nu, zi-ka-ron l'ma-a-sei	הִנְחִילָנוּ, זִכָּרוֹן לְמַעֲשֵׂה
v'rei-sheet. Ki hu yom t'chi-la	בְרֵאשִׁית. כִּי הוּא יוֹם תְּחִלָּה
l'mik-ra-ei ko-desh, zei-cher	לְמִקְרָאֵי קֹדֶשׁ, זֵכֶר
li-tzi-at Mitz-ra-yim. Ki va-nu	לִיצִיאַת מִצְרָיִם. כִּי־בָנוּ
va-char-ta v'o-ta-nu ki-dash-ta mi-kol	בָחַרְתָּ וְאוֹתָנוּ קִדַּשְׁתָּ מִכָּל־
ha-a-mim, v'sha-bat kod-sh'cha	הָעַמִּים, וְשַׁבַּת קָדְשְׁךָ
b'a-ha-va u-v'ra-tzon hin-chal-ta-nu.	בְּאַהֲבָה וּבְרָצוֹן הִנְחַלְתָּנוּ.
Ba-ruch a-ta Adonai, m'ka-deish	בָּרוּךְ אַתָּה יי מְקַדֵּשׁ
ha-shabbat.	הַשַּׁבָּת.

We praise You, Eternal God, Sovereign of the universe, Creator of the fruit of the vine.

We praise You, Eternal God, Sovereign of the universe: You call us to holiness with the Mitzvah of Shabbat: the sign of Your love, a reminder of Your creative work, and of our liberation from Egyptian bondage: our day of days. On Shabbat especially, we hearken to Your call to serve You as a holy people. We praise You, O God, for the holiness of Shabbat.

Before partaking of food

Ba-ruch a-ta Adonai, Eh-lo-hei-nu	בָּרוּךְ אַתָּה יי אֱלֹהֵינוּ
meh-lech ha-o-lam, ha-mo-tzi	מֶלֶךְ הָעוֹלָם, הַמּוֹצִיא
leh-chem min ha-a-retz.	לֶחֶם מִן הָאָרֶץ.

We praise You, Eternal God, Sovereign of the universe, for You cause bread to come forth from the earth.

Kiddush for Shabbat Morning

קִדּוּשׁ לְשַׁחֲרִית שֶׁל שַׁבָּת

🌱 *It is customary to recite the following before the midday meal.*

🌱 *Wine and grape juice are equally "fruit of the vine."*

WE HOLD THE CUP AND SAY:

*V'sham'ru v'nei Yis-ra-el et
ha-sha-bat, la-a-sot et ha-shabbat
l'do-ro-tam, b'rit o-lam. Bei-ni
u-vein b'nei Yis-ra-el ot hi
l'o-lam, ki shei-shet ya-mim a-sa
Adonai et ha-sha-ma-yim v'et
ha-a-retz, u-va-yom ha-sh'vi-i
sha-vat va-yi-na-fash.*

וְשָׁמְרוּ בְנֵי־יִשְׂרָאֵל אֶת־
הַשַּׁבָּת, לַעֲשׂוֹת אֶת־הַשַּׁבָּת
לְדֹרֹתָם בְּרִית עוֹלָם. בֵּינִי
וּבֵין בְּנֵי יִשְׂרָאֵל אוֹת הִוא
לְעֹלָם, כִּי־שֵׁשֶׁת יָמִים עָשָׂה
יהוה אֶת־הַשָּׁמַיִם וְאֶת־
הָאָרֶץ, וּבַיּוֹם הַשְּׁבִיעִי
שָׁבַת וַיִּנָּפַשׁ.

The people of Israel shall keep the Sabbath, observing the Sabbath in every generation as a covenant for all time. It is a sign between Me and the people of Israel forever. For in six days the Eternal God made heaven and earth, but on the seventh day God rested and was refreshed.

*Al kein bei-rach Adonai et yom
ha-shabbat va-y'ka-d'shei-hu.*

עַל־כֵּן בֵּרַךְ יהוה אֶת־יוֹם
הַשַּׁבָּת וַיְקַדְּשֵׁהוּ.

Therefore the Eternal One blessed the seventh day and called it holy.

*Ba-ruch a-ta Adonai, Eh-lo-hei-nu
meh-lech ha-o-lam, bo-rei p'ri
ha-ga-fen.*

בָּרוּךְ אַתָּה יי אֱלֹהֵינוּ
מֶלֶךְ הָעוֹלָם, בּוֹרֵא פְּרִי
הַגָּפֶן.

We praise You, Eternal God, Sovereign of the universe, Creator of the fruit of the vine.

43

Before partaking of food

Ba-ruch a-ta Adonai, Eh-lo-hei-nu
meh-lech ha-o-lam, ha-mo-tzi
leh-chem min ha-a-retz.

בָּרוּךְ אַתָּה יי אֱלֹהֵינוּ
מֶלֶךְ הָעוֹלָם, הַמּוֹצִיא
לֶחֶם מִן הָאָרֶץ.

We praise You, Eternal God, Sovereign of the universe, for You cause bread to come forth from the earth.

Songs for Shabbat

שָׁלוֹם עֲלֵיכֶם

שָׁלוֹם עֲלֵיכֶם, מַלְאֲכֵי הַשָּׁרֵת, מַלְאֲכֵי עֶלְיוֹן,
מִמֶּלֶךְ מַלְכֵי הַמְּלָכִים, הַקָּדוֹשׁ בָּרוּךְ הוּא.

Sha-lom a-lei-chem mal-a-chei ha-sha-reit, mal-a-chei el-yon,
Mi-meh-lech ma-l'chei ha-m'la-chim, ha-ka-dosh ba-ruch hu.

בּוֹאֲכֶם לְשָׁלוֹם, מַלְאֲכֵי הַשָּׁלוֹם, מַלְאֲכֵי עֶלְיוֹן,
מִמֶּלֶךְ מַלְכֵי הַמְּלָכִים, הַקָּדוֹשׁ בָּרוּךְ הוּא.

Bo-a-chem l'sha-lom, mal-a-chei ha-sha-lom, mal-a-chei el-yon,
Mi-meh-lech ma-l'chei ha-m'la-chim, ha-ka-dosh ba-ruch hu.

בָּרְכוּנִי לְשָׁלוֹם, מַלְאֲכֵי הַשָּׁלוֹם, מַלְאֲכֵי עֶלְיוֹן,
מִמֶּלֶךְ מַלְכֵי הַמְּלָכִים, הַקָּדוֹשׁ בָּרוּךְ הוּא.

Ba-r'chu-ni l'sha-lom, mal-a-chei ha-sha-lom, mal-a-chei el-yon,
Mi-meh-lech ma-l'chei ha-m'la-chim, ha-ka-dosh ba-ruch hu.

צֵאתְכֶם לְשָׁלוֹם, מַלְאֲכֵי הַשָּׁלוֹם, מַלְאֲכֵי עֶלְיוֹן,
מִמֶּלֶךְ מַלְכֵי הַמְּלָכִים, הַקָּדוֹשׁ בָּרוּךְ הוּא.

Tzei-t'chem l'sha-lom, mal-a-chei ha-sha-lom, mal-a-chei el-yon,
Mi-meh-lech ma-l'chei ha-m'la-chim, ha-ka-dosh ba-ruch hu.

❧ *For translation, see page 37.*

שַׁבָּת הַמַּלְכָּה

הַחַמָּה מֵרֹאשׁ הָאִילָנוֹת נִסְתַּלְּקָה,
בֹּאוּ וְנֵצֵא לִקְרַאת שַׁבָּת הַמַּלְכָּה.
הִנֵּה הִיא יוֹרֶדֶת, הַקְּדוֹשָׁה הַבְּרוּכָה.
וְעִמָּהּ מַלְאָכִים, צְבָא שָׁלוֹם וּמְנוּחָה.
בֹּאִי בֹּאִי הַמַּלְכָּה, בֹּאִי בֹּאִי הַכַּלָּה.
שָׁלוֹם עֲלֵיכֶם מַלְאֲכֵי הַשָּׁלוֹם.

The sun on the treetops no longer is seen,
Come gather to welcome the Sabbath, our queen.
Behold her descending, the holy, the blessed,
And with her the angels of peace and of rest.
Draw near, draw near, and here abide,
Draw near, draw near, O Sabbath bride.
Peace also to you, you angels of peace.

יוֹם זֶה לְיִשְׂרָאֵל

יוֹם זֶה לְיִשְׂרָאֵל אוֹרָה וְשִׂמְחָה, שַׁבַּת מְנוּחָה.

צִוִּיתָ פִּקּוּדִים בְּמַעֲמַד סִינַי,

שַׁבָּת וּמוֹעֲדִים לִשְׁמוֹר בְּכָל־שָׁנַי,

לַעֲרוֹךְ לְפָנַי מַשְׂאֵת וַאֲרוּחָה,

שַׁבַּת מְנוּחָה.

יוֹם זֶה לְיִשְׂרָאֵל אוֹרָה וְשִׂמְחָה, שַׁבַּת מְנוּחָה.

קִדַּשְׁתָּ בֵּרַכְתָּ אוֹתוֹ מִכָּל־יָמִים

בְּשֵׁשֶׁת כִּלִּיתָ מְלֶאכֶת עוֹלָמִים,

בּוֹ מָצְאוּ עֲגוּמִים הַשְׁקֵט וּבִטְחָה,

שַׁבַּת מְנוּחָה.

יוֹם זֶה לְיִשְׂרָאֵל אוֹרָה וְשִׂמְחָה, שַׁבַּת מְנוּחָה.

Yom zeh l'yis-ra-el, o-ra v'sim-cha, shabbat m'nu-cha.

Tzi-vi-ta pi-ku-dim b'ma-a-mad si-nai,
shabbat u-mo-a-dim lish-mor b'chol sha-nai,
la-ar-och l'fa-nai mas-eit va-a-ru-cha,
shabbat m'nu-cha.

Yom zeh l'yis-ra-el, o-ra v'sim-cha, shabbat m'nu-cha.

Ki-dash-ta bei-rach-ta o-to mi-kol ya-mim,
b'shei-shet ki-li-ta m'leh-chet o-la-mim,
bo matz-u a-gu-mim hash-keit u-vi-t'-cha,
shabbat m'nu-cha.

Yom zeh l'yis-ra-el, o-ra v'sim-cha, shabbat m'nu-cha.

This day is one of light and gladness, a Sabbath of rest . . .

46

❧

יְדִיד נֶפֶשׁ, אָב הָרַחֲמָן
מְשׁוֹךְ עַבְדְּךָ אֶל רְצוֹנֶךָ.
יָרוּץ עַבְדְּךָ כְּמוֹ אַיָל
יִשְׁתַּחֲוֶה אֶל מוּל הֲדָרֶךָ.

Y'did neh-fesh, av ha-ra-cha-man
m'shoch av-d'cha el r'tzo-neh-cha.
Ya-rutz av-d'cha k'mo a-yal,
yish-ta-cha-veh el mul ha-da-reh-cha.

Heart's delight, Source of mercy, draw Your servant into Your arms . . .

❧

כִּי אֶשְׁמְרָה שַׁבָּת, אֵל יִשְׁמְרֵנִי.

Ki esh-m'ra Shabbat, El yish-m'rei-ni.

כִּי אֶשְׁמְרָה שַׁבָּת, אֵל יִשְׁמְרֵנִי.

Ki esh-m'ra Shabbat, El yish-m'rei-ni.

אוֹת הִיא לְעוֹלְמֵי עַד, בֵּינוֹ וּבֵינִי.

Ot hi l'o-l'mei ad, bei-no u-vei-ni.

אוֹת הִיא לְעוֹלְמֵי עַד, בֵּינוֹ וּבֵינִי.

Ot hi l'o-l'mei ad, bei-no u-vei-ni.

Shabbat is the bond forever between us and our God.

❧

וְטַהֵר לִבֵּנוּ לְעָבְדְּךָ בֶּאֱמֶת.

V'ta-heir li-bei-nu l'ov-d'cha beh-eh-met.

Purify our hearts to serve You in truth.

❧

47

עַל שְׁלֹשָׁה דְבָרִים הָעוֹלָם עוֹמֵד:

Al sh'lo-sha d'va-rim ha-o-lam o-meid:

עַל הַתּוֹרָה וְעַל הָעֲבוֹדָה וְעַל גְּמִילוּת חֲסָדִים.

al ha-torah, v'al ha-a-vo-dah, v'al g'mi-lut cha-sa-dim.

The world stands on three things: on Torah, on worship, and on loving kindness.

❧

דָּוִד מֶלֶךְ יִשְׂרָאֵל חַי וְקַיָּם.

Da-vid meh-lech Yis-ra-el chai v'ka-yam.

David, king of Israel, lives and endures.

COME, O SABBATH DAY

Come, O Sabbath day and bring
Peace and healing on your wing;
And to every weary one
Let your word of blessing come:
You shall rest, You shall rest.

Welcome Sabbath, let depart
Every care of troubled heart;
Now the daily task is done,
Let your word of comfort come:
You shall rest, You shall rest.

Wipe from ev'ry cheek the tear,
Banish care and silence fear;
All hearts turning to the best,
Teach us the divine behest:
You shall rest, You shall rest.

O HOLY SABBATH DAY

O holy Sabbath day, draw near,
You are the source of bliss and cheer;
The first in God's creative thought,
The final aim of all God wrought.

    Welcome, welcome, day of rest,
    Day of joy that God has blessed.

Let all rejoice with all their might,
The Sabbath, freedom brings and light;
Let songs of praise to God ascend,
And voices sweet in chorus blend.

    Welcome, welcome, day of rest,
    Day of joy that God has blessed.

Now come, O blessed Sabbath-Bride,
Our joy, our comfort, and our pride;
All cares and sorrow now bid cease,
And fill our waiting hearts with peace.

    Welcome, welcome, day of rest,
    Day of joy that God has blessed.

COME, O HOLY SABBATH EVENING

Come, O holy Sabbath evening,
Crown our toil with well earned rest;
Bring us hallowed hours of gladness,
Day of days beloved and blest.

Weave your mystic spell around us
With the glow of Sabbath light:
As we read the ancient wisdom,
Learn its laws of truth and right.

Come, O holy Sabbath spirit,
Radiant shine from every eye;
Lending us your benediction,
Filling every heart with joy.

Havdalah I

❧ *The leader lights the candle and hands it to the youngest person present.*

הִנֵּה אֵל יְשׁוּעָתִי,
אֶבְטַח וְלֹא אֶפְחָד.
כִּי־עָזִּי וְזִמְרָת יָהּ יהוה,
וַיְהִי־לִי לִישׁוּעָה.
וּשְׁאַבְתֶּם־מַיִם בְּשָׂשׂוֹן
מִמַּעַיְנֵי הַיְשׁוּעָה.
לַיהוה הַיְשׁוּעָה,
עַל־עַמְּךָ בִרְכָתֶךָ, סֶּלָה.
יהוה צְבָאוֹת עִמָּנוּ,
מִשְׂגָּב־לָנוּ אֱלֹהֵי יַעֲקֹב, סֶלָה.
יהוה צְבָאוֹת,
אַשְׁרֵי אָדָם בֹּטֵחַ בָּךְ.
יהוה הוֹשִׁיעָה;
הַמֶּלֶךְ יַעֲנֵנוּ בְיוֹם־קָרְאֵנוּ.
לַיְּהוּדִים הָיְתָה אוֹרָה וְשִׂמְחָה
וְשָׂשׂוֹן וִיקָר;
כֵּן תִּהְיֶה לָּנוּ.
כּוֹס־יְשׁוּעוֹת אֶשָּׂא,
וּבְשֵׁם יהוה אֶקְרָא.

Behold, God is my Help;

> *trusting in the Eternal One, I am not afraid.*

For the Eternal One is my strength and my song,

> *and has become my salvation.*

With joy we draw water

> *from the wells of salvation.*

The Eternal One brings deliverance,

> *and blessing to the people.*

The God of the hosts of heaven is with us;

the God of Jacob is our stronghold.

God of the hosts of heaven,

happy is the one who trusts in You!

Save us, Eternal One;

answer us, when we call upon You.

Give us light and joy, gladness and honor,

as in the happiest days of our people's past.

Then shall we lift up the cup to rejoice in Your saving power,

and call out Your name in praise.

THE LEADER RAISES THE CUP OF WINE OR GRAPE JUICE AND SAYS:

Ba-ruch a-ta Adonai, Eh-lo-hei-nu meh-lech ha-o-lam, bo-rei p'ri ha-ga-fen.

בָּרוּךְ אַתָּה יי אֱלֹהֵינוּ מֶלֶךְ הָעוֹלָם, בּוֹרֵא פְּרִי הַגָּפֶן.

We praise You, Eternal God, Sovereign of the universe, Creator of the fruit of the vine.

THE LEADER HOLDS UP THE SPICE-BOX AND SAYS:

Ba-ruch a-ta Adonai, Eh-lo-hei-nu meh-lech ha-o-lam, bo-rei mi-nei v'sa-mim.

בָּרוּךְ אַתָּה יי אֱלֹהֵינוּ מֶלֶךְ הָעוֹלָם, בּוֹרֵא מִינֵי בְשָׂמִים.

We praise You, Eternal God, Sovereign of the universe, Creator of the world's spices.

THE SPICE BOX IS CIRCULATED AND ALL PRESENT INHALE ITS FRAGRANCE.

THE LEADER HOLDS UP THE CANDLE AND SAYS:

*Ba-ruch a-ta Adonai, Eh-lo-hei-nu
meh-lech ha-o-lam, bo-rei m'o-rei
ha-eish.*

בָּרוּךְ אַתָּה יי אֱלֹהֵינוּ
מֶלֶךְ הָעוֹלָם, בּוֹרֵא מְאוֹרֵי
הָאֵשׁ.

We praise You, Eternal God, Sovereign of the universe, Creator of fire.

THE CANDLE IS HELD HIGH AS THE LEADER SAYS:

בָּרוּךְ אַתָּה יי אֱלֹהֵינוּ מֶלֶךְ הָעוֹלָם, הַמַּבְדִּיל בֵּין קֹדֶשׁ לְחוֹל, בֵּין אוֹר
לְחֹשֶׁךְ, בֵּין יִשְׂרָאֵל לָעַמִּים, בֵּין יוֹם הַשְּׁבִיעִי לְשֵׁשֶׁת יְמֵי הַמַּעֲשֶׂה.

We praise You, Eternal God, Sovereign of the universe: You make distinctions, teaching us to distinguish the commonplace from the holy; You create light and darkness, Israel and the nations, the seventh day of rest and the six days of labor.

בָּרוּךְ אַתָּה יי הַמַּבְדִּיל בֵּין קֹדֶשׁ לְחוֹל.

We praise You, O God: You call us to distinguish the commonplace from the holy.

ALL PRESENT SIP FROM THE CUP.

THE CANDLE IS EXTINGUISHED BY IMMERSING IT IN THE CUP.

We give thanks for the Sabbath day now ending. We are grateful for its many blessings: for peace and joy, rest for the body, and refreshment for the soul. May something of its meaning remain with us as we enter the new week, lifting all that we do to a higher plane, and inspiring us to work with new heart for the coming of the day of redemption from every form of oppression. Of this redemption the prophet Elijah is a symbol:

אֵלִיָּהוּ הַנָּבִיא, אֵלִיָּהוּ הַתִּשְׁבִּי,

Ei-li-ya-hu ha-na-vi, Ei-li-ya-hu ha-tish-bi;

אֵלִיָּהוּ, אֵלִיָּהוּ, אֵלִיָּהוּ הַגִּלְעָדִי.

Ei-li-ya-hu, Ei-li-ya-hu, Ei-li-ya-hu ha-gil-adi.

בִּמְהֵרָה בְיָמֵינוּ, יָבֹא אֵלֵינוּ;

Bi-m'hei-ra v'ya-mei-nu, ya-vo ei-lei-nu;

עִם מָשִׁיחַ בֶּן דָּוִד, עִם מָשִׁיחַ בֶּן דָּוִד.

im ma-shi-ach ben Da-vid, im ma-shi-ach ben Da-vid.

אֵלִיָּהוּ הַנָּבִיא . . .

Ei-li-ya-hu ha-na-vi . . .

❧

הַמַּבְדִּיל בֵּין קֹדֶשׁ לְחוֹל, חַטֹּאתֵינוּ הוּא יִמְחֹל,
זַרְעֵנוּ וְכַסְפֵּנוּ יַרְבֶּה כַחוֹל, וְכַכּוֹכָבִים בַּלָּיְלָה.
שָׁבוּעַ טוֹב . . .

Ha-mav-dil bein ko-desh l'chol, cha-to-tei-nu hu yim-chol,
zar-ei-nu v'chas-pei-nu yar-beh ka-chol, v'cha-ko-cha-vim ba-
lai-la.
Sha-vu-ah tov . . .

יוֹם פָּנָה כְּצֵל תֹּמֶר, אֶקְרָא לָאֵל, עָלַי גֹמֵר;
אָמַר שׁוֹמֵר, אָתָא בֹקֶר וְגַם־לָיְלָה.
שָׁבוּעַ טוֹב . . .

Yom pa-na k'tzeil to-mer, ek-ra la-eil, a-lai go-meir;
a-mar sho-meir, a-ta vo-ker, v'gam lai-la.
Sha-vu-ah tov . . .

צִדְקָתְךָ כְּהַר תָּבוֹר, עַל חֲטָאַי עָבוֹר תַּעֲבוֹר,

כְּיוֹם אֶתְמוֹל כִּי יַעֲבוֹר, וְאַשְׁמוּרָה בַלֵּיְלָה.

שָׁבְוּעַ טוֹב . . .

Tzid-ka-t'cha k'har ta-vor, al cha-ta-ai a-vor ta-a-vor,
k'yom et-mol ki ya-a-vor, v'ash-mu-ra va-lai-la.
Sha-vu-ah tov . . .

הַעָתֵר, נוֹרָא וְאָיוֹם, אֲשַׁוֵּעַ, תְּנָה פִדְיוֹם,

בְּנֶשֶׁף, בְּעֶרֶב יוֹם, בְּאִישׁוֹן לָיְלָה.

שָׁבְוּעַ טוֹב . . .

Hei-a-teir, no-ra v'a-yom, a-sha-vei-a, t'na fid-yom,
b'neh-shef, b'eh-rev yom, b'i-shon lai-la.
Sha-vu-ah tov . . .

❦

You teach us to distinguish between the commonplace and the holy: teach us also to transform our sins to merits. Let those who love you be numerous as the sands and the stars.

Day has declined, the shadows are gone; we call to the One whose word is good. The sentry says: 'Morning will come, though the night seems long.'

Your righteousness is a majestic mountain: forgive our sins. Let them be as yesterday when it is past, as a watch in the night.

Hear our prayer, O awesome God, and grant redemption: in the twilight, in the waning of the day, or in the blackness of the night!

שָׁבְוּעַ טוֹב . . .

Sha-vu-ah tov, Sha-vu-ah tov, Sha-vu-ah tov, Sha-vu-ah tov.

A good week, a week of peace;
may gladness reign and light increase.

Havdalah II

🍂 *The following is an interpretive version of Havdalah.*

In the Torah we read: The Eternal One spoke to Aaron: 'You shall distinguish between the sacred and the profane.' Like Aaron, first of the priests, we who were called at Sinai to be a kingdom of priests are charged to make Havdalah.

We must distinguish between sacred and profane, between holy and common.

To this end has Shabbat been set aside:

Shabbat, most precious of days; Shabbat, the day of holiness.

Shabbat is blessed rest from daily toil. More than rest, Shabbat is freedom:

To reach out to God, to family and friends.

To search and hope to find goodness and beauty, holiness and truth.

Our fathers knew Shabbat as refuge from this world's compromises, from the brutalities and hurts of competition.

It was refuge, haven, oasis for our mothers: a day of release from earthbound pursuits, from the relentless struggle for daily bread.

A foretaste of heaven which they called: 'Yom sheh-ku-lo Shabbat,' a time that is all Shabbat.

But our Shabbat is here on earth, this day's earth, and end it does.

With all reluctance we say farewell to this foretaste of heaven.

Let us carry into the coming week some Shabbat hope and joy, and bring them into our offices and shops, the choices we make, our hours of leisure.

VERSES OF THANKS

The ancients took words from Scripture to voice their thanks to God who sustains us during the week. Within their words of praise was the hint of prayer for life and health in the week to come. May their loving faith be ours, as we make their words of praise our own.

**THE LEADER LIGHTS THE CANDLE AND HANDS IT
TO THE YOUNGEST PERSON PRESENT.**

הִנֵּה אֵל יְשׁוּעָתִי,

אֶבְטַח וְלֹא אֶפְחָד.

כִּי־עָזִּי וְזִמְרָת יָהּ יהוה,

וַיְהִי־לִי לִישׁוּעָה.

וּשְׁאַבְתֶּם־מַֽיִם בְּשָׂשׂוֹן

מִמַּעַיְנֵי הַיְשׁוּעָה.

לַיהוה הַיְשׁוּעָה,

עַל־עַמְּךָ בִרְכָתֶֽךָ, סֶּֽלָה.

יהוה צְבָאוֹת עִמָּֽנוּ,

מִשְׂגָּב־לָֽנוּ אֱלֹהֵי יַעֲקֹב, סֶּֽלָה.

יהוה צְבָאוֹת,

אַשְׁרֵי אָדָם בֹּטֵחַ בָּךְ.

יהוה הוֹשִׁיעָה;

הַמֶּֽלֶךְ יַעֲנֵֽנוּ בְיוֹם־קָרְאֵֽנוּ.

לַיְּהוּדִים הָיְתָה אוֹרָה וְשִׂמְחָה

וְשָׂשֹׂן וִיקָר;

כֵּן תִּהְיֶה לָֽנוּ.

כּוֹס־יְשׁוּעוֹת אֶשָּׂא,

וּבְשֵׁם יהוה אֶקְרָא.

Behold, God is my Help;

trusting in the Eternal One, I am not afraid.

For the Eternal One is my strength and my song,

and has become my salvation.

With joy we draw water

from the wells of salvation.

The Eternal One brings deliverance,

and blessing to the people.

The God of the hosts of heaven is with us;

the God of Jacob is our stronghold.

56

God of the hosts of heaven,

happy is the one who trusts in You!

Save us, Eternal One;

answer us, when we call upon You.

Give us light and joy, gladness and honor,

as in the happiest days of our people's past.

Then shall we lift up the cup to rejoice in Your saving power,

and call out Your name in praise.

THE LEADER RAISES THE CUP OF WINE OR GRAPE JUICE AND SAYS:

The fruit of the vine gladdens the heart. In our gladness, we see beyond the ugliness and misery which stain the world. Our eyes open to unnoticed grace, blessings till now unseen, and the promise of goodness we can bring to flower.

Ba-ruch a-ta Adonai, Eh-lo-hei-nu meh-lech ha-o-lam, bo-rei p'ri ha-ga-fen.

בָּרוּךְ אַתָּה יי אֱלֹהֵינוּ מֶלֶךְ הָעוֹלָם, בּוֹרֵא פְּרִי הַגָּפֶן.

° We give thanks for the goodness of fruit, for sun, air, and earth, and for all who labor on the soil.

THE LEADER HOLDS UP THE SPICE-BOX AND SAYS:

The added soul Shabbat confers is leaving now, and these spices will console us at the moment of its passing. They remind us that the six days will pass, and Shabbat return. And their bouquet will make us yearn with thankful heart for the sweetness of rest and the fragrance of growing things; for the clean smell of rainwashed earth and the sad innocence of childhood; and for the dream of a world healed of pain, pure and wholesome as on that first Shabbat, when God, finding all things good, rested from the work of creation.

° This signifies that the English is a variation on the theme of the Hebrew.

57

Ba-ruch a-ta Adonai, Eh-lo-hei-nu
meh-lech ha-o-lam, bo-rei mi-nei
ve-sa-mim.

בָּרוּךְ אַתָּה יי אֱלֹהֵינוּ
מֶלֶךְ הָעוֹלָם, בּוֹרֵא מִינֵי
בְשָׂמִים.

° We give thanks for this world and its sweetness, and for Shabbat, which gives fragrance to all the days.

THE SPICE BOX IS CIRCULATED AND ALL PRESENT INHALE ITS FRAGRANCE.

THE LEADER HOLDS UP THE CANDLE AND SAYS:

The Rabbis tell us: As night descended at the end of the world's first Sabbath, Adam feared and wept. Then God showed him how to make fire, and by its light and warmth to dispel the darkness and its terrors. Kindling light is a symbol of our first labor upon the earth.

Shabbat departs as we kindle fire and the workday begins. We, who dread the night no more, thank God for the flame by which we turn earth's raw stuff into things of use and beauty.

The Havadalah candle's double wick reminds us that all qualities are paired. We have the power to kindle many fires, some useful, others baneful. Let us be on guard never to let this gift of fire devour human life, sear cities, forests, and fields. Let the fire we kindle be holy; let it bring light and warmth to all humanity.

Ba-ruch a-ta Adonai, Eh-lo-hei-nu
meh-lech ha-o-lam, bo-rei m'o-rei
ha-eish.

בָּרוּךְ אַתָּה יי אֱלֹהֵינוּ
מֶלֶךְ הָעוֹלָם, בּוֹרֵא מְאוֹרֵי
הָאֵשׁ.

°We give thanks for all that gives light and warmth to flesh and blood.

58

SEPARATION

The light will soon be gone, and Shabbat with it, yet hope illumines the night for us, who are prisoners of hope. Amid the reality of a world shrouded in deep darkness, our hope is steadfast and our faith sure. There will come a Shabbat without Havdalah, when the glory of Shabbat, its peace and its love, will endure for ever.

THE CANDLE IS HELD HIGH AS THE LEADER SAYS:

בָּרוּךְ אַתָּה יי אֱלֹהֵינוּ מֶלֶךְ הָעוֹלָם, הַמַּבְדִּיל בֵּין קֹדֶשׁ לְחוֹל, בֵּין אוֹר לְחֹשֶׁךְ, בֵּין יִשְׂרָאֵל לָעַמִּים, בֵּין יוֹם הַשְּׁבִיעִי לְשֵׁשֶׁת יְמֵי הַמַּעֲשֶׂה. בָּרוּךְ אַתָּה יי הַמַּבְדִּיל בֵּין קֹדֶשׁ לְחוֹל.

° We give thanks to the One who makes distinctions, teaching us to transform the commonplace into the holy; creating light and darkness, Israel and the nations, the seventh day of rest and the six days of labor.

ALL PRESENT SIP FROM THE CUP.

THE CANDLE IS EXTINGUISHED BY IMMERSING IT IN THE CUP.

Elijah!
Week after week we wait,
at Sabbath's end we wait for you,
we wait to be redeemed:
from guilt and oppression redeemed;
from empty nights redeemed;
and from the stuttering of our hearts,
from that, too, redeemed.
Do you wait for us?
Do you await one sign,
one deed, one surprise?
Yes, yes! You wait for us,
you wait for us to wait no more.
Your presence now we invoke in song:

אֵלִיָּהוּ הַנָּבִיא, אֵלִיָּהוּ הַתִּשְׁבִּי,

Ei-li-ya-hu ha-na-vi, Ei-li-ya-hu ha-tish-bi;

אֵלִיָּהוּ, אֵלִיָּהוּ, אֵלִיָּהוּ הַגִּלְעָדִי.

Ei-li-ya-hu, Ei-li-ya-hu, Ei-li-ya-hu ha-gil-adi.

בִּמְהֵרָה בְיָמֵינוּ, יָבֹא אֵלֵינוּ;

Bi-m'hei-ra v'ya-mei-nu, ya-vo ei-lei-nu;

עִם מָשִׁיחַ בֶּן דָּוִד, עִם מָשִׁיחַ בֶּן דָּוִד.

im ma-shi-ach ben Da-vid, im ma-shi-ach ben Da-vid.

. . . אֵלִיָּהוּ הַנָּבִיא

Ei-li-ya-hu ha-na-vi . . .

שָׁבוּעַ טוֹב . . .

Sha-vu-ah tov, Sha-vu-ah tov, Sha-vu-ah tov, Sha-vu-ah tov.

A good week, a week of peace;
may gladness reign and light increase.

For the New Moon

קִדּוּשׁ לְבָנָה

❧ *It is customary, at the beginning of the new (lunar) month, to go outdoors in celebration of the first appearance of the New Moon, and to recite the following:*

הַלְלוּיָהּ!

הַלְלוּ אֶת־יהוה מִן־הַשָּׁמַיִם,

הַלְלוּהוּ בַּמְּרוֹמִים.

הַלְלוּהוּ שֶׁמֶשׁ וְיָרֵחַ,

הַלְלוּהוּ כָּל־כּוֹכְבֵי אוֹר.

הַלְלוּ אֶת־יהוה מִן־הָאָרֶץ,

תַּנִּינִים וְכָל־תְּהֹמוֹת,

אֵשׁ וּבָרָד, שֶׁלֶג וְקִיטוֹר,

רוּחַ סְעָרָה עֹשָׂה דְבָרוֹ.

הֶהָרִים וְכָל־גְּבָעוֹת,

עֵץ פְּרִי וְכָל־אֲרָזִים,

הַחַיָּה וְכָל־בְּהֵמָה,

רֶמֶשׂ וְצִפּוֹר כָּנָף,

מַלְכֵי־אֶרֶץ וְכָל־לְאֻמִּים,

שָׂרִים וְכָל־שֹׁפְטֵי אָרֶץ,

בַּחוּרִים וְגַם־בְּתוּלוֹת,

זְקֵנִים עִם־נְעָרִים.

יְהַלְלוּ אֶת־שֵׁם יהוה,

כִּי־נִשְׂגָּב שְׁמוֹ לְבַדּוֹ,

הוֹדוֹ עַל־אֶרֶץ וְשָׁמָיִם.

הַלְלוּיָהּ!

Praise the Eternal One!

Praise God in the high heavens, give praise in deep space. Give praise, sun and moon, give praise, you shining stars. Let earth resound with praise of God: teeming oceans, fire and hail, snow and mist, storm and wind, mountains and hills, fruit trees and cedars, wild beasts and cattle, reptiles and birds, rulers of nations, judges and leaders, women and men, the old and the young. Let all give praise to God, whose name alone is exalted, whose glory pervades heaven and earth. Halleluyah! Praise the Eternal God!

בָּרוּךְ אַתָּה יי אֱלֹהֵינוּ מֶלֶךְ הָעוֹלָם, אֲשֶׁר בְּמַאֲמָרוֹ בָּרָא שְׁחָקִים, וּבְרוּחַ פִּיו כָּל־צְבָאָם. חֹק וּזְמַן נָתַן לָהֶם, שֶׁלֹּא יְשַׁנּוּ אֶת־תַּפְקִידָם. שָׂשִׂים וּשְׂמֵחִים לַעֲשׂוֹת רְצוֹן קוֹנָם, פּוֹעֵל אֱמֶת, שֶׁפְּעֻלָּתוֹ אֱמֶת. וְלַלְּבָנָה אָמַר שֶׁתִּתְחַדֵּשׁ; עֲטֶרֶת תִּפְאֶרֶת לַעֲמוּסֵי בָטֶן. שֶׁהֵם עֲתִידִים לְהִתְחַדֵּשׁ כְּמוֹתָהּ וּלְפָאֵר לְיוֹצְרָם עַל שֵׁם כְּבוֹד מַלְכוּתוֹ.

We praise You, Eternal God, Sovereign of the universe: Your word made the heavens; the breath of Your lips, their starry hosts. Your law immutable fixed their orbits; they delight in Your will, O faithful Creator whose work holds true. To the moon You say: 'Renew yourself.' To us, O God, You are a crown of glory.

We too will find renewal in time to come, to honor our Maker in a world You have redeemed.

בָּרוּךְ אַתָּה, יי, מְחַדֵּשׁ חֳדָשִׁים.

We praise You, O God, Renewer of time, for every new month.

Welcoming Yom Tov

קַבָּלַת יוֹם טוֹב

❧ *It is customary, before the beginning of Yom Tov, for each member of the household to put money aside for some worthy cause.*

Happy are those who consider the poor.

[Psalm 41:2]

We hereby vow to fulfill the Mitzvah of Tzedakah as we begin this festival. We remember the words of Your prophet, who called us to share our bread with the hungry, to clothe the naked, and never to hide ourselves from our own kin.

May we, together with the whole House of Israel, be mindful of the needs of others, sharing with them the fruits of our labor and helping to sustain them. May the promise be fulfilled:

Then your light shall blaze forth like the dawn, and your wounds shall quickly heal; your righteousness shall walk before you, the glory of the Eternal One shall follow you.

We praise You, O God. Let Your light shine upon us. May our hearts and our homes be illumined by the assurance of Your love, and sanctified by our sense of Your presence.

הַדְלָקַת הַנֵּרוֹת

We praise You, Eternal God, Sovereign of the universe: You hallow us with Your Mitzvot, and command us to kindle (the Sabbath and) Festival lights.

Ba-ruch a-ta Adonai, Eh-lo-hei-nu	בָּרוּךְ אַתָּה יי אֱלֹהֵינוּ
meh-lech ha-o-lam, ah-sher	מֶלֶךְ הָעוֹלָם, אֲשֶׁר
ki-d'sha-nu b'mitz-vo-tav v'tzi-va-nu	קִדְּשָׁנוּ בְּמִצְוֹתָיו וְצִוָּנוּ
l'had-lik ner shel (Shabbat v'shel)	לְהַדְלִיק נֵר שֶׁל [שַׁבָּת וְשֶׁל]
yom tov.	יוֹם טוֹב.

We thank You, O God, for the joy of Yom Tov, and for the opportunity to celebrate it in the company of those we love.

We give thanks, therefore, for our home, where we find rest from the day's work, and refuge from cares. May it be warm with love and companionship; may our joys be heightened and our sorrows softened by the love we give and receive.

THE PARENTS BLESS THE CHILDREN

Blessed is the parent, and blessed the child, when their hearts are turned to one another. Blessed is the home filled with gladness and light, the spirit of Yom Tov. May God bless you and guide you. Seek truth always, be charitable in your words, just and loving in your deeds. A noble heritage has been entrusted to you; guard it well.

FOR A BOY

יְשִׂמְךָ אֱלֹהִים כְּאֶפְרַיִם וְכִמְנַשֶּׁה.

May God inspire you to live in the tradition of Ephraim and Menasheh, who carried forward the life of our people.

FOR A GIRL

יְשִׂמֵךְ אֱלֹהִים כְּשָׂרָה, רִבְקָה, לֵאָה וְרָחֵל.

May God inspire you to live in the tradition of Sarah, Rebekah, Leah, and Rachel, who carried forward the life of our people.

FOR BOTH

Y'va-reh-ch'cha Adonai v'yish-m'reh-cha. יְבָרֶכְךָ יהוה וְיִשְׁמְרֶךָ.
Ya-eir Adonai pa-nav ei-leh-cha יָאֵר יהוה פָּנָיו אֵלֶיךָ
vi-chu-neh-ka. וִיחֻנֶּךָּ.
Yi-sa Adonai pa-nav ei-leh-cha יִשָּׂא יהוה פָּנָיו אֵלֶיךָ
v'ya-seim l'cha sha-lom. וְיָשֵׂם לְךָ שָׁלוֹם.

May God bless you and keep you. May God look kindly upon you, and be gracious to you. May God reach out to you in tenderness, and give you peace.

❧ *There may now be a moment of silence, in which all present think of one another with blessing.*

Kiddush for Yom Tov Evening

קִדּוּשׁ

❧ *Wine and grape juice are equally "fruit of the vine."*

ON PESACH

Pesach teaches that all people must be free to serve God, free from oppression, free to live in their own land.

With the fruit of the vine, our symbol of joy, we celebrate this day, and give thanks for the liberating power that redeemed Israel from Egyptian bondage. May our celebration make us aware of the blessing and responsibility of freedom; may it teach us concern for all human beings.

❧ *On Shabbat, continue on page 66.*
Otherwise, continue on page 67.

ON SHAVUOT

Shavuot calls upon us to hallow our lives by seeking truth and establishing justice in our community.

With the fruit of the vine, our symbol of joy, we celebrate this day by giving thanks for Torah and for the first fruits of earth's goodness. May our celebration help us to live by the light of Torah, giving of the first fruits of our strength for the well-being of our community and our people.

❧ *On Shabbat, continue on page 66.*
Otherwise, continue on page 67.

ON SUKKOT

❧ *On Sukkot it is customary to recite the Kiddush in the Sukkah.*

Sukkot teaches us to give thanks for the harvest of fruit and grain, and to share our blessings with others.

With the fruit of the vine, our symbol of joy, we celebrate this day, and give thanks that God has been with us throughout all our people's wanderings, sustaining us from year to year by the fruitfulness of our world. Thankful for God's goodness, may we be inspired to bring blessing to those who are in need.

❧ *On Shabbat, continue below. Otherwise, continue on page 67.*

ON SH'MINI ATZERET-SIMCHAT TORAH

This festival teaches that the study of Torah never ends, and that its influence can fill our lives with the beauty of holiness.

With the fruit of the vine, our symbol of joy, we celebrate this day, giving thanks for the great teachers of every generation. May our celebration make us eager to study our heritage and to use what we learn in the service of humanity.

❧ *On Shabbat, continue below. Otherwise, continue on page 67.*

ON SHABBAT

❧ *When Shabbat coincides with Yom Tov, add this passage:*

WE HOLD THE CUP AND SAY:

Va-y'chu-lu ha-sha-ma-yim	וַיְכֻלּוּ הַשָּׁמַיִם
v'ha-a-retz v'chol tz'va-am,	וְהָאָרֶץ וְכָל־צְבָאָם:
va-y'chal Eh-lo-him ba-yom	וַיְכַל אֱלֹהִים בַּיּוֹם
ha-sh'vi-i m'lach-to a-sher	הַשְּׁבִיעִי מְלַאכְתּוֹ אֲשֶׁר
a-sa, va-yish-bot ba-yom	עָשָׂה וַיִּשְׁבֹּת בַּיּוֹם
ha-sh'vi-i mi-kol m'lach-to	הַשְּׁבִיעִי מִכָּל־מְלַאכְתּוֹ
a-sher a-sa. Va-y'va-rech	אֲשֶׁר עָשָׂה: וַיְבָרֶךְ
Eh-lo-him et yom ha-sh'vi-i	אֱלֹהִים אֶת־יוֹם הַשְּׁבִיעִי
va-y'ka-deish o-to, ki vo sha-vat	וַיְקַדֵּשׁ אֹתוֹ כִּי בוֹ שָׁבַת
mi-kol m'lach-to a-sher ba-ra	מִכָּל־מְלַאכְתּוֹ אֲשֶׁר־בָּרָא
Eh-lo-him la-a-sot.	אֱלֹהִים לַעֲשׂוֹת:

Now the whole universe—sky, earth, and all their array—
was completed. With the seventh day God ended the work
of creation, resting on the seventh day, with all the work
completed. Then God blessed the seventh day and
sanctified it, this day having completed the work of creation.

৺

ON ALL OCCASIONS

WE HOLD THE CUP AND SAY:

*Ba-ruch a-ta Adonai, Eh-lo-hei-nu
meh-lech ha-o-lam, bo-rei p'ri
ha-ga-fen.*

בָּרוּךְ אַתָּה יי אֱלֹהֵינוּ
מֶלֶךְ הָעוֹלָם, בּוֹרֵא פְּרִי
הַגָּפֶן.

We praise You, Eternal God, Sovereign of the universe, Creator of the
fruit of the vine.

*Baruch ata Adonai, Eh-lo-hei-nu
meh-lech ha-o-lam, a-sher ba-char
ba-nu mi-kol am, v'ro-m'ma-nu
mi-kol la-shon, v'kid'sha-nu
b'mitz-vo-tav. Va-ti-ten la-nu, Adonai
Eh-lohei-nu, b'a-ha-va (sha-ba-tot
li-m'nu-cha u-) mo-a-dim l'sim-cha,
cha-gim u-z'ma-nim l'sa-son, et yom
(ha-shabbat ha-zeh v'et yom)*

♦ *chag ha-su-kot ha-zeh,
z'man sim-cha-tei-nu,*

♦ *ha-sh'mi-nu chag ha-a-tzeh-ret
ha-zeh, z'man sim-cha-tei-nu,*

♦ *chag ha-ma-tzot ha-zeh,
z'man chei-ru-tei-nu,*

♦ *chag ha-sha-vu-ot ha-zeh,
z'man ma-tan to-ra-tei-nu,*

בָּרוּךְ אַתָּה יי אֱלֹהֵינוּ
מֶלֶךְ הָעוֹלָם, אֲשֶׁר בָּחַר
בָּנוּ מִכָּל־עָם, וְרוֹמְמָנוּ
מִכָּל־לָשׁוֹן, וְקִדְּשָׁנוּ
בְּמִצְוֹתָיו. וַתִּתֶּן לָנוּ, יי
אֱלֹהֵינוּ, בְּאַהֲבָה [שַׁבָּתוֹת
לִמְנוּחָה וּ] מוֹעֲדִים לְשִׂמְחָה,
חַגִּים וּזְמַנִּים לְשָׂשׂוֹן אֶת־יוֹם
[הַשַּׁבָּת הַזֶּה וְאֶת־יוֹם]

♦ חַג הַסֻּכּוֹת הַזֶּה,
זְמַן שִׂמְחָתֵנוּ,

♦ הַשְּׁמִינִי חַג הָעֲצֶרֶת
הַזֶּה, זְמַן שִׂמְחָתֵנוּ,

♦ חַג הַמַּצּוֹת הַזֶּה,
זְמַן חֵרוּתֵנוּ,

♦ חַג הַשָּׁבוּעוֹת הַזֶּה,
זְמַן מַתַּן תּוֹרָתֵנוּ,

mik-ra ko-desh, zei-cher li-tzi-at   מִקְרָא קֹדֶשׁ, זֵכֶר לִיצִיאַת

mitz-ra-yim. Ki va-nu va-char-ta   מִצְרָיִם. כִּי־בָנוּ בָחַרְתָּ

v'o-ta-nu ki-dash-ta mi-kol   וְאוֹתָנוּ קִדַּשְׁתָּ מִכָּל־

ha-a-mim, (v'sha-bat u-) mo-a-dei   הָעַמִּים, [וְשַׁבָּת וּ] מוֹעֲדֵי

kod-sh'cha (b'a-ha-va u-v'ra-tzon,)   קָדְשֶׁךָ [בְּאַהֲבָה וּבְרָצוֹן,]

b'sim-cha u-v'sa-son hin-chal-ta-nu.   בְּשִׂמְחָה וּבְשָׂשׂוֹן הִנְחַלְתָּנוּ.

Ba-ruch ata Adonai, m'ka-deish   בָּרוּךְ אַתָּה יי מְקַדֵּשׁ

(ha-shabbat v') Yis-ra-eil   [הַשַּׁבָּת וְ] יִשְׂרָאֵל

v'ha-z'ma-nim.   וְהַזְּמַנִּים.

Eternal God, You call us to Your service and hallow us with Mitzvot. In Your love You have given us (the Sabbath and its rest,) festive times and seasons, together with their joys. They are sacred meeting-days, reminders of our liberation from Egyptian bondage.

We praise You, O God, for these days sacred to Israel.

❦ *The following blessing is not recited on the last day of Pesach:*

Ba-ruch a-ta Adonai, Eh-lo-hei-nu   בָּרוּךְ אַתָּה יי אֱלֹהֵינוּ

meh-lech ha-o-lam, sheh-heh-cheh-ya-nu,   מֶלֶךְ הָעוֹלָם, שֶׁהֶחֱיָנוּ,

v'ki-y'manu, v'higi-anu la-z'man hazeh.   וְקִיְּמָנוּ וְהִגִּיעָנוּ לַזְּמַן הַזֶּה.

We praise You, Eternal God, Sovereign of the universe, for giving us life, for sustaining us, and for enabling us to reach this season.

ON SUKKOT

❦ *On Sukkot, the following is added:*

Ba-ruch a-ta Adonai, Eh-lo-hei-nu   בָּרוּךְ אַתָּה יי אֱלֹהֵינוּ

meh-lech ha-o-lam, ah-sher   מֶלֶךְ הָעוֹלָם, אֲשֶׁר

ki-d'sha-nu b'mitz-vo-tav   קִדְּשָׁנוּ בְּמִצְוֹתָיו

v'tzi-va-nu lei-sheiv ba-su-kah.   וְצִוָּנוּ לֵישֵׁב בַּסֻּכָּה.

We praise You, Eternal God, Sovereign of the universe: You hallow us with Your Mitzvot and command us to celebrate in the Sukkah.

Before partaking of food

Ba-ruch a-ta Adonai, Eh-lo-hei-nu
meh-lech ha-o-lam, ha-mo-tzi
leh-chem min ha-a-retz.

בָּרוּךְ אַתָּה יי אֱלֹהֵינוּ
מֶלֶךְ הָעוֹלָם, הַמּוֹצִיא
לֶחֶם מִן הָאָרֶץ.

We praise You, Eternal God, Sovereign of the universe, for You cause bread to come forth from the earth.

Kiddush for Yom Tov Morning

❧ *It is customary to recite the following before the midday meal.*
❧ *On Sukkot it is customary to recite the Kiddush in the Sukkah.*

ON SHABBAT

WE HOLD THE CUP AND SAY:

V'sham'ru v'nei Yis-ra-el et
ha-shabbat, la-a-sot et
ha-shabbat l'do-ro-tam, b'rit
o-lam. Bei-ni u-vein b'nei
Yis-ra-el ot hi l'o-lam, ki
shei-shet ya-mim a-sa Adonai
et ha-sha-ma-yim v'et ha-a-retz,
u-va-yom ha-sh'vi-i sha-vat
va-yi-na-fash.

וְשָׁמְרוּ בְנֵי־יִשְׂרָאֵל אֶת־
הַשַּׁבָּת, לַעֲשׂוֹת אֶת־
הַשַּׁבָּת לְדֹרֹתָם בְּרִית
עוֹלָם. בֵּינִי וּבֵין בְּנֵי
יִשְׂרָאֵל אוֹת הִוא לְעֹלָם, כִּי־
שֵׁשֶׁת יָמִים עָשָׂה יהוה
אֶת־הַשָּׁמַיִם וְאֶת־הָאָרֶץ,
וּבַיּוֹם הַשְּׁבִיעִי שָׁבַת
וַיִּנָּפַשׁ.

The people of Israel shall keep the Sabbath, observing the Sabbath in every generation as a covenant for all time. It is a sign between Me and the people of Israel forever. For in six days the Eternal God made heaven and earth, but on the seventh day God rested and was refreshed.

Al kein bei-rach Adonai et
yom ha-shabbat va-y'ka-d'shei-hu.

עַל־כֵּן בֵּרַךְ יהוה אֶת־
יוֹם הַשַּׁבָּת וַיְקַדְּשֵׁהוּ.

Therefore the Eternal One blessed the seventh day and called it holy.

ON ALL OCCASIONS

WE HOLD THE CUP AND SAY:

*Ei-leh mo-a-dei Adonai, mik-ra-ei
ko-desh, a-sher tik-r'u o-tam
b'mo-a-dam.
Va-y'da-beir Mo-sheh et mo-a-dei
Adonai el b'nei Yis-ra-eil.*

אֵלֶּה מוֹעֲדֵי יהוה, מִקְרָאֵי
קֹדֶשׁ, אֲשֶׁר תִּקְרְאוּ אֹתָם
בְּמוֹעֲדָם.
וַיְדַבֵּר מֹשֶׁה אֶת־מוֹעֲדֵי
יהוה אֶל־בְּנֵי יִשְׂרָאֵל.

'These are the appointed seasons of the Eternal One, the sacred days, that you shall proclaim at their appointed times.'

Then Moses taught the people of Israel to celebrate God's Festivals.

*Ba-ruch a-ta Adonai, Eh-lo-hei-nu
meh-lech ha-o-lam, bo-rei p'ri
ha-ga-fen.*

בָּרוּךְ אַתָּה יי אֱלֹהֵינוּ
מֶלֶךְ הָעוֹלָם, בּוֹרֵא פְּרִי
הַגָּפֶן.

We praise You, Eternal God, Sovereign of the universe, Creator of the fruit of the vine.

ON SUKKOT

❧ *On Sukkot, the following is added:*

*Ba-ruch a-ta Adonai, Eh-lo-hei-nu
meh-lech ha-o-lam ah-sher
ki-d'sha-nu b'mitz-vo-tav
v'tzi-va-nu lei-sheiv ba-su-kah.*

בָּרוּךְ אַתָּה יי אֱלֹהֵינוּ
מֶלֶךְ הָעוֹלָם, אֲשֶׁר
קִדְּשָׁנוּ בְּמִצְוֹתָיו
וְצִוָּנוּ לֵישֵׁב בַּסֻּכָּה.

We praise You, Eternal God, Sovereign of the universe: You hallow us with Your Mitzvot and command us to celebrate in the Sukkah.

Before partaking of food

Ba-ruch a-ta Adonai, Eh-lo-hei-nu
meh-lech ha-o-lam, ha-mo-tzi
leh-chem min ha-a-retz.

בָּרוּךְ אַתָּה יי אֱלֹהֵינוּ
מֶלֶךְ הָעוֹלָם, הַמּוֹצִיא
לֶחֶם מִן הָאָרֶץ.

We praise You, Eternal God, Sovereign of the universe, for You cause
bread to come forth from the earth.

Building a Sukkah

❧ *Immediately after the Havdalah for Yom Kippur (if this is recited at home), a symbolic beginning might be made with the building of the Sukkah, so that the first act after the conclusion of Yom Kippur may be the performance of a Mitzvah. This is followed by the breaking of the fast. The actual building of the Sukkah is preceded by the following ritual:*

יהוה מִי־יָגוּר בְּאָהֳלֶךָ? מִי־יִשְׁכֹּן בְּהַר קָדְשֶׁךָ?
הוֹלֵךְ תָּמִים וּפֹעֵל צֶדֶק, וְדֹבֵר אֱמֶת בִּלְבָבוֹ,
לֹא־רָגַל עַל־לְשֹׁנוֹ, לֹא־עָשָׂה לְרֵעֵהוּ רָעָה,
וְחֶרְפָּה לֹא־נָשָׂא עַל־קְרֹבוֹ. נִשְׁבַּע לְהָרַע וְלֹא יָמִר,
כַּסְפּוֹ לֹא־נָתַן בְּנֶשֶׁךְ, וְשֹׁחַד עַל־נָקִי לֹא לָקָח.
עֹשֵׂה־אֵלֶּה לֹא יִמּוֹט לְעוֹלָם.

Eternal God:
Who may abide in Your house?

Who may dwell in Your holy mountain?

Those who are upright; who do justly,

all whose hearts are true.

Who do not slander others, nor wrong them,

nor bring shame upon their kin.

Who give their word and, come what may, do not retract it.

Who do not exploit others, who never take bribes.

Those who live in this way shall never be shaken.

From Psalm 15

Eternal God, let Your presence dwell among us, and let us abide always in the shelter of Your peace. Be with us on this festival, as with love and awe we celebrate Your goodness to all the living.

We build this Sukkah with joy and gratitude for the gift of life and for all that sustains our bodies and enriches our spirits.

Ba-ruch a-ta Adonai, Eh-lo-hei-nu
meh-lech ha-o-lam ah-sher
ki-d'sha-nu b'mitz-vo-tav
v'tzi-va-nu lei-sheiv ba-su-kah.

בָּרוּךְ אַתָּה יי אֱלֹהֵינוּ
מֶלֶךְ הָעוֹלָם, אֲשֶׁר
קִדְּשָׁנוּ בְּמִצְוֹתָיו
וְצִוָּנוּ לֵישֵׁב בַּסֻּכָּה.

We praise You, Eternal God, Sovereign of the universe: You hallow us with your Mitzvot, and command us to fulfill the Mitzvah of building a Sukkah.

🍃 *Kiddush is said on the eve of the first day of Sukkot. The ritual begins on page 65.*

Ba-ruch a-ta Adonai, Eh-lo-hei-nu
meh-lech ha-o-lam, sheh-heh-cheh-ya-nu,
v'ki-y'manu, v'higi-a-nu la-z'man
ha-zeh

בָּרוּךְ אַתָּה יי אֱלֹהֵינוּ
מֶלֶךְ הָעוֹלָם, שֶׁהֶחֱיָנוּ
וְקִיְּמָנוּ וְהִגִּיעָנוּ לַזְּמַן
הַזֶּה.

We praise You, Eternal God, Sovereign of the universe, for giving us life, for sustaining us, and for enabling us to reach this season.

Welcoming Guests in the Sukkah (Ushpizin)

❧ *According to the Zohar, the great men and women of Scripture are our invisible companions in the Sukkah, and we are urged to invite the poor to share our meals with us, in gratitude for the gift of spirit that comes to us from entering into the Sukkah with the great ones of our past.*

Eternal One, our God, God of our mothers and fathers, be present among us, let us dwell always in the shelter of Your peace, and surround us with Your radiance. Inspire us to feed the hungry and to give drink to all who thirst. Praised be the Eternal One for ever. Amen and Amen.

To this meal we summon sublime guests; their memory blesses us, their presence inspires us:
Abraham, Isaac, and Jacob; Joseph, Moses, Aaron, and David.
Sarah, Rebekah, Leah, and Rachel; Miriam, Hannah, and Deborah.

❧ *The following passages are said on the appropriate day:*

1

בְּמָטוּ מִנָּךְ, אַבְרָהָם, אֻשְׁפִּיזִי עִלָּאִי, דְּיֵיתְבוּ עִמִּי וְעִמָּךְ כָּל אֻשְׁפִּיזֵי
עִלָּאֵי: יִצְחָק, יַעֲקֹב, יוֹסֵף, מֹשֶׁה, אַהֲרֹן וְדָוִד.

בְּמָטוּ מִינִיךְ, שָׂרָה, אֻשְׁפִּיזְתִּי עִלֵּיתָא, דְּיֵיתְבָן עִמִּי וְעִמָּךְ כָּל אֻשְׁפִּיזָתָא
עִלָּהָתָא: רִבְקָה, לֵאָה, רָחֵל, מִרְיָם, חַנָּה וּדְבוֹרָה.

Abraham, exalted guest, you are welcome here, along with Isaac, Jacob, Joseph, Moses, Aaron and David.

Sarah, exalted guest, you are welcome here, along with Rebekah, Leah, Rachel, Miriam, Hannah and Deborah.

2

בְּמָטוּ מִנָּךְ, יִצְחָק, אֻשְׁפִּיזִי עִלָּאִי, דְּיֵתְבוּ עִמִּי וְעִמָּךְ כָּל אֻשְׁפִּיזֵי עִלָּאִי:
אַבְרָהָם, יַעֲקֹב, יוֹסֵף, מֹשֶׁה, אַהֲרֹן וְדָוִד.

בְּמָטוּ מִינִיךְ, רִבְקָה, אֻשְׁפִּיזְתִּי עִלֵּיתָא, דְּיֵתְבָן עִמִּי וְעִמָּךְ כָּל אֻשְׁפִּיזָתָא
עִלָּתָא: שָׂרָה, לֵאָה, רָחֵל, מִרְיָם, חַנָּה וּדְבוֹרָה.

Isaac, exalted guest, you are welcome here, along with Abraham,
Jacob, Joseph, Moses, Aaron and David.

Rebekah, exalted guest, you are welcome here, along with Sarah,
Leah, Rachel, Miriam, Hannah and Deborah.

3

בְּמָטוּ מִנָּךְ, יַעֲקֹב, אֻשְׁפִּיזִי עִלָּאִי, דְּיֵתְבוּ עִמִּי וְעִמָּךְ כָּל אֻשְׁפִּיזֵי עִלָּאִי:
אַבְרָהָם, יִצְחָק, יוֹסֵף, מֹשֶׁה, אַהֲרֹן וְדָוִד.

בְּמָטוּ מִינִיךְ, לֵאָה, אֻשְׁפִּיזְתִּי עִלֵּיתָא, דְּיֵתְבָן עִמִּי וְעִמָּךְ כָּל אֻשְׁפִּיזָתָא
עִלָּתָא: שָׂרָה, רִבְקָה, רָחֵל, מִרְיָם, חַנָּה וּדְבוֹרָה.

Jacob, exalted guest, you are welcome here, along with Abraham,
Isaac, Joseph, Moses, Aaron and David.

Leah, exalted guest, you are welcome here, along with Sarah,
Rebekah, Rachel, Miriam, Hannah and Deborah.

4

בְּמָטוּ מִנָּךְ, יוֹסֵף, אֻשְׁפִּיזִי עִלָּאִי, דְּיֵתְבוּ עִמִּי וְעִמָּךְ כָּל אֻשְׁפִּיזֵי עִלָּאִי:
אַבְרָהָם, יִצְחָק, יַעֲקֹב, מֹשֶׁה, אַהֲרֹן וְדָוִד.

בְּמָטוּ מִינִיךְ, רָחֵל, אֻשְׁפִּיזְתִּי עִלֵּיתָא, דְּיֵתְבָן עִמִּי וְעִמָּךְ כָּל אֻשְׁפִּיזָתָא
עִלָּתָא: שָׂרָה, רִבְקָה, לֵאָה, מִרְיָם, חַנָּה וּדְבוֹרָה.

Joseph, exalted guest, you are welcome here, along with Abraham,
Isaac, Jacob, Moses, Aaron and David.

Rachel, exalted guest, you are welcome here, along with Sarah,
Rebekah, Leah, Miriam, Hannah and Deborah.

5

בְּמָטוּ מִנָּךְ, מֹשֶׁה, אֻשְׁפִּיזִי עִלָּאִי, דְּיֵיתְבוּ עִמִּי וְעִמָּךְ כָּל אֻשְׁפִּיזֵי עִלָּאֵי: אַבְרָהָם, יִצְחָק, יַעֲקֹב, יוֹסֵף, אַהֲרֹן וְדָוִד.

בְּמָטוּ מִינִיךְ, מִרְיָם, אֻשְׁפִּיזָתִי עִלֵּיתָא, דְּיֵיתְבָן עִמִּי וְעִמָּךְ כָּל אֻשְׁפִּיזָתָא עִלָּתָא: שָׂרָה, רִבְקָה, לֵאָה, רָחֵל, חַנָּה וּדְבוֹרָה.

Moses, exalted guest, you are welcome here, along with Abraham, Isaac, Jacob, Joseph, Aaron and David.

Miriam, exalted guest, you are welcome here, along with Sarah, Rebekah, Leah, Rachel, Hannah and Deborah.

6

בְּמָטוּ מִנָּךְ, אַהֲרֹן, אֻשְׁפִּיזִי עִלָּאִי, דְּיֵיתְבוּ עִמִּי וְעִמָּךְ כָּל אֻשְׁפִּיזֵי עִלָּאֵי: אַבְרָהָם, יִצְחָק, יַעֲקֹב, יוֹסֵף, מֹשֶׁה וְדָוִד.

בְּמָטוּ מִינִיךְ, חַנָּה, אֻשְׁפִּיזָתִי עִלֵּיתָא, דְּיֵיתְבָן עִמִּי וְעִמָּךְ כָּל אֻשְׁפִּיזָתָא עִלָּתָא: שָׂרָה, רִבְקָה, לֵאָה, רָחֵל, מִרְיָם וּדְבוֹרָה.

Aaron, exalted guest, you are welcome here, along with Abraham, Isaac, Jacob, Joseph, Moses and David.

Hannah, exalted guest, you are welcome here, along with Sarah, Rebekah, Leah, Rachel, Miriam and Deborah.

7

בְּמָטוּ מִנָּךְ, דָוִד, אֻשְׁפִּיזִי עִלָּאִי, דְּיֵיתְבוּ עִמִּי וְעִמָּךְ כָּל אֻשְׁפִּיזֵי עִלָּאֵי: אַבְרָהָם, יִצְחָק, יַעֲקֹב, יוֹסֵף, מֹשֶׁה וְאַהֲרֹן.

בְּמָטוּ מִינִיךְ, דְבוֹרָה, אֻשְׁפִּיזָתִי עִלֵּיתָא, דְּיֵיתְבָן עִמִּי וְעִמָּךְ כָּל אֻשְׁפִּיזָתָא עִלָּתָא: שָׂרָה, רִבְקָה, לֵאָה, רָחֵל, מִרְיָם וְחַנָּה.

David, exalted guest, you are welcome here, along with Abraham, Isaac, Jacob, Joseph, Moses and Aaron.

Deborah, exalted guest, you are welcome here, along with Sarah, Rebekah, Leah, Rachel, Miriam and Hannah.

Lulav

❧ *The Lulav and Etrog may be taken up, except on Shabbat, and the following meditation recited silently or aloud:*

I take Lulav and Etrog, in remembrance of these words of Torah: *On the first day, take for yourselves the fruit of a goodly tree, branches of palms, leaves of the myrtle and willows of the brook.*

With these four species I reach out to the Source of all life, the Sovereign of all creation. Let the graciousness of our Eternal God be with us, and may our work have lasting value.

Ba-ruch a-ta Adonai, Eh-lo-hei-nu	בָּרוּךְ אַתָּה יי אֱלֹהֵינוּ
meh-lech ha-o-lam ah-sher	מֶלֶךְ הָעוֹלָם, אֲשֶׁר
ki-d'sha-nu b'mitz-vo-tav	קִדְּשָׁנוּ בְּמִצְוֹתָיו
v'tzi-va-nu al n'ti-lat lu-lav.	וְצִוָּנוּ עַל נְטִילַת לוּלָב.

We praise You, Eternal God, Sovereign of the universe: You hallow us and command us to fulfill the Mitzvah of the Lulav.

Havdalah for a Festival

❧ *Wine and grape juice are equally "fruit of the vine."*

THE LEADER RAISES THE CUP OF WINE OR GRAPE JUICE AND SAYS:

*Ba-ruch a-ta Adonai, Eh-lo-hei-nu
meh-lech ha-o-lam, bo-rei p'ri
ha-ga-fen.*

בָּרוּךְ אַתָּה יי אֱלֹהֵינוּ
מֶלֶךְ הָעוֹלָם, בּוֹרֵא פְּרִי
הַגָּפֶן.

We praise You, Eternal God, Sovereign of the universe, Creator of the fruit of the vine.

We thank You, O God, for the Festival we now conclude, and for the blessings we have received from it. May its influence remain with us from this day until we celebrate it again. May its beauty and its joyful message remain in our hearts.

THE CANDLE IS HELD HIGH AS THE LEADER SAYS:

בָּרוּךְ אַתָּה יי אֱלֹהֵינוּ מֶלֶךְ הָעוֹלָם, הַמַּבְדִּיל בֵּין קֹדֶשׁ לְחוֹל.

We praise You, Eternal God, Sovereign of the universe: You teach us to distinguish between the commonplace and the holy.

ALL PRESENT SIP FROM THE CUP.

THE CANDLE IS EXTINGUISHED BY IMMERSING IT IN THE CUP.

Welcoming Rosh Hashanah

🌱 *It is customary, before the beginning of Rosh Hashanah, for each member of the household to put money aside for some worthy cause.*

Happy are those who consider the poor.

[Psalm 41:2]

We hereby vow to fulfill the Mitzvah of Tzedakah as we begin this festival. We remember the words of Your prophet, who called us to share our bread with the hungry, to clothe the naked, and never to hide ourselves from our own kin.

May we, together with the whole House of Israel, be mindful of the needs of others, sharing with them the fruits of our labor and helping to sustain them, so that the promise may be fulfilled:

Then your light shall blaze forth like the dawn, and your wounds shall quickly heal; your righteousness shall walk before you, the glory of the Eternal One shall follow you.

Fountain of life, as we begin a new year, let Your light and Your truth come forth to lead us. We look back upon the days that are past and see troubled times and days of celebration. Now we look ahead with the prayer that the new year be one of health and prosperity. When pains and troubles beset us, may we find strength to face them with courage; and when times are good for us, may we have the wisdom to be grateful for our blessings. Amen.

הַדְלָקַת הַנֵּרוֹת

Ba-ruch a-ta Adonai, Eh-lo-hei-nu	בָּרוּךְ אַתָּה יי אֱלֹהֵינוּ
meh-lech ha-o-lam a-sher	מֶלֶךְ הָעוֹלָם, אֲשֶׁר
ki-d'sha-nu b'mitz-vo-tav v'tzi-va-nu	קִדְּשָׁנוּ בְּמִצְוֹתָיו וְצִוָּנוּ
l'had-lik ner shel (Shabbat v'shel)	לְהַדְלִיק נֵר שֶׁל [שַׁבָּת וְשֶׁל]
yom tov.	יוֹם טוֹב.

We praise You, Eternal God, Sovereign of the universe: You hallow us with your Mitzvot and command us to kindle (the Sabbath and) Festival lights.

THE PARENTS BLESS THE CHILDREN

May God bless you and guide you. Seek truth always, be charitable in your words, just and loving in your deeds. A noble heritage has been entrusted to you; guard it well.

FOR A BOY

יְשִׂמְךָ אֱלֹהִים כְּאֶפְרַיִם וְכִמְנַשֶּׁה.

May God inspire you to live in the tradition of Ephraim and Menasheh, who carried forward the life of our people.

FOR A GIRL

יְשִׂמֵךְ אֱלֹהִים כְּשָׂרָה, רִבְקָה, לֵאָה וְרָחֵל.

May God inspire you to live in the tradition of Sarah, Rebekah, Leah, and Rachel, who carried forward the life of our people.

FOR BOTH

Y'va-reh-ch'cha Adonai v'yish-m'reh-cha. יְבָרֶכְךָ יהוה וְיִשְׁמְרֶךָ.

Ya-eir Adonai pa-nav ei-leh-cha יָאֵר יהוה פָּנָיו אֵלֶיךָ

vi-chu-neh-ka. וִיחֻנֶּךָּ.

Yi-sa Adonai pa-nav ei-leh-cha יִשָּׂא יהוה פָּנָיו אֵלֶיךָ

v'ya-seim l'cha sha-lom. וְיָשֵׂם לְךָ שָׁלוֹם.

May God bless you and keep you. May God look kindly upon you, and be gracious to you. May God reach out to you in tenderness, and give you peace.

❧ *There may now be a moment of silence, in which all present think of one another with blessing.*

Kiddush for Rosh Hashanah Evening

❧ *Wine and grape juice are equally "fruit of the vine."*

WE HOLD THE CUP AND SAY:

The observance of Rosh Hashanah reminds us to judge our words and our deeds by a divine standard. It calls us to turn from old errors and failures, and to look ahead with fresh hope and determination.

Let us praise God with this symbol of joy, the fruit of the vine, and give thanks for the gift of life. May our observance on this day fill us with eagerness to embrace life and to hallow it. May the new year bring renewed strength to our people Israel, and peace to the world.

ON SHABBAT

Va-y'chu-lu ha-sha-ma-yim	וַיְכֻלּוּ הַשָּׁמַיִם
v'ha-a-retz v'chol tz'va-am,	וְהָאָרֶץ וְכָל־צְבָאָם:
va-y'chal Eh-lo-him ba-yom	וַיְכַל אֱלֹהִים בַּיּוֹם
ha-sh'vi-i m'lach-to a-sher	הַשְּׁבִיעִי מְלַאכְתּוֹ אֲשֶׁר
a-sa, va-yish-bot ba-yom	עָשָׂה וַיִּשְׁבֹּת בַּיּוֹם
ha-sh'vi-i mi-kol m'lach-to	הַשְּׁבִיעִי מִכָּל־מְלַאכְתּוֹ
a-sher a-sa. Va-y'va-rech	אֲשֶׁר עָשָׂה: וַיְבָרֶךְ
Eh-lo-him et yom ha-sh'vi-i	אֱלֹהִים אֶת־יוֹם הַשְּׁבִיעִי
va-y'ka-deish o-to, ki vo sha-vat	וַיְקַדֵּשׁ אֹתוֹ כִּי בוֹ שָׁבַת
mi-kol m'lach-to a-sher ba-ra	מִכָּל־מְלַאכְתּוֹ אֲשֶׁר־בָּרָא
Eh-lo-him la-a-sot.	אֱלֹהִים לַעֲשׂוֹת:

Now the whole universe—sky, earth, and all their array—was completed. With the seventh day God ended the work of creation, resting on the seventh day, with all the work completed. Then God blessed the seventh day and sanctified it, this day having completed the work of creation.

ON ALL OCCASIONS

Ba-ruch a-ta Adonai, Eh-lo-hei-nu
meh-lech ha-o-lam, bo-rei p'ri
ha-ga-fen.

בָּרוּךְ אַתָּה יי אֱלֹהֵינוּ
מֶלֶךְ הָעוֹלָם, בּוֹרֵא פְּרִי
הַגָּפֶן.

We praise You, Eternal God, Sovereign of the universe, Creator of the fruit of the vine.

Ba-ruch ata Adonai, Eh-lo-hei-nu
meh-lech ha-o-lam, a-sher ba-char
ba-nu mi-kol am, v'ro-m'ma-nu
mi-kol la-shon, v'kid'sha-nu
b'mitz-vo-tav. Va-ti-ten la-nu, Adonai
Eh-lohei-nu, b'a-ha-va et yom
(ha-shabbat ha-zeh v'et yom)
ha-zi-ka-ron ha-zeh, yom t'ru-ah,
mik-ra ko-desh, zei-cher li-tzi-at
mitz-ra-yim. Ki va-nu va-char-ta
v'o-ta-nu ki-dash-ta mi-kol
ha-a-mim, u-d'va-r'cha eh-met
v'ka-yam la-ad.

בָּרוּךְ אַתָּה יי אֱלֹהֵינוּ
מֶלֶךְ הָעוֹלָם, אֲשֶׁר בָּחַר
בָּנוּ מִכָּל־עָם, וְרוֹמְמָנוּ
מִכָּל־לָשׁוֹן, וְקִדְּשָׁנוּ
בְּמִצְוֹתָיו. וַתִּתֶּן לָנוּ, יי
אֱלֹהֵינוּ, בְּאַהֲבָה אֶת־יוֹם
[הַשַּׁבָּת הַזֶּה וְאֶת־יוֹם]
הַזִּכָּרוֹן הַזֶּה, יוֹם תְּרוּעָה,
מִקְרָא קֹדֶשׁ, זֵכֶר לִיצִיאַת
מִצְרָיִם. כִּי־בָנוּ בָחַרְתָּ
וְאוֹתָנוּ קִדַּשְׁתָּ מִכָּל־
הָעַמִּים, וּדְבָרְךָ אֱמֶת
וְקַיָּם לָעַד.

Ba-ruch ata Adonai, m'ka-deish
(ha-shabbat v') Yis-ra-eil
v'yom ha-zi-ka-ron.

בָּרוּךְ אַתָּה יי מְקַדֵּשׁ
[הַשַּׁבָּת וְ] יִשְׂרָאֵל
וְיוֹם הַזִּכָּרוֹן.

Eternal God, You call us to Your service and hallow us with Mitzvot. In Your love You have given us (the Sabbath and its rest and,) this Day of Remembrance, to hear the sound of the Shofar, unite in worship, and recall our liberation from Egyptian bondage.

We praise You, O God, for this day sacred to Israel.

Ba-ruch a-ta Adonai, Eh-lo-hei-nu
meh-lech ha-o-lam, sheh-heh-cheh-ya-nu,
v'ki-y'manu, v'higi-anu la-z'man ha-zeh..

בָּרוּךְ אַתָּה יי אֱלֹהֵינוּ
מֶלֶךְ הָעוֹלָם, שֶׁהֶחֱיָנוּ,
וְקִיְּמָנוּ וְהִגִּיעָנוּ לַזְּמַן הַזֶּה.

We praise You, Eternal God, Sovereign of the universe, for giving us life, for sustaining us, and for enabling us to reach this season.

❧ *Many observe the custom of eating a round Challah with raisins after saying:*

Ba-ruch a-ta Adonai, Eh-lo-hei-nu
meh-lech ha-o-lam, ha-mo-tzi
le-chem min ha-a-retz.

בָּרוּךְ אַתָּה יי אֱלֹהֵינוּ
מֶלֶךְ הָעוֹלָם, הַמּוֹצִיא
לֶחֶם מִן הָאָרֶץ.

We praise You, Eternal God, Sovereign of the universe, for You cause bread to come forth from the earth.

❧ *An apple dipped in honey is eaten after saying:*

Ba-ruch a-ta Adonai, Eh-lo-hei-nu
meh-lech ha-o-lam, bo-rei p'ri
ha-eitz.

בָּרוּךְ אַתָּה יי אֱלֹהֵינוּ
מֶלֶךְ הָעוֹלָם, בּוֹרֵא פְּרִי
הָעֵץ.

We praise You, Eternal God, Sovereign of the universe, Creator of the fruit of the tree.

❧ *It is customary to add:*

יְהִי רָצוֹן מִלְּפָנֶיךָ יי אֱלֹהֵינוּ וֵאלֹהֵי אֲבוֹתֵינוּ וְאִמּוֹתֵינוּ, שֶׁתְּחַדֵּשׁ עָלֵינוּ
שָׁנָה טוֹבָה וּמְתוּקָה.

Our God and God of our people, may this new year be good for us, and sweet.

Kiddush for Rosh Hashanah Morning

🍃 *It is customary to recite the following before the midday meal.*

ON SHABBAT

WE HOLD THE CUP AND SAY:

V'sham'ru v'nei Yis-ra-el et ha-
la-a-sot et ha-shabbat
l'do-ro-tam, b'rit o-lam. Bei-ni
u-vein b'nei Yis-ra-el ot hi
l'o-lam, ki shei-shet ya-mim
a-sa Adonai et ha-sha-ma-yim
v'et ha-a-retz, u-va-yom
ha-sh'vi-i sha-vat va-yi-na-fash.

וְשָׁמְרוּ בְנֵי־יִשְׂרָאֵל אֶת־
הַשַּׁבָּת, לַעֲשׂוֹת אֶת־הַשַּׁבָּת
לְדֹרֹתָם בְּרִית עוֹלָם. בֵּינִי
וּבֵין בְּנֵי יִשְׂרָאֵל אוֹת הִוא
לְעֹלָם, כִּי־שֵׁשֶׁת יָמִים
עָשָׂה יהוה אֶת־הַשָּׁמַיִם
וְאֶת־הָאָרֶץ, וּבַיּוֹם
הַשְּׁבִיעִי שָׁבַת וַיִּנָּפַשׁ.

The people of Israel shall keep the Sabbath, observing the Sabbath in every generation as a covenant for all time. It is a sign between Me and the people of Israel forever. For in six days the Eternal God made heaven and earth, but on the seventh day God rested and was refreshed.

ON ALL OCCASIONS

WE HOLD THE CUP AND SAY:

U-v'yom sim-cha-t'chem
u-v'mo-a-dei-chem u-v'ra-shei
chod-shei-chem, u-t'ka-tem
ba-cha-tzo-tz'rot . . . v'ha-yu la-chem
l'zi-ka-ron lif-nei Eh-lo-hei-chem; a-ni,
Adonai, Eh-lo-hei-chem.

וּבְיוֹם שִׂמְחַתְכֶם
וּבְמוֹעֲדֵיכֶם וּבְרָאשֵׁי
חָדְשֵׁיכֶם, וּתְקַעְתֶּם
בַּחֲצֹצְרֹת . . . וְהָיוּ לָכֶם
לְזִכָּרוֹן לִפְנֵי אֱלֹהֵיכֶם; אֲנִי,
יהוה, אֱלֹהֵיכֶם.

On your day of rejoicing, on your festivals and new moons, you shall sound the trumpets . . . as a remembrance before your God; I, the Eternal One, am your God.

Ti-k'u va-cho-desh sho-far, ba-keh-seh   תִּקְעוּ בַחֹדֶשׁ שׁוֹפָר, בַּכֶּסֶה
l'yom cha-gei-nu. Ki chok l'yis-ra-eil   לְיוֹם חַגֵּנוּ. כִּי חֹק לְיִשְׂרָאֵל
hu, mish-pat lei-lo-hei Ya-a-kov.   הוּא, מִשְׁפָּט לֵאלֹהֵי יַעֲקֹב.

Sound the Shofar when the new moon appears, at the turning of the year, at the return of our celebration. For this is a statute binding on Israel, an ordinance of Israel's God.

Ba-ruch a-ta Adonai, Eh-lo-hei-nu   בָּרוּךְ אַתָּה יי אֱלֹהֵינוּ
meh-lech ha-o-lam, bo-rei p'ri   מֶלֶךְ הָעוֹלָם, בּוֹרֵא פְּרִי
ha-ga-fen.   הַגָּפֶן.

We praise You, Eternal God, Sovereign of the universe, Creator of the fruit of the vine.

Before partaking of food

Ba-ruch a-ta Adonai, Eh-lo-hei-nu   בָּרוּךְ אַתָּה יי אֱלֹהֵינוּ
meh-lech ha-o-lam, ha-mo-tzi   מֶלֶךְ הָעוֹלָם, הַמּוֹצִיא
leh-chem min ha-a-retz.   לֶחֶם מִן הָאָרֶץ.

We praise You, Eternal God, Sovereign of the universe, for You cause bread to come forth from the earth.

Kindling the Yom Kippur Lights

❧ *It is customary, before the beginning of Yom Kippur, for each member of the household to put money aside for some worthy cause.*

Happy are those who consider the poor.

[Psalm 41:2]

We hereby vow to fulfill the Mitzvah of Tzedakah as we begin this festival. We remember the words of Your prophet, who called us to share our bread with the hungry, to clothe the naked, and never to hide ourselves from our own kin.

May we, together with the whole House of Israel, be mindful of the needs of others, sharing with them the fruits of our labor and helping to sustain them, so that the promise may be fulfilled:

Then your light shall blaze forth like the dawn, and your wounds shall quickly heal; your righteousness shall walk before you, the glory of the Eternal One shall follow you.

הַדְלָקַת הַנֵּרוֹת

❧ *The lights are kindled after the meal and before leaving for the synagogue.*

The holiest day of the year is about to begin. May it be for each one of us a day of renewal. We seek this day to overcome what wrong we have done, and to strengthen what is good in our lives. May it bring us closer to one another, and make us more loyal to our community and our faith.

*Ba-ruch a-ta Adonai, Eh-lo-hei-nu
meh-lech ha-o-lam, a-sher
ki-d'sha-nu b'mitz-vo-tav v'tzi-va-nu
l'had-lik ner shel (Shabbat v'shel)
yom tov.*

בָּרוּךְ אַתָּה יי אֱלֹהֵינוּ
מֶלֶךְ הָעוֹלָם, אֲשֶׁר
קִדְּשָׁנוּ בְּמִצְוֹתָיו וְצִוָּנוּ
לְהַדְלִיק נֵר שֶׁל [שַׁבָּת וְשֶׁל]
יוֹם טוֹב.

We praise You, Eternal God, Sovereign of the universe: You hallow us with your Mitzvot, and command us to kindle the lights of (the Sabbath and) the Day of Atonement.

Ba-ruch a-ta Adonai, Eh-lo-hei-nu
meh-lech ha-o-lam, sheh-heh-cheh-ya-nu,
v'ki-y'manu, v'higi-anu la-z'man ha-zeh.

בָּרוּךְ אַתָּה יי אֱלֹהֵינוּ
מֶלֶךְ הָעוֹלָם, שֶׁהֶחֱיָנוּ,
וְקִיְּמָנוּ וְהִגִּיעָנוּ לַזְּמַן הַזֶּה.

We praise You, Eternal God, Sovereign of the universe, for giving us life, for sustaining us, and for enabling us to reach this season.

THE PARENTS BLESS THE CHILDREN

May God bless you and guide you. Seek truth always, be charitable in your words, just and loving in your deeds. A noble heritage has been entrusted to you; guard it well.

FOR A BOY

יְשִׂמְךָ אֱלֹהִים כְּאֶפְרַיִם וְכִמְנַשֶּׁה.

May God inspire you to live in the tradition of Ephraim and Menasheh, who carried forward the life of our people.

FOR A GIRL

יְשִׂמֵךְ אֱלֹהִים כְּשָׂרָה, רִבְקָה, לֵאָה וְרָחֵל.

May God inspire you to live in the tradition of Sarah, Rebekah, Leah, and Rachel, who carried forward the life of our people.

FOR BOTH

Y'va-reh-ch'cha Adonai v'yish-m'reh-cha.
Ya-eir Adonai pa-nav ei-leh-cha
vi-chu-neh-ka.
Yi-sa Adonai pa-nav ei-leh-cha
v'ya-seim l'cha sha-lom.

יְבָרֶכְךָ יהוה וְיִשְׁמְרֶךָ.
יָאֵר יהוה פָּנָיו אֵלֶיךָ
וִיחֻנֶּךָּ.
יִשָּׂא יהוה פָּנָיו אֵלֶיךָ
וְיָשֵׂם לְךָ שָׁלוֹם.

May God bless you and keep you. May God look kindly upon you, and be gracious to you. May God reach out to you in tenderness, and give you peace.

❦ *There may now be a moment of silence, in which all present think of one another with blessing.*

Havdalah for Rosh Hashanah and Yom Kippur

🍂 *Two passages, marked "On Shabbat," are recited only when the conclusion of Rosh Hashanah or Yom Kippur concides with the conclusion of Shabbat.*

ON SHABBAT

הִנֵּה אֵל יְשׁוּעָתִי,

אֶבְטַח וְלֹא אֶפְחָד.

כִּי־עָזִּי וְזִמְרָת יָהּ יהוה,

וַיְהִי־לִי לִישׁוּעָה.

וּשְׁאַבְתֶּם־מַיִם בְּשָׂשׂוֹן

מִמַּעַיְנֵי הַיְשׁוּעָה.

לַיהוה הַיְשׁוּעָה,

עַל־עַמְּךָ בִרְכָתֶךָ, סֶּלָה.

יהוה צְבָאוֹת עִמָּנוּ,

מִשְׂגָּב־לָנוּ אֱלֹהֵי יַעֲקֹב, סֶלָה.

יהוה צְבָאוֹת,

אַשְׁרֵי אָדָם בֹּטֵחַ בָּךְ.

יהוה הוֹשִׁיעָה;

הַמֶּלֶךְ יַעֲנֵנוּ בְיוֹם־קָרְאֵנוּ.

לַיְּהוּדִים הָיְתָה אוֹרָה וְשִׂמְחָה

וְשָׂשׂוֹן וִיקָר;

כֵּן תִּהְיֶה לָּנוּ.

כּוֹס־יְשׁוּעוֹת אֶשָּׂא,

וּבְשֵׁם יהוה אֶקְרָא.

Behold, God is my Help;

   trusting in the Eternal One, I am not afraid.

For the Eternal One is my strength and my song,

   and has become my salvation.

With joy we draw water

   from the wells of salvation.

The Eternal One brings deliverance,

and blessing to the people.

The God of the hosts of heaven is with us;

the God of Jacob is our stronghold.

God of the hosts of heaven,

happy is the one who trusts in You!

Save us, Eternal One;

answer us, when we call upon You.

Give us light and joy, gladness and honor,

as in the happiest days of our people's past.

Then shall we lift up the cup to rejoice in Your saving power,

and call out Your name in praise.

ON ALL OCCASIONS

THE LEADER RAISES THE CUP OF WINE OR GRAPE JUICE AND SAYS:

*Ba-ruch a-ta Adonai, Eh-lo-hei-nu
meh-lech ha-o-lam, bo-rei p'ri
ha-ga-fen.*

בָּרוּךְ אַתָּה יי אֱלֹהֵינוּ
מֶלֶךְ הָעוֹלָם, בּוֹרֵא פְּרִי
הַגָּפֶן.

We praise You, Eternal God, Sovereign of the universe, Creator of the fruit of the vine.

ON SHABBAT

THE LEADER HOLDS UP THE SPICE-BOX AND SAYS:

*Ba-ruch a-ta Adonai, Eh-lo-hei-nu
meh-lech ha-o-lam, bo-rei
mi-nei v'sa-mim.*

בָּרוּךְ אַתָּה יי אֱלֹהֵינוּ
מֶלֶךְ הָעוֹלָם, בּוֹרֵא
מִינֵי בְשָׂמִים.

We praise You, Eternal One, Sovereign God of the universe, Creator of the world's spices.

**THE SPICE BOX IS CIRCULATED
AND ALL PRESENT INHALE ITS FRAGRANCE.**

ON ALL OCCASIONS

THE LEADER HOLDS UP THE CANDLE AND SAYS:

Ba-ruch a-ta Adonai, Eh-lo-hei-nu meh-lech ha-o-lam, bo-rei m'o-rei ha-eish.

בָּרוּךְ אַתָּה יי אֱלֹהֵינוּ מֶלֶךְ הָעוֹלָם, בּוֹרֵא מְאוֹרֵי הָאֵשׁ.

We praise You, Eternal God, Sovereign of the universe, Creator of fire.

THE CANDLE IS HELD HIGH AS THE LEADER SAYS:

בָּרוּךְ אַתָּה יי אֱלֹהֵינוּ מֶלֶךְ הָעוֹלָם, הַמַּבְדִּיל בֵּין קֹדֶשׁ לְחוֹל, בֵּין אוֹר לְחֹשֶׁךְ, בֵּין יִשְׂרָאֵל לָעַמִּים, בֵּין יוֹם הַשְּׁבִיעִי לְשֵׁשֶׁת יְמֵי הַמַּעֲשֶׂה. בָּרוּךְ אַתָּה יי הַמַּבְדִּיל בֵּין קֹדֶשׁ לְחוֹל.

We praise You, Eternal God, Sovereign of the universe: You make distinctions, teaching us to distinguish the commonplace from the holy; You create light and darkness, Israel and the nations, the seventh day of rest and the six days of labor.

We praise You, O God: You call us to distinguish the commonplace from the holy.

ALL PRESENT SIP FROM THE CUP.

THE CANDLE IS EXTINGUISHED BY IMMERSING IT IN THE CUP.

הַמַּבְדִּיל בֵּין קֹדֶשׁ לְחוֹל, חַטֹּאתֵינוּ הוּא יִמְחֹל,
זַרְעֵנוּ וְכַסְפֵּנוּ יַרְבֶּה כַחוֹל, וְכַכּוֹכָבִים בַּלָּיְלָה.
שָׁבוּעַ טוֹב . . .

Ha-mav-dil bein ko-desh l'chol, cha-to-tei-nu hu yim-chol,
zar-ei-nu v'chas-pei-nu yar-beh ka-chol, v'cha-ko-cha-vim ba-
lai-la.

Sha-vu-ah tov . . .

יוֹם פָּנָה כְּצֵל תֹּמֶר, אֶקְרָא לָאֵל, עָלַי גֹּמֵר;
אָמַר שׁוֹמֵר, אָתָא בֹקֶר וְגַם־לָיְלָה.
שָׁבוּעַ טוֹב . . .

Yom pa-na k'tzeil to-mer, ek-ra la-eil, a-lai go-meir;
a-mar sho-meir, a-ta vo-ker, v'gam lai-la.

Sha-vu-ah tov . . .

צִדְקָתְךָ כְּהַר תָּבוֹר עַל חֲטָאַי עָבוֹר תַּעֲבוֹר,
כְּיוֹם אֶתְמוֹל כִּי יַעֲבוֹר, וְאַשְׁמוּרָה בַלָּיְלָה.
שָׁבוּעַ טוֹב . . .

Tzid-ka-t'cha k'har ta-vor, al cha-ta-ai a-vor ta-a-vor,
k'yom et-mol ki ya-a-vor, v'ash-mu-ra va-lai-la.
Sha-vu-ah tov . . .

הַעְתֵּר, נוֹרָא וְאָיוֹם, אֲשַׁוֵּעַ, תְּנָה פִדְיוֹם,
בְּנֶשֶׁף, בְּעֶרֶב יוֹם, בְּאִישׁוֹן לָיְלָה.
שָׁבוּעַ טוֹב . . .

Hei-a-teir, no-ra v'a-yom, a-sha-vei-a, t'na fid-yom,
b'neh-shef, b'eh-rev yom, b'i-shon lai-la.
Sha-vu-ah tov . . .

☙

92

You teach us to distinguish between the commonplace and the holy: teach us also to transform our sins to merits. Let those who love you be numerous as the sands, and the stars of heaven.

Day has declined, the shadows are gone; we call to the One whose word is good. The sentry says: 'Morning will come, though the night seems long.'

Your righteousness is a majestic mountain: forgive our sins. Let them be as yesterday when it is past, as a watch in the night.

Hear our prayer, O awesome God, and grant redemption: in the twilight, in the waning of the day, or in the blackness of the night!

❧ *Some begin building the Sukkah immediately after the Havdalah for Yom Kippur. See p. 73.*

Thanksgiving Day

Creative Source of all being, from You come our blessings from day to day and from year to year. The towering mountains and the shaded forests, the abundant streams and the fruitful earth are Your gift to us. May we preserve this gift for our children, that they, too, may give thanks for the blessings that will be theirs.

For this land so richly blessed, we raise our voice in thanks. Your children have come to these shores from many lands in quest of liberty and new life. Many have been pilgrims to this western world. Here they found a safe haven, soil on which to prosper, and the opportunity to outgrow old fears and superstitions. For our country, for its freedom promised, attained, and yet to be enlarged, for the richness of its natural blessings, and for a growing harmony that we pray will ever increase among its citizens, we give thanks.

God of justice and right, inspire all who dwell in our land with loyalty to the ideals of its founders. Give us wisdom and strength to labor for its well-being, on the firm foundation of justice and truth. Fill us with the spirit of kindness, generosity, and peace, that this land may be a beacon-light to many peoples.

Ba-ruch a-ta Adonai, Eh-lo-hei-nu　　　בָּרוּךְ אַתָּה יי אֱלֹהֵינוּ

meh-lech ha-o-lam, ha-mo-tzi　　　מֶלֶךְ הָעוֹלָם, הַמּוֹצִיא

leh-chem min ha-a-retz.　　　לֶחֶם מִן הָאָרֶץ.

We praise You, Eternal God, Sovereign of the universe, for You cause bread to come forth from the earth.

Chanukah

The lights of Chanukah are a symbol of our joy. In time of darkness, our ancestors had the courage to struggle for freedom. Theirs was a victory of the weak over the strong, the few over the many. It was a victory for all ages and all peoples.

אַשְׁרֵי הַגַּפְרוּר שֶׁנִּשְׂרַף וְהִצִּית לְהָבוֹת.

אַשְׁרֵי הַלֶּהָבָה שֶׁבָּעֲרָה בְּסִתְרֵי לְבָבוֹת.

אַשְׁרֵי הַלְּבָבוֹת שֶׁיָּדְעוּ לַחֲדוֹל בְּכָבוֹד.

אַשְׁרֵי הַגַּפְרוּר שֶׁנִּשְׂרַף וְהִצִּית לְהָבוֹת.

Blessed is the match consumed in kindling flame.
Blessed is the flame that burns in the heart's secret places.
Blessed is the heart with strength to stop its beating for
    honor's sake.
Blessed is the match consumed in kindling flame.

Zion hears and is glad;
The daughters of Judah rejoice,
Eternal One, in Your judgments.

שָׁמְעָה וַתִּשְׂמַח צִיּוֹן;

וַתָּגֵלְנָה בְּנוֹת יְהוּדָה,

לְמַעַן מִשְׁפָּטֶיךָ, יהוה.

The light of our faith burns brightly now; our people Israel has survived all who sought to destroy us. In every generation, we are called, through love and self-sacrifice, to renew ourselves and the life of our people.

Let the lights we kindle shine forth for the world to see. May they illumine our lives and fill us with gratitude for those who came before us, whose will and courage, time and again, kept the flame of faith from extinction.

❧ *The candles are placed in the Menorah from right to left, and kindled from left to right.*

Ba-ruch a-ta Adonai, Eh-lo-hei-nu	בָּרוּךְ אַתָּה יי אֱלֹהֵינוּ
meh-lech ha-o-lam a-sher	מֶלֶךְ הָעוֹלָם, אֲשֶׁר
ki-d'sha-nu b'mitz-vo-tav v'tzi-va-nu	קִדְּשָׁנוּ בְּמִצְוֹתָיו וְצִוָּנוּ
l'had-lik ner shel Chanukah.	לְהַדְלִיק נֵר שֶׁל חֲנֻכָּה.

We praise You, Eternal God, Sovereign of the universe: You hallow us with Your Mitzvot, and command us to kindle the Chanukah lights.

Ba-ruch a-ta Adonai, Eh-lo-hei-nu	בָּרוּךְ אַתָּה יי אֱלֹהֵינוּ
meh-lech ha-o-lam, sheh-a-sa ni-sim	מֶלֶךְ הָעוֹלָם, שֶׁעָשָׂה נִסִּים
la-a-vo-tei-nu/l'i-mo-tei-nu	לַאֲבוֹתֵינוּ/לְאִמּוֹתֵינוּ
ba-ya-mim ha-heim ba-z'man ha-zeh.	בַּיָּמִים הָהֵם בַּזְּמַן הַזֶּה.

We praise You, Eternal God, Sovereign of the universe: You showed wonders to our fathers/mothers in days of old, at this season.

ON THE FIRST NIGHT ONLY

Ba-ruch a-ta A-do-nai, E-lo-hei-nu	בָּרוּךְ אַתָּה יי אֱלֹהֵינוּ
me-lech ha-o-lam, she-hecheyanu,	מֶלֶךְ הָעוֹלָם, שֶׁהֶחֱיָנוּ
v'ki-y'manu, v'higi-anu	וְקִיְּמָנוּ וְהִגִּיעָנוּ
la-z'man hazeh.	לַזְּמַן הַזֶּה.

We praise You, Eternal One, Sovereign God of the universe, for giving us life, for sustaining us, and for enabling us to reach this season.

❧ *The following verses may be recited as the lights are kindled*

1

הָעָם הַהֹלְכִים בַּחֹשֶׁךְ רָאוּ אוֹר גָּדוֹל.

The people who walked in darkness have seen a great light.

2

כִּי נָפַלְתִּי קֶמְתִּי; כִּי־אֵשֵׁב בַּחֹשֶׁךְ יהוה אוֹר לִי.

Though I fall, I shall rise; though I sit in darkness, God shall be a light to me.

3

כִּי־אַתָּה תָּאִיר נֵרִי; יהוה אֱלֹהַי יַגִּיהַּ חָשְׁכִּי.

For You light my lamp; the everlasting God makes bright my darkness.

4

זָרַח בַּחֹשֶׁךְ אוֹר לַיְשָׁרִים; חַנּוּן וְרַחוּם וְצַדִּיק.

Light dawns in the darkness for the upright; for the one who is gracious, compassionate, and just.

5

יהוה אוֹרִי וְיִשְׁעִי; מִמִּי אִירָא?

God is my light and my help; whom shall I fear?

6

כִּי נֵר מִצְוָה, וְתוֹרָה אוֹר.

For the Mitzvah is a lamp, and Torah is light.

7

קוּמִי, אוֹרִי, כִּי בָא אוֹרֵךְ, וּכְבוֹד יהוה עָלַיִךְ זָרַח.

Arise, shine, for your light has come, and God's splendor shall dawn upon you.

8

בֵּית יַעֲקֹב, לְכוּ וְנֵלְכָה בְּאוֹר יהוה.

O House of Jacob, come, let us walk by the light of our God.

THE FOLLOWING IS SUNG:

הַנֵּרוֹת הַלָּלוּ אֲנַחְנוּ מַדְלִיקִין עַל הַנִּסִּים, וְעַל הַפֻּרְקָן, וְעַל הַגְּבוּרוֹת, וְעַל הַתְּשׁוּעוֹת, וְעַל הַמִּלְחָמוֹת, שֶׁעָשִׂיתָ לַאֲבוֹתֵינוּ וְשֶׁעָשִׂיתָ לְאִמּוֹתֵינוּ בַּיָּמִים הָהֵם, בַּזְּמַן הַזֶּה.

וְכָל־שְׁמוֹנַת יְמֵי חֲנֻכָּה הַנֵּרוֹת הַלָּלוּ קֹדֶשׁ הֵם; וְאֵין לָנוּ רְשׁוּת לְהִשְׁתַּמֵּשׁ בָּהֶם אֶלָּא לִרְאוֹתָם בִּלְבָד, כְּדֵי לְהוֹדוֹת וּלְהַלֵּל לְשִׁמְךָ הַגָּדוֹל עַל נִסֶּיךָ וְעַל נִפְלְאוֹתֶיךָ וְעַל יְשׁוּעָתֶךָ.

We kindle these lights in remembrance of the wondrous deliverance You inspired our ancestors to struggle for and to attain.

During the eight days of Chanukah these lights are sacred; we are not to use them but only to gaze upon them, so that their glow may rouse us to give thanks for Your wondrous saving power.

Chanukah Songs

מִי יְמַלֵּל

מִי יְמַלֵּל גְּבוּרוֹת יִשְׂרָאֵל, אוֹתָן מִי יִמְנֶה?

Mi y'ma-leil g'vu-rot Yis-ra-eil, o-tan mi yim-neh?

הֵן בְּכָל דּוֹר יָקוּם הַגִּבּוֹר, גּוֹאֵל הָעָם.

Hein b'chol dor ya-kum ha-gi-bor go-eil ha-am.

שְׁמַע! בַּיָּמִים הָהֵם בַּזְּמַן הַזֶּה, מַכַּבִּי מוֹשִׁיעַ וּפוֹדֶה.

Sh'ma! ba-ya-mim ha-heim ba-z'man ha-zeh,
Ma-ka-bi mo-shi-a u-fo-deh,

וּבְיָמֵינוּ כָּל עַם יִשְׂרָאֵל, יִתְאַחֵד יָקוּם לְהִגָּאֵל!

U-v'ya-mei-nu kol am Yis-ra-eil, yit-a-cheid ya-kum l'hi-ga-eil.

Who can retell the things that befell us,
Who can count them?
In every age a hero or sage
Came to our aid.

Hark! In days of yore, in Israel's ancient land,
Brave Maccabeus led his faithful band,
And now all Israel must as one arise,
Redeem itself through deed and sacrifice!

Who can retell the things that befell us,
Who can count them?
In every age a hero or sage
Came to our aid.

מָעוֹז צוּר

Ma-oz tzur y'shu-a-ti,

l'cha na-eh l'sha-bei-ach,

ti-kon beit t'fi-la-ti

v'sham to-da n'za-bei-ach.

L'eit tash-bit mat-bei-ach

v'tzar ha-m'na-bei-ach,

az eg-mor, b'shir miz-mor

cha-nu-kat ha-miz-bei-ach.

מָעוֹז צוּר יְשׁוּעָתִי,

לְךָ נָאֶה לְשַׁבֵּחַ,

תִּכּוֹן בֵּית תְּפִלָּתִי,

וְשָׁם תּוֹדָה נְזַבֵּחַ.

לְעֵת תַּשְׁבִּית מַטְבֵּחַ

וְצָר הַמְנַבֵּחַ,

אָז אֶגְמוֹר, בְּשִׁיר מִזְמוֹר,

חֲנֻכַּת הַמִּזְבֵּחַ.

Rock of ages, let our song
Praise Your saving power;
You, amid the raging foes,
Were our sheltering tower.
Furious, they assailed us
Bur Your arm availed us,
  And Your word
  Broke their sword,
When our own strength failed us.

Kindling new the holy lamps,
  Priests approved in suffering,
  Purified the nation's shrines,
Brought to You their offering.
And Your courts surrounding
  Hear, in joy abounding,
    Happy throngs,
    Singing songs,
With a mighty sounding.

Children of the Maccabees,
Whether free or fettered,
Wake the echoes of the songs,
Where you may be scattered.
Yours the message cheering,
That the day is nearing,
  Which will see,
  All go free,
Tyrants disappearing.

עַל הַנִּסִּים

Al ha-ni-sim, v'al ha-pur-kan,   עַל הַנִּסִּים, וְעַל הַפֻּרְקָן,

v'al ha-g'vu-rot, v'al ha-t'shu-ot,   וְעַל הַגְּבוּרוֹת, וְעַל הַתְּשׁוּעוֹת,

v'al ha-neh-cha-mot,   וְעַל הַנֶּחָמוֹת,

sheh-a-si-ta la-a-vo-tei-nu   שֶׁעָשִׂיתָ לַאֲבוֹתֵינוּ

ve-sheh-a-si-ta l'i-mo-tei-nu   וְשֶׁעָשִׂיתָ לְאִמּוֹתֵינוּ

ba-ya-min ha-heim, ba-z'man ha-zeh.   בַּיָּמִים הָהֵם, בַּזְּמַן הַזֶּה.

Bi-mei Ma-tit-ya-hu ben Yo-cha-nan   בִּימֵי מַתִּתְיָהוּ בֶּן־יוֹחָנָן

ko-hein ga-dol, chash-mo-nai   כֹּהֵן גָּדוֹל, חַשְׁמוֹנַאִי

u-va-nav,   וּבָנָיו,

k'sheh-a-m'da mal-chut Ya-van   כְּשֶׁעָמְדָה מַלְכוּת יָוָן

al a-m'cha Yis-ra-eil,   עַל עַמְּךָ יִשְׂרָאֵל,

l'hash-ki-cham To-ra-teh-cha,   לְהַשְׁכִּיחָם תּוֹרָתֶךָ,

u-l'ha-a-vi-ram mei-chu-kei   וּלְהַעֲבִירָם מֵחֻקֵּי

r'tzo-neh-cha.   רְצוֹנֶךָ.

V'a-ta b'ra-cha-meh-cha ha-ra-bim,   וְאַתָּה בְּרַחֲמֶיךָ הָרַבִּים,

a-ma-d'ta la-hem b'eit tza-ra-tam.   עָמַדְתָּ לָהֶם בְּעֵת צָרָתָם.

We kindle these lights in remembrance of the wondrous deliverance You inspired our ancestors to struggle for and to attain.

In the time of the Hasmoneans, a tyrant rose up against our ancestors, determined to make them forget Your Torah, and to turn them away from obedience to Your will. But You were at their side in time of trouble.

Purim

❧ *Before the evening meal.*

We come before You, O God, with words of thanksgiving for the blessing You have been to our people Israel and to all humanity.

This day brings to mind the suffering we have endured in many generations. Painful trials and bitter struggles, torments of body and soul have often been our portion. But sustained by the hope that goodness and love would triumph over evil and hate, we have overcome.

Remembering the courage of Esther and the devotion of Mordechai, we give thanks for the women and men of every age who have helped to keep our people alive.

We shall yet see the forces of destruction—cruel Amalek and vindictive Haman—vanish before the mighty onrush of Your light and Your love. And although many a bitter experience may await us before prejudice and hate disappear, still we trust that in the end all humanity will unite in love, knowing that they are one, children all of the Eternal God. Amen.

Ba-ruch a-ta Adonai, Eh-lo-hei-nu
meh-lech ha-o-lam, ha-mo-tzi
leh-chem min ha-a-retz.

בָּרוּךְ אַתָּה יי אֱלֹהֵינוּ
מֶלֶךְ הָעוֹלָם, הַמּוֹצִיא
לֶחֶם מִן הָאָרֶץ.

We praise You, Eternal God, Sovereign of the universe, for You cause bread to come forth from the earth.

Ba-ruch a-ta Adonai, Eh-lo-hei-nu
meh-lech ha-o-lam, sheh-heh-cheh-ya-nu,
v'ki-y'manu, v'higi-anu la-z'man
ha-zeh.

בָּרוּךְ אַתָּה יי אֱלֹהֵינוּ
מֶלֶךְ הָעוֹלָם, שֶׁהֶחֱיָנוּ,
וְקִיְּמָנוּ וְהִגִּיעָנוּ לַזְּמַן
הַזֶּה.

We praise You, Eternal God, Sovereign of the universe, for giving us life, for sustaining us, and for enabling us to reach this season.

The Path
of Life

THE PATH OF LIFE

Beginnings

New life-cycle benedictions

Menarche blessing

יְהִי רָצוֹן מִלְפָנֶיךָ, יי אֱלֹהֵינוּ וֵאלֹהֵי אֲבוֹתֵינוּ וְאִמוֹתֵינוּ, שֶׁתִּשְׁכּוֹן עִמָּדִי בְּהִכָּנְסִי לְמַעֲגַל הַנָּשִׁים.

Our God and God of our mothers and our fathers, be with me as I begin the cycle of women.

Ba-ruch a-ta Adonai,   בָּרוּךְ אַתָּה יי
Eh-lo-hei-nu meh-lech ha-o-lam,   אֱלֹהֵינוּ מֶלֶךְ הָעוֹלָם,
sheh-heh-cheh-ya-nu, v'ki-y'ma-nu,   שֶׁהֶחֱיָנוּ וְקִיְּמָנוּ
v'higi-a-nu la-z'man ha-zeh.   וְהִגִּיעָנוּ לַזְּמַן הַזֶּה.

I praise You, Eternal God, Sovereign of the universe, for giving me life, for sustaining me, and for enabling me to reach this season of my life.

At the onset of each menstrual period

בָּרוּךְ אַתָּה יי אֱלֹהֵינוּ מֶלֶךְ הָעוֹלָם, שֶׁעָשַׂנִי אִשָּׁה.

I praise You, Eternal God, Sovereign of the universe, for making me a woman.

❧ *See also related prayers in 'The Path of Life,' page 126.*

On having had confirmation of a pregnancy

יְהִי רָצוֹן מִלְפָנֶיךָ, יי אֱלֹהֵינוּ וֵאלֹהֵי אֲבוֹתֵינוּ וְאִמוֹתֵינוּ, שֶׁתִּקְוַת חַיִּים חֲדָשָׁה זוֹ תִּתְמַמֵּשׁ לִבְרָכָה בִּמְלֹאת הַיָּמִים.

Our God and God of our mothers and our fathers, may this promise of new life be realized in the fullness of time, and be to us a blessing.

❧ *See also related prayers in 'The Path of Life', pages 107–108.*

Upon a miscarriage

מִמַּעֲמַקִּים קְרָאנוּ לָךְ, יהוה, כִּי הָיִינוּ כְּאֵלָה נֹבֶלֶת עָלֶהָ וּכְגַנָּה אֲשֶׁר־מַיִם
אֵין לָהּ. עֲנֵנוּ, אֱלֹהֵי צִדְקֵנוּ, כִּי תִקְוָתֵנוּ נִפָּצָה. בָּרוּךְ אַתָּה יי מִקְוֵה
יִשְׂרָאֵל.

Out of the depths we cry out to You, for we are 'like a withered oak tree, like a garden that is parched' [*Psalm 130:1, Isaiah 1:30*]. Answer us, O God who upholds us, for our hopes have been shattered. Praised be the Eternal God, the Hope of Israel.

❦ *See also related prayers in 'The Path of Life,' page 162.*

Upon giving birth

❦ *May be said by one or both parents.*

Ba-ruch a-ta Adonai,	בָּרוּךְ אַתָּה יי
Eh-lo-hei-nu meh-lech ha-o-lam,	אֱלֹהֵינוּ מֶלֶךְ הָעוֹלָם,
sheh-heh-cheh-ya-nu, v'ki-y'ma-nu,	שֶׁהֶחֱיָנוּ וְקִיְּמָנוּ
v'higi-a-nu la-z'man ha-zeh.	וְהִגִּיעָנוּ לַזְּמַן הַזֶּה.

We praise You, Eternal God, Sovereign of the universe, for giving us life, for sustaining us, and for enabling us to reach this time.

יוֹם חַג הוּא יוֹם זֶה לָנוּ, כַּכָּתוּב: יִשְׂמַח־אָבִיךָ וְאִמֶּךָ וְתָגֵל יוֹלַדְתֶּךָ.

This is our day of joy. As it is said: 'Your father and mother will be jubilant; the woman who bore you will exult' [*Proverbs 23:25*].

❦ *See also related prayers in 'The Path of Life,' pages 109–110.*

Upon breast feeding

בָּרוּךְ אַתָּה יי אֱלֹהֵינוּ מֶלֶךְ הָעוֹלָם, הַמְאַפְשֵׁר לִי לְהֵינִיק אֶת־פְּרִי
בִּטְנִי.

Eternal God, Sovereign of the universe, I praise You, for You are the One who makes me able to nurse the fruit of my womb.

Upon experiencing any profound change in one's life

יְהִי רָצוֹן מִלְּפָנֶיךָ, יי אֱלֹהֵינוּ וֵאלֹהֵי אֲבוֹתֵינוּ וְאִמּוֹתֵינוּ, שֶׁתַּנְחֵנִי בְּדַרְכֵי נֹעַם בִּשְׁאֵרִית יָמַי. בָּרוּךְ הַיּוֹצֵר שִׁנּוּי בְּכָל בְּרִיּוֹתָיו.

Be my Guide, O God and God of my ancestors, and lead me in ways of pleasantness along my life's path. Praised be the Source of all change.

On learning of a pregnancy

MAN AND WOMAN:

We stand humbled before the Power of Creation that works through us to bring forth new life. We tremble with fear and with joy.

WOMAN:

Deep inside me a seed is growing. I am at once afraid and filled with ecstasy.

MAN:

I stand with you in awe before the wonder of existence.

MAN AND WOMAN:

May this promise of life come to be—our child. At this tender moment, at the threshold of new life, we proclaim our trust in the Source of Being, and ask for wisdom and strength to nurture this gift of life. Sheltered under the wings of transcendent love, may we grow as partners with the Source of life in the miracle of creation.

Ba-ruch a-ta Adonai,
Eh-lo-hei-nu meh-lech ha-o-lam,
sheh-heh-cheh-ya-nu, v'ki-y'ma-nu,
v'higi-a-nu la-z'man ha-zeh.

בָּרוּךְ אַתָּה יי
אֱלֹהֵינוּ מֶלֶךְ הָעוֹלָם,
שֶׁהֶחֱיָנוּ וְקִיְּמָנוּ
וְהִגִּיעָנוּ לַזְּמַן הַזֶּה.

We praise You, Eternal God, Sovereign of the universe, for giving us life, for sustaining us, and for enabling us to reach this day.

During pregnancy

❦ *A prayer for prospective parents.*

God of all generations, You have blessed our life with companionship and mutual love. For all Your past gifts we are thankful; now our hearts are full, in this time of expectant hope.

We await the birth of a new life and You are with us. As a parent holds the hand of a child, so now make our spirits serene. Let us wait in confidence and calm, with hearts unafraid. Let our child be born to health and happiness. Help us to be worthy parents, and bless us with a long life nourished and sustained by the sweetness of family love. Amen.

By a couple who fear they may be infertile

Our God and God of our ancestors . . .

We say these words with sadness, for we feel the pain of our ancestors, Abraham and Sarah, who were childless many long years. We feel their yearning and know their despair. We know, too, that they were blessed with a child after all hope had disappeared. As You blessed them with a child, we pray that You will bless us with a child.

Guide all who seek to help us. Enlighten and bless our physicians and nurses, our family and friends. Whatever lies ahead, sustain us with Your love and Your mercy. Strengthen the bonds between the two of us so that whatever may result from our endeavors and our prayers, our hearts will always be filled with love, one for the other. Amen.

By those seeking to adopt a child

God of mercy, we come before You, seeking to embrace a new life, to love and nurture a child. We wish to give of our heart, and to experience the gifts and responsibilities of parenthood.

O God, give us the fortitude and patience we need at this hour and in the days and weeks to come. Help us to wait in trust that somewhere in the world, our child awaits us.

COUPLE:

God of mercy, in mercy hear our prayer and bless us with a child.

On the birth or adoption of a child

❦ *You may select either of the two versions.*

I

Source of all life, our hearts are filled with joy for the child that has been entrusted to us. May we be thankful always, and speak our thanks not with words alone, but with the love, understanding, and tender care with which we hope to raise our child.

Be gracious to our child, that he (she) may grow in strength of body, mind, and spirit. May he (she) learn to love all that is good and beautiful and true, and so live a life of blessing.

May our child find his (her) way in the paths of Torah and good deeds as a loyal member of his (her) people. Give us, O God, the wisdom, courage, and faith that we as parents will need to help our child become a strong, confident, and loving person. Amen.

Ba-ruch a-ta Adonai,   בָּרוּךְ אַתָּה יי
Eh-lo-hei-nu meh-lech ha-o-lam,   אֱלֹהֵינוּ מֶלֶךְ הָעוֹלָם,
sheh-heh-cheh-ya-nu, v'ki-y'ma-nu,   שֶׁהֶחֱיָנוּ וְקִיְּמָנוּ
v'higi-a-nu la-z'man ha-zeh.   וְהִגִּיעָנוּ לַזְּמַן הַזֶּה.

We praise You, Eternal God, Sovereign of the universe, for giving us life, for sustaining us, and for enabling us to reach this day.

II

How small you are, our child, and how beautiful! You grasp our finger; we hold you close. Let our arms be your loving cradle; our whispered prayer, your lullaby.

Our hearts overflow with joy, and we give thanks:

בָּרוּךְ אַתָּה יי אֱלֹהֵינוּ מֶלֶךְ הָעוֹלָם, שֶׁעָשָׂה לָנוּ נֵס בַּמָּקוֹם הַזֶּה.

Sovereign God of the universe, for the wonder we have experienced, we give thanks.

On the birth or adoption of a grandchild

We are thankful for the blessing You have bestowed upon us in our lives. Now we have been granted a [new] grandchild to love, the opening of a new page in our family's chronicle. May this child grow up in health and happiness.

May her (his) dear parents find much joy in the years that lie before them. O God of life, may they raise their child with wisdom and understanding, teaching her (him) the ways of righteousness, leading her (him) to the study of Torah and the practice of love and kindness.

May we, too, be granted the joy of seeing her (him) develop all her (his) gifts, and the gratification of helping her (him) to fulfill the best that is in her (him). Then our prayer shall have found its answer: the days and years to come shall be for us times of peace and fulfillment. Amen.

Ba-ruch a-ta Adonai,
Eh-lo-hei-nu meh-lech ha-o-lam,
sheh-heh-cheh-ya-nu, v'ki-y'ma-nu,
v'higi-a-nu la-z'man ha-zeh.

בָּרוּךְ אַתָּה יי
אֱלֹהֵינוּ מֶלֶךְ הָעוֹלָם,
שֶׁהֶחֱיָנוּ וְקִיְּמָנוּ
וְהִגִּיעָנוּ לַזְּמַן הַזֶּה.

We praise You, Eternal God, Sovereign of the universe, for giving us life, for sustaining us, and for enabling us to reach this day.

On bringing a new child home

מַה־טֹּבוּ אֹהָלֶיךָ, יַעֲקֹב, מִשְׁכְּנֹתֶיךָ יִשְׂרָאֵל!

How lovely are your tents, O Jacob,
your dwelling-places, O Israel!

May our home always be a small sanctuary, O God, filled with Your presence.

May this home be your sanctuary, child, a place where loving arms

110

will cradle you, hands uphold you, and eyes delight in you.

Let this home be filled with love.

Here let the hearts of parents and children ever be turned to one another.

Here may the bonds of trust and caring keep us together as a family.

בָּרְכֵנוּ, אָבֵנוּ, כֻּלָּנוּ כְּאֶחָד בְּאוֹר פָּנֶיךָ.

As a loving Parent, bless all of us together with the light of Your presence.

The Covenant of Milah
בְּרִית מִילָה

🍂 *This ritual is conducted on the eighth day.*

בָּרוּךְ הַבָּא.

Blessed be the child whom we now welcome.

The rite of circumcision has been enjoined on us as a sign of our covenant with God, as it is written, 'And God said to Abraham: You shall keep My covenant, you and your children after you. He who is eight days old shall be circumcised, every male throughout your generations.'

We recall the Prophetic promise that one day this sign of our covenant with God will be imprinted not only upon our flesh, but upon our hearts and the hearts of our children. So shall we rise to the selfless love of God, and therein find new life.

May we, like our father Abraham, obey the command of God: Walk with integrity before Me *[Genesis 17:1]*.

A PARENT:

Joyfully we present our son for the covenant of circumcision:

וַיָּקֶם עֵדוּת בְּיַעֲקֹב, וְתוֹרָה שָׂם בְּיִשְׂרָאֵל, אֲשֶׁר צִוָּה אֶת־אֲבוֹתֵינוּ
לְהוֹדִיעָם לִבְנֵיהֶם; לְמַעַן יֵדְעוּ דוֹר אַחֲרוֹן בָּנִים יִוָּלֵדוּ. זָכַר לְעוֹלָם
בְּרִיתוֹ, דָּבָר צִוָּה לְאֶלֶף דּוֹר: אֲשֶׁר כָּרַת אֶת־אַבְרָהָם, וּשְׁבוּעָתוֹ
לְיִצְחָק, וַיַּעֲמִידֶהָ לְיַעֲקֹב לְחֹק, לְיִשְׂרָאֵל בְּרִית עוֹלָם.

Eternal One, You established a testimony in Jacob, You placed a Teaching in Israel, commanding our ancestors to make them known to their children; that the generations to come—children yet unborn—might know them.

You are for ever mindful of Your covenant, the word You commanded for a thousand generations: the covenant You made with Abraham; Your sworn promise to Isaac: the commitment You made to Jacob; Your everlasting covenant with Israel.

הוֹדוּ לַיהוה כִּי־טוֹב, כִּי לְעוֹלָם חַסְדּוֹ.

Give thanks to the Eternal One, who is good, whose love is ever-lasting.

MOHEL OR A PARENT:

Ba-ruch a-ta Adonai,
Eh-lo-hei-nu meh-lech ha-o-lam,
a-sher ki-d'sha-nu b'mitz-vo-tav
v'tzi-va-nu al ha-mi-lah.

בָּרוּךְ אַתָּה יי
אֱלֹהֵינוּ מֶלֶךְ הָעוֹלָם,
אֲשֶׁר קִדְּשָׁנוּ בְּמִצְוֹתָיו
וְצִוָּנוּ עַל הַמִּילָה.

We praise You, Eternal God, Sovereign of the universe: You hallow us with Your Mitzvot, and command us to fulfill the Mitzvah of circumcision.

THE CIRCUMCISION IS PERFORMED

A PARENT:

Ba-ruch a-ta Adonai,
Eh-lo-hei-nu meh-lech ha-o-lam,
a-sher ki-d'sha-nu b'mitz-vo-tav
v'tzi-va-nu l'hach-ni-so bi-v'ri-to
shel Av-ra-ham a-vi-nu.

בָּרוּךְ אַתָּה יי
אֱלֹהֵינוּ מֶלֶךְ הָעוֹלָם,
אֲשֶׁר קִדְּשָׁנוּ בְּמִצְוֹתָיו
וְצִוָּנוּ לְהַכְנִיסוֹ בִּבְרִיתוֹ
שֶׁל אַבְרָהָם אָבִינוּ.

We praise You, Eternal God, Sovereign of the universe: You hallow us with Your Mitzvot, and command us to bring our sons into the Covenant of Abraham.

MOHEL OR OTHER PARTICIPANT:

Ba-ruch a-ta Adonai,
Eh-lo-hei-nu meh-lech ha-o-lam,
bo-rei p'ri ha-ga-fen.

בָּרוּךְ אַתָּה יי
אֱלֹהֵינוּ מֶלֶךְ הָעוֹלָם,
בּוֹרֵא פְּרִי הַגָּפֶן.

We praise You, Eternal God, Sovereign of the universe, Creator of the fruit of the vine.

113

אֱלֹהֵינוּ וֵאלֹהֵי אֲבוֹתֵינוּ וְאִמּוֹתֵינוּ, קַיֵּם אֶת־הַיֶּלֶד הַזֶּה לְאָבִיו וּלְאִמּוֹ,
וְיִקָּרֵא שְׁמוֹ בְּיִשְׂרָאֵל . . . . יִשְׂמַח הָאָב בְּיוֹצֵא חֲלָצָיו וְתָגֵל
אִמּוֹ בִּפְרִי בִטְנָהּ. זֶה הַקָּטָן גָּדוֹל יִהְיֶה. כְּשֵׁם שֶׁנִּכְנַס לַבְּרִית כֵּן יִכָּנֵס
לְתוֹרָה, לְחֻפָּה, וּלְמַעֲשִׂים טוֹבִים.

Our God and God of our mothers and fathers, sustain this child, and
let him be known in the House of Israel as . . . . May he bring
much joy to his parents. As he has entered into the Covenant of
Abraham, so may he enter into the life of Torah, the blessing of
family life, and the practice of goodness.

מִי שֶׁבֵּרַךְ אֲבוֹתֵינוּ אַבְרָהָם, יִצְחָק, וְיַעֲקֹב, וְאִמּוֹתֵינוּ שָׂרָה, רִבְקָה,
לֵאָה, וְרָחֵל, הוּא יְבָרֵךְ אֶת־הַיֶּלֶד הָרַךְ הַנִּמּוֹל וִירַפֵּא אוֹתוֹ רְפוּאָה
שְׁלֵמָה. וִיזַכּוּ הוֹרָיו לְגַדְּלוֹ, לְחַנְּכוֹ וּלְחַכְּמוֹ. וְיִהְיוּ יָדָיו וְלִבּוֹ לְאֵל
אֱמוּנָה, וְנֹאמַר: אָמֵן.

May the One who blessed our fathers Abraham, Isaac, and Jacob, and
our mothers Sarah, Rebekah, Leah, and Rachel, bless this child and
keep him from all harm. May his parents help him to dedicate his
life in faithfulness to God, his heart receptive always to Torah and
Mitzvot. Then shall he bring blessing to his parents, his people,
and all the world. Amen.

Y'va-reh-ch'cha Adonai v'yish-m'reh-cha.	יְבָרֶכְךָ יהוה וְיִשְׁמְרֶךָ.
Ya-eir Adonai pa-nav ei-leh-cha	יָאֵר יהוה פָּנָיו אֵלֶיךָ
vi-chu-neh-ka.	וִיחֻנֶּךָּ.
Yi-sa Adonai pa-nav ei-leh-cha	יִשָּׂא יהוה פָּנָיו אֵלֶיךָ
v'ya-seim l'cha sha-lom.	וְיָשֵׂם לְךָ שָׁלוֹם.

May God bless you and keep you. May God look kindly upon you,
and be gracious to you. May God reach out to You in tenderness, and
give you peace.

❧ *The service might conclude with a reading in the form of an alphabetical
acrostic of the child's name, selected from Psalm 119 or other Scriptural verses.*

In the event that one of the parents is not present at the service of circumcision, this prayer may be offered when the child is taken to her/him.

We give thanks, O God, Fountain of life, for the gift of our child, who has entered into the Covenant of Abraham. Keep him from harm, and grant that he may be a source of joy to us and all his loved ones. May he have health and length of days. Teach us to rear our child with care and affection, with wisdom and understanding, that he may be a faithful child of our people, and a blessing to the world. Amen.

The Covenant of Life

בְּרִית הַחַיִּים

❧ *This ritual is conducted on the eighth day.*

בְּרוּכָה הַבָּאָה.

Blessed be the child whom we now welcome.

Reverence for life has been enjoined on us as a fulfillment of our covenant with God, as it is written, 'And God said to Israel: Choose life, that you and your descendants may live.'

The birth of a daughter brings us joy and hope, and the courage to reaffirm our enduring covenant with life and its Creator.

❧ *The mother kindles a light and takes her daughter in her arms:*

כִּי נֵר מִצְוָה וְתוֹרָה אוֹר.

The Mitzvah is a lamp; Torah is a light.

בָּרוּךְ אַתָּה יי, הַמֵּאִיר לָעוֹלָם כֻּלּוֹ בִּכְבוֹדוֹ.

We praise You, O God, whose presence gives light to all the world.

Joyfully I bring my daughter into the covenant of our people: a covenant with God, with Torah, and with our people.

Ba-ruch a-ta Adonai,
Eh-lo-hei-nu meh-lech ha-o-lam,
a-sher ki-d'sha-nu b'mitz-vo-tav
v'tzi-va-nu l'hach-ni-sah bi-v'rit
ha-cha-yim.

בָּרוּךְ אַתָּה יי
אֱלֹהֵינוּ מֶלֶךְ הָעוֹלָם,
אֲשֶׁר קִדְּשָׁנוּ בְּמִצְוֹתָיו
וְצִוָּנוּ לְהַכְנִיסָהּ בִּבְרִית
הַחַיִּים.

We praise You, Eternal God, Sovereign of the universe: You hallow us with Your Mitzvot, and command us to bring our daughters into the Covenant of Life.

❧ *The father kindles a light and takes his daughter in his arms:*

אֲנִי יהוה, וְאֶתֶּנְךָ לִבְרִית עָם, לְאוֹר גּוֹיִם.

I, the Eternal One, have called you to be a covenant people, a light to the nations.

Joyfully I bring my daughter into the Covenant of our people: a covenant with God, with Torah, and with the people Israel.

בָּרוּךְ אַתָּה יי
אֱלֹהֵינוּ מֶלֶךְ הָעוֹלָם,
אֲשֶׁר קִדְּשָׁנוּ בְּמִצְוֹתָיו
וְצִוָּנוּ עַל קִדּוּשׁ הַחַיִּים.

Ba-ruch a-ta Adonai,
Eh-lo-hei-nu meh-lech ha-o-lam,
a-sher ki-d'sha-nu b'mitz-vo-tav
v'tzi-va-nu al ki-dush ha-cha-yim.

We praise You, Eternal God, Sovereign of the universe: You hallow us with Your Mitzvot, and command us to sanctify our life.

BOTH PARENTS SAY:

בָּרוּךְ אַתָּה יי
אֱלֹהֵינוּ מֶלֶךְ הָעוֹלָם,
שֶׁהֶחֱיָנוּ וְקִיְּמָנוּ
וְהִגִּיעָנוּ לַזְּמַן הַזֶּה.

Ba-ruch a-ta Adonai,
E-lo-hei-nu meh-lech ha-o-lam,
sheh-heh-cheh-ya-nu, v'ki-y'ma-nu,
v'hi-gi-a-nu la-z'man ha-zeh.

We praise You, Eternal God, Sovereign of the universe, for giving us life, for sustaining us, and for enabling us to reach this season.

זֶה הַיּוֹם עָשָׂה יהוה; נָגִילָה וְנִשְׂמְחָה בוֹ.

This is the day the Eternal God has made; let us rejoice and be glad in it.

כִּי זֹאת הַבְּרִית אֲשֶׁר אֶכְרֹת אֶת־בֵּית יִשְׂרָאֵל אַחֲרֵי הַיָּמִים הָהֵם,
נְאֻם־יהוה: נָתַתִּי אֶת־תּוֹרָתִי בְּקִרְבָּם, וְעַל־לִבָּם אֶכְתֲּבֶנָּה, וְהָיִיתִי לָהֶם
לֵאלֹהִים, וְהֵמָּה יִהְיוּ־לִי לְעָם.

This is the covenant I will make with the House of Israel in time to come, says the Eternal One: I will put My Teaching within them, and engrave it on their hearts; I will be their God, and they shall be My people.

וְלֹא יְלַמְּדוּ עוֹד אִישׁ אֶת־רֵעֵהוּ וְאִישׁ אֶת־אָחִיו לֵאמֹר, דְּעוּ אֶת־
יהוה, כִּי־כֻלָּם יֵדְעוּ אוֹתִי, לְמִקְטַנָּם וְעַד־גְּדוֹלָם, נְאֻם־יהוה.

No longer shall you need to teach one another to know Me, for all shall know Me, young and old!

הוֹדוּ לַיהוה כִּי־טוֹב, כִּי לְעוֹלָם חַסְדּוֹ.

Give thanks to the Eternal One, who is good, whose love is everlasting.

Ba-ruch a-ta Adonai,　　　　　　　בָּרוּךְ אַתָּה יי
Eh-lo-hei-nu meh-lech ha-o-lam,　אֱלֹהֵינוּ מֶלֶךְ הָעוֹלָם,
bo-rei p'ri ha-ga-fen.　　　　　　בּוֹרֵא פְּרִי הַגָּפֶן.

We praise You, Eternal God, Sovereign of the universe, Creator of the fruit of the vine.

אֱלֹהֵינוּ וֵאלֹהֵי אֲבוֹתֵינוּ וְאִמּוֹתֵינוּ, קַיֵּם אֶת־הַיַּלְדָּה הַזֹּאת לְאָבִיהָ וּלְאִמָּהּ,
וְיִקָּרֵא שְׁמָהּ בְּיִשְׂרָאֵל . . . . יִשְׂמַח הָאָב בְּיוֹצֵאת חֲלָצָיו
וְתָגֵל אִמָּהּ בִּפְרִי בִטְנָהּ. זֹאת הַקְּטַנָּה גְּדוֹלָה תִּהְיֶה. כְּשֵׁם שֶׁנִּכְנְסָה
לַבְּרִית כֵּן תִּכָּנֵס לַתּוֹרָה, לְחֻפָּה, וּלְמַעֲשִׂים טוֹבִים.

Our God and God of our mothers and fathers, sustain this child, and let her be known in the House of Israel as . . . . May she bring much joy to her parents. As she has entered into the Covenant of Life, so may she enter into the life of Torah, the blessing of family life, and the practice of goodness.

מִי שֶׁבֵּרַךְ אֲבוֹתֵינוּ אַבְרָהָם, יִצְחָק, וְיַעֲקֹב, וְאִמּוֹתֵינוּ שָׂרָה, רִבְקָה,
לֵאָה, וְרָחֵל, הוּא יְבָרֵךְ אֶת־הַיַּלְדָּה הָרַכָּה וְיִשְׁמְרֶהָ מִכָּל־צָרָה וְצוּקָה.
וְיִזְכּוּ הוֹרֶיהָ לְגַדְּלָהּ, לְחַנְּכָהּ וּלְחַכְּמָהּ. וְיִהְיוּ יָדֶיהָ וְלִבָּהּ לְאֵל אֱמוּנָה,
וְנֹאמַר: אָמֵן.

May the One who blessed our fathers Abraham, Isaac, and Jacob, and
our mothers Sarah, Rebekah, Leah, and Rachel, bless this child and
keep her from all harm. May her parents help her to dedicate her life
in faithfulness to God, her heart receptive always to Torah and
Mitzvot. Then shall she bring blessing to her parents, her people,
and all the world. Amen.

Y'va-reh-ch'cha Adonai v'yish-m'reh-cha.   יְבָרֶכְךָ יהוה וְיִשְׁמְרֶךָ.

Ya-eir Adonai pa-nav ei-leh-cha   יָאֵר יהוה פָּנָיו אֵלֶיךָ

vi-chu-neh-ka.   וִיחֻנֶּךָּ.

Yi-sa Adonai pa-nav ei-leh-cha   יִשָּׂא יהוה פָּנָיו אֵלֶיךָ

v'ya-seim l'cha sha-lom.   וְיָשֵׂם לְךָ שָׁלוֹם.

May God bless you and keep you. May God look kindly upon you,
and be gracious to you. May God reach out to You in tenderness, and
give you peace.

❧ *The service might conclude with a reading in the form of an alphabetical
acrostic of the child's name, selected from Psalm 119 or other Scriptural verses.*

*In the event that one of the parents is not present at the service, this prayer may
be offered later:*

> We give thanks, O God, Fountain of life, for the gift of our
> child, who has entered into the Covenant of Life. Keep her
> from harm, and grant that she may be a source of joy to us
> and all her loved ones. May she have health and length of
> days. Teach us to bring up our child with care and affection,
> with wisdom and understanding, that she may be a faithful
> child of our people, and a blessing to the world. Amen.

For the Naming of a Child

❧ *This ceremony may be performed in the synagogue or at home.*

God and Creator, Your children have come into Your presence with grateful hearts, to reflect on their responsibilities as parents. Give them the wisdom to teach their child to be faithful to the heritage of the Household of Israel, that he (she) may grow up with the knowledge that You are always near to him (her), guiding and sustaining him (her). Keep open his (her) eyes and spirit, that he (she) may ever be conscious of the beauty and wonder of Your world. And let him (her) learn to love the goodness that is in man and woman, that he (she) may ever nourish the goodness that has been implanted within him (her). Though none can escape sorrow and pain, we humbly ask for him (her) the courage to face evil, the faith to transcend it, and the strength to subdue it. Grant him (her) health of mind and of body, that he (she) may enjoy fullness of years and live to do Your will in faithfulness. Amen.

בָּרוּךְ אַתָּה יי אֱלֹהֵינוּ מֶלֶךְ הָעוֹלָם, גוֹמֵל חֲסָדִים טוֹבִים.

We praise You, Eternal God, Sovereign of the universe: Your love and kindness extend to all the world.

Ba-ruch a-ta Adonai,
Eh-lo-hei-nu meh-lech ha-o-lam,
sheh-heh-cheh-ya-nu, v'ki-y'ma-nu,
v'higi-a-nu la-z'man ha-zeh.

בָּרוּךְ אַתָּה יי
אֱלֹהֵינוּ מֶלֶךְ הָעוֹלָם,
שֶׁהֶחֱיָנוּ וְקִיְּמָנוּ
וְהִגִּיעָנוּ לַזְּמַן הַזֶּה.

We praise You, Eternal God, Sovereign of the universe, for giving us life, for sustaining us, and for enabling us to reach this season.

FOR A GIRL

מִי שֶׁבֵּרַךְ אֲבוֹתֵינוּ אַבְרָהָם, יִצְחָק, וְיַעֲקֹב, וְאִמּוֹתֵינוּ שָׂרָה,
רִבְקָה, לֵאָה, וְרָחֵל, הוּא יְבָרֵךְ אֶת־הַיַּלְדָּה הַזֹּאת. הַקָּדוֹשׁ
בָּרוּךְ הוּא יִשְׁמְרֶהָ וְיִטָּה אֶת־לֵב הַיַּלְדָּה לָלֶכֶת בְּדַרְכֵי יֹשֶׁר,
וִיהִי יי עִמָּהּ, וְיִתֶּן לָהּ דֵּעָה, בִּינָה, וְהַשְׂכֵּל, חַיִּים וָחֶסֶד,

בְּרָכָה וְשָׁלוֹם, וְיִזְכּוּ הוֹרֶיהָ לְגַדְּלָהּ לְחֻנְּכָה וּלְחַכְּמָהּ לְתוֹרָה לְחֻפָּה וּלְמַעֲשִׂים טוֹבִים, וְנֹאמַר: אָמֵן.

May the One who blessed our fathers Abraham, Isaac, and Jacob, and our mothers Sarah, Rebekah, Leah, and Rachel, bless this child with life and health. May she be a joy to her parents. May she live to bring honor to the House of Israel, blessing to humanity, and glory to the name of God. Amen.

FOR A BOY

מִי שֶׁבֵּרַךְ אֲבוֹתֵינוּ אַבְרָהָם, יִצְחָק, וְיַעֲקֹב, וְאִמּוֹתֵינוּ שָׂרָה, רִבְקָה, לֵאָה, וְרָחֵל, הוּא יְבָרֵךְ אֶת־הַיֶּלֶד הַזֶּה. הַקָּדוֹשׁ בָּרוּךְ הוּא יִשְׁמְרֵהוּ וְיִטֶּה אֶת־לֵב הַיֶּלֶד לָלֶכֶת בְּדַרְכֵי יֹשֶׁר, וִיהִי יי עִמּוֹ, וְיִתֶּן לוֹ דֵעָה, בִּינָה וְהַשְׂכֵּל, חַיִּים וְחֶסֶד, בְּרָכָה וְשָׁלוֹם, וְיִזְכּוּ הוֹרָיו לְגַדְּלוֹ לְחֻנְּכוֹ וּלְחַכְּמוֹ לְתוֹרָה לְחֻפָּה וּלְמַעֲשִׂים טוֹבִים, וְנֹאמַר: אָמֵן.

May the One who blessed our fathers Abraham, Isaac, and Jacob, and our mothers Sarah, Rebekah, Leah, and Rachel, bless this child with life and health. May he be a joy to his parents. May he live to bring honor to the House of Israel, blessing to humanity, and glory to the name of God. Amen.

BY THE PARENTS:

O God, for the gift of this child we give thanks, and pray that we may be worthy of the blessing and responsibility of parenthood.

For a boy

May we lead our son in the way of righteousness. Teach us to guide and instruct him, that he may grow up to be loyal to Judaism and a worthy member of the Jewish community.

For a girl

May we lead our daughter in the way of righteousness. Teach us to guide and instruct her, that she may grow up to be loyal to Judaism and a worthy member of the Jewish community.

TO THE PARENTS:

Friends, may You dedicate yourselves to give your holiest gifts—love and respect—to this new person, whom you have brought to be named, and may you ever give freely of yourselves, so that in time's fullness your love will bestow upon this child the gift of freedom. May joy ever accompany such giving and receiving.

TO THE CHILD:

Now, in the presence of loved ones, we give to you the name
. . . . Let it become a name honored and respected for wisdom and good deeds. . . . . , we commit ourselves to the unfolding of your promise; may you walk the path of goodness, beauty, and truth. Do justly and love mercy, and be humble before the mystery of life and the grandeur of the universe into which you have been born.

May God's blessing rest on you now and always.

Y'va-reh-ch'cha Adonai v'yish-m'reh-cha.	יְבָרֶכְךָ יהוה וְיִשְׁמְרֶךָ.
Ya-eir Adonai pa-nav ei-leh-cha	יָאֵר יהוה פָּנָיו אֵלֶיךָ
vi-chu-neh-ka.	וִיחֻנֶּךָּ.
Yi-sa Adonai pa-nav ei-leh-cha	יִשָּׂא יהוה פָּנָיו אֵלֶיךָ
v'ya-seim l'cha sha-lom.	וְיָשֵׂם לְךָ שָׁלוֹם.

May God bless you and keep you. May God look kindly upon you, and be gracious to you. May God reach out to You in tenderness, and give you peace.

❧ *Wine and grape juice are equally "fruit of the vine."*

Ba-ruch a-ta Adonai,	בָּרוּךְ אַתָּה יי
Eh-lo-hei-nu meh-lech ha-o-lam,	אֱלֹהֵינוּ מֶלֶךְ הָעוֹלָם,
bo-rei p'ri ha-ga-fen.	בּוֹרֵא פְּרִי הַגָּפֶן.

We praise You, Eternal God, Sovereign of the universe, Creator of the fruit of the vine.

❧ *A few drops might be given to the child. The cup might be shared by parents and loved ones.*

At a birthday celebration

God of days and years, Author of life, our times are in Your hand. We thank You for the blessing of life, and for all that enriches our lives.

We gather today in special thankfulness to share in the happiness of . . . . Be with him (her) always as the joy of his (her) life. May he (she) be blessed with health and happiness, and with the strength to overcome sickness and sorrow.

May we have the joy of coming together for many more years, united by mutual reverence and love. Then will our lives be filled with abundance of blessing.

❧ *Wine and grape juice are equally "fruit of the vine."*

Ba-ruch a-ta Adonai,
Eh-lo-hei-nu meh-lech ha-o-lam,
bo-rei p'ri ha-ga-fen.

בָּרוּךְ אַתָּה יי
אֱלֹהֵינוּ מֶלֶךְ הָעוֹלָם,
בּוֹרֵא פְּרִי הַגָּפֶן.

We praise You, Eternal God, Sovereign of the universe, Creator of the fruit of the vine.

Ba-ruch a-ta Adonai,
Eh-lo-hei-nu meh-lech ha-o-lam,
sheh-heh-cheh-ya-nu, v'ki-y'ma-nu,
v'higi-a-nu la-z'man ha-zeh.

בָּרוּךְ אַתָּה יי
אֱלֹהֵינוּ מֶלֶךְ הָעוֹלָם,
שֶׁהֶחֱיָנוּ וְקִיְמָנוּ
וְהִגִּיעָנוּ לַזְּמַן הַזֶּה.

We praise You, Eternal God, Sovereign of the universe, for giving us life, for sustaining us, and for enabling us to reach this season.

Before partaking of the birthday cake

Ba-ruch a-ta Adonai,
Eh-lo-hei-nu meh-lech ha-o-lam,
bo-rei mi-nei m'zo-not.

בָּרוּךְ אַתָּה יי
אֱלֹהֵינוּ מֶלֶךְ הָעוֹלָם,
בּוֹרֵא מִינֵי מְזוֹנוֹת.

We praise You, Eternal God, Sovereign of the universe, Creator of many kinds of food.

At the beginning of a child's religious education

❦ *A prayer for parents in the home or in the synagogue.*

> 'Let these words, which I command you this day, be always in your heart. Teach them faithfully to your children . . .'

Source of all knowledge, Teacher of Israel and all the world, You reveal Yourself to us in the order and beauty of nature, in the call of conscience, and in the truths of sacred tradition. The hearts and minds of children sense Your presence. This religious instinct we would foster through education, that through knowledge it may gain strength, through worship take root in the soul, and through deeds of mercy and justice ennoble human life.

Therefore we bring our child to Your house to study Your Teaching, to be among those who seek to know Your ways and to follow the path of Your Mitzvot.

We pray that our child will grow in heart and mind. May the story of our people inspire him (her). May the truths of Torah guide him (her). And may the grandeur of the Prophetic word of truth and righteousness enter his (her) spirit and be for him (her) a lasting benediction. Amen.

Ba-ruch a-ta Adonai,	בָּרוּךְ אַתָּה יי
Eh-lo-hei-nu meh-lech ha-o-lam,	אֱלֹהֵינוּ מֶלֶךְ הָעוֹלָם,
a-sher ki-d'sha-nu b'mitz-vo-tav	אֲשֶׁר קִדְּשָׁנוּ בְּמִצְוֹתָיו
v'tzi-va-nu l'ga-deil ba-nim	וְצִוָּנוּ לְגַדֵּל בָּנִים
u-va-not la-Torah.	וּבָנוֹת לַתּוֹרָה.

We praise You, Eternal God, Sovereign of the universe: You hallow us with Your Mitzvot, and command us to bring up our children to love Torah.

At Bar Mitzvah, Bat Mitzvah, or Confirmation

❧ *A prayer for parents in the home or in the synagogue.*

'And all your children shall be taught about God, and great shall be the peace of Your children.'

We give thanks for this day, and for the years of growth and learning that have preceded it. Now as our child steps forth to affirm her (his) commitment to the ideals and Mitzvot of our faith, our soul is joyful, our mind is at peace.

Ba-ruch a-ta Adonai,

Eh-lo-hei-nu meh-lech ha-o-lam,

sheh-heh-cheh-ya-nu, v'ki-y'ma-nu,

v'higi-a-nu la-z'man ha-zeh.

בָּרוּךְ אַתָּה יי

אֱלֹהֵינוּ מֶלֶךְ הָעוֹלָם,

שֶׁהֶחֱיָנוּ וְקִיְּמָנוּ

וְהִגִּיעָנוּ לַזְּמַן הַזֶּה.

We praise You, Eternal God, Sovereign of the universe, for giving us life, for sustaining us, and for enabling us to reach this season.

We pray that this day's service may long echo in our child's memory. May it engrave on her (his) heart the understanding that this day initiates a life more firmly dedicated to the study of Torah and the fulfillment of Mitzvot, to deeds of justice and kindness, to faithful membership in the Household of Israel.

AN INDIVIDUAL SAYS:

> O God, make me a worthy example to my children. Let nothing estrange me from them and from You. Help me, too, again and again to renew my attachment to the Covenant of Israel, to walk hand in hand with my child in the ways of righteousness and truth. Amen.

A COUPLE SAYS:

> O God, make each of us a worthy example to our children. Let nothing estrange us from them and from You. Help us, too, again and again to renew our attachment to the Covenant of Israel, to walk hand in hand with our child in the ways of righteousness and truth. Amen.

By a Bar Mitzvah or a Bat Mitzvah

🐫 *At home or in the synagogue.*

O God of Israel, like Jews of generations past, I take my place as a Bar (Bat) Mitzvah. Grant that with them I may understand my responsibility as a Jew, to show love to my family and friends, to learn more and more about the traditions of my people.

O God, make me grateful for all that I have, and ready always to share with those who are in need. Then I will be able to say:

I am a Jew because a hundred generations before me were steadfast in their faith. I am a Jew because the faith of Israel teaches love and kindness. I am a Jew because the faith of Israel teaches justice, compassion, and truth.

Ba-ruch a-ta Adonai,	בָּרוּךְ אַתָּה יי
Eh-lo-hei-nu meh-lech ha-o-lam,	אֱלֹהֵינוּ מֶלֶךְ הָעוֹלָם,
sheh-heh-cheh-ya-nu, v'ki-y'ma-nu,	שֶׁהֶחֱיָנוּ וְקִיְּמָנוּ
v'higi-a-nu la-z'man ha-zeh.	וְהִגִּיעָנוּ לַזְּמַן הַזֶּה.

We praise You, Eternal God, Sovereign of the universe, for giving us life, for sustaining us, and for enabling us to reach this season.

Menstruation

Holy One, as the circle of my life revolves, renew me.
Give me
length of days,
a rich and honorable life,
a life of peace,
of goodness,
a life of blessing.

Grant me
sustenance and strength,
a sense of awe, wonder
at the miracle of my body and my being.

Give me
eyes to see the light of Torah,
a heart where Your Presence abides,
a mind unafraid of questions and their answers,
a life of wholeness, of harmony, of peace.

Ba-ruch a-ta Adonai,

Eh-lo-hei-nu meh-lech ha-o-lam

sheh-a-sa-ni i-sha

בָּרוּךְ אַתָּה יי

אֱלֹהֵינוּ מֶלֶךְ הָעוֹלָם,

שֶׁעָשַׂנִי אִשָּׁה.

I praise You, Eternal God, Sovereign of the universe, for making me a woman.

On entering college

אַתָּה חוֹנֵן לְאָדָם דַּעַת וּמְלַמֵּד לֶאֱנוֹשׁ בִּינָה. חָנֵּנוּ מֵאִתְּךָ דֵּעָה, בִּינָה וְהַשְׂכֵּל. בָּרוּךְ אַתָּה יי חוֹנֵן הַדָּעַת.

By your grace we have the power to gain knowledge and to grow in understanding. Favor us with knowledge, understanding and wisdom, for You are their Source.

We praise You, O God, gracious giver of knowledge.

I pray for wisdom to hold all truth sacred, whether it comes from the Torah and its interpreters of old, or from the scholars of our own age. Help me, Eternal God, to see beyond the surface of things, to understand that their beauty is but a reflection of Your wondrous creative power at work in me and in all the universe. Give me, also, a discerning mind, that I may recognize what is good, and reject what is false and harmful. And grant me a heart of wisdom, that, as Your partner in the work of creation, I may learn to use my knowledge for righteous purpose.

Wherever I go, and whatever I do, let me be a true child of my people Israel, faithful to justice and truth, eager for knowledge and insight. And may the study of Torah be sweet as honey on my lips. Amen.

Marriage Prayers

In contemplation of marriage

❧ *Read one or more of the following.*

I

I have agreed to enter into marriage with one whom I love, and who loves me. We have committed ourselves to one another with joy and in hope. May I be worthy of my beloved's trust; may we be faithful friends, each a help and support to the other in all that befalls us. And may we be blessed with children, a new generation which will grow in health and in beauty of spirit.

II

I have agreed to enter into marriage with one whom I love, and who loves me. We have committed ourselves to one another with joy and in hope. May there be tenderness between us; gentleness and understanding; a readiness to forgive each other's faults. We would create a union of hands for honest labor and fruitful effort. In joy and sorrow we shall work together to achieve the happiness for which we yearn.

III

God of compassion, give us wisdom to look beyond ourselves, to see ourselves as part of the greater family of the House of Israel, and as part of the larger human family. Then we shall abide in faithfulness, truth and peace.

Before the wedding

❦ *Read one or more of the following.*

I

In mercy You have touched me with Your love, O God, and in compassion You are with me on the path of my life. Now, in hope and in need I stand before You. Let the life I am about to enter be good and true, and filled with devotion. In dark moments as in light, may my beloved and I lean upon each other with perfect confidence.

II

O God, give us Your blessing! Let us each come to understand what is in the heart of the other, and gain insight into our own hearts. Keep us loyal to the ideals with which we begin this union, and help us to honor and sustain one another. Smile upon us and teach us to give and receive love with hearts joyful and unafraid.

III

For all the lessons that life has taught me, for the good I have known and the happiness that is yet to come, I give thanks and praise. Amen.

On the marriage of a son or daughter

How can I give thanks enough for this blessed day? How can I express what I feel for my beloved child? My heart is full to overflowing.

I remember so much anxiety, so many joys.

Now, as my child joins hands with another on the threshold of a new life, I pray that the home they establish will be built on firm foundations. May their love grow deeper through the years. And may their union mature through shared tasks and constant effort, to bring them blessing.

May the family they create be a strong part of our larger family, united in lasting affection. God of life, let the Divine Presence illumine their home and their lives always, blessing them with unfailing love. Amen.

Wedding Service

❦ *There are four parts to the service.*

I

בָּרוּךְ הַבָּא בְּשֵׁם יהוה, בֵּרַכְנוּכֶם מִבֵּית יהוה.

Blessed are you who come in the name of God; may you be blessed this day and every day of your lives together.

מִי אַדִּיר עַל הַכֹּל
מִי בָּרוּךְ עַל הַכֹּל,
מִי גָדוֹל עַל הַכֹּל
יְבָרֵךְ אֶת־הֶחָתָן וְאֶת־הַכַּלָּה.

May the One supreme in majesty, beyond all praise and infinitely great, bless this man and this woman who now enter into marriage.

TO THE BRIDE:

Do you, ..., now affirm your marriage with . . . ., and do you promise to love and honor him, to sustain and help him, and to keep faith with him always?

TO THE GROOM:

Do you, ..., now affirm your marriage with . . . ., and do you promise to love and honor her, to sustain and help her, and to keep faith with her always?

The following benediction is not traditional here, and may be omitted.

Ba-ruch a-ta Adonai,   בָּרוּךְ אַתָּה יי
Eh-lo-hei-nu meh-lech ha-o-lam,   אֱלֹהֵינוּ מֶלֶךְ הָעוֹלָם,
sheh-heh-cheh-ya-nu, v'ki-y'ma-nu,   שֶׁהֶחֱיָנוּ וְקִיְּמָנוּ
v'higi-a-nu la-z'man ha-zeh.   וְהִגִּיעָנוּ לַזְּמַן הַזֶּה.

We praise You, Eternal God, Sovereign of the universe, for giving us life, for sustaining us, and for enabling us to reach this season.

Ba-ruch a-ta Adonai,
Eh-lo-hei-nu meh-lech ha-o-lam,
bo-rei p'ri ha-ga-fen.

בָּרוּךְ אַתָּה יי
אֱלֹהֵינוּ מֶלֶךְ הָעוֹלָם,
בּוֹרֵא פְּרִי הַגָּפֶן.

We praise You, Eternal God , Sovereign of the universe, Creator of the fruit of the vine.

בָּרוּךְ אַתָּה יי אֱלֹהֵינוּ מֶלֶךְ הָעוֹלָם, אֲשֶׁר קִדְּשָׁנוּ בְּמִצְוֹתָיו וְצִוָּנוּ עַל פְּרִיָּה וּרְבִיָּה, וּקְרָאָנוּ לְקַדֵּשׁ אֶת־הַחַיִּים, וְזִמֵּן אוֹתָנוּ לַעֲבוֹדָתוֹ, בָּרוּךְ אַתָּה יי מְקַדֵּשׁ הַחַיִּים.

We praise You, Eternal God, Sovereign of the universe: You call us to holiness and invite us to be fruitful and multiply; and You summon us to Your service, inspiring us to sanctify our life. We praise You, O God: You sanctify our life.

II

❧ *The following passages, to the bottom of this page, are optional.*

שִׂימֵנִי כַחוֹתָם עַל־לִבֶּךָ,
כַּחוֹתָם עַל־זְרוֹעֶךָ,
כִּי־עַזָּה כַמָּוֶת אַהֲבָה,
שַׁלְהֶבֶת־יָהּ.

Set me as a seal upon your heart,
like the seal upon your hand,
for love is strong as death,
it is the flame of God.

וְאֵרַשְׂתִּיךְ לִי לְעוֹלָם,
וְאֵרַשְׂתִּיךְ לִי בְּצֶדֶק וּבְמִשְׁפָּט,
וּבְחֶסֶד וּבְרַחֲמִים,
וְאֵרַשְׂתִּיךְ לִי בֶּאֱמוּנָה . . .

I betroth you to me forever;
I betroth you to me
in righteousness and justice,
in love and compassion;
I betroth you to me
in everlasting faithfulness.

❦

THE GROOM SAYS TO THE BRIDE:

Ha-rei at m'ku-deh-shet li
b'ta-ba-at zo k'dat mo-sheh
v'yis-ra-el.

הֲרֵי אַתְּ מְקֻדֶּשֶׁת לִי
בְּטַבַּעַת זוֹ כְּדַת מֹשֶׁה
וְיִשְׂרָאֵל.

By this ring you are consecrated to me according to the tradition of Israel.

THE BRIDE SAYS TO THE GROOM:

Ha-rei a-ta m'ku-dash li
b'ta-ba-at zo k'dat mo-sheh
v'yis-ra-el.

הֲרֵי אַתָּה מְקֻדָּשׁ לִי
בְּטַבַּעַת זוֹ כְּדַת מֹשֶׁה
וְיִשְׂרָאֵל.

By this ring you are consecrated to me according to the tradition of Israel.

❦

בָּרוּךְ אַתָּה יי אֱלֹהֵינוּ מֶלֶךְ הָעוֹלָם, מְקַדֵּשׁ עַמּוֹ יִשְׂרָאֵל עַל־יְדֵי חֻפָּה
וְקִדּוּשִׁין.

We praise You, Eternal God, Sovereign of the universe: You sanctify Your people Israel under the sacred marriage canopy.

III

❦ *An alternative set of benedictions is on page 134.*

Ba-ruch a-ta Adonai,
Eh-lo-hei-nu meh-lech ha-o-lam,
bo-rei p'ri ha-ga-fen.

בָּרוּךְ אַתָּה יי
אֱלֹהֵינוּ מֶלֶךְ הָעוֹלָם,
בּוֹרֵא פְּרִי הַגָּפֶן.

We praise You, Eternal God, Sovereign of the universe, Creator of the fruit of the vine.

בָּרוּךְ אַתָּה יי אֱלֹהֵינוּ מֶלֶךְ הָעוֹלָם, שֶׁהַכֹּל בָּרָא לִכְבוֹדוֹ.

Praised be the One whose glory we find in all that we behold.

בָּרוּךְ אַתָּה יי אֱלֹהֵינוּ מֶלֶךְ הָעוֹלָם יוֹצֵר הָאָדָם.

Praised be the Creator of human kind.

בָּרוּךְ אַתָּה יי אֱלֹהֵינוּ מֶלֶךְ הָעוֹלָם, אֲשֶׁר יָצַר אֶת־הָאָדָם בְּצַלְמוֹ,
בְּצֶלֶם דְּמוּת תַּבְנִיתוֹ, וְהִתְקִין לוֹ מִמֶּנּוּ בִּנְיָן עֲדֵי־עַד.
בָּרוּךְ אַתָּה יי יוֹצֵר הָאָדָם.

Praised be our God, Creator of woman and man, a single human fabric woven of love. You have made us in Your own image, Your own likeness, and we give thanks and praise.

שׂוֹשׂ תָּשִׂישׂ וְתָגֵל הָעֲקָרָה, בְּקִבּוּץ בָּנֶיהָ לְתוֹכָהּ בְּשִׂמְחָה.
בָּרוּךְ אַתָּה יי מְשַׂמֵּחַ צִיּוֹן בְּבָנֶיהָ.

You have filled Zion's mouth with song: her children have come back to her in joy! We give thanks to the One who gladdens Zion through her children.

שַׂמֵּחַ תְּשַׂמַּח רֵעִים הָאֲהוּבִים, כְּשַׂמֵּחֲךָ יְצִירְךָ בְּגַן עֵדֶן מִקֶּדֶם.
בָּרוּךְ אַתָּה יי מְשַׂמֵּחַ חָתָן וְכַלָּה.

To these Your children, by love made one, all delight and gladness give. Renew their lives, refresh their hearts, show them both the joy of Eden. Eternal God, we praise You, for You cause man and woman to rejoice in marriage.

בָּרוּךְ אַתָּה יי אֱלֹהֵינוּ מֶלֶךְ הָעוֹלָם, אֲשֶׁר בָּרָא שָׂשׂוֹן וְשִׂמְחָה, חָתָן
וְכַלָּה, גִּילָה רִנָּה דִּיצָה וְחֶדְוָה, אַהֲבָה וְאַחֲוָה, שָׁלוֹם וְרֵעוּת. מְהֵרָה, יי
אֱלֹהֵינוּ, יִשָּׁמַע בְּעָרֵי יְהוּדָה וּבְחוּצוֹת יְרוּשָׁלָיִם, קוֹל שָׂשׂוֹן וְקוֹל שִׂמְחָה,
קוֹל חָתָן וְקוֹל כַּלָּה, קוֹל מִצְהֲלוֹת חֲתָנִים מֵחֻפָּתָם, וּנְעָרִים מִמִּשְׁתֵּה
נְגִינָתָם. בָּרוּךְ אַתָּה יי מְשַׂמֵּחַ חָתָן עִם הַכַּלָּה.

We give thanks for joy and gladness, happiness and exaltation, love and harmony, peace and friendship. Speedily let there be heard in the streets of Jerusalem and the cities of Judah, in earth's four corners, the cry of joy and the shout of gladness, the tender song of woman and man, the happy sounds of the wedding feast. Praised be the One who causes woman and man to rejoice in marriage.

IV

Y'va-reh-ch'cha Adonai v'yish-m'reh-cha.

יְבָרֶכְךָ יהוה וְיִשְׁמְרֶךָ.

Ya-eir Adonai pa-nav ei-leh-cha
vi-chu-neh-ka.

יָאֵר יהוה פָּנָיו אֵלֶיךָ
וִיחֻנֶּךָּ.

Yi-sa Adonai pa-nav ei-leh-cha
v'ya-seim l'cha sha-lom.

יִשָּׂא יהוה פָּנָיו אֵלֶיךָ
וְיָשֵׂם לְךָ שָׁלוֹם.

May God bless you and keep you. May God look kindly upon you, and be gracious to you. May God reach out to You in tenderness, and give you peace.

❧ *The breaking of glass concludes the service. The breaking of glass may be performed by either the woman or the man, or by both of them.*

Alternative Benedictions

בָּרוּךְ אַתָּה יי אֱלֹהֵינוּ מֶלֶךְ הָעוֹלָם, שֶׁהַכֹּל בָּרָא לִכְבוֹדוֹ.

בָּרוּךְ אַתָּה יי אֱלֹהֵינוּ מֶלֶךְ הָעוֹלָם, יוֹצֵר הָאָדָם.

בָּרוּךְ אַתָּה יי אֱלֹהֵינוּ מֶלֶךְ הָעוֹלָם, אֲשֶׁר יָצַר אֶת־הָאָדָם בְּצַלְמוֹ, בְּצֶלֶם דְּמוּת תַּבְנִיתוֹ, וְהִתְקִין לוֹ מִמֶּנּוּ בִּנְיָן עֲדֵי־עַד. בָּרוּךְ אַתָּה יי יוֹצֵר הָאָדָם.

שַׂמֵּחַ תְּשַׂמַּח רֵעִים הָאֲהוּבִים, כְּשַׂמֵּחֲךָ יְצִירְךָ בְּגַן עֵדֶן מִקֶּדֶם. בָּרוּךְ אַתָּה יי מְשַׂמֵּחַ חָתָן וְכַלָּה.

שׂוֹשׂ תָּשִׂישׂ וְתָגֵל צִיּוֹן, בְּקִבּוּץ בָּנֶיהָ וּבְנוֹתֶיהָ לְתוֹכָהּ בְּשִׂמְחָה. בָּרוּךְ אַתָּה יי מְשַׂמֵּחַ צִיּוֹן בְּבָנֶיהָ וּבִבְנוֹתֶיהָ.

בָּרוּךְ אַתָּה יי אֱלֹהֵינוּ מֶלֶךְ הָעוֹלָם, אֲשֶׁר בָּרָא שָׂשׂוֹן וְשִׂמְחָה, חָתָן וְכַלָּה, גִּילָה רִנָּה דִּיצָה וְחֶדְוָה, אַהֲבָה וְאַחֲוָה, שָׁלוֹם וְרֵעוּת. מְהֵרָה, יי אֱלֹהֵינוּ, יִשָּׁמַע בְּעָרֵי יְהוּדָה וּבְחוּצוֹת יְרוּשָׁלַיִם, קוֹל שָׂשׂוֹן וְקוֹל שִׂמְחָה, קוֹל חָתָן וְקוֹל כַּלָּה, קוֹל מִצְהֲלוֹת חֲתָנִים מֵחֻפָּתָם, וּנְעָרִים מִמִּשְׁתֵּה נְגִינָתָם. בָּרוּךְ אַתָּה יי מְשַׂמֵּחַ חָתָן עִם הַכַּלָּה.

בָּרוּךְ אַתָּה יי אֱלֹהֵינוּ מֶלֶךְ הָעוֹלָם, בּוֹרֵא פְּרִי הַגָּפֶן.

We give thanks for life, for health, for all that sustains us, and for this joyous day.

We honor the mystery and wonder in creation's every breath.

We praise human being: its yearning for tomorrow's wine, and for the taste of this morning's bread.

We celebrate the divine energy that pours through our separate selves and makes us one.

We sing of these friends, whose life renews itself in their communion of body and mind and heart.

We pray that like joy be found in earth's four corners. Justice, freedom, laughter, truth; peace, and love, and hope—the human heritage become at last the human way.

We rejoice with our friends who now share the fruit that gladdens the heart.

Fragrance — בְּשָׂמִים

🌸 *A wedding custom.*

מַה־יָּקָר חַסְדְּךָ אֱלֹהִים. . .
וְנַחַל עֲדָנֶיךָ תַשְׁקֵם.

How precious is Your faithful love, O God!
We drink from the fountain of Your delights.

[Psalms 36:8–9]

Life's pleasures, the delights of the senses, and the beauty of creation we now celebrate by enjoying the fragrance of a tree that possesses an especially sweet aroma. . . . . and. . . . ., may your love be fragrant; may it enable you to savor the sweetness of the earth. Drink deep of the fountain of delight that God has caused to flow.

בָּרוּךְ אַתָּה יי אֱלֹהֵינוּ מֶלֶךְ הָעוֹלָם, בּוֹרֵא עֲצֵי בְשָׂמִים.

We praise You, Eternal God, Sovereign of the universe, for trees and their fragrance.

Anniversary Prayers

For a wedding anniversary

'I am my beloved's and my beloved is mine.' God of all generations, we give thanks for the blessings that have graced our marriage, and we look back upon the day of our union with thankfulness. So may this joy be with us always: our way of life loving and good, as we help each other bear burdens and as we share our joys.

Give us, O God, a peaceful dwelling where contentment and love find a resting-place. May we maintain a home in which glows the light of faith, one which honors our membership in the House of Israel, our people.

O God, grant that we may grow old together in health, and live in gratitude for our marriage. Amen.

Silver or golden wedding anniversary

❧ *There are two versions.*

1

In the fullness of this day's joy, we turn in thanksgiving to the Eternal Source of blessing. We give thanks for the strength that has preserved and sustained us and permitted us to reach this hour. In the midst of family and loved ones, we look back in reverent and grateful reminiscence upon the years that have passed since first we pledged our hearts to one another. Many and varied have been our experiences since that hour; many the mingled occasions of satisfaction and disappointment. We recall the joys that sweetened our lives; we remember the storms that shook us to our very roots. In bliss and trial alike, O God, You have been with us and in us; so may You continue to bless us with Your presence in the years to come.

Let these be years of health and contentment; of unclouded happiness in the circle of our family and loved ones; of unbroken service of love and caring to those who are far and to those who are near. Amen.

Ba-ruch a-ta Adonai,
Eh-lo-hei-nu meh-lech ha-o-lam,
sheh-heh-cheh-ya-nu, v'ki-y'ma-nu,
v'higi-a-nu la-z'man ha-zeh.

בָּרוּךְ אַתָּה יי
אֱלֹהֵינוּ מֶלֶךְ הָעוֹלָם,
שֶׁהֶחֱיָנוּ וְקִיְּמָנוּ
וְהִגִּיעָנוּ לַזְּמַן הַזֶּה.

We praise You, Eternal God, Sovereign of the universe, for giving us life, for sustaining us, and for enabling us to reach this season.

2

❧ *The following text is used if a third person is asked to bless the couple.*

In the fullness of this day's joy, we turn in thanksgiving to the Eternal Source of blessing. We give thanks for the strength that has preserved and sustained you, ... and ...., and permitted you to reach this hour. In the midst of family and loved ones, we look back in reverent and grateful reminiscence upon the years that have passed since first you pledged your hearts to one another. Many and varied have been your experiences since that hour; many the mingled occasions of satisfaction and disappointment. You recall the joys that sweetened your lives; you remember the storms that shook you to your very roots. In bliss and trial alike, O God, You have been with them; so may You continue to bless them with Your presence in the years to come.

Let these be years of health and contentment; of unclouded happiness in the circle of your family and loved ones; of unbroken service of love and caring to those who are far and to those who are near. Amen.

Ba-ruch a-ta Adonai,
Eh-lo-hei-nu meh-lech ha-o-lam,
sheh-heh-cheh-ya-nu, v'ki-y'ma-nu,
v'higi-a-nu la-z'man ha-zeh.

בָּרוּךְ אַתָּה יי
אֱלֹהֵינוּ מֶלֶךְ הָעוֹלָם,
שֶׁהֶחֱיָנוּ וְקִיְּמָנוּ
וְהִגִּיעָנוּ לַזְּמַן הַזֶּה.

We praise You, Eternal God, Sovereign of the universe, for giving us life, for sustaining us, and for enabling us to reach this season.

Other Personal Occasions

Consecration of a House

❧ *For the ceremony of Consecration, a Mezuzah, a Bible, wine or grape juice, Challah, and salt are required. Members of the household and guests participate in the ritual.*

❧ *To affix a Mezuzah to a room (the house having already been consecrated) begin on page 141.*

In the spirit of our Jewish faith, we consecrate this house with prayers of thanksgiving and invoke upon it God's blessing.

שְׁמַע יִשְׂרָאֵל: יהוה אֱלֹהֵינוּ יהוה אֶחָד!

Hear, O Israel: the Eternal One is our God,
the Eternal God alone!

בָּרוּךְ שֵׁם כְּבוֹד מַלְכוּתוֹ לְעוֹלָם וָעֶד!

Blessed is God's glorious majesty for ever and ever!

❧ *Transliteration of the V'ahavta is on page 5.*

וְאָהַבְתָּ אֵת יהוה אֱלֹהֶיךָ בְּכָל־לְבָבְךָ וּבְכָל־נַפְשְׁךָ וּבְכָל־מְאֹדֶךָ: וְהָיוּ הַדְּבָרִים הָאֵלֶּה אֲשֶׁר אָנֹכִי מְצַוְּךָ הַיּוֹם עַל־לְבָבֶךָ: וְשִׁנַּנְתָּם לְבָנֶיךָ וְדִבַּרְתָּ בָּם בְּשִׁבְתְּךָ בְּבֵיתֶךָ וּבְלֶכְתְּךָ בַדֶּרֶךְ וּבְשָׁכְבְּךָ וּבְקוּמֶךָ: וּקְשַׁרְתָּם לְאוֹת עַל־יָדֶךָ וְהָיוּ לְטֹטָפֹת בֵּין עֵינֶיךָ: וּכְתַבְתָּם עַל־מְזוּזֹת בֵּיתֶךָ וּבִשְׁעָרֶיךָ:

You shall love your Eternal God with all your heart, with all your mind, with all your being. Set these words, which I command you this day, upon your heart. Teach them faithfully to your children; speak of them in your home and on your way, when you lie down and when you rise up. Bind them as a sign upon your hand; let them be a symbol before your eyes; inscribe them on the doorposts of your house, and on your gates.

138

לְמַעַן תִּזְכְּרוּ וַעֲשִׂיתֶם אֶת־כָּל־מִצְוֹתָי וִהְיִיתֶם קְדֹשִׁים לֵאלֹהֵיכֶם: אֲנִי יְהוָה אֱלֹהֵיכֶם אֲשֶׁר הוֹצֵאתִי אֶתְכֶם מֵאֶרֶץ מִצְרַיִם לִהְיוֹת לָכֶם לֵאלֹהִים.אֲנִי יְהוָה אֱלֹהֵיכֶם:

Be mindful of all My Mitzvot, and do them: so shall you consecrate yourselves to your God. I am your Eternal God who led you out of Egypt to be your God; I am your Eternal God.

❧

Our homes have always been the dwelling place of the Jewish spirit. Our tables have been altars of faith and love. It is written: 'When words of Torah pass between us, the Divine Presence is in our midst.' Our doors have been open to the stranger and the needy. May this home we now consecrate keep alive the beauty of our heritage.

CHALLAH IS DIPPED IN SALT AND DISTRIBUTED

Ba-ruch a-ta Adonai,
Eh-lo-hei-nu meh-lech ha-o-lam,
ha-mo-tzi leh-chem min ha-a-retz.

בָּרוּךְ אַתָּה יי
אֱלֹהֵינוּ מֶלֶךְ הָעוֹלָם,
הַמּוֹצִיא לֶחֶם מִן הָאָרֶץ.

We praise You, Eternal God, Sovereign of the universe, for You cause bread to come forth from the earth.

WINE OR GRAPE JUICE IS GIVEN TO EACH GUEST

❧ *Wine and grape juice are equally "fruit of the vine."*

Ba-ruch a-ta Adonai,
Eh-lo-hei-nu meh-lech ha-o-lam,
bo-rei p'ri ha-ga-fen.

בָּרוּךְ אַתָּה יי
אֱלֹהֵינוּ מֶלֶךְ הָעוֹלָם,
בּוֹרֵא פְּרִי הַגָּפֶן.

We praise You, Eternal God, Sovereign of the universe, Creator of the fruit of the vine.

THE OPEN BIBLE IS RAISED

The Torah has been our life; it has taught us how to live. May this home be a place for learning and doing. May the hearts of all who dwell here be filled with a love of Torah and its teachings.

Ba-ruch a-ta Adonai,

Eh-lo-hei-nu meh-lech ha-o-lam,

a-sher ki-d'sha-nu b'mitz-vo-tav

v'tzi-va-nu la-a-sok b'di-v'rei To-rah.

בָּרוּךְ אַתָּה יי

אֱלֹהֵינוּ מֶלֶךְ הָעוֹלָם,

אֲשֶׁר קִדְּשָׁנוּ בְּמִצְוֹתָיו

וְצִוָּנוּ לַעֲסוֹק בְּדִבְרֵי תוֹרָה.

We praise You, Eternal God, Sovereign of the universe: You hallow us with Your Mitzvot, and command us to immerse ourselves in Your teachings.

❧

יהוה מִי־יָגוּר בְּאָהֳלֶךְ?

מִי־יִשְׁכֹּן בְּהַר קָדְשֶׁךְ?

הוֹלֵךְ תָּמִים וּפֹעֵל צֶדֶק,

וְדֹבֵר אֱמֶת בִּלְבָבוֹ.

לֹא־רָגַל עַל־לְשֹׁנוֹ,

לֹא־עָשָׂה לְרֵעֵהוּ רָעָה,

וְחֶרְפָּה לֹא־נָשָׂא עַל־קְרֹבוֹ.

נִשְׁבַּע לְהָרַע וְלֹא יָמִר,

כַּסְפּוֹ לֹא־נָתַן בְּנֶשֶׁךְ,

וְשֹׁחַד עַל־נָקִי לֹא לָקָח.

עֹשֵׂה־אֵלֶּה לֹא יִמּוֹט לְעוֹלָם.

Eternal God:

Who may abide in Your house?

Who may dwell in Your holy mountain?

Those who are upright; who do justly,

all whose hearts are true.

Who do not slander others, nor wrong them,

nor bring shame upon their kin.

Who give their word and, come whay may, do not retract it.

Who do not exploit others, who never take bribes.

Those who live in this way shall never be shaken.

[From Psalm 15]

❧ *An additional Scriptural passage, such as First Kings 8:54–61, might be read here.*

❧

THE MEZUZAH IS RAISED

This ancient symbol speaks to us of our need to live by the words of the Eternal One. We affix the Mezuzah to the doorposts of this house with the hope that it will always remind us of our duties to one another as members of the Household of Israel. May the divine spirit fill this house—the spirit of love and kindness and consideration for all people.

Ba-ruch a-ta Adonai,	בָּרוּךְ אַתָּה יי
Eh-lo-hei-nu meh-lech ha-o-lam,	אֱלֹהֵינוּ מֶלֶךְ הָעוֹלָם,
a-sher ki-d'sha-nu b'mitz-vo-tav	אֲשֶׁר קִדְּשָׁנוּ בְּמִצְוֹתָיו
v'tzi-va-nu lik-bo-a m'zu-zah.	וְצִוָּנוּ לִקְבּוֹעַ מְזוּזָה.

We praise You, Eternal God, Sovereign of the universe: You hallow us with Your Mitzvot, and command us to affix the Mezuzah.

❧ *The Mezuzah, its top inclining inward, is affixed to the upper part of the doorpost on the right, as one enters the house. If desired, a Mezuzah may be affixed to the right doorpost of the principal rooms.*

Ba-ruch a-ta Adonai,	בָּרוּךְ אַתָּה יי
Eh-lo-hei-nu meh-lech ha-o-lam,	אֱלֹהֵינוּ מֶלֶךְ הָעוֹלָם,
sheh-heh-cheh-ya-nu, v'ki-y'ma-nu,	שֶׁהֶחֱיָנוּ וְקִיְּמָנוּ
v'higi-a-nu la-z'man ha-zeh.	וְהִגִּיעָנוּ לַזְּמַן הַזֶּה.

We praise You, Eternal God, Sovereign of the universe, for giving us life, for sustaining us, and for enabling us to reach this season.

꩜

אִם־יהוה לֹא יִבְנֶה בַֽיִת, שָׁוְא עָמְלוּ בוֹנָיו בּוֹ.

Unless the Eternal One builds the house,
its builders labor in vain.

[Psalm 127:1]

In this awareness we pray that our home be blessed by the sense of God's presence.

We offer thanksgiving for the promise of security and contentment this home represents, and express our resolve to make it a temple dedicated to godliness. Let it be filled with the beauty of holiness and the warmth of love. May the guest and stranger find within it welcome and friendship. So will it ever merit the praise: 'How lovely are your tents, O Jacob, your dwelling places, O Israel!'

For all who are assembled here, and for all who will enter these doors, we invoke God's blessing:

יהוה יִשְׁמָר־צֵאתְךָ וּבוֹאֶֽךָ מֵעַתָּה וְעַד־עוֹלָם.

May the Eternal One guard your going out and your coming in, now and always. Amen.

[Psalm 121:7]

Before a journey

יהוה יִשְׁמָר־צֵאתְךָ וּבוֹאֶךָ מֵעַתָּה וְעַד־עוֹלָם.

'The Eternal One shall guard your coming and your going
from this time forth and for ever.'

[Psalm 121:7]

God within and beyond me, Your presence pervades the world.
Wherever I go, You are near to me. 'If I take up the wings of the
morning, and dwell on the ocean's farthest shore, even there Your
hand will lead me, Your strong hand will hold me.' *[Psalm 139:9-10]*

Now that I begin a new journey, I turn to You in confidence and
trust, for You have always been a light to my path. May I go forth
in health and safely reach my destination. May this journey not be
in vain; and let me return in contentment to my home and my dear
ones. Then will my travels be truly blessed. Amen.

בָּרוּךְ אַתָּה, יי, שׁוֹמֵר הַנּוֹסְעִים.

We praise You, O God, Protector of wayfarers.

Upon arriving in Israel

On this soil sacred to memory, in the millenial home of our people, we pray for the welfare of this land:

Eternal God, our Rock and Redeemer, grant blessing to the State of
Israel, created as a haven for the oppressed and as the fulfillment of
a dream. Inspire its leaders and citizens with faithfulness to the
aims of its founders: to develop the land for the benefit of all its
inhabitants, and to implement the Prophetic ideals of liberty and
justice. May they live in harmony with one another and in peace
with their neighbors. Help our people to realize the ancient vision,
that 'Out of Zion shall go forth Torah and the word of God from
Jerusalem.'

FROM PSALMS 122 AND 128

שָׂמַחְתִּי בְּאֹמְרִים לִי: בֵּית יהוה נֵלֵךְ.

עֹמְדוֹת הָיוּ רַגְלֵינוּ בִּשְׁעָרַיִךְ, יְרוּשָׁלָיִם.

I rejoiced when they said to me: Let us go up to the House of the Eternal One.

Now we stand within your gates, O Jerusalem!

יְרוּשָׁלַיִם הַבְּנוּיָה כְּעִיר שֶׁחֻבְּרָה־לָּהּ יַחְדָּו.

יְרוּשָׁלַיִם הַבְּנוּיָה כְּעִיר שֶׁחֻבְּרָה־לָּהּ יַחְדָּו.

Jerusalem restored! The city united and whole!

Jerusalem, built to be a city where people come together as one.

שַׁאֲלוּ שְׁלוֹם יְרוּשָׁלָיִם: יִשְׁלָיוּ אֹהֲבָיִךְ.

יְהִי־שָׁלוֹם בְּחֵילֵךְ, שַׁלְוָה בְּאַרְמְנוֹתָיִךְ.

Pray for the peace of Jerusalem: may those who love you prosper.

Let there be peace in your homes, safety within your borders.

לְמַעַן אַחַי וְרֵעָי אֲדַבְּרָה־נָּא שָׁלוֹם בָּךְ.

וְנִרְאֶה בְּטוֹב יְרוּשָׁלָיִם כֹּל יְמֵי חַיֵּינוּ.

For the sake of my people, my friends, I pray you find peace.

And let us see the good of Jerusalem all the days of our lives.

יְבָרֶכְנוּ יהוה מִצִּיּוֹן, עֹשֵׂה שָׁמַיִם וָאָרֶץ.

שָׁלוֹם עַל־יִשְׂרָאֵל.

May the Eternal One, Maker of heaven and earth, bless us from Zion.

Let Israel have peace.

On beginning a new enterprise

❧ *Such as a new business, profession, or other endeavor.*

'Unless the Eternal One builds the house,
its builders labor in vain.'

[Psalm 127:1]

Creator of the universe, by whose goodness the world is renewed day by day, You have implanted in us a spark of Your creative will. You have made us Your partners in the building of the world.

My heart is full—how wonderful to open my eyes, my life, to new vistas. I give thanks for the opportunities that lie ahead, and pray for strength and skill. May I gain my living honorably; and, as I strive for myself, let me add to the contentment and well-being of others.

In this enterprise I need a clear vision and a wise judgment, and the wisdom not to neglect my dear ones or injure my health or close myself off from You, O God. May I walk with those I love in the light of Your presence and use all my powers for blessing. Amen.

At a time of achievement

I have aspired, and labored, and achieved! My heart is filled with joy, for I said:

'God, give me hills to climb, and strength to climb them.'

My prayer was granted.

You have given me so much, have given me the strength of will to achieve. Give me one thing more, O God—a grateful heart. And give me a wise and constant spirit, one aware of my debt to others for what I have achieved. You are the strength of my hands, O God, and the light of my life. All that I am and all that I may yet be, I owe to the creative power that You have implanted within me.

Even as I exult in the success of my labors, so may I glory to be kind in thought, gentle in word, and generous in deed, that others may have cause to rejoice in my accomplishments. Give me a grateful heart and a loving disposition, that I may be Your messenger of blessing for the poor, the helpless, and the sick. Thus would I give thanks for the blessings that have come to me. Amen.

At a time of disappointment

חִזְקוּ וְאִמְצוּ; אַל־תִּירְאוּ . . . כִּי יהוה אֱלֹהֶיךָ הוּא הַהֹלֵךְ עִמָּךְ, לֹא יַרְפְּךָ וְלֹא יַעַזְבֶךָ.

Be strong and of good courage; have no fear . . . for the Eternal One, your God, is the One who goes with you, never failing you or forsaking you.

[Deuteronomy 31:5]

My high hopes have been brought low, and in place of contentment I feel pain and distress. O God of life, even as You renew the work of creation day by day, so, now, help me find renewal in my time of sadness and disappointment. Now, especially, I need the healing touch of Your love. It is written *[Psalm 46:1]*, *God is my refuge and my strength, a very present help in time of trouble.* Help me to feel that help. Let Your presence be a light within to dispel the darkness. Let Your nearness, Your silent speech within the heart, be a comfort to me.

I pray for the courage to carry on in the face of disappointment, for the wisdom to learn from adversity, for the strength to build a new and better life. Your spirit can transform affliction into salvation; enlighten me, therefore, that I may look to the dawn of a new day with confidence and trust. May hope abide beyond the moment's loss. For You, O God of hope, are my sustaining power, even when I have fallen. Keep me from self-recrimination. Give me peace of mind and contentment of spirit. Amen.

At a time of anxiety

Eternal God, You abide though all things change. I am anxious and fearful, and I turn my heart to You, looking to You and leaning on Your strength,.

It is written *[Psalm 84:5]*, *Blessed is the one whose strength is in You.* Bless me now with faith and courage. Help me to feel that You are with me, steadying and sustaining me with the assurance that I am loved. Be with me and bring me hope, that in the days to come, my aspirations may be fulfilled for my good and the good of those I love who depend on me. Banish my fears with the sense that You are always present, to uphold and sustain me, as it is written *[Isaiah 41:10]: Have no fear, for I am with you; be not dismayed, for I am your God. I will strengthen you, I will help you, I will uphold you with the power of My righteousness.* Amen.

When our burdens seem too heavy

I come to You, O God, for Your gracious help. You dwell within my heart, You feel my distress, You know my pain, and how burdened I am. Give me strength to bear my burdens with courage, wisdom, and grace. Help me to be true to my better self, to discern my real work in life, and to do it with all my might. When I struggle within my own heart, stay by my side. Then I shall be able to say with Your prophet *[Isaiah 40:31]*, *But those who hold fast to the Eternal shall renew their strength; they shall mount up with wings as eagles; they shall run and not be weary; they shall walk, and not faint.*

May my work, and the ties that bind me to family and friends, make life rich in meaning for me, so that each day I live may be yet another step leading me nearer to You. Amen.

After a trauma

> Just and holy God,
> receive our fear, our shame, our grief, our anger.
> Help us to to overcome them,
> to use these energies in the service of healing.

THIS IS SAID TO A PERSON WHO HAS SUFFERED A TRAUMA:

You are in need of healing.

You seek comfort in your distress.

You would wash yourself clean of the memory of pain, of anger, of fear.

Know that you are loved. Know that God sustains you by giving you the strength to heal your wounds of body and spirit.

RESPONSE:

I have been wounded, but I can heal. Let my hurt not keep me from caring about the hurt that others feel.

I have been helpless, but I can act. Let my suffering not keep me from reaching out to help others.

God, give me wisdom to know that You are with me even now, to overcome my pain, my anger, and my fear, to accept the help of those who care for me.

God, give me strength to return the love of family and friends.

TO THE PERSON:

The God who has implanted within you the power of healing, be with you now and heal you.

RESPONSE:

Heal me, O God, and I shall be healed; save me, and I shall be saved.

[Jeremiah 17:14]

TO THE PERSON:

The God who created the world with light, bring light to your eyes.

RESPONSE:

The Eternal One is my light and my salvation; whom shall I fear? God is the stronghold of my life; of whom shall I be afraid?

[Psalm 27:1]

TO THE PERSON:

May the God whom we call the Hope of Israel, plant hope in your heart.

RESPONSE:

You show me the path of life. In Your presence there is fullness of joy.

[Psalm 16:11]

❧ *The following may be added:*

TO A WOMAN:

> When we are born, God is with our mother in her travail; and God is with us, even with those who feel born to pain and abandonment, as it is said: . . . "on the day you were born, no eye pitied you, and you were left lying, rejected, in the open field. . . . And as you lay in your blood, I said to you: Live! Live! Grow up like a flower. And you grew up and became tall and arrived at full womanhood. . . ."
>
> *[Ezekiel 16:4a, 4–5b, 6b–7a]*

Her response:

> I have grown, and God remains with me, as it is said: . . . "You were at the age for love: . . . I pledged Myself to you and entered into a covenant with you, and you became Mine. Then I bathed you with water, and washed off the blood from you, and anointed you with oil."
>
> *[Ezekiel 16:8b,d–9]*

May the Holy One be midwife now to my rebirth.

TO A MAN:

> God is not far off, but near, within your heart and mind, even in your darkest moments. Kindle a light, that you may see gifts that you never knew you had. For it is said: "God, Your love does not cease, Your compassion does not

end; they are new every morning: great is Your faithfulness. 'The Eternal One is my portion,' says my soul, 'therefore I hope in You.' "   [Lamentations 3:22–24]

His response:

As I know that God is with me now and always, I say: "My tears have been my food day and night, while people say to me continually, 'Where is your God?' But I have calmed and quieted my soul, like a child at its mother's breast; my soul is like a comforted child."   [Psalms 42:3, 131:2]

May the Holy One heal me now, and help me to love.

If this ritual takes place in a Mikveh or by a body of water, the following blessing may be said:

בָּרוּךְ אַתָּה יי אֱלֹהֵינוּ מֶלֶךְ הָעוֹלָם, אֲשֶׁר קִדְּשָׁנוּ בְּמִצְוֹתָיו וְצִוָּנוּ עַל הַטְּבִילָה.

We praise You, Eternal God, Sovereign of the universe: You hallow us with Your Mitzvot, and command us to immerse ourselves in healing waters.

On life with others

Loving God, how much I need the balm of friendship and the warmth of understanding! How greatly I need to be needed and cherished! I pray therefore that my soul may know the joy of love given and received.

Open my eyes to the beauty within all who walk the earth. When I feel lonely and forsaken, let the faith that You are with me give me strength, and the solace of friendship bring me courage. Keep me from imagined hurts, from seeing only foes where friends are to be found. And give me insight into my own heart, that I may uproot my weaknesses. Help me to be patient when I am misunderstood, open to the thoughts of others, and quick to forgive hurts. As a friend to others, may I neither judge them too harshly, nor slavishly follow them in paths that are not mine. And as we walk through life together, let me and my dear ones go with that integrity which leads to peace, that love which brings harmony and joy, that regard whose fruit is enduring friendship. Amen.

Upon retirement

As I look back over the years that have gone, I ask to see life as a continuum from youth to age: What lies before me now? I look ahead not knowing what will be given me to see. Sustain me, Eternal God, Fountain of Life, with faith that the best is yet to be, for opportunities now await me. There is blessing that only the maturity of age can bring; there is a ripeness that experience alone can yield. May I find the sweetness of that joy which is reserved for those who serve others through the counsel and guidance learned in the school of life. Out of the lessons drawn from disappointment and success alike, may I be able to help them to discover value in life's struggles, and find joys and triumphs that endure.

Now I have precious time to give to those I love, to family and friends. I pray for insight and a warm heart: let me be with them when they need me, let me respond when they call to me. And let me use my leisure to explore new worlds of thought and feeling, or to rediscover old ones. Now I can study my heritage of Torah, savor the beauties of nature and art, find new meaning and inspiration in the book of life. Let the passage of time continually deepen within me the spirit of wisdom and understanding, the spirit of knowledge and reverence for life.

And let me never lose that sense of wonder which stirs within me in the presence of Your creation and which beckons me to greet each day with zest and eager welcome. Thus will my life be renewed and blessed; and thus will I bring blessing to many in the years to come. Amen.

Simchat Chochmah

❧ *To be said on a significant birthday (such as the sixtieth or seventieth) to celebrate one's arrival at an 'age of wisdom.'*

River of light and truth, You have sustained me these many years and brought me to this place in my life's journey. Let me look out with wisdom, from the high ground of my years and experiences, over the terrain of my life. Let me gaze out toward the past and the future with a heightened sense of Your presence as my Guide. Let me see that growth is not reserved for any one season, and that love and fulfillment are not the exclusive provinces of the young.

As today I celebrate my life's continued unfolding, I am awestruck by the wonder of my being. And so I pray that kindness and compassion may be on my lips, that strength and courage may be with me in my comings and goings, and that I may continue to learn from and to teach those dear to me.

O God my Creator, as You are the first and the last, may my life ever be a song of praise to You.

בָּרוּךְ אַתָּה יי אֱלֹהֵינוּ מֶלֶךְ הָעוֹלָם, שֶׁנָּתַן מֵחָכְמָתוֹ לְבָשָׂר וָדָם.

We praise You, Eternal God, Sovereign of the universe: You give of Your wisdom to flesh and blood.

Illness and Recovery

In illness

In sickness I turn to You, O God, for comfort and help. Strengthen within me the wondrous power of healing that You have implanted in Your children. Guide my doctors and nurses that they may speed my recovery. Let my dear ones find comfort and courage in the knowledge that You are with us at all times, in sickness as in health.

May my sickness not weaken my faith in You, nor diminish my love for others. From my illness may I gain a fuller sympathy for all who suffer.

Ba-ruch a-ta Adonai,
ro-fei ha-cho-lim.

בָּרוּךְ אַתָּה, יי,
רוֹפֵא הַחוֹלִים.

I praise You, O God, the Source of healing.

In prolonged illness

My God and God of all generations, in my great need I pour out my heart to You. The days and weeks of suffering are hard to endure. In my struggle, let me feel that You are near, a presence whose care enfolds me. Rouse in me the strength to overcome fear and anxiety, and brighten my spirit with the assurance of Your love. Help me to help my dear ones in their striving to strengthen and encourage me. Let the healing power within me—Your gift to me—give me strength to recover, that I and all who love me may rejoice.

Ba-ruch a-ta Adonai,
ro-fei ha-cho-lim.

בָּרוּךְ אַתָּה, יי,
רוֹפֵא הַחוֹלִים.

I praise You, O God, the Source of healing.

In chronic illness or disability

Sunday

רַבִּים אֹמְרִים: מִי־יַרְאֵנוּ טוֹב,

נְסָה־עָלֵינוּ אוֹר פָּנֶיךָ, יהוה.

There are many who say: 'Oh, that we could see some good,
but the light of Your presence, O God, has fled from us!'

[Psalm 4:7]

'Light that makes some things seen, makes some things invisible.
Were it not for the darkness and the shadow of the earth, the noblest
part of the Creation would remain unseen, and the stars in heaven
invisible.'

What is it that the darkness I live in can help make me see which
otherwise I would not see?

בָּרוּךְ אַתָּה, יי, הַמֵּאִיר לָעוֹלָם כֻּלּוֹ בִּכְבוֹדוֹ.

I praise you, O God: in Your glory You give light to all the world.

Monday

לָמָה, יהוה, תַּעֲמֹד בְּרָחוֹק?

תַּעְלִים לְעִתּוֹת בַּצָּרָה?

Why do You stand far off, Eternal One?
Why do You hide Yourself in time of trouble?

[Psalm 10:1]

You know how much I suffer, the difficulties that surround me:

Renew a steadfast spirit within me—renew it, and help me to overcome the bitterness I sometimes feel. When I am tempted to give
up the struggle, let me feel Your hand holding mine, giving me
courage and strength.

בָּרוּךְ אַתָּה, יי, הַנּוֹתֵן לַיָּעֵף כֹּחַ.

I praise you, O God: You give strength to the weary.

Tuesday

חָנֵּנִי, יהוה, כִּי אֻמְלַל אָנִי . . .
וְנַפְשִׁי נִבְהֲלָה מְאֹד,
וְאַתָּה, יהוה, עַד־מָתָי?

Be gracious to me, Eternal One, for I am languishing;
I am so afraid, while You, O God—how long?

[Psalm 6:3a, 4]

Let these words guide me:
Know how sublime a thing it is
To suffer and be strong.

O God, teach me to be strong in spirit, to find a moment in the day when my heart is light enough to let me smile. Even in affliction I would have the grace of a loving spirit.

בָּרוּךְ אַתָּה, יי, שׁוֹמֵעַ תְּפִלָּה.

I praise you, O God: You hearken to prayer.

Wednesday

צָרוֹת לְבָבִי הִרְחִיבוּ:
דְּרָכֶיךָ, יהוה, הוֹדִיעֵנִי;
אֹרְחוֹתֶיךָ לַמְּדֵנִי.

Many are my heart's distresses: let me know Your paths,
Eternal One; teach me Your ways.

[Psalm 25:4,17]

May I not think merely of what I cannot do, being sick or weak, but what I can do, in spite of weakness and sickness.

Everyone can do *something*.

Helen Keller said: 'I thank God for my handicaps, for, through them, I have found myself, my work, and my God.' May something of her wisdom be mine, so that I can say: I take what is given and make my life out of it.

בָּרוּךְ אַתָּה, יי, הַנּוֹתֵן לַיָּעֵף כֹּחַ.

I praise you, O God: You give strength to the weary.

155

Thursday

הַדְרִיכֵנִי בַאֲמִתֶּךָ, וְלַמְּדֵנִי,
כִּי־אַתָּה אֱלֹהֵי יִשְׁעִי;
אוֹתְךָ קִוִּיתִי כָּל־הַיּוֹם.

Lead me in Your truth and teach me,
for You are the God of my salvation;
In You do I hope all the day.

[Psalm 25:5]

'The times of our lives which hold the deepest meaning for us, from which we learn the most, are very often those when we are face to face with problems which seem too great for our strength, with illness, and with death.'

May I find meaning in all that I sense and feel—whether it be pain or joy.

בָּרוּךְ אַתָּה, יי, הַטּוֹב וְהַמֵּטִיב.

I praise you, O God: You are the Source of all good.

Friday

בְּשָׁלוֹם יַחְדָּו אֶשְׁכְּבָה וְאִישָׁן;
כִּי־אַתָּה, יהוה, לְבָדָד לָבֶטַח תּוֹשִׁיבֵנִי.

Now I will lie down in peace, and sleep; for You alone,
Eternal One, make me live unafraid.

[Psalm 4:9]

As the week turns toward Shabbat, I pray that my mind be less troubled. My thoughts are more peaceful and tranquil, and my courage grows, as I reflect on these words *[Psalm 71:14]*:

> *I will hope continually, and will praise You*
> *more and more.*
> Yes, there is hope in me, for it may be that
> Tomorrow I shall put forth buds again,
> And clothe myself in fruit.

בָּרוּךְ אַתָּה, יי, שׁוֹמֵעַ תְּפִלָּה.

I praise you, O God: You hearken to prayer.

Shabbat

שְׁמַע־יהוה וְחָנֵּנִי;

יהוה, הֱיֵה־עֹזֵר לִי.

הָפַכְתָּ מִסְפְּדִי לְמָחוֹל לִי,

פִּתַּחְתָּ שַׂקִּי וַתְּאַזְּרֵנִי שִׂמְחָה,

לְמַעַן יְזַמֶּרְךָ כָבוֹד וְלֹא יִדֹּם.

Hear me and be gracious to me, Eternal One; O God, be my helper; then I will know that You have turned my mourning into dancing, taken off my sackcloth and clothed me with joy, so that my soul may praise You and not be silent.

[Psalm 30:11–12]

On Shabbat I see that what life has given to me matters less than what I can give to life. So I know that my illness is not what defines me; my heart and soul can rejoice, for I can find ways to be useful, I can love and be loved.

Yes, these words are true: 'They are ill discoverers who think there is no land, when they can see nothing but sea.'

O God, help me to remember the good I can do, even when I am weak and in pain. And help me, on this and every Shabbat, to see beyond my troubles, that I may be a blessing to others—and to myself.

בָּרוּךְ אַתָּה, יי, הַטּוֹב וְהַמֵּטִיב.

I praise you, O God: You are the Source of all good.

In convalescence

Loving God, the healing power that You have placed within me from birth onward has sustained me in my weakness, supported me in my suffering, and set me on the road to recovery. By Your grace, I have found the strength to endure the hours of pain and distress. Now I need patience and peace of mind. These, too, I know You have implanted within me. And after I have recovered, may the understanding that You are with me in sickness and in health fill me with gratitude, and help me to use the insights I have gained from my illness in my own life and to counsel others. Thus will I be serving You, who in love have created and sustained me to this day.

Ba-ruch a-ta Adonai,   בָּרוּךְ אַתָּה, יְיָ,
ro-fei ha-cho-lim.   רוֹפֵא הַחוֹלִים.

I praise you, O God, the Source of healing.

On recovery

❧ *See also page 30.*

For health of body and spirit, I thank You, my God. I was broken and now am whole; weary, but now am rested; anxious, but now am reassured.

Teach me to show my thankfulness to all who helped me in my need, who heartened me when I was afraid, and who visited me when I was lonely. For the strength You created within me, O God, I give thanks to You.

Ba-ruch a-ta Adonai,   בָּרוּךְ אַתָּה, יְיָ,
ro-fei ha-cho-lim.   רוֹפֵא הַחוֹלִים.

I praise you, O God, the Source of healing.

By a sick child

O God, help me to become well. Make me brave when I feel pain, and teach me to help my parents, the doctor, and all who love and care for me by doing what they ask. In that way, I know, I will feel better more quickly.

Ba-ruch a-ta Adonai,
ro-fei ha-cho-lim.

בָּרוּךְ אַתָּה, יי,
רוֹפֵא הַחוֹלִים.

Thank You, O God, for the power of healing that You have made a part of me.

By a child on recovery

I thank all who helped me become well and strong again, O God, and I thank You for life and health.

Ba-ruch a-ta Adonai,
ro-fei ha-cho-lim.

בָּרוּךְ אַתָּה, יי,
רוֹפֵא הַחוֹלִים.

Thank You, O God, for the power of healing that You have made a part of me.

On behalf of the sick

We are grateful, O God, for the gift of life and for the healing powers that You have implanted within Your creatures. Sustain ...., our loved one, through these days of illness with the courage and fortitude he (she) needs to endure weakness and pain. Help us to find ways to show our love and concern for him (her), so that we may be an influence for good in his (her) time of need. And may all who suffer illness of body or mind know that You are with them, giving them strength of spirit as they struggle to recover. May their afflictions soon be ended, and may they return in health to family and friends.

Ba-ruch a-ta Adonai,
ro-fei ha-cho-lim.

בָּרוּךְ אַתָּה, יי,
רוֹפֵא הַחוֹלִים.

We praise You, the Source of healing.

The Valley of the Shadow

In contemplation of death

Everlasting God, Creator of all that lives: although I pray for healing and continued life, still I know that I am mortal. Give me courage to accept my kinship with all who have come before me.

Alas, over the years, I have committed many wrongs; I know, too, I left much undone. Yet I also know the good I did or tried to do. That goodness imparts an eternal meaning to my life.

And, as You are with me, so, I know, are You with my loved ones. This comforts my soul, O God my Rock and Redeemer.

B'ya-do af-kid ru-chi,	בְּיָדוֹ אַפְקִיד רוּחִי,
b'eit i-shan v'a-i-ra,	בְּעֵת אִישַׁן וְאָעִירָה,
v'im ru-chi g'vi-ya-ti:	וְעִם רוּחִי גְוִיָּתִי;
Adonai li, v'lo i-ra.	יי לִי, וְלֹא אִירָא.

Into Your hands I commend my spirit, both when I sleep and when I wake. Body and soul are Yours, O God, and in Your presence I cast off fear and am at rest.

Adonai meh-lech, Adonai ma-lach,	יי מֶלֶךְ, יי מָלָךְ,
Adonai yim-loch l'o-lam va-ed.	יי יִמְלוֹךְ לְעוֹלָם וָעֶד.
Ba-ruch sheim k'vod mal'chu-toh	בָּרוּךְ שֵׁם כְּבוֹד מַלְכוּתוֹ
l'o-lam va-ed!	לְעוֹלָם וָעֶד!

Eternal One: You reign, You have reigned, You will reign for ever. Praised for ever be God's glorious majesty!

יהוה הוּא הָאֱלֹהִים.

Adonai hu ha-Eh-lo-him

The Eternal One alone is God.

שְׁמַע יִשְׂרָאֵל: יהוה אֱלֹהֵינוּ, יהוה אֶחָד!

Sh'mah Yis-ra-eil: Adonai Eh-lo-hei-nu, Adonai Eh-chad!

**Hear, O Israel: the Eternal One is our God,
the Eternal God is One!**

On hearing of a death

Ba-ruch a-ta Adonai,　　　　　　　　בָּרוּךְ אַתָּה יי

Eh-lo-hei-nu meh-lech ha-o-lam,　　אֱלֹהֵינוּ מֶלֶךְ הָעוֹלָם,

da-yan ha-eh-met.　　　　　　　　　דַּיַּן הָאֱמֶת.

We praise You, Eternal God, Sovereign of the universe, the righteous judge.

　　—*or*—

Ba-ruch a-ta Adonai,　　　　　　　　בָּרוּךְ אַתָּה, יי,

no-tei-a b'to-chei-nu cha-yei o-lam　נוֹטֵעַ בְּתוֹכֵנוּ חַיֵּי עוֹלָם.

We praise You, Eternal One: You have implanted within us eternal
life.

After a stillbirth or upon the death of a young child

מִמַּעֲמַקִּים קְרָאתֶיךָ, יהוה.

אֲדֹנָי, שִׁמְעָה בְקוֹלִי.

Out of the depths I call to You, Eternal One. O God,
hearken to my voice. *[Psalm 130:1]*

> We looked for joy,
> and now, suddenly,
> birds sing
> but not our child.
>
> We looked for life
> and now, suddenly,
> trees bloom,
> but not our child.

How our laughter has turned into grief, our mirth to tears! Hope was
full within us: now it is turned to sorrow and lamentation. O God,
from You we come, to You we go; You have been our refuge in all generations. Take our grief, and make us whole again, as it is written:
You shall forget your misery, and remember it only as waters that
pass away. *[Job 11.16]*

❧

MEDITATION

A woman lost her child and came to a teacher for comfort. She
poured out her grief as he listened patiently. Then he said to her:
My dear, I cannot wipe away your tears. I can only show you how
to make them holy.

❧

מִמַּעֲמַקִּים קְרָאתֶיךָ, יהוה.

אֲדֹנָי, שִׁמְעָה בְקוֹלִי.

Out of the depths I call to You, Eternal One.
O God, hearken to my voice.

[Psalm 130:1]

162

Upon terminating a pregnancy

Mother of all life: I need You. I need Your comfort and love; I yearn to rest my head on Your tender breast. Rock me in Your arms as I reflect upon the meanings of life and loss.

Awed by the creative powers within my body, I look back with sadness on the life that could not be. Like a wanderer in a desert I need help: give me shade, quench my thirst. I seek Your warm embrace, that I may drift into healing sleep and arise again, ready to re-enter the garden of Your world.

Readings from Scripture at a time of bereavement

❦ *Some of the following passages from Scripture will usually be read; in addition, there will be other prayers and readings chosen for the occasion.*

1

שִׁוִּיתִי, יהוה, לְנֶגְדִּי תָמִיד, כִּי מִימִינִי בַּל־אֶמּוֹט. לָכֵן שָׂמַח לִבִּי וַיָּגֶל
כְּבוֹדִי; אַף־בְּשָׂרִי יִשְׁכֹּן לָבֶטַח. כִּי לֹא־תַעֲזֹב נַפְשִׁי לִשְׁאוֹל; לֹא־תִתֵּן
חֲסִידְךָ לִרְאוֹת שָׁחַת. תּוֹדִיעֵנִי אֹרַח חַיִּים. שֹׂבַע שְׂמָחוֹת אֶת־פָּנֶיךָ;
נְעִמוֹת בִּימִינְךָ נֶצַח.

I have set You, Eternal One, continually before me, ever at my side; I shall not be moved.

Therefore my heart is glad and my soul can rejoice, for I am safe in Your presence.

For You will not abandon me to death nor send Your faithful one to destruction.

You show me the path of life. Your presence brings fullness of joy; enduring happiness is Your gift.

[*From Psalm 16*]

2

אַשְׁרֵי הָאִישׁ אֲשֶׁר לֹא הָלַךְ בַּעֲצַת רְשָׁעִים, וּבְדֶרֶךְ חַטָּאִים לֹא עָמָד,
וּבְמוֹשַׁב לֵצִים לֹא יָשָׁב. כִּי אִם־בְּתוֹרַת יהוה חֶפְצוֹ, וּבְתוֹרָתוֹ יֶהְגֶּה יוֹמָם
וָלָיְלָה. וְהָיָה כְּעֵץ שָׁתוּל עַל־פַּלְגֵי מָיִם, אֲשֶׁר פִּרְיוֹ יִתֵּן בְּעִתּוֹ, וְעָלֵהוּ
לֹא־יִבּוֹל, וְכֹל אֲשֶׁר־יַעֲשֶׂה יַצְלִיחַ.

Happy are those who have not followed the counsel of the wicked,
or taken the path of sinners, or joined the company of the insolent;

Who have made God's Teaching their delight, and have meditated
on it day and night.

They are like trees planted by streams of water, that yield their fruit
in season, whose leaves do not wither.

Their fruit is always good.

[Psalm 1]

3

יהוה, מָה־אָדָם וַתֵּדָעֵהוּ, בֶּן־אֱנוֹשׁ וַתְּחַשְּׁבֵהוּ?
אָדָם לַהֶבֶל דָּמָה, יָמָיו כְּצֵל עוֹבֵר.
זְרַמְתָּם; שֵׁנָה, יִהְיוּ; בַּבֹּקֶר כֶּחָצִיר יַחֲלֹף.
בַּבֹּקֶר יָצִיץ וְחָלָף, לָעֶרֶב יְמוֹלֵל וְיָבֵשׁ.
תָּשֵׁב אֱנוֹשׁ עַד־דַּכָּא, וַתֹּאמֶר: שׁוּבוּ בְנֵי־אָדָם.

What are we, Eternal One, that You take note of us;
what is our worth, that You take account of us?
We are like a breath, our days are as a passing shadow.
You sweep us away; we are like a dream,
like grass which springs up in the morning:
in the morning it flourishes and is renewed;
in the evening it fades and withers.
You cause us to return to dust, saying: Return, O mortal creatures!

4

מַה־יָּקָר חַסְדְּךָ, אֱלֹהִים, וּבְנֵי אָדָם בְּצֵל כְּנָפֶיךָ יֶחֱסָיוּן.

יִרְוְיֻן מִדֶּשֶׁן בֵּיתֶךָ, וְנַחַל עֲדָנֶיךָ תַשְׁקֵם.

כִּי־עִמְּךָ מְקוֹר חַיִּים; בְּאוֹרְךָ נִרְאֶה־אוֹר.

How precious is Your loving kindness, O God;
men and women take refuge in the shadow of Your wings.
They feast on the abundance of Your house,
and You give them drink from the river of Your delights.
For with You is the fountain of life;
in Your light shall we see light.

[From Psalm 36]

5

אֲדֹנָי, מָעוֹן אַתָּה הָיִיתָ לָּנוּ בְּדֹר וָדֹר.

בְּטֶרֶם הָרִים יֻלָּדוּ,

וַתְּחוֹלֵל אֶרֶץ וְתֵבֵל,

וּמֵעוֹלָם עַד־עוֹלָם אַתָּה אֵל.

כִּי אֶלֶף שָׁנִים בְּעֵינֶיךָ כְּיוֹם אֶתְמוֹל כִּי יַעֲבֹר,

וְאַשְׁמוּרָה בַלָּיְלָה.

כְּלִינוּ שָׁנֵינוּ כְמוֹ־הֶגֶה.

כִּי־גָז חִישׁ וַנָּעֻפָה.

לִמְנוֹת יָמֵינוּ כֵּן הוֹדַע,

וְנָבִא לְבַב חָכְמָה.

שַׂבְּעֵנוּ בַבֹּקֶר חַסְדֶּךָ,

וּנְרַנְּנָה וְנִשְׂמְחָה בְּכָל־יָמֵינוּ.

יֵרָאֶה אֶל־עֲבָדֶיךָ פָעֳלֶךָ,

וַהֲדָרְךָ עַל־בְּנֵיהֶם.

וִיהִי נֹעַם אֲדֹנָי אֱלֹהֵינוּ עָלֵינוּ, וּמַעֲשֵׂה יָדֵינוּ כּוֹנְנָה עָלֵינוּ,

וּמַעֲשֵׂה יָדֵינוּ כּוֹנְנֵהוּ.

Eternal One, You have been our refuge in all generations.

Before the mountains were born,

Or earth and universe brought forth,

from eternity to eternity You are God.

A thousand years in Your sight are but as yesterday when it is past,

or as a watch in the night.

Our years come to an end like a sigh.

They are soon gone, and we fly away.

So teach us to number our days,

that we may grow wise in heart.

Satisfy us in the morning with Your loving kindness,

that we may rejoice and be glad all our days

Let Your servants understand Your ways,

and their children see Your glory.

Let Your favor, Eternal One, our God, be with us, and may our work have lasting value.

Let the work of our hands be enduring!

[From Psalm 90]

6

יהוה, מִי־יָגוּר בְּאָהֳלֶךָ?
מִי־יִשְׁכֹּן בְּהַר קָדְשֶׁךָ?

הוֹלֵךְ תָּמִים וּפֹעֵל צֶדֶק,
וְדֹבֵר אֱמֶת בִּלְבָבוֹ.
לֹא־רָגַל עַל־לְשֹׁנוֹ,
לֹא־עָשָׂה לְרֵעֵהוּ רָעָה,
וְחֶרְפָּה לֹא־נָשָׂא עַל־קְרֹבוֹ.
נִשְׁבַּע לְהָרַע וְלֹא יָמִר,
כַּסְפּוֹ לֹא־נָתַן בְּנֶשֶׁךְ,
וְשֹׁחַד עַל־נָקִי לֹא לָקָח.
עֹשֵׂה־אֵלֶּה לֹא יִמּוֹט לְעוֹלָם.

Eternal God:
Who may abide in Your house?
Who may dwell in Your holy mountain?
Those who are upright; who do justly,
all whose hearts are true.
Who do not slander others, nor wrong them,
nor bring shame upon their kin.
Who give their word and, come what may, do not retract it.
Who do not exploit others, who never take bribes.
Those who live in this way shall never be shaken.

   [From Psalm 15]

7

קוֹל אֹמֵר: קְרָא!

וְאָמַר: מָה אֶקְרָא?

כָּל־הַבָּשָׂר חָצִיר,

וְכָל־חַסְדּוֹ כְּצִיץ הַשָּׂדֶה.

יָבֵשׁ חָצִיר, נָבֵל צִיץ,

כִּי רוּחַ יהוה נָשְׁבָה בּוֹ.

אָכֵן חָצִיר הָעָם.

יָבֵשׁ חָצִיר, נָבֵל צִיץ,

וּדְבַר־אֱלֹהֵינוּ יָקוּם לְעוֹלָם.

A voice says: Cry out!

   And I say: What shall I cry?

All flesh is grass, and all its beauty is like the flower of the field.

   The grass withers, the flower fades, when a wind from Beyond blows upon it.

Surely the people are grass.

   The grass withers, the flower fades, but the word of our God abides for ever.

   [Isaiah 40:6–8]

8

מִזְמוֹר לְדָוִד

יהוה רֹעִי, לֹא אֶחְסָר.

בִּנְאוֹת דֶּשֶׁא יַרְבִּיצֵנִי,

עַל־מֵי מְנֻחוֹת יְנַהֲלֵנִי.

נַפְשִׁי יְשׁוֹבֵב;

יַנְחֵנִי בְמַעְגְּלֵי־צֶדֶק לְמַעַן שְׁמוֹ.

גַּם כִּי־אֵלֵךְ בְּגֵיא צַלְמָוֶת

לֹא־אִירָא רָע, כִּי־אַתָּה עִמָּדִי:

שִׁבְטְךָ וּמִשְׁעַנְתֶּךָ, הֵמָּה יְנַחֲמֻנִי.

תַּעֲרֹךְ לְפָנַי שֻׁלְחָן נֶגֶד צֹרְרָי,

דִּשַּׁנְתָּ בַשֶּׁמֶן רֹאשִׁי, כּוֹסִי רְוָיָה.

אַךְ טוֹב וָחֶסֶד יִרְדְּפוּנִי כָּל־יְמֵי חַיָּי,

וְשַׁבְתִּי בְּבֵית־יהוה לְאֹרֶךְ יָמִים.

Eternal God, You are my shepherd, I shall not want. You make me lie down in green pastures, You lead me beside still waters. You restore my soul; You guide me in paths of righteousness for Your name's sake. Yes, even when I walk through the valley of the shadow of death, I shall fear no evil, for You are with me; with rod and staff You comfort me. You prepare a table before me in the presence of my enemies; You have anointed my head with oil; my cup overflows. Surely, goodness and mercy shall follow me all the days of my life, and I shall dwell in the house of the Eternal God for ever.

[Psalm 23]

9

כִּי יֵשׁ לַכֶּסֶף מוֹצָא,

וּמָקוֹם לַזָּהָב יָזֹקּוּ.

בַּרְזֶל מֵעָפָר יֻקָּח,

וְאֶבֶן יָצוּק נְחוּשָׁה.

וְהַחָכְמָה מֵאַיִן תָּבוֹא?

וְאֵי זֶה מְקוֹם בִּינָה?

הֵן יִרְאַת אֲדֹנָי הִיא חָכְמָה,

וְסוּר מֵרָע בִּינָה.

אַשְׁרֵי נֹצְרֵי עֵדֹתָיו,

בְּכָל־לֵב יִדְרְשׁוּהוּ.

There is a mine for silver,
And a place for gold to be refined.
Iron is taken out of the earth,
And copper is smelted from ore.
But where does wisdom come from?
And where is the place of understanding?
Truly, the fear of God is wisdom,
And to depart from evil is understanding.
Happy are those who follow Your teachings,
Who seek You with a whole heart.

10

אֶשָּׂא עֵינַי אֶל־הֶהָרִים:

מֵאַיִן יָבֹא עֶזְרִי?

עֶזְרִי מֵעִם יהוה,

עֹשֵׂה שָׁמַיִם וָאָרֶץ.

אַל־יִתֵּן לַמּוֹט רַגְלֶךָ,

אַל־יָנוּם שֹׁמְרֶךָ.

הִנֵּה לֹא־יָנוּם וְלֹא יִישָׁן שׁוֹמֵר יִשְׂרָאֵל.

יהוה שֹׁמְרֶךָ,

יהוה צִלְּךָ עַל־יַד יְמִינֶךָ.

יוֹמָם הַשֶּׁמֶשׁ לֹא־יַכֶּכָּה,

וְיָרֵחַ בַּלָּיְלָה.

יהוה יִשְׁמָרְךָ מִכָּל־רָע,

יִשְׁמֹר אֶת־נַפְשֶׁךָ.

יהוה יִשְׁמָר־צֵאתְךָ וּבוֹאֶךָ

מֵעַתָּה וְעַד־עוֹלָם.

I lift up my eyes to the mountains:
Where will I find my help?
My help is the Eternal One,
Maker of heaven and earth.
God will keep your foot from slipping,
Your Guardian does not slumber.
Behold, the Guardian of Israel neither slumbers nor sleeps.
The Eternal One is your shield,
The Eternal One is your shade at your side.
The sun will not strike you by day,
Nor the moon by night.
The Eternal One is your shield against evil,
the Guardian of your spirit.
The Eternal One is your shield,
   when you come in and when you go out,
Now and for ever.

[Psalm 121]

11

אֵשֶׁת־חַיִל מִי יִמְצָא,

וְרָחֹק מִפְּנִינִים מִכְרָהּ.

כַּפָּהּ פָּרְשָׂה לֶעָנִי,

וְיָדֶיהָ שִׁלְּחָה לָאֶבְיוֹן.

עֹז־וְהָדָר לְבוּשָׁהּ,

וַתִּשְׂחַק לְיוֹם אַחֲרוֹן.

פִּיהָ פָּתְחָה בְחָכְמָה,

וְתוֹרַת־חֶסֶד עַל־לְשׁוֹנָהּ.

קָמוּ בָנֶיהָ וַיְאַשְּׁרוּהָ,

בַּעְלָהּ וַיְהַלְלָהּ.

רַבּוֹת בָּנוֹת עָשׂוּ חָיִל,

וְאַתְּ עָלִית עַל־כֻּלָּנָה.

שֶׁקֶר הַחֵן וְהֶבֶל הַיֹּפִי,

אִשָּׁה יִרְאַת־יְהוָה הִיא תִתְהַלָּל.

תְּנוּ־לָהּ מִפְּרִי יָדֶיהָ,

וִיהַלְלוּהָ בַשְּׁעָרִים מַעֲשֶׂיהָ.

A woman of valor—seek her out; she is to be valued above rubies.

She opens her hand to those in need, and offers her help to the poor.

Adorned with strength and dignity, she looks to the future with cheerful trust.

Her speech is wise, and the law of kindness is on her lips.

Those who love her rise up with praise, and call her blessed:

Many women have done well, but you surpass them all.

Charm is deceptive and beauty short-lived, but a woman loyal to God has truly earned praise.

Honor her for her work; her life proclaims her praise.

[From Proverbs 31]

12

לַכֹּל זְמָן, וְעֵת לְכָל־חֵפֶץ תַּחַת הַשָּׁמָיִם:

עֵת לָלֶדֶת וְעֵת לָמוּת;

עֵת לָטַעַת וְעֵת לַעֲקוֹר נָטוּעַ;

עֵת לִפְרוֹץ וְעֵת לִבְנוֹת;

עֵת לִבְכּוֹת וְעֵת לִשְׂחוֹק;

עֵת סְפוֹד וְעֵת רְקוֹד;

עֵת לְהַשְׁלִיךְ אֲבָנִים וְעֵת כְּנוֹס אֲבָנִים;

עֵת לַחֲבוֹק וְעֵת לִרְחֹק מֵחַבֵּק;

עֵת לְבַקֵּשׁ וְעֵת לְאַבֵּד;

עֵת לִשְׁמוֹר וְעֵת לְהַשְׁלִיךְ;

עֵת לִקְרוֹעַ וְעֵת לִתְפּוֹר;

עֵת לַחֲשׁוֹת וְעֵת לְדַבֵּר.

For everything there is a season,
and a time for every desire under heaven:

A time to be born

and a time to die;

A time to plant

and a time to uproot what has been planted;

A time to tear down

and a time to build up;

A time to weep

and a time to laugh;

A time to grieve

and a time to dance;

A time to cast away stones

and a time to gather stones;

A time to embrace

and a time to refrain from embracing;

A time to seek

and a time to lose;

A time to keep

and a time to give away;

A time to rend

and a time to mend;

A time to keep silence

and a time to speak.

[From Ecclesiastes 3]

13

אַשְׁרֵי־אִישׁ יָרֵא אֶת־יְהוָה,

בְּמִצְוֹתָיו חָפֵץ מְאֹד!

גִּבּוֹר בָּאָרֶץ יִהְיֶה זַרְעוֹ;

דּוֹר יְשָׁרִים יְבֹרָךְ.

הוֹן־וָעֹשֶׁר בְּבֵיתוֹ,

וְצִדְקָתוֹ עֹמֶדֶת לָעַד.

זָרַח בַּחֹשֶׁךְ אוֹר לַיְשָׁרִים;

חַנּוּן וְרַחוּם וְצַדִּיק.

נָכוֹן לִבּוֹ, בָּטֻחַ בַּיהוָה.

סָמוּךְ לִבּוֹ; לֹא יִירָא.

פִּזַּר נָתַן לָאֶבְיוֹנִים;

צִדְקָתוֹ עֹמֶדֶת לָעַד;

קַרְנוֹ תָּרוּם בְּכָבוֹד.

Happy is the man loyal to God, who greatly delights in the Eternal One's commandments!

His descendants will be honored in the land; the generation of the upright will be blessed.

His household prospers, and his righteousness endures for ever.

Light dawns in the darkness for the upright; for the man who is gracious, merciful, and just.

His mind is firm, trusting in the Eternal One.

His heart is steady, he is not afraid.

He has been generous, has given freely to the poor; his righteousness endures for ever; his life is exalted in honor.

[From Psalm 112]

14

אָנָה אֵלֵךְ מֵרוּחֶךָ?

וְאָנָה מִפָּנֶיךָ אֶבְרָח?

אִם־אֶסַּק שָׁמַיִם, שָׁם אָתָּה!

וְאַצִּיעָה שְּׁאוֹל, הִנֶּךָּ!

אֶשָּׂא כַנְפֵי־שָׁחַר,

אֶשְׁכְּנָה בְּאַחֲרִית יָם,

גַּם־שָׁם יָדְךָ תַנְחֵנִי,

וְתֹאחֲזֵנִי יְמִינֶךָ.

וָאֹמַר: אַךְ־חֹשֶׁךְ יְשׁוּפֵנִי,

וְלַיְלָה אוֹר בַּעֲדֵנִי,

גַּם־חֹשֶׁךְ לֹא־יַחְשִׁיךְ מִמֶּךָ,

וְלַיְלָה כַּיּוֹם יָאִיר!

אוֹדְךָ, עַל כִּי נוֹרָאוֹת נִפְלֵיתִי;

נִפְלָאִים מַעֲשֶׂיךָ,

וְנַפְשִׁי יֹדַעַת מְאֹד.

חָקְרֵנִי, אֵל, וְדַע לְבָבִי;

בְּחָנֵנִי, וְדַע שַׂרְעַפָּי.

וּרְאֵה אִם־דֶּרֶךְ־עֹצֶב בִּי,

וּנְחֵנִי בְּדֶרֶךְ עוֹלָם.

Whither can I go from Your spirit? Whither can I flee from Your
    presence?

If I go up to the heavens, You are there! If I make my home in the
    lowest depths, behold, You are there!

If I fly on the wings of the morning, and dwell on the ocean's far-
    thest shore,

even there Your hand leads me, Your strong hand holds me.

If I say: Yes, the darkness will hide me, the light will turn into
    night—

even darkness is not dark for You, for whom the night is bright as
    day!

I, who am a miracle of Your making, praise You; wonderful are Your
    works; my heart knows it full well.

Search me, O God, and know my heart; test me, and consider my
    thoughts. See if my ways lead to sorrow, and lead me, rather, on
    a way that is everlasting.

[From Psalm 139]

❦ *Kaddish is on page 190. El Malei Rachamim is on page 191.*

On returning home after a funeral

🍃 *In Jewish tradition, a mourner is identified as being a child, spouse, sibling, or parent of the deceased. Others, however, may also wish to use the following prayers and meditations.*

Out of the depths I cry to You, Eternal One;
hear my supplication.

A heavy burden has fallen upon us and sorrow has bowed our heads. And now we turn to You, the Source of life, for comfort and help. Give us the eyes to see that pain is not Your will, that somewhere there weeps with us One who feels our trouble and knows the suffering of our souls. We seek the light that will dispel the darkness that has overtaken us. Let us find it in the love of family and friends, in the sources of healing that are implanted within all the living, in the mind that conquers infirmity and trouble. Grant us the strength to endure what is inescapable, the wisdom to accept what cannot be undone, and the courage to go on without bitterness or despair. Amen.

Neir l'rag-li d'va-reh-cha, v'or
li-n'ti-va-ti. B'o-r'cha nir-eh or.

נֵר לְרַגְלִי דְבָרֶךָ, וְאוֹר
לִנְתִיבָתִי. בְּאוֹרְךָ נִרְאֶה אוֹר.

Your word, O God, is a lamp to my feet, a light to my path.
By Your light shall we see light.

THE MEMORIAL LIGHT IS KINDLED

Neir Adonai nish-mat a-dam.

נֵר יי נִשְׁמַת אָדָם.

Your light, O God, burns in the human soul.

Ba-ruch a-ta Adonai,
no-tei-a b'to-chei-nu cha-yei o-lam.

בָּרוּךְ אַתָּה, יי,
נוֹטֵעַ בְּתוֹכֵנוּ חַיֵּי עוֹלָם.

We praise You, O God: You have implanted within us eternal life.

The other days of mourning

❧ *In Jewish tradition, a mourner is identified as being a child, spouse, sibling, or parent of the deceased. Others, however, may also wish to use the following prayers and meditations.*

The second day

לַכֹּל זְמָן, וְעֵת לְכָל־חֵפֶץ
תַּחַת הַשָּׁמָיִם:
עֵת לָלֶדֶת וְעֵת לָמוּת;
עֵת לִבְכּוֹת וְעֵת לִשְׂחוֹק;
עֵת סְפוֹד וְעֵת רְקוֹד;
עֵת לִשְׁמוֹר וְעֵת לְהַשְׁלִיךְ.

For everything there is a season,
and a time for every desire under heaven:

A time to be born

and a time to die;

A time to weep

and a time to laugh;

A time to grieve

and a time to dance;

A time to keep

and a time to give away.

[*Ecclesiastes 3*]

You once brought wholeness to my life and now you have gone. Yet in the emptiness your passing leaves behind, I am not alone. For I have the companionship of the living, and even you, beloved, remain alive in my heart and mind, and what you did is part of what I have become. I will honor you when I live most fully, even in the shadow of my loss, and so draw closer to the Source of life, in whom every life finds meaning, purpose, and hope.

The third day

דּוֹר הֹלֵךְ וְדוֹר בָּא,

וְהָאָרֶץ לְעוֹלָם עֹמָדֶת.

כָּל־הַנְּחָלִים הֹלְכִים אֶל־הַיָּם,

וְהַיָּם אֵינֶנּוּ מָלֵא . . .

A generation goes, a generation comes,
but the earth remains forever.
All streams run to the sea, but the sea is not full. . .

[Ecclesiastes 1]

You have gone, now, beloved, yet your life within me is strong and vital. There is something of you that can never be lost, so long as the breath of life is within me. May I so live that my actions will reflect my gratitude for Your life and influence.

For it has been said: 'We cannot tell what may happen to us in the strange medley of life. But we can decide what happens in us—how we take it, what we do with it—and that is what really counts in the end. How to take the raw stuff of life and make it a thing of worth and beauty—that is the test of living.'

The fourth day

וְהָפַכְתִּי אֶבְלָם לְשָׂשׂוֹן,

וְנִחַמְתִּים וְשִׂמַּחְתִּים מִיגוֹנָם.

I will turn their mourning into joy,
I will comfort them, and give them gladness for sorrow.

[Jeremiah 31]

At this hour, as I think of you, the sorrow of bereavement begins to be softened by the love that continues to unite us, and by cherished memories of you which I will always carry in my heart. Soon I return to the world, though I know that the sense of loss will remain with me. Yet return I must, and I pray that my memory of all that was kind and beautiful in your thoughts, words, and deeds will remain in my life as an influence for good and a source of blessing. Amen.

The fifth day

טוֹב שֵׁם מִשֶּׁמֶן טוֹב;

וְיוֹם הַמָּוֶת מִיּוֹם הִוָּלְדוֹ.

Better a good name than all else;
and the day of death than the day of birth.

[*Ecclesiastes 7*]

'We come into this world crying while all around us are smiling. May we so live that we go out of this world smiling while everybody around us is crying.'

Beloved, as I think back upon your life, I see there was much goodness. And surely there was kindness I did not perceive, generosity to others unknown to me. I hope and trust that God has taken you in with a smile of welcome, knowing the many times you made others smile.

The sixth day

מַצְרֵף לַכֶּסֶף;

וְכוּר לַזָּהָב;

וּבֹחֵן לִבּוֹת יהוה.

For silver, the crucible;
for gold, the furnace;
for the heart, the living God.

[*Proverbs 17:3*]

Creator of the universe, You give me life, in which joys and sorrows are commingled in accordance with Your wisdom; and You send death, with its promise of eternal peace. Teach me to accept humbly and courageously whatever burden is laid upon me. Comfort me and all who mourn, and let the light of faith illumine the darkness of our sorrow with the hope of immortality. Strengthen us at all times with an unfailing trust in Your providence.

At the end of the mourning period

לֹא־יָבוֹא עוֹד שִׁמְשֵׁךְ,

וִירֵחֵךְ לֹא יֵאָסֵף;

כִּי יהוה יִהְיֶה־לָּךְ לְאוֹר עוֹלָם,

וְשָׁלְמוּ יְמֵי אֶבְלֵךְ.

Your sun will not go down again,
your moon will not depart;
for the Eternal One will be your light for ever,
and your days of mourning ended.

[Isaiah 60]

God of spirit and flesh, we (I) have turned to You for comfort in these days of grief. When the cup of sorrow passed into our (my) hands, Your Presence was with us (me). Now we (I) rise up to face the tasks of life once more. There will be moments of woe and loneliness. May the continued sense of Your Presence be for us (me) a source of comfort, and let the pain of our (my) loss subside. May the memory of our (my) loved one be more and more a cause of joy and gratitude. Teach us (me), O God, to give thanks for all that was deathless in the life of our (my) dear companion and friend, and which now is revealed to us (me) more clearly in all its beauty.

For the ties of love that death cannot sever; for the friendship we shared along life's path; for those gifts of heart and mind which have now become a precious heritage—for all this and more, we are (I am) grateful. Now help us (me), O compassionate God, not to dwell on sorrow and pain; help us (me), instead, to find within our hearts (my heart) the courage to return to the tasks of life, and its joys. Amen.

Consecration of a memorial

❧ *Begin with one or more of the following passages, then continue on page 188.*

1

יְהֹוָה, אֲדֹנֵינוּ, מָה־אַדִּיר שִׁמְךָ בְּכָל־הָאָרֶץ!
אֲשֶׁר תְּנָה הוֹדְךָ עַל־הַשָּׁמָיִם.
כִּי־אֶרְאֶה שָׁמֶיךָ, מַעֲשֵׂי אֶצְבְּעֹתֶיךָ;
יָרֵחַ וְכוֹכָבִים אֲשֶׁר כּוֹנָנְתָּה,
מָה־אֱנוֹשׁ כִּי־תִזְכְּרֶנּוּ,
וּבֶן־אָדָם כִּי תִפְקְדֶנּוּ?
וַתְּחַסְּרֵהוּ מְּעַט מֵאֱלֹהִים,
וְכָבוֹד וְהָדָר תְּעַטְּרֵהוּ.
תַּמְשִׁילֵהוּ בְּמַעֲשֵׂי יָדֶיךָ,
כֹּל שַׁתָּה תַחַת־רַגְלָיו:
צֹנֶה וַאֲלָפִים, כֻּלָּם, וְגַם בַּהֲמוֹת שָׂדָי, צִפּוֹר שָׁמַיִם, וּדְגֵי הַיָּם,
עֹבֵר אָרְחוֹת יַמִּים.
יְהֹוָה, אֲדֹנֵינוּ, מָה־אַדִּיר שִׁמְךָ בְּכָל־הָאָרֶץ!

Eternal One, our God, how glorious is Your name in all the earth!
You have stamped Your glory upon the heavens!
When I look at the heavens, the work of Your fingers;
the moon and the stars that You have established,
What are we, that You are mindful of us,
we human beings, that You care for us?
Yet You have made us little lower than the angels,
and crowned us with glory and honor!
You have appointed us to look after all that You have made,
You have placed all creation in our care:
Sheep and cattle, all of them; beasts and birds and fish,
and all who travel the ocean's paths.
Eternal One, our God, how glorious is Your name in all the earth!

[From Psalm 8]

2

בָּרְכִי, נַפְשִׁי, אֶת־יהוה, וְכָל־קְרָבַי אֶת־שֵׁם קָדְשׁוֹ.

בָּרְכִי, נַפְשִׁי, אֶת־יהוה, וְאַל־תִּשְׁכְּחִי כָּל־גְּמוּלָיו.

הַגּוֹאֵל מִשַּׁחַת חַיָּיְכִי, הַמְעַטְּרֵכִי חֶסֶד וְרַחֲמִים.

עֹשֵׂה צְדָקוֹת יהוה, וּמִשְׁפָּטִים לְכָל־עֲשׁוּקִים.

רַחוּם וְחַנּוּן יהוה, אֶרֶךְ אַפַּיִם וְרַב־חָסֶד.

כִּי־הוּא יָדַע יִצְרֵנוּ, זָכוּר כִּי־עָפָר אֲנָחְנוּ.

אֱנוֹשׁ כֶּחָצִיר יָמָיו; כְּצִיץ הַשָּׂדֶה כֵּן יָצִיץ.

כִּי רוּחַ עָבְרָה־בּוֹ, וְאֵינֶנּוּ; וְלֹא־יַכִּירֶנּוּ עוֹד מְקוֹמוֹ.

וְחֶסֶד יהוה מֵעוֹלָם וְעַד־עוֹלָם עַל־יְרֵאָיו, וְצִדְקָתוֹ לִבְנֵי בָנִים,

לְשֹׁמְרֵי בְרִיתוֹ וּלְזֹכְרֵי פִקֻּדָיו לַעֲשׂוֹתָם.

יהוה בַּשָּׁמַיִם הֵכִין כִּסְאוֹ, וּמַלְכוּתוֹ בַּכֹּל מָשָׁלָה.

בָּרְכוּ יהוה, מַלְאָכָיו, גִּבֹּרֵי כֹחַ עֹשֵׂי דְבָרוֹ, לִשְׁמֹעַ בְּקוֹל דְּבָרוֹ.

בָּרְכוּ יהוה כָּל־צְבָאָיו, מְשָׁרְתָיו עֹשֵׂי רְצוֹנוֹ.

בָּרְכוּ יהוה כָּל־מַעֲשָׂיו, בְּכָל־מְקֹמוֹת מֶמְשַׁלְתּוֹ.

בָּרְכִי, נַפְשִׁי, אֶת־יהוה.

Praise the Eternal One, O my soul, and let all that is in me praise God's holy name.

Praise the Eternal One, and never forget the blessings of God,

who forgives your sins and heals your wounds,

who redeems your life from futility, and surrounds you with love and compassion.

The Eternal One is just, demanding justice for the oppressed;

God is merciful and gracious, endlessly patient and full of love.

For God knows how we are made, and remembers that we are dust.

Our days are like grass; we blossom like the flower of the field.

The wind blows, and it is gone; its place knows it no more.

But Your love, Eternal God, rests for ever on all who revere You, and Your goodness rests on their children's children,

who keep Your covenant and remember to observe Your precepts.

Eternal One, You have established Your throne in the heavens, and You reign in all the universe.

Let the ministering angels praise You, the mighty ones, who do Your bidding, who hearken to Your voice.

Let all the Hosts of Heaven, Your ministers, praise You.

Let all Your works praise You in all creation.

Praise the Eternal One, O my soul!

[From Psalm 103]

3

אֵשֶׁת־חַיִל מִי יִמְצָא,
וְרָחֹק מִפְּנִינִים מִכְרָהּ.
כַּפָּהּ פָּרְשָׂה לֶעָנִי,
וְיָדֶיהָ שִׁלְּחָה לָאֶבְיוֹן.
עֹז־וְהָדָר לְבוּשָׁהּ,
וַתִּשְׂחַק לְיוֹם אַחֲרוֹן.
פִּיהָ פָּתְחָה בְחָכְמָה,
וְתוֹרַת־חֶסֶד עַל־לְשׁוֹנָהּ.
קָמוּ בָנֶיהָ וַיְאַשְּׁרוּהָ,
בַּעְלָהּ וַיְהַלְלָהּ.
רַבּוֹת בָּנוֹת עָשׂוּ חָיִל
וְאַתְּ עָלִית עַל־כֻּלָּנָה.
שֶׁקֶר הַחֵן וְהֶבֶל הַיֹּפִי,
אִשָּׁה יִרְאַת־יהוה הִיא תִתְהַלָּל.
תְּנוּ־לָהּ מִפְּרִי יָדֶיהָ,
וִיהַלְלוּהָ בַשְּׁעָרִים מַעֲשֶׂיהָ.

A woman of valor—seek her out; she is to be valued above rubies.

She opens her hand to those in need, and offers her help to the poor.

Adorned with strength and dignity, she looks to the future with cheerful trust.

Her speech is wise, and the law of kindness is on her lips.

Those who love her rise up with praise, and call her blessed:

Many women have done well, but you surpass them all.

Charm is deceptive and beauty short-lived, but a woman loyal to God has truly earned praise.

Honor her for her work; her life proclaims her praise.

[From Proverbs 31]

4

יהוה, מִי־יָגוּר בְּאָהֳלֶךָ?
מִי־יִשְׁכֹּן בְּהַר קָדְשֶׁךָ?

הוֹלֵךְ תָּמִים וּפֹעֵל צֶדֶק,
וְדֹבֵר אֱמֶת בִּלְבָבוֹ.
לֹא־רָגַל עַל־לְשֹׁנוֹ,
לֹא־עָשָׂה לְרֵעֵהוּ רָעָה,
וְחֶרְפָּה לֹא־נָשָׂא עַל־קְרֹבוֹ.
נִשְׁבַּע לְהָרַע וְלֹא יָמִר,
כַּסְפּוֹ לֹא־נָתַן בְּנֶשֶׁךְ,
וְשֹׁחַד עַל־נָקִי לֹא לָקָח.
עֹשֵׂה־אֵלֶּה לֹא יִמּוֹט לְעוֹלָם.

Eternal God:
Who may abide in Your house?
Who may dwell in Your holy mountain?
Those who are upright; who do justly,
all whose hearts are true.
Who do not slander others, nor wrong them,
nor bring shame upon their kin.
Who give their word and, come what may, do not retract it.
Who do not exploit others, who never take bribes.
Those who live in this way shall never be shaken.

[From Psalm 15]

5

אַשְׁרֵי־אִישׁ יָרֵא אֶת־יְהֹוָה,

בְּמִצְוֹתָיו חָפֵץ מְאֹד!

גִּבּוֹר בָּאָרֶץ יִהְיֶה זַרְעוֹ;

דּוֹר יְשָׁרִים יְבֹרָךְ.

הוֹן־וָעֹשֶׁר בְּבֵיתוֹ,

וְצִדְקָתוֹ עֹמֶדֶת לָעַד.

זָרַח בַּחֹשֶׁךְ אוֹר לַיְשָׁרִים;

חַנּוּן וְרַחוּם וְצַדִּיק.

נָכוֹן לִבּוֹ, בָּטֻחַ בַּיהֹוָה.

סָמוּךְ לִבּוֹ; לֹא יִירָא.

פִּזַּר נָתַן לָאֶבְיוֹנִים;

צִדְקָתוֹ עֹמֶדֶת לָעַד;

קַרְנוֹ תָּרוּם בְּכָבוֹד.

Happy is the man loyal to God, who greatly delights in the Eternal One's commandments!

His descendants will be honored in the land; the generation of the upright will be blessed.

His household prospers, and his righteousness endures for ever.

Light dawns in the darkness for the upright; for the man who is gracious, merciful, and just.

His mind is firm, trusting in the Eternal One.

His heart is steady, he is not afraid.

He has been generous, has given freely to the poor; his righteousness endures for ever; his life is exalted in honor.

[From Psalm 112]

6

A SONG OF DAVID

מִזְמוֹר לְדָוִד

יהוה רֹעִי, לֹא אֶחְסָר.

בִּנְאוֹת דֶּשֶׁא יַרְבִּיצֵנִי,

עַל־מֵי מְנֻחוֹת יְנַהֲלֵנִי.

נַפְשִׁי יְשׁוֹבֵב;

יַנְחֵנִי בְמַעְגְּלֵי־צֶדֶק לְמַעַן שְׁמוֹ.

גַּם כִּי־אֵלֵךְ בְּגֵיא צַלְמָוֶת

לֹא־אִירָא רָע, כִּי־אַתָּה עִמָּדִי:

שִׁבְטְךָ וּמִשְׁעַנְתֶּךָ, הֵמָּה יְנַחֲמֻנִי.

תַּעֲרֹךְ לְפָנַי שֻׁלְחָן נֶגֶד צֹרְרָי,

דִּשַּׁנְתָּ בַשֶּׁמֶן רֹאשִׁי, כּוֹסִי רְוָיָה.

אַךְ טוֹב וָחֶסֶד יִרְדְּפוּנִי כָּל־יְמֵי חַיָּי,

וְשַׁבְתִּי בְּבֵית־יהוה לְאֹרֶךְ יָמִים.

Eternal God, You are my shepherd, I shall not want. You make me lie down in green pastures, You lead me beside still waters. You restore my soul; You guide me in paths of righteousness for Your name's sake. Yes, even when I walk through the valley of the shadow of death, I will fear no evil, for You are with me; with rod and staff You comfort me. You prepare a table before me in the presence of my enemies; You have anointed my head with oil; my cup overflows. Surely, goodness and mercy shall follow me all the days of my life, and I shall dwell in the house of the Eternal God for ever.

[Psalm 23]

7

אֶשָּׂא עֵינַי אֶל־הֶהָרִים:

מֵאַיִן יָבֹא עֶזְרִי?

עֶזְרִי מֵעִם יהוה,

עֹשֵׂה שָׁמַיִם וָאָרֶץ.

אַל־יִתֵּן לַמּוֹט רַגְלֶךָ,

אַל־יָנוּם שֹׁמְרֶךָ.

הִנֵּה לֹא־יָנוּם וְלֹא יִישָׁן שׁוֹמֵר יִשְׂרָאֵל.

יהוה שֹׁמְרֶךָ,

יהוה צִלְּךָ עַל־יַד יְמִינֶךָ.

יוֹמָם הַשֶּׁמֶשׁ לֹא־יַכֶּכָּה, וְיָרֵחַ בַּלָּיְלָה.

יהוה יִשְׁמָרְךָ מִכָּל־רָע,

יִשְׁמֹר אֶת־נַפְשֶׁךָ.

יהוה יִשְׁמָר־צֵאתְךָ וּבוֹאֶךָ

מֵעַתָּה וְעַד־עוֹלָם.

I lift up my eyes to the mountains:
Where will I find my help?
My help is the Eternal One,
Maker of heaven and earth.
God will keep your foot from slipping,
Your Guardian does not slumber.
Behold, the Guardian of Israel neither slumbers nor sleeps.
The Eternal One is your shield,
The Eternal One is your shade at your side.
The sun will not strike you by day,
Nor the moon by night.
The Eternal One is your shield against evil,
the Guardian of your spirit.
The Eternal One is your shield, when you come in
    and when you go out,
Now and for ever.

   [Psalm 121]

CONTINUE HERE

BY A FAMILY MEMBER

> On behalf of our family, and in the presence of our relatives and friends, we consecrate this memorial to . . . . as a sign of undying love.

ON BEHALF OF THE FAMILY

> On behalf of the family of . . . ., and in the presence of his (her) relatives and friends, we consecrate this memorial as a sign of undying love.

FOR A MALE

נִשְׁמָתוֹ צְרוּרָה בִּצְרוֹר הַחַיִּים.

His soul is bound up in the bond of eternal life.

FOR A FEMALE

נִשְׁמָתָהּ צְרוּרָה בִּצְרוֹר הַחַיִּים.

Her soul is bound up in the bond of eternal life.

FOR AN ADULT

> God of infinite love, in whose hands are the souls of all the living and the spirits of all flesh, standing at the grave of . . . . we gratefully recall the goodness in him (her) and we give thanks for the consolation of memory.

> Strengthen us, that, walking through the valley of the shadow of death, we may be guided by Your light. May our actions and aspirations honor our loved one as surely as does this monument, which will ever be a symbol of abiding devotion. So will he (she) live on for blessing among us.

FOR A CHILD

To You, O Source of peace, we turn in our time of need. Give us strength and patience to bear our burden of sorrow. Deepen our love for one another; teach us to open our hearts to all who need us; move us to reach out to them with our hands; and guide us in our path, helping us to find the abiding love that survives all loss and sustains us through every trial.

In Your everlasting spirit are all spirits bound together: grant consolation to sorrowing parents and to all who mourn. Send us healing: renew our hope and our faith. May the memory of this child make all children more precious to us.

As we dedicate this memorial to . . . ., we sanctify Your name.

Kaddish

יִתְגַּדַּל וְיִתְקַדַּשׁ שְׁמֵהּ רַבָּא בְּעָלְמָא דִי־בְרָא כִרְעוּתֵהּ, וְיַמְלִיךְ מַלְכוּתֵהּ בְּחַיֵּיכוֹן וּבְיוֹמֵיכוֹן וּבְחַיֵּי דְכָל־בֵּית יִשְׂרָאֵל, בַּעֲגָלָא וּבִזְמַן קָרִיב, וְאִמְרוּ: אָמֵן.

Yit-ga-dal v'yit-ka-dash sh'mei ra-ba b'al-ma di-v'ra chir-u-tei, v'yam-lich mal-chu-tei b'cha-yei-chon u-v'yo-mei-chon u-v'cha-yei d'chol beit Yis-ra-eil, ba-a-ga-la u-viz-man ka-riv, v'im-ru: A-mein.

יְהֵא שְׁמֵהּ רַבָּא מְבָרַךְ לְעָלַם וּלְעָלְמֵי עָלְמַיָּא.

Y'hei sh'mei ra-ba m'va-rach l'a-lam u-l'al-mei al-ma-ya.

יִתְבָּרַךְ וְיִשְׁתַּבַּח, וְיִתְפָּאַר וְיִתְרוֹמַם וְיִתְנַשֵּׂא, וְיִתְהַדָּר וְיִתְעַלֶּה וְיִתְהַלָּל שְׁמֵהּ דְּקוּדְשָׁא, בְּרִיךְ הוּא,

Yit-ba-rach v'yish-ta-bach v'yit-pa-ar, v'yit-ro-mam, v'yit-na-sei, v'yit-ha-dar, v'yit-a-leh, v'yit-ha-lal sh'mei d'ku-d'sha, b'rich hu,

לְעֵלָּא מִן־כָּל־בִּרְכָתָא וְשִׁירָתָא, תֻּשְׁבְּחָתָא וְנֶחֱמָתָא דַּאֲמִירָן בְּעָלְמָא, וְאִמְרוּ: אָמֵן.

l'ei-la min kol bir-cha-ta v'shi-ra-ta, tush-b'cha-ta v'neh-cheh-ma-ta da-a-mi-ran b'al-ma, v'im-ru: A-mein.

יְהֵא שְׁלָמָא רַבָּא מִן־שְׁמַיָּא וְחַיִּים עָלֵינוּ וְעַל־כָּל־יִשְׂרָאֵל, וְאִמְרוּ: אָמֵן.

Y'hei sh'la-ma ra-ba min sh'ma-ya v'cha-yim, a-lei-nu v'al kol Yis-ra-eil, v'im-ru: A-mein.

עֹשֶׂה שָׁלוֹם בִּמְרוֹמָיו, הוּא יַעֲשֶׂה שָׁלוֹם עָלֵינוּ וְעַל־כָּל־יִשְׂרָאֵל, וְאִמְרוּ: אָמֵן.

O-seh sha-lom bi-m'ro-mav, hu ya-a-seh sha-lom a-lei-nu v'al kol Yis-ra-eil, v'im-ru: A-mein.

Magnified and sanctified be the great name of the One by whose will the world was created. May God's rule become effective in your lives, and in the life of the whole House of Israel. May it be so soon, and let us say:

Amen. May God's great name be praised to all eternity.

Blessed and praised; glorified, exalted and extolled; lauded, honored and acclaimed be the name of the Holy One, who is ever to be praised, though far above the eulogies and songs of praise and consolation that human lips can utter; and let us say: Amen.

May great peace descend from heaven, and abundant life be granted, to us and all Israel; and let us say: Amen.

May the Most High, Source of perfect peace, grant peace to us, to all Israel, and to all the world.

אֵל מָלֵא רַחֲמִים, שׁוֹכֵן בַּמְּרוֹמִים, הַמְצֵא מְנוּחָה נְכוֹנָה תַּחַת כַּנְפֵי
הַשְּׁכִינָה עִם קְדוֹשִׁים וּטְהוֹרִים כְּזֹהַר הָרָקִיעַ מַזְהִירִים אֶת־נִשְׁמַת
שֶׁהָלַךְ לְעוֹלָמוֹ [שֶׁהָלְכָה לְעוֹלָמָהּ]. בַּעַל הָרַחֲמִים
יַסְתִּירֵהוּ [וְיַסְתִּירֶהָ] בְּסֵתֶר כְּנָפָיו לְעוֹלָמִים, וְיִצְרוֹר בִּצְרוֹר הַחַיִּים אֶת־
נִשְׁמָתוֹ [נִשְׁמָתָהּ]. יְיָ הוּא נַחֲלָתוֹ [נַחֲלָתָהּ] וְיָנוּחַ [וְתָנוּחַ] בְּשָׁלוֹם עַל
מִשְׁכָּבוֹ [מִשְׁכָּבָהּ] וְנֹאמַר: אָמֵן.

Eil ma-lei ra-cha-mim, sho-chein ba-m'ro-mim, ham-tzei m'nu-cha n'cho-na ta-chat ka-n'fei ha-sh'chi-na im k'do-shim u-t'ho-rim k'zo-har ha-ra-ki-a maz-hi-rim et nish-mat . . . . sheh-ha-lach l'o-la-mo (sheh-ha-l'cha l'o-la-mah). Ba-al ha-ra-cha-mim yas-ti-rei-hu b'sei-ter k'na-fav l'o-la-mim, v'yitz-ror bi-tz'ror ha-cha-yim et nish-ma-toh (nish-ma-tah). Adonai hu na-cha-la-toh (na-cha-la-tah) v'ya-nu-ach (v'ta-nu-ach) b'sha-lom al mish-ka-vo (mish-ka-vah) v'no-mar: A-mein.

God full of compassion, dwelling in the heights and in the depths, grant perfect rest under the wings of Your Presence to . . . ., our loved one who has entered eternity. She (he) has found refuge for ever in the shadow of Your wings, and her (his) soul is bound up in the bond of eternal life; for You, the Everlasting God, are her (his) inheritance. May she (he) rest in peace, as we say: Amen.

For a Yahrzeit

❧ *The family is gathered at dusk, on the evening before the anniversary of the death.*

A GROUP SAYS:

> At this moment, in memory of our beloved . . . .,
> we join hands in love and remembrance. A link has been
> broken in the chain that has bound us together, yet strong
> bonds of home and love hold us each to the other.
>
> We give thanks for the blessing of life, of companionship,
> and of memory. We are grateful for the strength and faith
> that sustained us in the hour of our bereavement. Though
> sorrow lingers, we have learned that love is stronger than
> death. Though our loved one is beyond our sight, we do
> not despair, for we sense our beloved in our hearts as a
> living presence.

AN INDIVIDUAL SAYS:

> At this moment, I pause for thought in memory of my
> beloved . . . .
>
> I give thanks for the blessing of life, of companionship,
> and of memory. I am grateful for the strength and faith
> that sustained me in the hour of my bereavement. Though
> sorrow lingers, I have learned that love is stronger than
> death. Though my loved one is beyond my sight, I do not
> despair, for I sense my beloved in my heart as a living
> presence.

❧ *The 23rd Psalm, page 186, or another favorite passage from the Bible or Prayerbook might now be recited.*

Sustained by words of faith, comforted by precious memories, we (I)
kindle the Yahrzeit light in remembrance. As this light burns pure
and clear, so may the blessed memory of the goodness of our (my)
dear . . . . illumine our souls (my soul).

THE LIGHT IS KINDLED

FOR A MALE

זִכְרוֹנוֹ לִבְרָכָה.

Zich-ro-no li-v'ra-cha.

His memory is a blessing.

FOR A FEMALE

זִכְרוֹנָה לִבְרָכָה.

Zich-ro-nah li-v'ra-cha.

Her memory is a blessing.

At the grave of a loved one

❦ *Either of the following might be said silently or aloud.*

God of all generations, what are we, that You care for us? What is our worth, that You take account of us? We are a breath, a passing shadow. But You are the God of heaven and earth; none who trust in You shall be forsaken.

Standing at the grave of . . . . , I give thanks for all that was good, true, and beautiful in his (her) life. May his (her) memory be a source of blessing and comfort to us all.

—*or*—

To this sacred place I come, drawn by the eternal ties that bind my soul to yours. Death has separated us. You are no longer at my side to share the beauty of the passing moment. I cannot look to you to lighten my burdens, to lend me your strength, your counsel, your faith. And yet what you mean to me neither withers nor fades. For a time we touched hands and hearts; still your voice abides within me, still your tender glance remains a joy to me. For you are part of me for ever; something of you has become a deathless song upon my lips. And so beyond the ache that tells how much I miss you, a deeper thought compels: we were together. I hold you still in mind, and give thanks for life and love. The happiness that was, the memories that do not fade, are a gift that cannot be lost. You continue to bless my days and years. I will always give thanks for you.

Weekday
Services

WEEKDAY SERVICES

Afternoon Service

מִנְחָה

אַשְׁרֵי

אַשְׁרֵי יוֹשְׁבֵי בֵיתֶךָ; עוֹד יְהַלְלוּךָ סֶּלָה.

אַשְׁרֵי הָעָם שֶׁכָּכָה לּוֹ; אַשְׁרֵי הָעָם שֶׁיהוה אֱלֹהָיו.

Happy are those who dwell in Your house;

they will sing Your praise for ever.

Happy the people to whom such blessing falls;

Happy the people of the Eternal God.

FROM PSALM 145

A PSALM OF DAVID   תְּהִלָּה לְדָוִד

אֲרוֹמִמְךָ, אֱלוֹהַי הַמֶּלֶךְ,

וַאֲבָרְכָה שִׁמְךָ לְעוֹלָם וָעֶד.

בְּכָל־יוֹם אֲבָרְכֶךָּ,

וַאֲהַלְלָה שִׁמְךָ לְעוֹלָם וָעֶד.

I will exalt You, my Sovereign God,

I will praise Your name for ever.

Every day I will praise You;

I will extol Your name for ever.

גָּדוֹל יהוה וּמְהֻלָּל מְאֹד,
וְלִגְדֻלָּתוֹ אֵין חֵקֶר.
דּוֹר לְדוֹר יְשַׁבַּח מַעֲשֶׂיךָ,
וּגְבוּרֹתֶיךָ יַגִּידוּ.

Great are You, Eternal One, and worthy of praise;
and infinite is Your greatness.
One generation shall acclaim Your work to the next;
they shall tell of Your mighty acts.

הֲדַר כְּבוֹד הוֹדֶךָ,
וְדִבְרֵי נִפְלְאֹתֶיךָ אָשִׂיחָה.
וֶעֱזוּז נוֹרְאֹתֶיךָ יֹאמֵרוּ,
וּגְדֻלָּתְךָ אֲסַפְּרֶנָּה.

They shall bring word of Your radiant glory;
and bear witness to Your wondrous works.
They shall speak of Your awesome might,
and make known Your greatness.

זֵכֶר רַב־טוּבְךָ יַבִּיעוּ,
וְצִדְקָתְךָ יְרַנֵּנוּ.
חַנּוּן וְרַחוּם יהוה,
אֶרֶךְ אַפַּיִם וּגְדָל־חָסֶד.
טוֹב־יהוה לַכֹּל,
וְרַחֲמָיו עַל־כָּל־מַעֲשָׂיו.

They shall tell the world of Your goodness,
and sing of Your righteousness.
"God is gracious and compassionate, endlessly patient,
overflowing with love."

*"You are good to all; Your compassion shelters all
Your creatures."*

יוֹדְוּךָ יהוה כָּל־מַעֲשֶׂיךָ,
וַחֲסִידֶיךָ יְבָרְכוּכָה.
כְּבוֹד מַלְכוּתְךָ יֹאמֵרוּ,
וּגְבוּרָתְךָ יְדַבֵּרוּ,

All Your works shall glorify You;

Your faithful ones shall praise You.

They shall proclaim Your majestic glory,

they shall tell of Your might:

לְהוֹדִיעַ לִבְנֵי הָאָדָם גְּבוּרֹתָיו,
וּכְבוֹד הֲדַר מַלְכוּתוֹ.
מַלְכוּתְךָ מַלְכוּת כָּל־עֹלָמִים
וּמֶמְשַׁלְתְּךָ בְּכָל־דּוֹר וָדֹר.

to reveal Your power to the world,

and the glorious splendor of Your rule.

You are sovereign to the end of time;

You reign through all generations.

סוֹמֵךְ יהוה לְכָל־הַנֹּפְלִים,
וְזוֹקֵף לְכָל־הַכְּפוּפִים.
עֵינֵי־כֹל אֵלֶיךָ יְשַׂבֵּרוּ,
וְאַתָּה נוֹתֵן־לָהֶם אֶת־אָכְלָם בְּעִתּוֹ.

You support the falling, Eternal One;

You raise up all who are bowed down.

The eyes of all are turned to You;

You sustain them in time of need.

פּוֹתֵחַ אֶת־יָדֶךָ

וּמַשְׂבִּיעַ לְכָל־חַי רָצוֹן.

צַדִּיק יהוה בְּכָל־דְּרָכָיו,

וְחָסִיד בְּכָל־מַעֲשָׂיו.

You open Your hand,

to fulfill the needs of all the living.

You are just in all Your ways,

loving in all Your deeds.

קָרוֹב יהוה לְכָל־קֹרְאָיו,

לְכֹל אֲשֶׁר יִקְרָאֻהוּ בֶאֱמֶת.

רְצוֹן־יְרֵאָיו יַעֲשֶׂה,

וְאֶת־שַׁוְעָתָם יִשְׁמַע וְיוֹשִׁיעֵם.

You are near to all who call upon You,

to all who call upon You in truth:

You fulfill the hope of all who revere You;

You hear their cry and help them.

תְּהִלַּת יהוה יְדַבֶּר־פִּי וִיבָרֵךְ כָּל־בָּשָׂר שֵׁם קָדְשׁוֹ לְעוֹלָם וָעֶד.

וַאֲנַחְנוּ נְבָרֵךְ יָהּ מֵעַתָּה וְעַד־עוֹלָם. הַלְלוּיָהּ!

My lips shall declare the glory of God;
let all flesh praise Your holy name for ever and ever.

We will praise Your name now and always. Halleluyah!

ALL RISE

READER'S KADDISH   חֲצִי קַדִּישׁ

יִתְגַּדַּל וְיִתְקַדַּשׁ שְׁמֵהּ רַבָּא בְּעָלְמָא דִי־בְרָא כִרְעוּתֵהּ, וְיַמְלִיךְ מַלְכוּתֵהּ בְּחַיֵּיכוֹן וּבְיוֹמֵיכוֹן וּבְחַיֵּי דְכָל־בֵּית יִשְׂרָאֵל, בַּעֲגָלָא וּבִזְמַן קָרִיב, וְאִמְרוּ: אָמֵן.

יְהֵא שְׁמֵהּ רַבָּא מְבָרַךְ לְעָלַם וּלְעָלְמֵי עָלְמַיָּא.

יִתְבָּרַךְ וְיִשְׁתַּבַּח, וְיִתְפָּאַר וְיִתְרוֹמַם וְיִתְנַשֵּׂא, וְיִתְהַדָּר וְיִתְעַלֶּה וְיִתְהַלָּל שְׁמֵהּ דְּקוּדְשָׁא, בְּרִיךְ הוּא, לְעֵלָּא מִן־כָּל־בִּרְכָתָא וְשִׁירָתָא, תֻּשְׁבְּחָתָא וְנֶחֱמָתָא דַּאֲמִירָן בְּעָלְמָא, וְאִמְרוּ: אָמֵן.

Yit-ga-dal v'yit-ka-dash sh'mei ra-ba b'al-ma di-v'ra chir-u-tei, v'yam-lich mal-chu-tei b'cha-yei-chon u-v'yo-mei-chon u-v'cha-yei d'chol beit Yis-ra-eil, ba-a-ga-la u-viz-man ka-riv, v'im' ru: A-mein.

Y'hei sh'mei ra-ba m'va-rach l'al-am u-l'al-mei al-ma-ya.

Yit-ba-rach v'yish-ta-bach v'yit-pa-ar, v'yit-ro-mam, v'yit-na-sei, v'yit-ha-dar, v'yit-a-leh, v'yit-ha-lal sh'mei d'ku-d'sha, b'rich hu, l'ei-la min kol bir-cha-ta v'shi-ra-ta, tush-b'cha-ta v'neh-cheh-ma-ta da-a-mi-ran b'al-ma, v'im' ru: A-mein.

Let the glory of God be extolled, let God's great name be hallowed in the world whose creation God willed. May God rule in our own day, in our own lives, and in the life of all Israel, and let us say: Amen.

Let God's great name be praised for ever and ever.

Beyond all the praises, songs, and adorations that we can utter is the Holy One, the Blessed One, whom yet we glorify, honor, and exalt. And let us say: Amen.

❧ *The T'filah is on page 228.*

201

Evening Service

תְּפִלַּת עַרְבִית

"And after the fire, a still, small voice."

[*1 Kings 19*]

You give meaning to our days, to our struggles and strivings. In the stillness of the night and in the press of the crowd, Yours is the voice within that brings joy and peace.

We do not ask for a life of ease, for happiness without alloy. We ask only to be uncomplaining and unafraid. In our darkness be our light, and in our loneliness help us discover the many souls akin to our own. Give us strength to face life with courage, to draw blessing even from its discords and conflicts. Make us understand that life calls us not merely to enjoy the richness of the earth, but to exult in heights gained after the toil of climbing.

Let our darkness be dispelled by Your love, that we may rise above fear and failure, our steps sustained by faith. You give meaning to our days; You are our support and our trust.

ALL RISE

The Sh'ma and its Blessings
שְׁמַע וּבִרְכוֹתֶיהָ

בָּרְכוּ אֶת־יי הַמְבֹרָךְ!

Ba-r'chu et Adonai ha-m'vo-rach!

Praise the One to whom our praise is due!

בָּרוּךְ יי הַמְבֹרָךְ לְעוֹלָם וָעֶד!

Ba-ruch A-do-nai ha-m'vo-rach l'o-lam va-ed!

Praised be the One to whom our praise is due, now and for ever!

CREATION

מַעֲרִיב עֲרָבִים

בָּרוּךְ אַתָּה יי, אֱלֹהֵינוּ מֶלֶךְ הָעוֹלָם, אֲשֶׁר בִּדְבָרוֹ מַעֲרִיב עֲרָבִים,
בְּחָכְמָה פּוֹתֵחַ שְׁעָרִים, וּבִתְבוּנָה מְשַׁנֶּה עִתִּים, וּמַחֲלִיף אֶת־הַזְּמַנִּים,
וּמְסַדֵּר אֶת־הַכּוֹכָבִים בְּמִשְׁמְרוֹתֵיהֶם בָּרָקִיעַ כִּרְצוֹנוֹ. בּוֹרֵא יוֹם וָלָיְלָה,
גּוֹלֵל אוֹר מִפְּנֵי חֹשֶׁךְ וְחֹשֶׁךְ מִפְּנֵי אוֹר, וּמַעֲבִיר יוֹם וּמֵבִיא לָיְלָה,
וּמַבְדִּיל בֵּין יוֹם וּבֵין לָיְלָה, יי צְבָאוֹת שְׁמוֹ. אֵל חַי וְקַיָּם, תָּמִיד יִמְלוֹךְ
עָלֵינוּ, לְעוֹלָם וָעֶד. בָּרוּךְ אַתָּה, יי, הַמַּעֲרִיב עֲרָבִים.

Praised be our Eternal God, Sovereign of the universe, whose word
brings on the evening. With wisdom You open heaven's gates, and
with understanding You make the ages pass and the seasons al-
ternate; Your will controls the stars as they travel through the skies.

*You are Creator of day and night, rolling light away from dark-
ness, and darkness from light; You cause day to pass and bring on
the night; separating day from night; You command the Hosts of
Heaven!*

*May the living and eternal God rule us always, to the end of time!
We praise You, O God, whose word makes evening fall.*

REVELATION

אַהֲבַת עוֹלָם

אַהֲבַת עוֹלָם בֵּית יִשְׂרָאֵל עַמְּךָ אָהָבְתָּ. תּוֹרָה וּמִצְוֹת, חֻקִּים וּמִשְׁפָּטִים
אוֹתָנוּ לִמַּדְתָּ. עַל־כֵּן, יי אֱלֹהֵינוּ, בְּשָׁכְבֵנוּ וּבְקוּמֵנוּ נָשִׂיחַ בְּחֻקֶּיךָ, וְנִשְׂמַח
בְּדִבְרֵי תוֹרָתֶךָ וּבְמִצְוֹתֶיךָ לְעוֹלָם וָעֶד. כִּי הֵם חַיֵּינוּ וְאֹרֶךְ יָמֵינוּ, וּבָהֶם
נֶהְגֶּה יוֹמָם וָלָיְלָה. וְאַהֲבָתְךָ אַל־תָּסוּר מִמֶּנּוּ לְעוֹלָמִים! בָּרוּךְ אַתָּה, יי,
אוֹהֵב עַמּוֹ יִשְׂרָאֵל.

Unending is Your love for Your people, the House of Israel: Torah and
Mitzvot, laws and precepts have You taught us.

Therefore, O God, when we lie down and when we rise up, we will
meditate on Your laws and rejoice in Your Torah and Mitzvot for
ever.

*Day and night we will reflect on them, for they are our life and
the length of our days. Then Your love shall never depart from our
hearts! We praise You, O God: You love Your people Israel.*

שְׁמַע יִשְׂרָאֵל: יהוה אֱלֹהֵינוּ יהוה אֶחָד!

**Hear, O Israel: the Eternal One is our God,
the Eternal God alone!**

בָּרוּךְ שֵׁם כְּבוֹד מַלְכוּתוֹ לְעוֹלָם וָעֶד!

Blessed is God's glorious majesty for ever and ever!

ALL ARE SEATED

V'a-hav-ta et Adonai eh-lo-heh-cha   וְאָהַבְתָּ אֵת יהוה אֱלֹהֶיךָ
b'chol l'va-v'cha u-v'chol naf-sh'cha   בְּכָל־לְבָבְךָ וּבְכָל־נַפְשְׁךָ
u-v'chol m'o-deh-cha. V'ha-yu   וּבְכָל־מְאֹדֶךָ: וְהָיוּ
ha-d'va-rim ha-ei-leh a-sher a-no-chi   הַדְּבָרִים הָאֵלֶּה אֲשֶׁר אָנֹכִי
m'tza-v'cha ha-yom al l'va-veh-cha.   מְצַוְּךָ הַיּוֹם עַל־לְבָבֶךָ:
V'shi-nan-tam l'va-neh-cha   וְשִׁנַּנְתָּם לְבָנֶיךָ
v'di-bar-ta bam b'shiv-t'cha   וְדִבַּרְתָּ בָּם בְּשִׁבְתְּךָ
b'vei-teh-cha u-v'lech-t'cha   בְּבֵיתֶךָ וּבְלֶכְתְּךָ
va-deh-rech u-v'shoch-b'cha   בַדֶּרֶךְ וּבְשָׁכְבְּךָ
u-v'ku-meh-cha. U-k'shar-tam l'ot   וּבְקוּמֶךָ: וּקְשַׁרְתָּם לְאוֹת
al ya-deh-cha v'ha-yu l'to-ta-fot bein   עַל־יָדֶךָ וְהָיוּ לְטֹטָפֹת בֵּין
ei-neh-cha; u-ch'tav-tam al m'zu-zot   עֵינֶיךָ: וּכְתַבְתָּם עַל־מְזֻזֹת
bei-teh-cha u-vi-sh'a-reh-cha.   בֵּיתֶךָ וּבִשְׁעָרֶיךָ:

You shall love your Eternal God with all your heart, with all your mind, with all your being. Set these words, which I command you this day, upon your heart. Teach them faithfully to your children; speak of them in your home and on your way, when you lie down and when you rise up. Bind them as a sign upon your hand; let them be a symbol before your eyes; inscribe them on the doorposts of your house, and on your gates.

L'ma-an tiz-k'ru va-a-si-tem   לְמַעַן תִּזְכְּרוּ וַעֲשִׂיתֶם
et kol mitz-vo-tai, vi-h'yi-tem   אֶת־כָּל־מִצְוֹתָי וִהְיִיתֶם
k'do-shim lei-lo-hei-chem. Ani   קְדֹשִׁים לֵאלֹהֵיכֶם: אֲנִי
Adonai Eh-lo-hei-chem a-sher   יהוה אֱלֹהֵיכֶם אֲשֶׁר
ho-tzei-ti et-chem mei-eh-retz   הוֹצֵאתִי אֶתְכֶם מֵאֶרֶץ

mitz-ra-yim li-h'yot la-chem

lei-lo-him. Ani Adonai

Eh-lo-hei-chem.

מִצְרַיִם לִהְיוֹת לָכֶם
לֵאלֹהִים. אֲנִי יהוה
אֱלֹהֵיכֶם:

Be mindful of all My Mitzvot, and do them: so shall you consecrate yourselves to your God. I am your Eternal God who led you out of Egypt to be your God; I am your Eternal God.

REDEMPTION

גְּאֻלָּה

אֱמֶת וֶאֱמוּנָה כָּל־זֹאת, וְקַיָּם עָלֵינוּ כִּי הוּא יי אֱלֹהֵינוּ וְאֵין זוּלָתוֹ,
וַאֲנַחְנוּ יִשְׂרָאֵל עַמּוֹ. הַפּוֹדֵנוּ מִיַּד מְלָכִים, מַלְכֵּנוּ הַגּוֹאֲלֵנוּ מִכַּף כָּל־
הֶעָרִיצִים. הָעֹשֶׂה גְדֹלוֹת עַד אֵין חֵקֶר, וְנִפְלָאוֹת עַד־אֵין מִסְפָּר. הַשָּׂם
נַפְשֵׁנוּ בַּחַיִּים, וְלֹא־נָתַן לַמּוֹט רַגְלֵנוּ. הָעֹשֶׂה לָנוּ נִסִּים בְּפַרְעֹה, אוֹתוֹת
וּמוֹפְתִים בְּאַדְמַת בְּנֵי חָם. וַיּוֹצֵא אֶת־עַמּוֹ יִשְׂרָאֵל מִתּוֹכָם לְחֵרוּת עוֹלָם.
וְרָאוּ בָנָיו וּבְנוֹתָיו גְּבוּרָתוֹ; שִׁבְּחוּ וְהוֹדוּ לִשְׁמוֹ. וּמַלְכוּתוֹ בְּרָצוֹן קִבְּלוּ
עֲלֵיהֶם. מֹשֶׁה וּמִרְיָם וּבְנֵי יִשְׂרָאֵל לְךָ עָנוּ שִׁירָה בְּשִׂמְחָה רַבָּה, וְאָמְרוּ
כֻלָם:

All this we hold to be true and sure; You alone are our God; there is none else, and we are Israel Your people.

You are our Sovereign: You deliver us from the hand of oppressors, and save us from the fist of tyrants,

You do wonders without number, marvels that pass our understanding.

You give us our life; by Your help we survive all who seek our destruction.

You did wonders for us in the land of Egypt, miracles and marvels in the land of Pharaoh,

You led Your people Israel out, forever to serve You in freedom.

When Your children witnessed Your power, they extolled You and gave You thanks; willingly they enthroned You; and, full of joy, Moses, Miriam, and all Israel sang this song:

Mi cha-mo-cha ba-ei-lim, Adonai?

מִי־כָמְכָה בָּאֵלִם, יהוה?

Mi ka-mo-cha, neh-dar ba-ko-desh,

מִי כָּמְכָה, נֶאְדָּר בַּקֹּדֶשׁ,

no-ra t'hi-lot, o-sei feh-leh?

נוֹרָא תְהִלֹּת, עֹשֵׂה פֶלֶא?

Who is like You, Eternal One, among the gods that are worshipped?

Who is like You, majestic in holiness, awesome in splendor, doing wonders?

Mal-chu-t'cha ra-u va-neh-cha,

מַלְכוּתְךָ רָאוּ בָנֶיךָ,

bo-kei-a yam lif-nei Mo-sheh;

בּוֹקֵעַ יָם לִפְנֵי מֹשֶׁה;

zeh ei-li! a-nu v'am-ru:

זֶה אֵלִי! עָנוּ וְאָמְרוּ:

Adonai yim-loch l'o-lam va-ed.

יהוה יִמְלֹךְ לְעֹלָם וָעֶד!

In their escape from the sea, Your children saw Your sovereign might displayed. "This is my God!" they cried. "The Eternal will reign for ever and ever!"

V'neh-eh-mar: Ki fa-da Adonai et

וְנֶאֱמַר: כִּי פָדָה יי אֶת־

Ya-a-kov, u-g'a-lo mi-yad cha-zak

יַעֲקֹב, וּגְאָלוֹ מִיַּד חָזָק

mi-meh-nu. Ba-ruch a-ta Adonai,

מִמֶּנּוּ. בָּרוּךְ אַתָּה, יי,

ga-al Yis-ra-eil.

גָּאַל יִשְׂרָאֵל.

And it has been said: The Eternal One delivered Jacob, and redeemed us from the hand of one stronger than ourselves. We praise You, O God, Redeemer of Israel.

DIVINE PROVIDENCE

הַשְׁכִּיבֵנוּ

הַשְׁכִּיבֵנוּ, יי אֱלֹהֵינוּ, לְשָׁלוֹם, וְהַעֲמִידֵנוּ, מַלְכֵּנוּ, לְחַיִּים. וּפְרוֹשׂ עָלֵינוּ סֻכַּת שְׁלוֹמֶךָ, וְתַקְּנֵנוּ בְּעֵצָה טוֹבָה מִלְּפָנֶיךָ, וְהוֹשִׁיעֵנוּ לְמַעַן שְׁמֶךָ, וְהָגֵן בַּעֲדֵנוּ. וְהָסֵר מֵעָלֵינוּ אוֹיֵב, דֶּבֶר וְחֶרֶב וְרָעָב וְיָגוֹן; וְהָסֵר שָׂטָן מִלְּפָנֵינוּ וּמֵאַחֲרֵינוּ, וּבְצֵל כְּנָפֶיךָ תַּסְתִּירֵנוּ, כִּי אֵל שׁוֹמְרֵנוּ וּמַצִּילֵנוּ אָתָּה, כִּי אֵל מֶלֶךְ חַנּוּן וְרַחוּם אָתָּה. וּשְׁמוֹר צֵאתֵנוּ וּבוֹאֵנוּ לְחַיִּים וּלְשָׁלוֹם, מֵעַתָּה וְעַד עוֹלָם. בָּרוּךְ אַתָּה, יי, שׁוֹמֵר עַמּוֹ יִשְׂרָאֵל לָעַד.

Grant that we may lie down in peace, Eternal God, and raise us up, O Sovereign, to life renewed. Spread over us the shelter of Your peace; guide us with Your good counsel; and for Your name's sake, be our Help.

Shield us from hatred and plague; keep us from war and famine and anguish; subdue our inclination to evil. O God, our Guardian and Helper, our gracious and merciful Ruler, give us refuge in the shadow of Your wings. O guard our coming and our going, that now and always we have life and peace.

We praise You, O God, the Guardian of Israel.

ALL RISE

READER'S KADDISH   חֲצִי קַדִּישׁ

יִתְגַּדַּל וְיִתְקַדַּשׁ שְׁמֵהּ רַבָּא בְּעָלְמָא דִי־בְרָא כִרְעוּתֵהּ, וְיַמְלִיךְ מַלְכוּתֵהּ בְּחַיֵּיכוֹן וּבְיוֹמֵיכוֹן וּבְחַיֵּי דְכָל־בֵּית יִשְׂרָאֵל, בַּעֲגָלָא וּבִזְמַן קָרִיב, וְאִמְרוּ: אָמֵן.

יְהֵא שְׁמֵהּ רַבָּא מְבָרַךְ לְעָלַם וּלְעָלְמֵי עָלְמַיָּא.

יִתְבָּרַךְ וְיִשְׁתַּבַּח, וְיִתְפָּאַר וְיִתְרוֹמַם וְיִתְנַשֵּׂא, וְיִתְהַדָּר וְיִתְעַלֶּה וְיִתְהַלָּל שְׁמֵהּ דְּקֻדְשָׁא, בְּרִיךְ הוּא, לְעֵלָּא מִן־כָּל־בִּרְכָתָא וְשִׁירָתָא, תֻּשְׁבְּחָתָא וְנֶחֱמָתָא דַּאֲמִירָן בְּעָלְמָא, וְאִמְרוּ: אָמֵן.

Yit-ga-dal v'yit-ka-dash sh'mei ra-ba b'al-ma di-v'ra chir-u-tei, v'yam-lich mal-chu-tei b'cha-yei-chon u-v'yo-mei-chon u-v'cha-yei d'chol beit Yis-ra-eil, ba-a-ga-la u-viz-man ka-riv, v'im' ru: A-mein.

    Y'hei sh'mei ra-ba m'va-rach l'al-am u-l'al-mei al-ma-ya.

Yit-ba-rach v'yish-ta-bach v'yit-pa-ar, v'yit-ro-mam, v'yit-na-sei, v'yit-ha-dar, v'yit-a-leh, v'yit-ha-lal sh'mei d'ku-d'sha, b'rich hu, l'ei-la min kol bir-cha-ta v'shi-ra-ta, tush-b'cha-ta v'neh-cheh-ma-ta da-a-mi-ran b'al-ma, v'im' ru: A-mein.

207

Let the glory of God be extolled, let God's great name be hallowed in the world whose creation God willed. May God rule in our own day, in our own lives, and in the life of all Israel, and let us say: Amen.

Let God's great name be praised for ever and ever.

Beyond all the praises, songs, and adorations that we can utter is the Holy One, the Blessed One, whom yet we glorify, honor, and exalt. And let us say: Amen.

T'filah
תְּפִלָּה

אֲדֹנָי, שְׂפָתַי תִּפְתָּח, וּפִי יַגִּיד תְּהִלָּתֶךָ:

Eternal God, open my lips,
that my mouth may declare Your glory.

GOD OF ALL GENERATIONS   אָבוֹת וְאִמָּהוֹת

Ba-ruch a-ta Adonai, Eh-lo-hei-nu   בָּרוּךְ אַתָּה יי, אֱלֹהֵינוּ
vei-lo-hei a-vo-tei-nu v'i-mo-tei-nu: וֵאלֹהֵי אֲבוֹתֵינוּ וְאִמּוֹתֵינוּ:
Eh-lo-hei Av-ra-ham, Eh-lo-hei   אֱלֹהֵי אַבְרָהָם, אֱלֹהֵי
Yitz-chak, vei-lo-hei Ya-a-kov.   יִצְחָק, וֵאלֹהֵי יַעֲקֹב.
Eh-lo-hei Sa-rah, Eh-lo-hei Riv-kah,   אֱלֹהֵי שָׂרָה, אֱלֹהֵי רִבְקָה,
Eh-lo-hei Lei-ah, vei-lo-hei Ra-cheil.   אֱלֹהֵי לֵאָה, וֵאלֹהֵי רָחֵל.
Ha-eil ha-ga-dol ha-gi-bor v'ha-no-ra,   הָאֵל הַגָּדוֹל הַגִּבּוֹר וְהַנּוֹרָא,
eil el-yon. Go-meil cha-sa-dim   אֵל עֶלְיוֹן, גּוֹמֵל חֲסָדִים
to-vim, v'ko-nei ha-kol, v'zo-cheir   טוֹבִים וְקוֹנֵה הַכֹּל, וְזוֹכֵר
chas-dei a-vot v'i-ma-hot, u-mei-vi   חַסְדֵי אָבוֹת וְאִמָּהוֹת, וּמֵבִיא
g'u-la li-v'nei v'nei-hem, l'ma-an   גְאֻלָּה לִבְנֵי בְנֵיהֶם, לְמַעַן
sh'mo, b'a-ha-vah.   שְׁמוֹ בְּאַהֲבָה.

Praised be our God, the God of our fathers and our mothers: God of Abraham, God of Isaac, and God of Jacob; God of Sarah, God of Rebekah, God of Leah and God of Rachel; great, mighty, and awesome God, God supreme.

Ruler of all the living, Your ways are ways of love. You remember the faithfulness of our ancestors, and in love bring redemption to their children's children for the sake of Your name.

BETWEEN ROSH HASHANAH AND YOM KIPPUR ADD:

Zoch-rei-nu l'cha-yim,   זָכְרֵנוּ לְחַיִּים,
meh-lech cha-feitz ba-cha-yim,   מֶלֶךְ חָפֵץ בַּחַיִּים,
v'chot'vei-nu b'sei-fer ha-cha-yim,   וְכָתְבֵנוּ בְּסֵפֶר הַחַיִּים,
l'ma-an-n'cha Eh-lo-him cha-yim.   לְמַעַנְךָ אֱלֹהִים חַיִּים.

Remember us unto life, Sovereign who delights in life, and inscribe us in the Book of Life, that Your will may prevail, O God of life.

Meh-lech o-zeir u-mo-shi-a u-ma-gein. מֶלֶךְ עוֹזֵר וּמוֹשִׁיעַ וּמָגֵן.

Ba-ruch a-ta Adonai, בָּרוּךְ אַתָּה, יי,

ma-gein Av-ra-ham v'ez-rat Sa-rah. מָגֵן אַבְרָהָם וְעֶזְרַת שָׂרָה.

You are our Sovereign and our Help, our Redeemer and our Shield.
We praise You, Eternal One, Shield of Abraham, Protector of Sarah.

GOD'S POWER גְּבוּרוֹת

A-ta gi-bor l'o-lam, Adonai, אַתָּה גִּבּוֹר לְעוֹלָם, אֲדֹנָי,

m'cha-yei ha-kol a-ta, rav- מְחַיֵּה הַכֹּל אַתָּה, רַב

l'ho-shi-a. M'chal-keil cha-yim לְהוֹשִׁיעַ. מְכַלְכֵּל חַיִּים

b'cheh-sed, m'cha-yei ha-kol בְּחֶסֶד, מְחַיֵּה הַכֹּל

b'ra-cha-mim ra-bim. So-meich בְּרַחֲמִים רַבִּים. סוֹמֵךְ

no-f'lim, v'ro-fei cho-lim, נוֹפְלִים, וְרוֹפֵא חוֹלִים,

u-ma-tir a-su-rim, u-m'ka-yeim וּמַתִּיר אֲסוּרִים, וּמְקַיֵּם

eh-mu-na-toh li-shei-nei a-far. אֱמוּנָתוֹ לִישֵׁנֵי עָפָר.

Mi cha-mo-cha ba-al g'vu-rot, מִי כָמוֹךָ בַּעַל גְּבוּרוֹת,

u-mi do-meh lach, meh-lech וּמִי דוֹמֶה לָּךְ, מֶלֶךְ

mei-mit u-m'cha-yeh u-matz-mi-ach מֵמִית וּמְחַיֶּה וּמַצְמִיחַ

y'shu-a! יְשׁוּעָה?

Eternal is Your might, O God; all life is Your gift; great is Your power to save!

With love You sustain the living, with great compassion give life to all. You send help to the falling and healing to the sick; You bring freedom to the captive and keep faith with those who sleep in the dust.

Who is like You, Mighty One, Author of life and death, Source of salvation!

BETWEEN ROSH HASHANAH AND YOM KIPPUR ADD:

Mi cha-mo-cha, av ha-ra-cha-mim,
zo-cheir y'tzu-rav l'cha-yim
b'ra-cha-mim?

מִי כָמוֹךָ, אַב הָרַחֲמִים,
זוֹכֵר יְצוּרָיו לְחַיִּים
בְּרַחֲמִים?

Who is like You, Source of mercy? In compassion You sustain the life of Your children.

V'neh-eh-man a-ta l'ha-cha-yot
ha-kol. Ba-ruch a-ta, Adonai,
m'cha-yei ha-kol.

וְנֶאֱמָן אַתָּה לְהַחֲיוֹת
הַכֹּל. בָּרוּךְ אַתָּה, יי,
מְחַיֵּה הַכֹּל.

We praise You, O God, the Source of life.

THE HOLINESS OF GOD   קְדוּשַׁת הַשֵּׁם

אַתָּה קָדוֹשׁ וְשִׁמְךָ קָדוֹשׁ, וּקְדוֹשִׁים בְּכָל־יוֹם יְהַלְלוּךָ סֶּלָה.
בָּרוּךְ אַתָּה, יי, הָאֵל הַקָּדוֹשׁ.

*BETWEEN ROSH HASHANAH AND YOM KIPPUR CONCLUDE:

בָּרוּךְ אַתָּה, יי, הַמֶּלֶךְ הַקָּדוֹשׁ.

You are holy, Your name is holy, and those who strive to be holy declare Your glory day by day.

*We praise You, Eternal One, the holy God.

*BETWEEN ROSH HASHANAH AND YOM KIPPUR CONCLUDE:

We praise You, Eternal One: You rule in holiness.

ALL ARE SEATED

INTERMEDIATE BENEDICTIONS

❧ *The Intermediate Benedictions, through page 215, may be recited silently.*

WISDOM   בִּינָה

אַתָּה חוֹנֵן לְאָדָם דַּעַת וּמְלַמֵּד לֶאֱנוֹשׁ בִּינָה. חָנֵּנוּ מֵאִתְּךָ דֵּעָה, בִּינָה וְהַשְׂכֵּל. בָּרוּךְ אַתָּה, יְיָ, חוֹנֵן הַדָּעַת.

BY YOUR GRACE we have the power to gain knowledge and to learn wisdom. Favor us with knowledge, wisdom, and insight, for You are their Source.

We praise You, O God, gracious giver of knowledge.

REPENTANCE   תְּשׁוּבָה

הֲשִׁיבֵנוּ אָבִינוּ לְתוֹרָתֶךָ, וְקָרְבֵנוּ מַלְכֵּנוּ לַעֲבוֹדָתֶךָ, וְהַחֲזִירֵנוּ בִּתְשׁוּבָה שְׁלֵמָה לְפָנֶיךָ. בָּרוּךְ אַתָּה, יְיָ, הָרוֹצֶה בִּתְשׁוּבָה.

HELP US, OUR CREATOR, to return to Your Teaching; draw us near, our Sovereign, to Your service; and bring us back into Your presence in perfect repentance.

We praise You, O God: You delight in repentance.

FORGIVENESS   סְלִיחָה

סְלַח־לָנוּ אָבִינוּ כִּי חָטָאנוּ, מְחַל־לָנוּ מַלְכֵּנוּ כִּי פָשָׁעְנוּ, כִּי מוֹחֵל וְסוֹלֵחַ אָתָּה. בָּרוּךְ אַתָּה, יְיָ, חַנּוּן הַמַּרְבֶּה לִסְלֹחַ.

FORGIVE US, OUR CREATOR, for we have sinned; pardon us, our Sovereign, for we have transgressed; for You are One who pardons and forgives.

We praise You, O God, gracious and quick to forgive.

REDEMPTION   גְּאֻלָּה

רְאֵה בְעָנְיֵנוּ וְרִיבָה רִיבֵנוּ, וּגְאָלֵנוּ מְהֵרָה לְמַעַן שְׁמֶךָ, כִּי גּוֹאֵל חָזָק אָתָּה. בָּרוּךְ אַתָּה, יְיָ, גּוֹאֵל יִשְׂרָאֵל.

LOOK UPON OUR AFFLICTION and help us in our need; O mighty Redeemer, redeem us speedily for Your name's sake.

We praise You, O God, Redeemer of Israel.

HEALTH   רְפוּאָה

רְפָאֵנוּ, יי, וְנֵרָפֵא, הוֹשִׁיעֵנוּ וְנִוָּשֵׁעָה, וְהַעֲלֵה רְפוּאָה שְׁלֵמָה לְכָל־
מַכּוֹתֵינוּ. בָּרוּךְ אַתָּה, יי, רוֹפֵא הַחוֹלִים.

HEAL US, O God, and we shall be healed; save us, and we shall be saved; grant us a perfect healing for all our infirmities.*

We praise You, O God, Healer of the sick.

*Here the worshipper might add a personal prayer for one who is ill.

ABUNDANCE   בִּרְכַּת הַשָּׁנִים

בָּרֵךְ עָלֵינוּ, יי אֱלֹהֵינוּ, אֶת־הַשָּׁנָה הַזֹּאת וְאֶת־כָּל־מִינֵי תְבוּאָתָה
לְטוֹבָה. וְתֵן בְּרָכָה עַל־פְּנֵי הָאֲדָמָה וְשַׂבְּעֵנוּ מִטּוּבֶךָ. בָּרוּךְ אַתָּה, יי,
מְבָרֵךְ הַשָּׁנִים.

BLESS THIS YEAR FOR US, Eternal God: may its produce bring us well-being. Bestow Your blessing on the earth that all Your children may share its abundance in peace.

We praise You, O God, for You bless earth's seasons from year to year.

FREEDOM   חֵרוּת

תְּקַע בְּשׁוֹפָר גָּדוֹל לְחֵרוּתֵנוּ, וְשָׂא נֵס לִפְדּוֹת עֲשׁוּקֵינוּ, וְקוֹל דְּרוֹר יִשָּׁמַע
בְּאַרְבַּע כַּנְפוֹת הָאָרֶץ. בָּרוּךְ אַתָּה, יי, פּוֹדֶה עֲשׁוּקִים.

SOUND THE GREAT SHOFAR to proclaim freedom, raise high the banner of liberation for the oppressed, and let the song of liberty be heard in the four corners of the earth.

We praise You, O God, Redeemer of the oppressed.

JUSTICE   מִשְׁפָּט

עַל שׁוֹפְטֵי אֶרֶץ שְׁפוֹךְ רוּחֶךָ, וְהַדְרִיכֵם בְּמִשְׁפְּטֵי צִדְקֶךָ, וּמְלוֹךְ עָלֵינוּ
אַתָּה לְבַדֶּךָ, בְּחֶסֶד וּבְרַחֲמִים. בָּרוּךְ אַתָּה, יי, מֶלֶךְ אוֹהֵב צְדָקָה
וּמִשְׁפָּט.

BESTOW YOUR SPIRIT upon the rulers of all lands; guide them, that they may govern justly. Then shall love and compassion be enthroned among us.

We praise You, Eternal One, the Sovereign God who loves righteousness and justice.

ON EVIL

עַל הָרִשְׁעָה

וְלָרִשְׁעָה אַל־תְּהִי תִקְוָה, וְהַתּוֹעִים אֵלֶיךָ יָשׁוּבוּ, וּמַלְכוּת זָדוֹן מְהֵרָה תְשַׁבֵּר. תַּקֵּן מַלְכוּתְךָ בְּתוֹכֵנוּ, בְּקָרוֹב בְּיָמֵינוּ לְעוֹלָם וָעֶד. בָּרוּךְ אַתָּה, יי, הַמַּשְׁבִּית רֶשַׁע מִן־הָאָרֶץ.

LET THE REIGN OF EVIL afflict us no more. May every errant heart find its way back to You. O help us to shatter the dominion of arrogance, to raise up a better world, where virtue will ennoble the life of Your children.

We praise You, O God, whose will it is that evil may vanish from the earth.

THE RIGHTEOUS

עַל הַצַּדִּיקִים

עַל־הַצַּדִּיקִים וְעַל־הַחֲסִידִים וְעַל גֵּרֵי הַצֶּדֶק וְעָלֵינוּ יֶהֱמוּ רַחֲמֶיךָ, יי אֱלֹהֵינוּ, וְתֵן שָׂכָר טוֹב לְכָל הַבּוֹטְחִים בְּשִׁמְךָ בֶּאֱמֶת, וְשִׂים חֶלְקֵנוּ עִמָּהֶם לְעוֹלָם. בָּרוּךְ אַתָּה, יי, מִשְׁעָן וּמִבְטָח לַצַּדִּיקִים.

FOR THE RIGHTEOUS AND FAITHFUL of all humankind, for all who join themselves to our people, for all who put their trust in You, and for all honest men and women, we ask Your favor, Eternal God. Grant that we may always be numbered among them.

We praise You, O God, Staff and Support of the righteous.

JERUSALEM

בּוֹנֵה יְרוּשָׁלַיִם

שְׁכוֹן, יי אֱלֹהֵינוּ, בְּתוֹךְ יְרוּשָׁלַיִם עִירֶךָ, וִיהִי שָׁלוֹם בִּשְׁעָרֶיהָ, וְשַׁלְוָה בְּלֵב יוֹשְׁבֶיהָ, וְתוֹרָתְךָ מִצִּיּוֹן תֵּצֵא, וּדְבָרְךָ מִירוּשָׁלָיִם. בָּרוּךְ אַתָּה, יי, בּוֹנֵה יְרוּשָׁלָיִם.

LET YOUR PRESENCE be manifest in Jerusalem, Your city. Establish peace in her gates and quietness in the hearts of all who dwell there. Let Your Torah go forth from Zion, Your word from Jerusalem.

We praise You, O God, Builder of Jerusalem.

DELIVERANCE   יְשׁוּעָה

אֶת־צֶמַח צְדָקָה מְהֵרָה תַצְמִיחַ, וְקֶרֶן יְשׁוּעָה תָּרוּם כִּנְאֻמֶךָ, כִּי לִישׁוּעָתְךָ קִוִּינוּ כָּל־הַיּוֹם. בָּרוּךְ אַתָּה, יי, מַצְמִיחַ קֶרֶן יְשׁוּעָה.

LET THE PLANT OF RIGHTEOUSNESS blossom and flourish, and let the light of deliverance shine forth according to Your word: we await Your deliverance all the day.

We praise You, O God: You will cause the light of deliverance to dawn for all the world.

PRAYER   שׁוֹמֵעַ תְּפִלָּה

שְׁמַע קוֹלֵנוּ, יי אֱלֹהֵינוּ, חוּס וְרַחֵם עָלֵינוּ, וְקַבֵּל בְּרַחֲמִים וּבְרָצוֹן אֶת־תְּפִלָּתֵנוּ כִּי אֵל שׁוֹמֵעַ תְּפִלּוֹת וְתַחֲנוּנִים אָתָּה. בָּרוּךְ אַתָּה, יי, שׁוֹמֵעַ תְּפִלָּה.

HEAR OUR VOICE, Eternal God; have compassion upon us, and accept our prayer with favor and mercy, for You are a God who hears prayer and supplication.

We praise You, O God: You hearken to prayer.

❧

WORSHIP   עֲבוֹדָה

רְצֵה, יי אֱלֹהֵינוּ, בְּעַמְּךָ יִשְׂרָאֵל, וּתְפִלָּתָם בְּאַהֲבָה תְקַבֵּל, וּתְהִי לְרָצוֹן תָּמִיד עֲבוֹדַת יִשְׂרָאֵל עַמֶּךָ. בָּרוּךְ אַתָּה, יי, הַמַּחֲזִיר שְׁכִינָתוֹ לְצִיּוֹן.

Eternal God, look with favor upon us, and may our service be acceptable to You. We praise You, O God, whom alone we serve with reverence.

ON ROSH CHODESH AND CHOL HA-MO-EID :

אֱלֹהֵינוּ וֵאלֹהֵי אֲבוֹתֵינוּ וְאִמּוֹתֵינוּ, יַעֲלֶה וְיָבֹא וְיִזָּכֵר זִכְרוֹנֵנוּ וְזִכְרוֹן כָּל־עַמְּךָ בֵּית יִשְׂרָאֵל לְפָנֶיךָ לְטוֹבָה לְחֵן לְחֶסֶד וּלְרַחֲמִים, לְחַיִּים וּלְשָׁלוֹם בְּיוֹם . . .

Our God , God of our fathers and our mothers, be mindful of Your people Israel on this . . .

♦ first day of the new month,   רֹאשׁ הַחֹדֶשׁ הַזֶּה.

♦ festival of Pesach,   חַג הַמַּצּוֹת הַזֶּה.

♦ festival of Sukkot,   חַג הַסֻּכּוֹת הַזֶּה.

and renew in us love and compassion, goodness, life, and peace.

זָכְרֵנוּ, יי אֱלֹהֵינוּ, בּוֹ לְטוֹבָה. אָמֵן.

This day remember us for well-being. *Amen.*

וּפָקְדֵנוּ בוֹ לִבְרָכָה. אָמֵן.

This day bless us with Your nearness. *Amen.*

וְהוֹשִׁיעֵנוּ בוֹ לְחַיִּים. אָמֵן.

This day help us to lead a full life. *Amen.*

THANKSGIVING   הוֹדָאָה

מוֹדִים אֲנַחְנוּ לָךְ, שָׁאַתָּה הוּא יי אֱלֹהֵינוּ וֵאלֹהֵי אֲבוֹתֵינוּ וְאִמּוֹתֵינוּ לְעוֹלָם וָעֶד. צוּר חַיֵּינוּ, מָגֵן יִשְׁעֵנוּ, אַתָּה הוּא לְדוֹר וָדוֹר. נוֹדֶה לְךָ וּנְסַפֵּר תְּהִלָּתֶךָ, עַל־חַיֵּינוּ הַמְּסוּרִים בְּיָדֶךָ, וְעַל־נִשְׁמוֹתֵינוּ הַפְּקוּדוֹת לָךְ, וְעַל־נִסֶּיךָ שֶׁבְּכָל־יוֹם עִמָּנוּ, וְעַל־נִפְלְאוֹתֶיךָ וְטוֹבוֹתֶיךָ שֶׁבְּכָל־עֵת, עֶרֶב וָבֹקֶר וְצָהֳרָיִם. הַטּוֹב: כִּי לֹא־כָלוּ רַחֲמֶיךָ, וְהַמְרַחֵם: כִּי־לֹא תַמּוּ חֲסָדֶיךָ, מֵעוֹלָם קִוִּינוּ לָךְ. וְעַל כֻּלָּם יִתְבָּרַךְ וְיִתְרוֹמַם שִׁמְךָ, מַלְכֵּנוּ, תָּמִיד לְעוֹלָם וָעֶד.

BETWEEN ROSH HASHANAH AND YOM KIPPUR ADD:

וּכְתוֹב לְחַיִּים טוֹבִים כָּל־בְּנֵי בְרִיתֶךָ.

וְכֹל הַחַיִּים יוֹדְוּךָ סֶּלָה, וִיהַלְלוּ אֶת שִׁמְךָ בֶּאֱמֶת, הָאֵל יְשׁוּעָתֵנוּ וְעֶזְרָתֵנוּ סֶלָה. בָּרוּךְ אַתָּה, יי, הַטּוֹב שִׁמְךָ וּלְךָ נָאֶה לְהוֹדוֹת.

We gratefully acknowledge that You are our God and the God of our people, the God of all the generations. You are the Rock of our life, the Power that shields us in every age. We thank You and sing Your praises: for our lives, which are in Your hand; for our souls, which are in Your keeping; for the signs of Your presence we encounter every day; and for Your wondrous gifts at all times, morning, noon, and night. You are Goodness: Your mercies never end; You are Compassion: Your love will never fail. You have always been our hope.

For all these things, O Sovereign God, let Your name be for ever exalted and blessed.

BETWEEN ROSH HASHANAH AND YOM KIPPUR ADD:

May all who are loyal to Your covenant be inscribed for a good life.

O God our Redeemer and Helper, let all who live affirm You and praise Your name in truth. Eternal God, whose nature is Goodness, we give You thanks and praise.

ON CHANUKAH ADD:

עַל הַנִּסִּים וְעַל הַפֻּרְקָן, וְעַל הַגְּבוּרוֹת וְעַל הַתְּשׁוּעוֹת, וְעַל הַמִּלְחָמוֹת, שֶׁעָשִׂיתָ לַאֲבוֹתֵינוּ וּלְאִמּוֹתֵינוּ בַּיָּמִים הָהֵם וּבַזְּמַן הַזֶּה. בִּימֵי מַתִּתְיָהוּ בֶּן־יוֹחָנָן כֹּהֵן גָּדוֹל, חַשְׁמוֹנַאי וּבָנָיו, כְּשֶׁעָמְדָה מַלְכוּת יָוָן הָרְשָׁעָה עַל עַמְּךָ יִשְׂרָאֵל, לְהַשְׁכִּיחָם תּוֹרָתֶךָ וּלְהַעֲבִירָם מֵחֻקֵּי רְצוֹנֶךָ. וְאַתָּה בְּרַחֲמֶיךָ הָרַבִּים עָמַדְתָּ לָהֶם בְּעֵת צָרָתָם. מַסַרְתָּ גִבּוֹרִים בְּיַד חַלָּשִׁים, וְרַבִּים בְּיַד מְעַטִּים, וְזֵדִים בְּיַד עוֹסְקֵי תוֹרָתֶךָ. וּלְךָ עָשִׂיתָ שֵׁם גָּדוֹל וְקָדוֹשׁ בְּעוֹלָמֶךָ, וּלְעַמְּךָ יִשְׂרָאֵל עָשִׂיתָ תְּשׁוּעָה גְדוֹלָה וּפֻרְקָן כְּהַיּוֹם הַזֶּה. וְאַחַר כֵּן בָּאוּ בָנֶיךָ לִדְבִיר בֵּיתֶךָ, וּפִנּוּ אֶת־הֵיכָלֶךָ, וְטִהֲרוּ אֶת־מִקְדָּשֶׁךָ, וְהִדְלִיקוּ נֵרוֹת בְּחַצְרוֹת קָדְשֶׁךָ, וְקָבְעוּ שְׁמוֹנַת יְמֵי חֲנֻכָּה אֵלּוּ, לְהוֹדוֹת וּלְהַלֵּל לְשִׁמְךָ הַגָּדוֹל.

In days of old at this season You saved our people by wonders and mighty deeds. In the days of Mattathias the Hasmonean, the tyrannic Empire sought to destroy our people Israel, by making them forget their Torah, and by forcing them to abandon their ancient way of life.

Through the power of Your spirit
the weak defeated the strong,
the few prevailed over the many,
and the righteous were victorious.
Then Your children returned to Your house
to purify the sanctuary
and to kindle its lights.
And they dedicated these days
to give thanks and praise
to Your majestic glory.

ON PURIM ADD:

עַל הַנִּסִּים וְעַל הַפֻּרְקָן, וְעַל הַגְּבוּרוֹת וְעַל הַתְּשׁוּעוֹת, וְעַל הַמִּלְחָמוֹת, שֶׁעָשִׂיתָ לַאֲבוֹתֵינוּ וּלְאִמּוֹתֵינוּ בַּיָּמִים הָהֵם בַּזְּמַן הַזֶּה. בִּימֵי מָרְדְּכַי וְאֶסְתֵּר בְּשׁוּשַׁן הַבִּירָה, כְּשֶׁעָמַד עֲלֵיהֶם הָמָן הָרָשָׁע, בִּקֵּשׁ לְהַשְׁמִיד לַהֲרוֹג וּלְאַבֵּד אֶת־כָּל־הַיְּהוּדִים, מִנַּעַר וְעַד־זָקֵן, טַף וְנָשִׁים, בְּיוֹם אֶחָד, בִּשְׁלֹשָׁה עָשָׂר לְחֹדֶשׁ שְׁנֵים־עָשָׂר, הוּא־חֹדֶשׁ אֲדָר, וּשְׁלָלָם לָבוֹז. וְאַתָּה בְּרַחֲמֶיךָ הָרַבִּים הֵפַרְתָּ אֶת־עֲצָתוֹ וְקִלְקַלְתָּ אֶת־מַחֲשַׁבְתּוֹ.

In days of old at this season You saved our people by wonders and mighty deeds.

In the days of Mordechai and Esther, the wicked Haman arose in Persia, plotting the destruction of all the Jews, young and old alike. He planned to destroy them in a single day, the thirteenth of Adar, and to plunder their possessions.

But through Your great mercy his plan was thwarted, his scheme frustrated. We therefore thank and bless You, the great and gracious God!

PEACE　　　　　　　　　　　　　　　　　　　　בִּרְכַּת שָׁלוֹם

שָׁלוֹם רָב עַל־יִשְׂרָאֵל עַמְּךָ תָּשִׂים לְעוֹלָם, כִּי אַתָּה הוּא מֶלֶךְ אֲדוֹן לְכָל־הַשָּׁלוֹם. וְטוֹב בְּעֵינֶיךָ לְבָרֵךְ אֶת־עַמְּךָ יִשְׂרָאֵל בְּכָל־עֵת וּבְכָל־שָׁעָה בִּשְׁלוֹמֶךָ. *בָּרוּךְ אַתָּה, יי, הַמְבָרֵךְ אֶת־עַמּוֹ יִשְׂרָאֵל בַּשָּׁלוֹם.

BETWEEN ROSH HASHANAH AND YOM KIPPUR CONCLUDE:

בְּסֵפֶר חַיִּים וּבְרָכָה נִכָּתֵב לְחַיִּים טוֹבִים וּלְשָׁלוֹם. בָּרוּךְ אַתָּה, יי, עוֹשֵׂה הַשָּׁלוֹם.

O Sovereign Source of peace, let Israel Your people know enduring peace, for it is good in Your sight to bless Israel and all the peoples continually with Your peace.

*We praise You, O God, the Source of peace.

BETWEEN ROSH HASHANAH AND YOM KIPPUR CONCLUDE:

Inscribe us in the Book of life, blessing, and peace. We praise You, O God, the Source of peace.

SILENT PRAYER

אֱלֹהַי, נְצֹר לְשׁוֹנִי מֵרָע, וּשְׂפָתַי מִדַּבֵּר מִרְמָה. וְלִמְקַלְלַי נַפְשִׁי תִדּוֹם וְנַפְשִׁי כֶּעָפָר לַכֹּל תִּהְיֶה. פְּתַח לִבִּי בְּתוֹרָתֶךָ, וּבְמִצְוֹתֶיךָ תִּרְדֹּף נַפְשִׁי. וְכָל־הַחוֹשְׁבִים עָלַי רָעָה, מְהֵרָה הָפֵר עֲצָתָם וְקַלְקֵל מַחֲשַׁבְתָּם. עֲשֵׂה לְמַעַן שְׁמֶךָ, עֲשֵׂה לְמַעַן יְמִינֶךָ, עֲשֵׂה לְמַעַן קְדֻשָּׁתֶךָ, עֲשֵׂה לְמַעַן תּוֹרָתֶךָ; לְמַעַן יֵחָלְצוּן יְדִידֶיךָ, הוֹשִׁיעָה יְמִינְךָ וַעֲנֵנִי.

O God, keep my tongue from evil and my lips from deceit. Help me to be silent in the face of derision, humble in the presence of all. Open my heart to Your Torah, and I will hasten to do Your Mitzvot. Save me with Your power; in time of trouble be my answer, that those who love You may rejoice.

ﭏ ﭏ

יִהְיוּ לְרָצוֹן אִמְרֵי־פִי וְהֶגְיוֹן לִבִּי לְפָנֶיךָ, יהוה, צוּרִי וְגֹאֲלִי.

May the words of my mouth, and the meditations of my heart, be acceptable to You, O God, my Rock and my Redeemer.

ﭏ

עֹשֶׂה שָׁלוֹם בִּמְרוֹמָיו, הוּא יַעֲשֶׂה שָׁלוֹם עָלֵינוּ וְעַל־כָּל־יִשְׂרָאֵל,
וְאִמְרוּ אָמֵן.

May the One who causes peace to reign in the high heavens, cause peace to reign among us, all Israel, and all the world.

ﭏ Prayers for the House of Mourning begin on page 233.

ﭏ Aleinu is on page 237 or page 239.

Morning Service

תְּפִלַּת שַׁחֲרִית

FOR THOSE WHO WEAR A TALLIT

בָּרְכִי נַפְשִׁי אֶת יְיָ! יְיָ אֱלֹהַי, גָּדַלְתָּ מְּאֹד! הוֹד וְהָדָר לָבָשְׁתָּ, עֹטֶה אוֹר כַּשַּׂלְמָה, נוֹטֶה שָׁמַיִם כַּיְרִיעָה.

Praise the Eternal One, O my soul! O God, You are very great! Arrayed in glory and majesty, You wrap Yourself in light as with a garment, You stretch out the heavens like a curtain.

בָּרוּךְ אַתָּה יְיָ, אֱלֹהֵינוּ מֶלֶךְ הָעוֹלָם, אֲשֶׁר קִדְּשָׁנוּ בְּמִצְוֹתָיו וְצִוָּנוּ לְהִתְעַטֵּף בַּצִּיצִת.

We praise You, Eternal God, Sovereign of the universe: You hallow us with Your Mitzvot, and teach us to wrap ourselves in the fringed Tallit.

❦ ❦

MEDITATION

Infinite One, Your greatness surpasses our understanding, yet at times we feel Your nearness.

The signs of Your presence overwhelm us; flooded by awe and wonder, still we feel within us a kinship with the divine.

And so we turn to You, looking at the world about us, and inward to the world within us, there to find You, and from Your presence gain life and strength.

Morning Blessings

ברכות הַשַׁחַר

FOR THE BLESSING OF WORSHIP   מה טבו

Mah to-vu o-ha-leh-cha Ya-a-kov,
mish-k'no-teh-cha, Yis-ra-eil!

מַה־טֹבוּ אֹהָלֶיךָ, יַעֲקֹב,
מִשְׁכְּנֹתֶיךָ, יִשְׂרָאֵל!

Va-a-ni, b'rov chas-d'cha
a-vo vei-teh-cha,
esh-ta-cha-veh el hei-chal kod-sh'cha
b'-yir-a-teh-cha.

וַאֲנִי, בְּרֹב חַסְדְּךָ
אָבֹא בֵיתֶךָ,
אֶשְׁתַּחֲוֶה אֶל־הֵיכַל קָדְשְׁךָ
בְּיִרְאָתֶךָ.

Adonai a-hav-ti m'on bei-te-cha
u-m'kom mish-kan k'vo-deh-cha.
Va-a-ni esh-ta-cha-veh v'ech-ra-ah,
ev-r'chah li-f'nei Adonai o-si.

יהוה, אָהַבְתִּי מְעוֹן בֵּיתֶךָ,
וּמְקוֹם מִשְׁכַּן כְּבוֹדֶךָ.
וַאֲנִי אֶשְׁתַּחֲוֶה וְאֶכְרָעָה,
אֶבְרְכָה לִפְנֵי־יהוה עֹשִׂי.

Va-a-ni t'fi-la-ti l'cha
Adonai eit ra-tson.
Eh-lo-him b'rov chas-deh-cha
a-nei-ni beh-eh-met yish-eh-cha.

וַאֲנִי תְפִלָּתִי לְךָ,
יהוה, עֵת רָצוֹן.
אֱלֹהִים בְּרָב־חַסְדֶּךָ,
עֲנֵנִי בֶּאֱמֶת יִשְׁעֶךָ.

How lovely are Your tents, O Jacob, your dwelling-places, O Israel!

As for me, O God abounding in grace, I enter Your house to worship with awe in Your sacred place.

I love Your house, Eternal One, the dwelling-place of Your glory; humbly I worship You, humbly I seek blessing from God my Maker.

To You, Eternal One, goes my prayer: may this be a time of Your favor. In Your great love, O God, answer me with Your saving truth.

FOR HEALTH   אֲשֶׁר יָצַר

בָּרוּךְ אַתָּה יי, אֱלֹהֵינוּ מֶלֶךְ הָעוֹלָם, אֲשֶׁר יָצַר אֶת־הָאָדָם בְּחָכְמָה,
וּבָרָא בוֹ נְקָבִים נְקָבִים, חֲלוּלִים חֲלוּלִים. גָּלוּי וְיָדוּעַ לִפְנֵי כִסֵּא כְבוֹדֶךָ,
שֶׁאִם יִפָּתֵחַ אֶחָד מֵהֶם, אוֹ יִסָּתֵם אֶחָד מֵהֶם, אִי אֶפְשָׁר לְהִתְקַיֵּם

וְלַעֲמוֹד לְפָנֶיךָ. בָּרוּךְ אַתָּה יי, רוֹפֵא כָל־בָּשָׂר וּמַפְלִיא לַעֲשׂוֹת.

We praise You, Eternal God, Sovereign of the universe: With divine wisdom You have made our bodies, combining veins, arteries, and vital organs into a finely balanced network.

Were one of them to fail, O wondrous Maker Sustainer of life—how well we are aware!—we would lack the strength to stand in life before You.

Source of our health and strength, we give You thanks and praise.

FOR TORAH   לַעֲסוֹק בְּדִבְרֵי תוֹרָה

בָּרוּךְ אַתָּה יי, אֱלֹהֵינוּ מֶלֶךְ הָעוֹלָם, אֲשֶׁר קִדְּשָׁנוּ בְּמִצְוֹתָיו וְצִוָּנוּ לַעֲסוֹק בְּדִבְרֵי תוֹרָה.

We praise You, Eternal God, Sovereign of the universe: You hallow us with the gift of Torah and command us to immerse ourselves in its words.

Eternal our God, make the words of Your Torah sweet to us, and to the House of Israel, Your people, that we and our children may be lovers of Your name and students of Your Torah. We praise You, O God, Teacher of Torah to Your people Israel.

ALL RISE

Sh'ma and its Blessings
שְׁמַע וּבְרְכוֹתֶיהָ

בָּרְכוּ אֶת־יי הַמְבֹרָךְ!

Ba-r'chu et Adonai ha-m'vo-rach!

Praise the One to whom our praise is due!

בָּרוּךְ יי הַמְבֹרָךְ לְעוֹלָם וָעֶד!

Baruch Adonai ha-m'vo-rach l'o-lam va-ed!

Praised be the One to whom our praise is due, now and for ever!

CREATION   יוֹצֵר

בָּרוּךְ אַתָּה יי, אֱלֹהֵינוּ מֶלֶךְ הָעוֹלָם, יוֹצֵר אוֹר וּבוֹרֵא חְשֶׁךְ, עֹשֶׂה שָׁלוֹם
וּבוֹרֵא אֶת־הַכֹּל. הַמֵּאִיר לָאָרֶץ וְלַדָּרִים עָלֶיהָ בְּרַחֲמִים, וּבְטוּבוֹ מְחַדֵּשׁ
בְּכָל־יוֹם תָּמִיד מַעֲשֵׂה בְרֵאשִׁית. מָה רַבּוּ מַעֲשֶׂיךָ, יי! כֻּלָּם
בְּחָכְמָה עָשִׂיתָ, מָלְאָה הָאָרֶץ קִנְיָנֶךָ. תִּתְבָּרַךְ, יי אֱלֹהֵינוּ, עַל־שֶׁבַח
מַעֲשֵׂה יָדֶיךָ, וְעַל־מְאוֹרֵי־אוֹר שֶׁעָשִׂיתָ: יְפָאֲרוּךָ. סֶלָה. בָּרוּךְ אַתָּה, יי,
יוֹצֵר הַמְּאוֹרוֹת.

°Heaven and earth, O God, are the work of Your hands. The roaring seas and the life within them issue forth from Your creative will. The universe is one vast wonder proclaiming Your wisdom and singing Your greatness.

The mysteries of life and death, of growth and decay, alike display the miracle of Your creative power. God of life, the whole universe is Your dwelling-place, all being a hymn to Your glory!

REVELATION אַהֲבָה רַבָּה

אַהֲבָה רַבָּה אֲהַבְתָּנוּ, יי אֱלֹהֵינוּ, חֶמְלָה גְדוֹלָה וִיתֵרָה חָמַלְתָּ עָלֵינוּ.
אָבִינוּ מַלְכֵּנוּ, בַּעֲבוּר אֲבוֹתֵינוּ וְאִמּוֹתֵינוּ שֶׁבָּטְחוּ בְךָ וַתְּלַמְּדֵם חֻקֵּי
חַיִּים, כֵּן תְּחָנֵּנוּ וּתְלַמְּדֵנוּ. וְתֵן בְּלִבֵּנוּ לִשְׁמֹעַ, לִהֲבִין וּלְהַשְׂכִּיל,
לִלְמֹד, לְשַׁמֵּר וְלַעֲשׂוֹת וּלְקַיֵּם אֶת־כָּל־דִּבְרֵי תוֹרָתֶךָ בְּאַהֲבָה.
וְהָאֵר עֵינֵינוּ בְּתוֹרָתֶךָ, וְדַבֵּק לִבֵּנוּ לְאַהֲבָה וּלְיִרְאָה אֶת־שְׁמֶךָ.
כִּי בָנוּ בָחַרְתָּ לְיַחֶדְךָ בְּאַהֲבָה. בָּרוּךְ אַתָּה, יי, הַבּוֹחֵר בְּעַמּוֹ
יִשְׂרָאֵל בְּאַהֲבָה.

°In the human heart, too, You reign supreme. Above the storms of anger and hate that shake our world, we hear Your voice proclaim the law of justice and love.

May our eyes be open to Your truth, our spirits alive to Your teaching, our hearts united to serve You.

May we find the will to consecrate ourselves anew to the task of all the generations: to speed the dawn of a new day when all will be united in friendship and peace, and with one accord acclaim You their Eternal God.

שְׁמַע יִשְׂרָאֵל: יהוה אֱלֹהֵינוּ יהוה אֶחָד!

**Hear, O Israel: the Eternal One is our God,
the Eternal God alone!**

בָּרוּךְ שֵׁם כְּבוֹד מַלְכוּתוֹ לְעוֹלָם וָעֶד!

Blessed is God's glorious majesty for ever and ever!

ALL ARE SEATED

V'a-hav-ta et Adonai eh-lo-heh-cha
b'chol l'va-v'cha u-v'chol naf-sh'cha
u-v'chol m'o-deh-cha. V'ha-yu
ha-d'va-rim ha-ei-leh a-sher a-no-chi
m'tza-v'cha ha-yom al l'va-veh-cha.
V'shi-nan-tam l'va-neh-cha
v'di-bar-ta bam b'shiv-t'cha
b'vei-teh-cha u-v'lech-t'cha
va-deh-rech u-v'shoch-b'cha
u-v'ku-meh-cha. U-k'shar-tam l'ot
al ya-deh-cha v'ha-yu l'to-ta-fot bein
ei-neh-cha; u-ch'tav-tam al m'zu-zot
bei-teh-cha u-vi-sh'a-reh-cha.

וְאָהַבְתָּ אֵת יהוה אֱלֹהֶיךָ
בְּכָל־לְבָבְךָ וּבְכָל־נַפְשְׁךָ
וּבְכָל־מְאֹדֶךָ: וְהָיוּ
הַדְּבָרִים הָאֵלֶּה אֲשֶׁר אָנֹכִי
מְצַוְּךָ הַיּוֹם עַל־לְבָבֶךָ:
וְשִׁנַּנְתָּם לְבָנֶיךָ
וְדִבַּרְתָּ בָּם בְּשִׁבְתְּךָ
בְּבֵיתֶךָ וּבְלֶכְתְּךָ
בַדֶּרֶךְ וּבְשָׁכְבְּךָ
וּבְקוּמֶךָ: וּקְשַׁרְתָּם לְאוֹת
עַל־יָדֶךָ וְהָיוּ לְטֹטָפֹת בֵּין
עֵינֶיךָ: וּכְתַבְתָּם עַל־מְזוּזֹת
בֵּיתֶךָ וּבִשְׁעָרֶיךָ:

You shall love Your Eternal God with all your heart, with all your mind, with all your being. Set these words, which I command you this day, upon your heart. Teach them faithfully to your children; speak of them in your home and on your way, when you lie down and when you rise up. Bind them as a sign upon your hand; let them be a symbol before your eyes; inscribe them on the doorposts of your house, and on your gates.

L'ma-an tiz-k'ru va-a-si-tem et
kol mitz-vo-tai, vi-h'yi-tem
k'do-shim lei-lo-hei-chem. Ani
Adonai Eh-lo-hei-chem a-sher
ho-tzei-ti et-chem mei-eh-retz
mitz-ra-yim li-h'yot la-chem
lei-lo-him. Ani Adonai
Eh-lo-hei-chem.

לְמַעַן תִּזְכְּרוּ וַעֲשִׂיתֶם אֶת־
כָּל־מִצְוֹתָי וִהְיִיתֶם
קְדֹשִׁים לֵאלֹהֵיכֶם: אֲנִי
יהוה אֱלֹהֵיכֶם אֲשֶׁר
הוֹצֵאתִי אֶתְכֶם מֵאֶרֶץ
מִצְרַיִם לִהְיוֹת לָכֶם
לֵאלֹהִים. אֲנִי יהוה
אֱלֹהֵיכֶם:

Be mindful of all My Mitzvot, and do them: so shall you consecrate yourselves to your God. I am your Eternal God who led you out of Egypt to be your God; I am your Eternal God.

REDEMPTION

גְּאֻלָּה

עֶזְרַת אֲבוֹתֵינוּ וְאִמּוֹתֵינוּ אַתָּה הוּא מֵעוֹלָם, מָגֵן וּמוֹשִׁיעַ לִבְנֵיהֶם
וְלִבְנוֹתֵיהֶם אַחֲרֵיהֶם בְּכָל־דּוֹר וָדוֹר. בְּרוּם עוֹלָם מוֹשָׁבֶךָ, וּמִשְׁפָּטֶיךָ
וְצִדְקָתְךָ עַד אַפְסֵי־אָרֶץ. אַשְׁרֵי אִישׁ שֶׁיִּשְׁמַע לְמִצְוֺתֶיךָ, וְתוֹרָתְךָ וּדְבָרְךָ
יָשִׂים עַל־לִבּוֹ.

°Infinite God, Creator and Redeemer of all being, You are Most
High, Most Near. In all generations we have cried out to You; we have
put our trust in You, we have borne witness to Your love before the
nations! O now let Your light and Your love appear to us and lead
us; bring us to Your holy mountain.

*Then, though earth itself should shake, though the mountains fall
into the heart of the sea, though its waters thunder and rage, though
the winds lift its waves to the very vault of heaven, we shall not
despair.*

We shall not lose hope, for You are with us; we shall rejoice in Your
deliverance. Then shall we know You, our Redeemer and our God,
and in the shadow of Your wings we shall sing with joy:

Mi cha-mo-cha ba-ei-lim, Adonai?

מִי־כָמֹכָה בָּאֵלִם, יהוה?

Mi ka-mo-cha, neh-dar ba-ko-desh,

מִי כָּמֹכָה, נֶאְדָּר בַּקֹּדֶשׁ,

no-ra t'hi-lot, o-sei feh-leh?

נוֹרָא תְהִלֹּת, עֹשֵׂה פֶלֶא?

Who is like You, Eternal One, among the gods that are worshipped?

Who is like You, majestic in holiness, awesome in splendor, doing
wonders?

Shi-ra cha-da-sha shi-b'chu g'u-lim
l'shi-m'cha al s'fat ha-yam; ya-chad
ku-lam ho-du v'him-li-chu v'a-m'ru:
Adonai yim-loch l'o-lam va-ed!

שִׁירָה חֲדָשָׁה שִׁבְּחוּ גְאוּלִים
לְשִׁמְךָ עַל־שְׂפַת הַיָּם; יַחַד
כֻּלָּם הוֹדוּ וְהִמְלִיכוּ וְאָמְרוּ:
יי יִמְלֹךְ לְעוֹלָם וָעֶד!

Tzur Yis-ra-eil, ku-ma b'ez-rat
Yis-ra-eil, u-f'dei chi-n'u-me-cha
Y'hu-dah v'yis-ra-eil. Go-a-lei-nu

צוּר יִשְׂרָאֵל, קוּמָה בְּעֶזְרַת
יִשְׂרָאֵל, וּפְדֵה כִנְאֻמֶךָ
יְהוּדָה וְיִשְׂרָאֵל. גֹּאֲלֵנוּ

Adonai tz'va-ot sh'mo, k'dosh   יי צְבָאוֹת שְׁמוֹ, קָדוֹשׁ
Yis-ra-eil. Ba-ruch a-tah Adonai,   יִשְׂרָאֵל. בָּרוּךְ אַתָּה, יי,
ga-al Yis-ra-eil.   גָּאַל יִשְׂרָאֵל.

When Your children perceived Your power they exclaimed: "This is my God!" "The Eternal will reign for ever and ever!"

ALL RISE

T'filah
תְּפִלָּה

אֲדֹנָי, שְׂפָתַי תִּפְתָּח, וּפִי יַגִּיד תְּהִלָּתֶךָ:

Eternal God, open my lips,
that my mouth may declare Your glory.

GOD OF ALL GENERATIONS   אָבוֹת וְאִמָּהוֹת

Ba-ruch a-ta Adonai, Eh-lo-hei-nu   בָּרוּךְ אַתָּה יי, אֱלֹהֵינוּ
vei-lo-hei a-vo-tei-nu v'i-mo-tei-nu: וֵאלֹהֵי אֲבוֹתֵינוּ וְאִמּוֹתֵינוּ:
Eh-lo-hei Av-ra-ham, Eh-lo-hei   אֱלֹהֵי אַבְרָהָם, אֱלֹהֵי
Yitz-chak, vei-lo-hei Ya-a-kov.   יִצְחָק, וֵאלֹהֵי יַעֲקֹב.
Eh-lo-hei Sa-rah, Eh-lo-hei Riv-kah,   אֱלֹהֵי שָׂרָה, אֱלֹהֵי רִבְקָה,
Eh-lo-hei Lei-ah, vei-lo-hei Ra-cheil.   אֱלֹהֵי לֵאָה, וֵאלֹהֵי רָחֵל.
Ha-eil ha-ga-dol ha-gi-bor v'ha-no-ra,   הָאֵל הַגָּדוֹל הַגִּבּוֹר וְהַנּוֹרָא,
eil el-yon. Go-meil cha-sa-dim   אֵל עֶלְיוֹן, גּוֹמֵל חֲסָדִים
to-vim, v'ko-nei ha-kol, v'zo-cheir   טוֹבִים וְקוֹנֵה הַכֹּל, וְזוֹכֵר
chas-dei a-vot v'i-ma-hot, u-mei-vi   חַסְדֵי אָבוֹת וְאִמָּהוֹת, וּמֵבִיא
g'u-la li-v'nei v'nei-hem, l'ma-an   גְאֻלָּה לִבְנֵי בְנֵיהֶם, לְמַעַן
sh'mo, b'a-ha-vah.   שְׁמוֹ בְּאַהֲבָה.

BETWEEN ROSH HASHANAH AND YOM KIPPUR ADD:

Zoch-rei-nu l'cha-yim,   זָכְרֵנוּ לְחַיִּים,
meh-lech cha-feitz ba-cha-yim,   מֶלֶךְ חָפֵץ בַּחַיִּים,
v'chot'vei-nu b'sei-fer ha-cha-yim,   וְכָתְבֵנוּ בְּסֵפֶר הַחַיִּים,
l'ma-an-n'cha Eh-lo-him cha-yim.   לְמַעַנְךָ אֱלֹהִים חַיִּים.

Meh-lech o-zeir u-mo-shi-a u-ma-gein.   מֶלֶךְ עוֹזֵר וּמוֹשִׁיעַ וּמָגֵן.
Ba-ruch a-ta Adonai,   בָּרוּךְ אַתָּה, יי,
ma-gein Av-ra-ham v'ez-rat Sa-rah.   מָגֵן אַבְרָהָם וְעֶזְרַת שָׂרָה.

°God of ages past and future, God of this day, as You were with our mothers and fathers, be with us as well.

As You strengthened them, strengthen us.

As you were their Guide, be ours as well.

Grant that we too may be bearers of Your teaching, teachers of Your truth.

Then our tradition shall endure, and Israel live: from mother and father to daughter and son, and all who follow them.

May students of Torah become teachers, that the people and its tradition endure. The people and its tradition will live.

GOD'S POWER   גְּבוּרוֹת

A-ta gi-bor l'o-lam, Adonai,   אַתָּה גִּבּוֹר לְעוֹלָם, אֲדֹנָי,
m'cha-yei ha-kol a-ta, rav-   מְחַיֵּה הַכֹּל אַתָּה, רַב
l'ho-shi-a. M'chal-keil cha-yim   לְהוֹשִׁיעַ. מְכַלְכֵּל חַיִּים
b'cheh-sed, m'cha-yei ha-kol   בְּחֶסֶד, מְחַיֵּה הַכֹּל
b'ra-cha-mim ra-bim. So-meich   בְּרַחֲמִים רַבִּים. סוֹמֵךְ
no-f'lim, v'ro-fei cho-lim,   נוֹפְלִים, וְרוֹפֵא חוֹלִים,
u-ma-tir a-su-rim, u-m'ka-yeim   וּמַתִּיר אֲסוּרִים, וּמְקַיֵּם
eh-mu-na-toh li-shei-nei a-far.   אֱמוּנָתוֹ לִישֵׁנֵי עָפָר.
Mi cha-mo-cha ba-al g'vu-rot,   מִי כָמוֹךָ בַּעַל גְּבוּרוֹת,
u-mi do-meh lach, meh-lech   וּמִי דּוֹמֶה לָּךְ, מֶלֶךְ
mei-mit u-m'cha-yeh u-matz-mi-ach   מֵמִית וּמְחַיֶּה וּמַצְמִיחַ
y'shu-a!   יְשׁוּעָה?

BETWEEN ROSH HASHANAH AND YOM KIPPUR ADD:

Mi cha-mo-cha, av ha-ra-cha-mim,   מִי כָמוֹךָ, אַב הָרַחֲמִים,
zo-cheir y'tzu-rav l'cha-yim   זוֹכֵר יְצוּרָיו לְחַיִּים
b'ra-cha-mim!   בְּרַחֲמִים?

V'neh-eh-man a-ta l'ha-cha-yot
ha-kol, Ba-ruch a-ta Adonai,
m'cha-yei ha-kol.

וְנֶאֱמָן אַתָּה לְהַחֲיוֹת
הַכֹּל. בָּרוּךְ אַתָּה, יי,
מְחַיֵּה הַכֹּל.

°Your might, O God, is everlasting;

Help us to use our strength for good.

You are the Source of life and blessing;

Help us to choose life for ourselves and our children.

You are the Support of the falling;

Help us to lift up the fallen.

You are the Author of freedom;

Help us to set free the captive;

You are our Hope in death as in life;

Help us to keep faith with those who sleep in the dust.

Your might, O God, is everlasting;

Help us to use our strength for good.

SANCTIFICATION   קְדוּשָׁה

נְקַדֵּשׁ אֶת־שִׁמְךָ בָּעוֹלָם, כְּשֵׁם שֶׁמַּקְדִּישִׁים אוֹתוֹ בִּשְׁמֵי מָרוֹם, כַּכָּתוּב
עַל־יַד נְבִיאֶךָ: וְקָרָא זֶה אֶל־זֶה וְאָמַר:

We sanctify Your name on earth, even as all things, to the ends of
the universe, proclaim Your holiness, and in the words of the prophet
we say:

Ka-dosh, ka-dosh, ka-dosh
Adonai tz'va-ot, m'lo chol
ha-a-retz k'vo-do.

קָדוֹשׁ, קָדוֹשׁ, קָדוֹשׁ
יהוה צְבָאוֹת, מְלֹא כָל־
הָאָרֶץ כְּבוֹדוֹ.

Holy, holy, holy is the Eternal One, God of the Hosts of Heaven! The
whole earth is filled with Your glory!

לְעֻמָּתָם בָּרוּךְ יֹאמֵרוּ:

All being recounts Your praise:

Ba-ruch k'vod Adonai mi-m'ko-mo.   בָּרוּךְ כְּבוֹד־יהוה מִמְּקוֹמוֹ.

Praised be the glory of God in heaven and earth.

וּבְדִבְרֵי קָדְשְׁךָ כָּתוּב לֵאמֹר:

And this is Your sacred word:

Yim-loch Adonai l'o-lam,   יִמְלֹךְ יהוה לְעוֹלָם,
Eh-lo-ha-yich Tzi-yon,   אֱלֹהַיִךְ צִיּוֹן,
l'dor va-dor. Ha-l'lu-yah!   לְדֹר וָדֹר. הַלְלוּיָהּ!

The Eternal One shall reign for ever; your God, O Zion, from generation to generation. Halleluyah!

לְדוֹר וָדוֹר נַגִּיד גָּדְלֶךָ וּלְנֵצַח נְצָחִים קְדֻשָּׁתְךָ נַקְדִּישׁ. וְשִׁבְחֲךָ, אֱלֹהֵינוּ, מִפִּינוּ לֹא יָמוּשׁ לְעוֹלָם וָעֶד. *בָּרוּךְ אַתָּה, יי, הָאֵל הַקָּדוֹשׁ.

To all generations we will make known Your greatness, and to all eternity proclaim Your holiness. Your praise, O God, shall never depart from our lips.

*We praise You, Eternal One, the holy God.

BETWEEN ROSH HASHANAH AND YOM KIPPUR CONCLUDE:

בָּרוּךְ אַתָּה, יי, הַמֶּלֶךְ הַקָּדוֹשׁ.

We praise You, Eternal One: You rule in holiness.

ALL ARE SEATED

INTERMEDIATE AND CONCLUDING BLESSINGS

We give thanks for the divine flame that glows within, the gift of reason that enables us to search after knowledge.

Blessed is the Eternal Source of wisdom and knowledge.

May our pride of intellect never be an idol turning us away from feeling wonder and awe. And may we remain aware that all our learning is but a handful of bright pebbles picked from the wide shore of the unknown.

Blessed is the One to whom all things are known.

May the beauty and mystery of the world move us to reverence and humility. Let the tree of knowledge bear good fruit for us and our children.

Blessed is the One from whom all blessings flow.

And let the consciousness of Your presence be the glory of our lives, making joyous our days and years.

Blessed is the One who hearkens to prayer.

❧ ❧

MEDITATION

❧ ❧

יִהְיוּ לְרָצוֹן אִמְרֵי־פִי וְהֶגְיוֹן לִבִּי לְפָנֶיךָ, יהוה, צוּרִי וְגֹאֲלִי.

May the words of my mouth, and the meditations of my heart, be acceptable to You, O God, my Rock and my Redeemer.

עֹשֶׂה שָׁלוֹם בִּמְרוֹמָיו, הוּא יַעֲשֶׂה שָׁלוֹם עָלֵינוּ וְעַל־כָּל־יִשְׂרָאֵל,
וְאִמְרוּ אָמֵן.

May the One who causes peace to reign in the high heavens cause peace to reign among us, all Israel, and all the world.

❧ *Prayers for the House of Mourning begin on page 233.*

❧ *Aleinu is on page 237 or page 239.*

At a House of Mourning

We are assembled with our friends in the shadow that has fallen on their home. We raise our voices together in prayer to the Source of life, asking for comfort and strength.

We need light when gloom darkens our home; to whom shall we look, if not to the Creator of light? We need fortitude and courage when pain and loss assail us; where shall we find them, if not in the thought of the One who preserves all that is good from destruction?

Who among us has not passed through trials and bereavements? Some bear fresh wounds in their hearts, and therefore feel more keenly the kinship of sorrow; Others, whose days of mourning are more remote, still recall the comfort that sympathy brought to their sorrowing hearts.

All things pass; all that lives must die. All that we prize is but lent to us, and the time comes when we must surrender it. We are travellers on the same road that leads us all to the same end.

MEDITATION

As in the world around us, so too in human life: darkness is followed by light, and sorrow by consolation. Life and death are twins; grief and hope walk hand in hand. Although we cannot know what lies beyond the body's death, we put our trust in the undying Spirit that calls us into life and abides to all eternity.

Eternal God of the spirits of all flesh, You are close to the hearts of the sorrowing, to strengthen and console them with the warmth of Your love, and with the assurance that the human spirit is enduring and indestructible. Even as we pray for perfect peace for those whose lives have ended, so do we ask You to give comfort and courage to the living.

May the knowledge of Your nearness be our strength, O God, for You are with us at all times: in joy and sorrow, in light and darkness, in life and death.

אָנָּא, יי, הָרוֹפֵא לִשְׁבוּרֵי לֵב וּמְחַבֵּשׁ לְעַצְּבוֹתָם, שַׁלֵּם נִחוּמִים
לָאֲבֵלִים. חַזְּקֵם וְאַמְּצֵם בְּיוֹם אֶבְלָם וִיגוֹנָם, וְזָכְרֵם לְחַיִּים טוֹבִים
וַאֲרֻכִּים. תֵּן בְּלִבָּם יִרְאָתְךָ וְאַהֲבָתְךָ לְעָבְדְּךָ בְּלֵבָב שָׁלֵם. וּתְהִי
אַחֲרִיתָם שָׁלוֹם. אָמֵן.

O God, Healer of the broken-hearted and Binder of their wounds,
grant consolation to those who mourn. Give them strength and
courage in the time of their grief, and restore to them a sense of
life's goodness.

Fill them with reverence and love, that they may serve You with a
whole heart, and let them soon know peace. Amen.

PSALM 23

יהוה רֹעִי, לֹא אֶחְסָר.

בִּנְאוֹת דֶּשֶׁא יַרְבִּיצֵנִי,

עַל־מֵי מְנֻחוֹת יְנַהֲלֵנִי.

נַפְשִׁי יְשׁוֹבֵב;

יַנְחֵנִי בְמַעְגְּלֵי־צֶדֶק לְמַעַן שְׁמוֹ.

גַּם כִּי־אֵלֵךְ בְּגֵיא צַלְמָוֶת

לֹא־אִירָא רָע, כִּי־אַתָּה עִמָּדִי:

שִׁבְטְךָ וּמִשְׁעַנְתֶּךָ, הֵמָּה יְנַחֲמֻנִי.

תַּעֲרֹךְ לְפָנַי שֻׁלְחָן נֶגֶד צֹרְרָי,

דִּשַּׁנְתָּ בַשֶּׁמֶן רֹאשִׁי, כּוֹסִי רְוָיָה.

אַךְ טוֹב וָחֶסֶד יִרְדְּפוּנִי

כָּל־יְמֵי חַיָּי,

וְשַׁבְתִּי בְּבֵית־יהוה לְאֹרֶךְ יָמִים.

Eternal God, You are my shepherd, I shall not want. You make me
lie down in green pastures, You lead me beside still waters. You
restore my soul; You guide me in paths of righteousness for Your
name's sake. Even when I walk through the valley of the shadow of
death, I shall fear no evil, for You are with me; with rod and staff
You comfort me. You prepare a table before me in the presence of

my enemies; You have anointed my head with oil; my cup over-flows. Surely, goodness and mercy shall follow me all the days of my life, and I shall dwell in the house of the Eternal God for ever.

❧

At this hour, especially, the blessed presence of family and friends brings us comfort and strength. It says to us: "Be sure that love, the spring of life, abides."

May all who mourn take heart, as they remember the goodness they have given and received. And when the days of their mourning are ended, may the memory of their loved ones come to be a bene-diction.

בָּרוּךְ אַתָּה, יי, מְחַיֵּה הַכֹּל.

Ba-ruch a-ta, Adonai, m'cha-yei ha-kol.

Praised be the Eternal Source of life.

ALL RISE

אֵל מָלֵא רַחֲמִים, שׁוֹכֵן בַּמְּרוֹמִים, הַמְצֵא מְנוּחָה נְכוֹנָה תַּחַת כַּנְפֵי הַשְּׁכִינָה עִם קְדוֹשִׁים וּטְהוֹרִים כְּזֹהַר הָרָקִיעַ מַזְהִירִים אֶת־נִשְׁמַת . . . . שֶׁהָלַךְ לְעוֹלָמוֹ [שֶׁהָלְכָה לְעוֹלָמָהּ]. בַּעַל הָרַחֲמִים יַסְתִּירֵהוּ [יַסְתִּירֶהָ] בְּסֵתֶר כְּנָפָיו לְעוֹלָמִים, וְיִצְרוֹר בִּצְרוֹר הַחַיִּים אֶת־נִשְׁמָתוֹ [נִשְׁמָתָהּ]. יי הוּא נַחֲלָתוֹ [נַחֲלָתָהּ] וְיָנוּחַ [וְתָנוּחַ] בְּשָׁלוֹם עַל מִשְׁכָּבוֹ [מִשְׁכָּבָהּ] וְנֹאמַר: אָמֵן.

Eil ma-lei ra-cha-mim, sho-chein ba-m'ro-mim, ham-tzei m'nu-cha n'cho-na ta-chat ka-n'fei ha-sh'chi-na im k'do-shim u-t'ho-rim k'zo-har ha-ra-ki-a maz-hi-rim et nish-mat . . . . sheh-ha-lach l'o-la-mo (sheh-ha-l'cha l'o-la-mah). Ba-al ha-ra-cha-mim yas-ti-rei-hu (yas-ti-reh-ha) b'sei-ter k'na-fav l'o-la-mim, v'yitz-ror bi-tz'ror ha-cha-yim et nish-ma-to (nish-ma-tah). Adonai hu na-cha-la-to (na-cha-la-tah) v'ya-nu-ach (v'ta-nu-ach) b'sha-lom al mish-ka-vo (mish-ka-vah) v'no-mar: A-mein.

God full of compassion, dwelling in the heights and in the depths, grant perfect rest under the wings of Your Presence to . . . ., our loved one who has entered eternity. She (he) has found refuge

235

for ever in the shadow of Your wings, and her (his) soul is bound up in the bond of eternal life; for You, the Everlasting God, are her (his) inheritance. May she (he) rest in peace, and let us say: Amen.

Aleinu I

עָלֵינוּ

ALL RISE

A-le-inu l'sha-bei-ach la-a-don ha-kol, עָלֵינוּ לְשַׁבֵּחַ לַאֲדוֹן הַכֹּל,
la-teit g'du-la l'yo-tzir b'rei-sheet, לָתֵת גְּדֻלָּה לְיוֹצֵר בְּרֵאשִׁית,
sheh-lo a-sa-nu k'go-yei ha-a-ra-tzot, שֶׁלֹא עָשָׂנוּ כְּגוֹיֵי הָאֲרָצוֹת,
v'lo sa-ma-nu k'mish-p'chot וְלֹא שָׂמָנוּ כְּמִשְׁפְּחוֹת
ha-a-da-mah; sheh-lo sam chel-kei-nu הָאֲדָמָה; שֶׁלֹא שָׂם חֶלְקֵנוּ
ka-hem, v'go-ra-lei-nu k'chol כָּהֶם, וְגוֹרָלֵנוּ כְּכָל־
ha-mo-nam. הֲמוֹנָם.

Va-a-nach-nu ko-r'im וַאֲנַחְנוּ כּוֹרְעִים
u-mish-ta-cha-vim u-mo-dim וּמִשְׁתַּחֲוִים וּמוֹדִים
lif-nei meh-lech ma-l'chei לִפְנֵי מֶלֶךְ מַלְכֵי
ha-m'la-chim, ha-ka-dosh הַמְּלָכִים, הַקָּדוֹשׁ
ba-ruch hu. בָּרוּךְ הוּא.

°We praise the One who gave us life. In our rejoicing You are God; You are God in our grief. In anguish and deliverance alike, we praise; in darkness and light we affirm our faith. Therefore we bow our heads in reverence before the Eternal God of life, the Holy One, the Blessed One.

Eternal God, we face the morrow with hope made stronger by the vision of Your deliverance, a world where poverty and war are banished, where injustice and hate are gone.

Teach us more and more to respond to the pain of others, to heed Your call for justice, to pursue the blessing of peace. And grant us wisdom and strength, O God, that we may bring nearer the day when all the world shall be one.

On that day the age-old dream shall come true. On that day, O God, You shall be One and Your name shall be One.

V'neh-eh-mar: V'ha-yah Adonai
l'meh-lech al kol ha-a-retz;
ba-yom ha-hu yi-h'yeh
Adonai eh-chad, u-sh'mo eh-chad!

וְנֶאֱמַר: "וְהָיָה יהוה
לְמֶֽלֶךְ עַל־כָּל־הָאָֽרֶץ;
בַּיּוֹם הַהוּא יִהְיֶה
יהוה אֶחָד וּשְׁמוֹ אֶחָד".

And it has been said: "The Eternal God shall reign over all the earth;
On that day You shall be One and Your name shall be One."

❧ Continue on page 241.

Aleinu II

עָלֵינוּ

ALL RISE

A-le-inu l'sha-bei-ach la-a-don ha-kol,   עָלֵינוּ לְשַׁבֵּחַ לַאֲדוֹן הַכֹּל,

la-teit g'du-la l'yo-tzer b'rei-sheet,   לָתֵת גְּדֻלָּה לְיוֹצֵר בְּרֵאשִׁית,

A-sher sam chel-kei-nu   אֲשֶׁר שָׂם חֶלְקֵנוּ

l'ya-cheid et sh'mo,   לְיַחֵד אֶת־שְׁמוֹ,

v'go-ra-lei-nu l'ham-lich mal-chu-toh.   וְגוֹרָלֵנוּ לְהַמְלִיךְ מַלְכוּתוֹ.

Va-a-nach-nu ko-r'im   וַאֲנַחְנוּ כּוֹרְעִים

u-mish-ta-cha-vim u-mo-dim   וּמִשְׁתַּחֲוִים וּמוֹדִים

lif-nei meh-lech ma-l'chei   לִפְנֵי מֶלֶךְ מַלְכֵי

ha-m'la-chim, ha-ka-dosh   הַמְּלָכִים, הַקָּדוֹשׁ

ba-ruch hu.   בָּרוּךְ הוּא.

°We celebrate the God of life, and sing the praise of Nature's Source, who spread out the heavens and established the earth, whose glory is proclaimed by the starry skies, and whose wonders are revealed in the human heart. You are our God; there is none else. With love and awe we acclaim the Eternal God, the Holy One, the Blessed One.

The day will come when all shall turn with trust to You, hearkening to Your voice, bearing witness to Your truth.

We pray with all our hearts: let violence be gone; let the day come soon when evil shall give way to goodness, when war shall be forgotten, hunger be no more, and all at last shall live in freedom.

O Source of life: may we, created in Your image, embrace one another in friendship and in joy. Then shall we be one family, and then shall Your dominion be established on earth, and the word of Your prophet fulfilled: "The Eternal God will reign for ever and ever."

V'neh-eh-mar: V'ha-yah Adonai
l'meh-lech al kol ha-a-retz;
ba-yom ha-hu yi-h'yeh
Adonai echad, u-sh'mo echad!

וְנֶאֱמַר: "וְהָיָה יהוה
לְמֶלֶךְ עַל־כָּל־הָאָרֶץ;
בַּיּוֹם הַהוּא יִהְיֶה
יהוה אֶחָד וּשְׁמוֹ אֶחָד."

On that day, O God, You shall be One and Your name shall be One.

The Kaddish

BEFORE THE KADDISH

Our thoughts turn to those who have departed this earth: our own loved ones, those whom our friends and neighbors have lost, the martyrs of our people, and those of every race and nation whose lives have been a blessing. As we remember them, we meditate on the meaning of love and loss, of life and death.

WHEN CHERISHED TIES are broken, and the chain of love is shattered, only trust and the strength of faith can lighten the heaviness of the heart. At times, the pain of separation seems more than we can bear; but love and understanding can help us pass through the darkness toward the light.

Out of affliction the Psalmist learned the law of God. And in truth, grief is a great teacher, when it sends us back to serve and bless the living. We learn how to counsel and comfort those who, like ourselves, are bowed with sorrow. We learn when to keep silence in their presence, and when a word will assure them of our love and concern.

Thus, even when they are gone, the departed are with us, moving us to live as, in their higher moments, they themselves wished to live. We remember them now; they live in our hearts; they are an abiding blessing.

—or—

IN NATURE'S EBB AND FLOW, Your eternal law abides. As You are our support in the struggles of life, so, also, are You our hope in death. In Your care, O God, are the souls of all the living and the spirits of all flesh. Your power gives us strength; Your love comforts us. O Life of our life, Soul of our soul, cause Your light to shine into our hearts. Fill us with trust in You, and turn us again to the tasks of life. And may the memory of our loved ones inspire us to continue their work for the coming of Your sovereign rule.

MOURNER'S KADDISH

קַדִּישׁ יָתוֹם

יִתְגַּדַּל וְיִתְקַדַּשׁ שְׁמֵהּ רַבָּא בְּעָלְמָא דִי־בְרָא כִרְעוּתֵהּ, וְיַמְלִיךְ מַלְכוּתֵהּ בְּחַיֵּיכוֹן וּבְיוֹמֵיכוֹן וּבְחַיֵּי דְכָל־בֵּית יִשְׂרָאֵל, בַּעֲגָלָא וּבִזְמַן קָרִיב, וְאִמְרוּ: אָמֵן.

Yit-ga-dal v'yit-ka-dash sh'mei ra-ba b'al-ma di-v'ra chir-u-tei, v'yam-lich mal-chu-tei b'cha-yei-chon u-v'yo-mei-chon u-v'cha-yei d'chol beit Yis-ra-eil, ba-a-ga-la u-viz-man ka-riv, v'im-ru: A-mein.

יְהֵא שְׁמֵהּ רַבָּא מְבָרַךְ לְעָלַם וּלְעָלְמֵי עָלְמַיָּא.

Y'hei sh'mei ra-ba m'va-rach l'a-lam u-l'al-mei al-ma-ya.

יִתְבָּרַךְ וְיִשְׁתַּבַּח, וְיִתְפָּאַר וְיִתְרוֹמַם וְיִתְנַשֵּׂא, וְיִתְהַדָּר וְיִתְעַלֶּה וְיִתְהַלָּל שְׁמֵהּ דְּקוּדְשָׁא, בְּרִיךְ הוּא,

Yit-ba-rach v'yish-ta-bach v'yit-pa-ar, v'yit-ro-mam, v'yit-na-sei, v'yit-ha-dar, v'yit-a-leh, v'yit-ha-lal sh'mei d'ku-d'sha, b'rich hu,

לְעֵלָּא מִן־כָּל־בִּרְכָתָא וְשִׁירָתָא, תֻּשְׁבְּחָתָא וְנֶחֱמָתָא דַּאֲמִירָן בְּעָלְמָא, וְאִמְרוּ: אָמֵן.

l'ei-la min kol bir-cha-ta v'shi-ra-ta, tush-b'cha-ta v'neh-cheh-ma-ta da-a-mi-ran b'al-ma, v'im-ru: A-mein.

יְהֵא שְׁלָמָא רַבָּא מִן־שְׁמַיָּא וְחַיִּים עָלֵינוּ וְעַל־כָּל־יִשְׂרָאֵל, וְאִמְרוּ: אָמֵן.

Y'hei sh'la-ma ra-ba min sh'ma-ya v'cha-yim, a-lei-nu v'al kol Yis-ra-eil, v'im-ru: A-mein.

עֹשֶׂה שָׁלוֹם בִּמְרוֹמָיו, הוּא יַעֲשֶׂה שָׁלוֹם עָלֵינוּ וְעַל־כָּל־יִשְׂרָאֵל, וְאִמְרוּ: אָמֵן.

O-seh sha-lom bi-m'ro-mav, hu ya-a-seh sha-lom a-lei-nu v'al kol Yis-ra-eil, v'im-ru: A-mein.

Let the glory of God be extolled, let God's great name be hallowed in the world whose creation God willed. May God rule in our own day, in our own lives, and in the life of all Israel, and let us say: Amen.

Let God's great name be praised for ever and ever.

Beyond all the praises, songs, and adorations that we can utter is the Holy One, the Blessed One, whom yet we glorify, honor, and exalt. And let us say: Amen.

For us and for all Israel, may the blessing of peace and the promise of life come true, and let us say: Amen.

May the One who causes peace to reign in the high heavens, cause peace to descend on us, on all Israel, and all the world, and let us say: Amen.

May the Source of peace send peace to all who mourn, and comfort to all who are bereaved. Amen.

Meditations for mourners

When you ease your neighbor's heart you make Heaven smile.

[Pirkei Avot]

❧

Like one who'd heal
a wound
with lye
is one who sings
to a heavy heart.

[Proverbs 25:20]

❧

Short the day and
hard the work and
slow the workers, yet
high the wage.
And the master urges them on.
You need not finish the work,
but you are not free to stop working.

[Pirkei Avot]

❧

When we are dead, and people weep for us and grieve,
let it be because we touched their lives with beauty
and simplicity. Let it not be said that life was good to us, but,
rather, that we were good to life.

[Jacob Philip Rudin]

❧

I see that under the sun the race is not to the swift,
nor the battle to the strong,
nor bread to the wise,
nor riches to the intelligent,
nor favor to the skillful;
but time and chance happen to them all.

[Ecclesiastes 9:11]

Days are scrolls; write on them what you want to be remembered.

[Bachya ibn Pakuda]

Private Weekday Prayers

🎐 *Additional worship resources are in 'Weekday Services' and in 'Poems, Prayers, and Readings'*

Sunday

THE FIRST DAY   יוֹם אֶחָד

בְּרֵאשִׁית בָּרָא אֱלֹהִים אֵת הַשָּׁמַיִם וְאֵת הָאָרֶץ. וְהָאָרֶץ הָיְתָה תֹהוּ וָבֹהוּ
וְחֹשֶׁךְ עַל־פְּנֵי תְהוֹם. וְרוּחַ אֱלֹהִים מְרַחֶפֶת עַל־פְּנֵי הַמָּיִם. וַיֹּאמֶר
אֱלֹהִים יְהִי אוֹר וַיְהִי־אוֹר. וַיַּרְא אֱלֹהִים אֶת־הָאוֹר כִּי־טוֹב וַיַּבְדֵּל
אֱלֹהִים בֵּין הָאוֹר וּבֵין הַחֹשֶׁךְ. וַיִּקְרָא אֱלֹהִים לָאוֹר יוֹם וְלַחֹשֶׁךְ קָרָא
לָיְלָה. וַיְהִי־עֶרֶב וַיְהִי־בֹקֶר יוֹם אֶחָד.

In the beginning God created the heavens and the earth.

The earth was empty and without form. Darkness covered the face of the deep. Then God's spirit moved over the waters.

And God said: Let there be light!—and there was light.

And God saw that the light was good, and God separated the light from the darkness.

Then God called the light Day, and the darkness, Night.

And there was evening and there was morning, one day.

FROM PSALM 24

A PSALM OF DAVID   לְדָוִד מִזְמוֹר

לַיהוה הָאָרֶץ וּמְלוֹאָהּ,
תֵּבֵל, וְיֹשְׁבֵי בָהּ.
מִי־יַעֲלֶה בְהַר־יהוה?
וּמִי־יָקוּם בִּמְקוֹם קָדְשׁוֹ?
נְקִי כַפַּיִם,
וּבַר־לֵבָב,

245

אֲשֶׁר לֹא־נָשָׂא לַשָּׁוְא נַפְשִׁי,

וְלֹא נִשְׁבַּע לְמִרְמָה.

יִשָּׂא בְרָכָה מֵאֵת יהוה,

וּצְדָקָה מֵאֱלֹהֵי יִשְׁעוֹ.

זֶה דּוֹר דֹּרְשָׁיו,

מְבַקְשֵׁי פָנֶיךָ,

יַעֲקֹב סֶלָה.

Yours is the earth,

    Yours the world, and all who dwell in it.

Who may ascend Your mountain, Eternal One,

    and who may stand in Your holy place?

Those with clean hands,

    and pure hearts,

Who do not lie to themselves,

    who swear only to the truth.

Them the Everlasting will bless,

    the God of their salvation will give them justice.

Such is the destiny of those who seek You,

    who seek Your presence, O God of Jacob.

Heaven and earth, O God, are the work of Your hands. The roaring seas and the life within them issue forth from Your creative will. The universe is one vast wonder proclaiming Your wisdom and singing Your greatness.

The mysteries of life and death, of growth and decay, alike display the miracle of Your creative power. God of life, the whole universe is Your dwelling-place, all being a hymn to Your glory!

בָּרוּךְ אַתָּה, יי, יוֹצֵר הַמְּאוֹרוֹת.

We praise You, Eternal one, for the new day and its light.

Monday

THE SECOND DAY

יוֹם שֵׁנִי

וַיֹּאמֶר אֱלֹהִים יְהִי רָקִיעַ בְּתוֹךְ הַמָּיִם וִיהִי מַבְדִּיל בֵּין מַיִם לָמָיִם. וַיִּקְרָא אֱלֹהִים לָרָקִיעַ שָׁמָיִם. וַיְהִי־עֶרֶב וַיְהִי־בֹקֶר יוֹם שֵׁנִי.

And God said: Let there be a firmament in the midst of the waters, to divide the upper from the lower waters.

God called the firmament Sky.

And there was evening and there was morning, a second day.

FROM PSALM 104

בָּרְכִי, נַפְשִׁי, אֶת־יהוה. יהוה אֱלֹהַי, גָּדַלְתָּ מְּאֹד.

הוֹד וְהָדָר לָבָשְׁתָּ.

עֹטֶה־אוֹר כַּשַּׂלְמָה,

נוֹטֶה שָׁמַיִם כַּיְרִיעָה.

הַשָּׁם־עָבִים רְכוּבוֹ,

הַמְהַלֵּךְ עַל־כַּנְפֵי־רוּחַ.

עֹשֶׂה מַלְאָכָיו רוּחוֹת,

מְשָׁרְתָיו אֵשׁ לֹהֵט.

מָה־רַבּוּ מַעֲשֶׂיךָ, יהוה, כֻּלָּם בְּחָכְמָה עָשִׂיתָ;

מָלְאָה הָאָרֶץ קִנְיָנֶךָ.

אָשִׁירָה לַיהוה בְּחַיָּי,

אֲזַמְּרָה לֵאלֹהַי בְּעוֹדִי.

Praise the Eternal One, O my soul! O God, You are very great!

    You are arrayed in glory and majesty.

You wrap Yourself in light as with a garment,

    You stretch out the heavens like a curtain.

The clouds are Your chariot;

> You ride on the wings of the wind.

You make the winds Your messengers;

> flames of fire are Your ministers.

How manifold are Your works, Eternal One!
In wisdom You have made them all;

> the earth is full of Your creations.

I will sing to the Eternal One all my days;

> I will sing praises to my God as long as I live.

Love lights our way through the dark passages of our lives.

Loving God, You reign supreme in the human heart. Above the storms of anger and hate that shake the world, I hear Your voice proclaim the law of justice and love.

May my eyes be open to Your truth, my spirit alive to Your teaching, my heart eager to serve You.

בָּרוּךְ אַתָּה, יי, הַבּוֹחֵר בְּעַמּוֹ יִשְׂרָאֵל בְּאַהֲבָה.

We praise You, Eternal One: in love You have called Your people Israel to serve You.

Tuesday

THE THIRD DAY   יוֹם שְׁלִישִׁי

וַיֹּאמֶר אֱלֹהִים יִקָּווּ הַמַּיִם מִתַּחַת הַשָּׁמַיִם אֶל־מָקוֹם אֶחָד וְתֵרָאֶה הַיַּבָּשָׁה וַיְהִי־כֵן. וַיִּקְרָא אֱלֹהִים לַיַּבָּשָׁה אֶרֶץ וּלְמִקְוֵה הַמַּיִם קָרָא יַמִּים וַיַּרְא אֱלֹהִים כִּי־טוֹב. וַיֹּאמֶר אֱלֹהִים תַּדְשֵׁא הָאָרֶץ דֶּשֶׁא עֵשֶׂב מַזְרִיעַ זֶרַע עֵץ פְּרִי עֹשֶׂה פְּרִי לְמִינוֹ אֲשֶׁר זַרְעוֹ־בוֹ עַל־הָאָרֶץ וַיְהִי־כֵן. וַתּוֹצֵא הָאָרֶץ דֶּשֶׁא עֵשֶׂב מַזְרִיעַ זֶרַע לְמִינֵהוּ וְעֵץ עֹשֶׂה־פְּרִי אֲשֶׁר זַרְעוֹ־בוֹ לְמִינֵהוּ וַיַּרְא אֱלֹהִים כִּי־טוֹב. וַיְהִי־עֶרֶב וַיְהִי־בֹקֶר יוֹם שְׁלִישִׁי.

And God said: Let the waters beneath the sky be gathered into a single place, so that the dry land may be seen. And it was so.

And God called the dry land Earth, and the gathered waters, Ocean. And God saw that it was good.

And God said: Let the earth put forth vegetation, plants yielding seed, and fruit trees upon the earth bearing fruit in which is their seed, each according to its kind. And it was so. The earth brought forth vegetation, plants yielding seed according to their kinds, and trees bearing fruit in which is their seed, each according to its kind. And God saw that it was good.

And there was evening and there was morning, a third day.

Those who came before me planted trees;
What shall I plant for those who will come after me?

FROM PSALM 33

שִׁירוּ־לוֹ שִׁיר חָדָשׁ,

הֵיטִֽיבוּ נַגֵּן בִּתְרוּעָה.

כִּי־יָשָׁר דְּבַר־יהוה,

וְכָל־מַעֲשֵׂהוּ בֶּאֱמוּנָה.

אֹהֵב צְדָקָה וּמִשְׁפָּט;

חֶֽסֶד יהוה מָלְאָה הָאָֽרֶץ.

בִּדְבַר יהוה שָׁמַֽיִם נַעֲשׂוּ,

וּבְרֽוּחַ פִּיו כָּל־צְבָאָם.

כִּי הוּא אָמַר וַיֶּֽהִי;

הוּא־צִוָּה וַיַּעֲמֹד.

נַפְשֵֽׁנוּ חִכְּתָה לַיהוה,

עֶזְרֵֽנוּ וּמָגִנֵּֽנוּ הוּא.

כִּי־בוֹ יִשְׂמַח לִבֵּֽנוּ,

כִּי בְשֵׁם קָדְשׁוֹ בָטָֽחְנוּ.

יְהִי־חַסְדְּךָ, יהוה, עָלֵֽינוּ,
כַּאֲשֶׁר יִחַֽלְנוּ לָךְ.

Sing to God a new song,

    play well, with shouts of joy.

For God's word holds good;

    God's every deed is done in faithfulness.

You love righteousness and justice, O God;

    the earth is full of Your kindness.

By Your word the heavens were made,

    and all their host by the breath of Your mouth.

For You spoke and it was,

    commanded, and it stood firm.

Our souls wait for You,

    our trust and our shield.

Our hearts are full of joy,

    for in Your holy name we trust.

Eternal God, let Your love rest on us,

    as we rest our hope in You.

❧

You are the notes, and we are the singer.
You are the singer, and we are the notes.

❧

Let me hear You, God, when I hear my spirit soaring in prayer. May I sing because I love, not afraid to waste my sweetness upon the void, but reflecting in my soul's flight the universal God who sings through me.

בָּרוּךְ אַתָּה יי אֱלֹהֵֽינוּ מֶֽלֶךְ הָעוֹלָם, שֶׁכֹּחוֹ וּגְבוּרָתוֹ מָלֵא עוֹלָם.

We praise You, Eternal One, whose power and might pervade the world.

Wednesday

THE FOURTH DAY   יוֹם רְבִיעִי

וַיֹּאמֶר אֱלֹהִים יְהִי מְאֹרֹת בִּרְקִיעַ הַשָּׁמַיִם לְהַבְדִּיל בֵּין הַיּוֹם וּבֵין
הַלָּיְלָה. וְהָיוּ לְאֹתֹת וּלְמוֹעֲדִים וּלְיָמִים וְשָׁנִים. וְהָיוּ לִמְאוֹרֹת בִּרְקִיעַ
הַשָּׁמַיִם לְהָאִיר עַל־הָאָרֶץ וַיְהִי־כֵן. וַיַּעַשׂ אֱלֹהִים אֶת־שְׁנֵי הַמְּאֹרֹת הַגְּדֹלִים
אֶת־הַמָּאוֹר הַגָּדֹל לְמֶמְשֶׁלֶת הַיּוֹם וְאֶת־הַמָּאוֹר הַקָּטֹן לְמֶמְשֶׁלֶת הַלַּיְלָה
וְאֵת הַכּוֹכָבִים.

וַיִּתֵּן אֹתָם אֱלֹהִים בִּרְקִיעַ הַשָּׁמָיִם לְהָאִיר עַל־הָאָרֶץ וְלִמְשֹׁל
בַּיּוֹם וּבַלַּיְלָה וּלֲהַבְדִּיל בֵּין הָאוֹר וּבֵין הַחֹשֶׁךְ וַיַּרְא אֱלֹהִים כִּי־טוֹב.
וַיְהִי־עֶרֶב וַיְהִי־בֹקֶר יוֹם רְבִיעִי.

And God said: Let there be luminaries in the firmament of the sky
to separate day from night, and let them be signs to mark the seasons, the days and the years. Let them be luminaries in the sky to
give light to the earth. And it was so.

God made the two great luminaries: the greater one to rule the day,
and the lesser one to rule the night; and God made the stars.

God put them in the dome of the sky to give light to the earth, to
hold sway over day and night, and to separate the light from the
dark. And God saw that it was good.

And there was evening and there was morning, a fourth day.

PSALM 148

הַלְלוּיָהּ!
הַלְלוּ אֶת־יהוה מִן־הַשָּׁמַיִם,
הַלְלוּהוּ בַּמְּרוֹמִים.
הַלְלוּהוּ כָל־מַלְאָכָיו,
הַלְלוּהוּ כָּל־צְבָאָיו.
הַלְלוּהוּ שֶׁמֶשׁ וְיָרֵחַ;
הַלְלוּהוּ כָּל־כּוֹכְבֵי אוֹר.

251

הַלְלוּהוּ, שְׁמֵי הַשָּׁמָיִם,

וְהַמַּיִם אֲשֶׁר מֵעַל הַשָּׁמָיִם.

יְהַלְלוּ אֶת־שֵׁם יהוה,

כִּי הוּא צִוָּה וְנִבְרָאוּ,

וַיַּעֲמִידֵם לָעַד לְעוֹלָם,

חָק־נָתַן וְלֹא יַעֲבוֹר.

הַלְלוּ אֶת־יהוה מִן־הָאָרֶץ:

תַּנִּינִים וְכָל־תְּהֹמוֹת,

אֵשׁ וּבָרָד, שֶׁלֶג וְקִיטוֹר,

רוּחַ סְעָרָה עֹשָׂה דְבָרוֹ;

הֶהָרִים וְכָל־גְּבָעוֹת,

עֵץ פְּרִי וְכָל־אֲרָזִים,

הַחַיָּה וְכָל־בְּהֵמָה,

רֶמֶשׂ וְצִפּוֹר כָּנָף:

מַלְכֵי־אֶרֶץ וְכָל־לְאֻמִּים,

שָׂרִים וְכָל־שֹׁפְטֵי אָרֶץ;

בַּחוּרִים וְגַם־בְּתוּלוֹת,

זְקֵנִים עִם־נְעָרִים!

יְהַלְלוּ אֶת־שֵׁם יהוה,

כִּי־נִשְׂגָּב שְׁמוֹ לְבַדּוֹ.

הוֹדוֹ עַל־אֶרֶץ וְשָׁמָיִם.

Halleluyah! Praise the Eternal One.

Praise God from the heavens,

praise God in the heights.

Give praise, all God's angels,

give praise, all God's hosts.

Give praise, sun and moon;

give praise, you shining stars.

Give praise, you highest heavens,

and you waters above the heavens.

Let them praise the name of the Eternal One,

    at whose command they were created,

Who established them to abide for ever,

    by a decree that does not change.

Praise God from the earth:

    crocodiles, creatures of the deep,

Fire and hail, snow and mist,

    storm winds that obey the divine command;

Mountains and hills,

    fruit trees and cedars,

Animals and cattle,

    creatures that creep and birds on the wing;

Rulers of every land and people,

    princes and judges of the earth;

Boys and girls together,

    old and young alike!

Let them praise the Eternal One, whose name is exalted,
whose majesty spans heaven and earth.

> Of all that God has shown me
> I can speak just the smallest word.
> Not more than a honey bee
> Takes on her foot
> From an overspilling jar.

> *The slant of winter light,*
> *Autumn's fall of leaf, soft summer and verdant spring,*
> *—are Yours: Your gift to me.*

בָּרוּךְ אַתָּה יי אֱלֹהֵינוּ מֶלֶךְ הָעוֹלָם, עֹשֶׂה מַעֲשֵׂה בְרֵאשִׁית.

We praise You, Eternal one, Source of creation and its wonders.

Thursday

THE FIFTH DAY   יוֹם חֲמִישִׁי

וַיֹּאמֶר אֱלֹהִים יִשְׁרְצוּ הַמַּיִם שֶׁרֶץ נֶפֶשׁ חַיָּה וְעוֹף יְעוֹפֵף עַל־הָאָרֶץ עַל־פְּנֵי רְקִיעַ הַשָּׁמָיִם. וַיִּבְרָא אֱלֹהִים אֶת־הַתַּנִּינִם הַגְּדֹלִים וְאֵת כָּל־נֶפֶשׁ הַחַיָּה הָרֹמֶשֶׂת אֲשֶׁר שָׁרְצוּ הַמַּיִם לְמִינֵהֶם וְאֵת כָּל־עוֹף כָּנָף לְמִינֵהוּ וַיַּרְא אֱלֹהִים כִּי־טוֹב. וַיְבָרֶךְ אֹתָם אֱלֹהִים לֵאמֹר פְּרוּ וּרְבוּ וּמִלְאוּ אֶת־הַמַּיִם בַּיַּמִּים וְהָעוֹף יִרֶב בָּאָרֶץ. וַיְהִי־עֶרֶב וַיְהִי־בֹקֶר יוֹם חֲמִישִׁי.

And God said: Let the oceans teem with living creatures, let birds fly above the earth, across the dome of heaven.

And God created the great sea–creatures, and every kind of living creature that teems in the waters, and every kind of winged bird. And God saw that it was good.

And God blessed them and said: Be fruitful and multiply and fill the waters of the sea; and let birds abound on the earth.

And there was evening and there was morning, a fifth day.

PSALM 146

הַלְלוּיָהּ!

הַלְלִי, נַפְשִׁי, אֶת־יהוה! אֲהַלְלָה יהוה בְּחַיָּי;

אֲזַמְּרָה לֵאלֹהַי בְּעוֹדִי.

אַל־תִּבְטְחוּ בִנְדִיבִים,

בְּבֶן־אָדָם שֶׁאֵין לוֹ תְשׁוּעָה.

תֵּצֵא רוּחוֹ, יָשֻׁב לְאַדְמָתוֹ;

בַּיּוֹם הַהוּא אָבְדוּ עֶשְׁתֹּנֹתָיו.

אַשְׁרֵי שֶׁאֵל יַעֲקֹב בְּעֶזְרוֹ,

שִׂבְרוֹ עַל־יהוה אֱלֹהָיו,

עֹשֶׂה שָׁמַיִם וָאָרֶץ,

אֶת־הַיָּם וְאֶת־כָּל־אֲשֶׁר־בָּם,

הַשֹּׁמֵר אֱמֶת לְעוֹלָם,

עֹשֶׂה מִשְׁפָּט לָעֲשׁוּקִים,

נֹתֵן לֶחֶם לָרְעֵבִים,

יהוה מַתִּיר אֲסוּרִים.

יהוה פֹּקֵחַ עִוְרִים;

יהוה זֹקֵף כְּפוּפִים;

יהוה אֹהֵב צַדִּיקִים;

יהוה שֹׁמֵר אֶת־גֵּרִים;

יָתוֹם וְאַלְמָנָה יְעוֹדֵד,

וְדֶרֶךְ רְשָׁעִים יְעַוֵּת.

יִמְלֹךְ יהוה לְעוֹלָם; אֱלֹהַיִךְ, צִיּוֹן, לְדֹר וָדֹר. הַלְלוּיָהּ.

Halleluyah!

Praise the Eternal One, O my soul!
I will sing to the Eternal One all my days;

I will sing praises to my God as long as I live.

Do not rely on earthly rulers,

on men or women who cannot save you.

Their breath departs, and they are dust;

that very day their plans perish.

Happy are those whose help is Israel's God,

whose hope is their Eternal God,

Maker of heaven and earth,

the sea and all that is in them,

Who keeps faith for ever,

who does justice for the oppressed,

Gives bread to the hungry,

and sets captives free.

O God: You open the eyes of the blind;

   You lift up the downtrodden;

You love the righteous;

   You care for the stranger,

You support the orphan and the widow,

   but frustrate the schemes of the wicked!

The Eternal One shall reign for ever;
your God, O Zion, through all generations. Halleluyah.

❧

The life so short, the craft so long to learn.

❧

O God, how can I know You? Where can I find You? You are as close
to me as breathing, yet You are farther than the farthermost star. You
are as mysterious as the vast solitudes of night, yet as familiar to me
as the light of the sun. To Moses You said: 'You cannot see My face,
but I will make all My goodness pass before you.' Even so does Your
goodness pass before me: in the realm of nature, and in the joys and
sorrows of life.

Let justice burn within me like a flaming fire; let love evoke will-
ing sacrifice from me; let me demonstrate my belief in the triumph
of truth and righteousness: then will Your goodness enter my life,
and then through righteousness will I behold Your presence.

בָּרוּךְ אַתָּה יי אֱלֹהֵינוּ מֶלֶךְ הָעוֹלָם, זוֹכֵר הַבְּרִית וְנֶאֱמָן בִּבְרִיתוֹ וְקַיָּם
בְּמַאֲמָרוֹ.

We praise You, Eternal One: true to Your word, You remember Your
covenant with creation.

Friday

THE SIXTH DAY   יוֹם הַשִּׁשִּׁי

וַיֹּאמֶר אֱלֹהִים תּוֹצֵא הָאָרֶץ נֶפֶשׁ חַיָּה לְמִינָהּ בְּהֵמָה וָרֶמֶשׂ וְחַיְתוֹ־אֶרֶץ
לְמִינָהּ וַיְהִי־כֵן. וַיַּעַשׂ אֱלֹהִים אֶת־חַיַּת הָאָרֶץ לְמִינָהּ וְאֶת־הַבְּהֵמָה
לְמִינָהּ וְאֵת כָּל־רֶמֶשׂ הָאֲדָמָה לְמִינֵהוּ וַיַּרְא אֱלֹהִים כִּי־טוֹב.

וַיֹּאמֶר אֱלֹהִים נַעֲשֶׂה אָדָם בְּצַלְמֵנוּ כִּדְמוּתֵנוּ וְיִרְדּוּ בִדְגַת הַיָּם וּבְעוֹף
הַשָּׁמַיִם וּבַבְּהֵמָה וּבְכָל־הָאָרֶץ וּבְכָל־הָרֶמֶשׂ הָרֹמֵשׂ עַל־הָאָרֶץ. וַיִּבְרָא
אֱלֹהִים ׀ אֶת־הָאָדָם בְּצַלְמוֹ בְּצֶלֶם אֱלֹהִים בָּרָא אֹתוֹ זָכָר וּנְקֵבָה בָּרָא
אֹתָם. וַיְבָרֶךְ אֹתָם אֱלֹהִים . . .

וַיַּרְא אֱלֹהִים אֶת־כָּל־אֲשֶׁר עָשָׂה וְהִנֵּה־טוֹב מְאֹד. וַיְהִי־עֶרֶב וַיְהִי־בֹקֶר
יוֹם הַשִּׁשִּׁי.

And God said: Let the earth bring forth every species of living creature: animals, reptiles and wild beasts. And it was so.

And God made the various species of animals, both wild and tame, and all that creeps upon the ground, and God saw that it was good.

And God said: Let us make a human being in our image, after our likeness, and let them take charge of the fish of the sea, the birds of the air, over the animals, over the whole earth, and over everything that creeps on the ground.

And God created human beings in the Divine Image, in the very image of God, making them male and female.

And God blessed them . . .

And God saw the whole creation, and it was very good.

And there was evening and there was morning, a sixth day.

FROM PSALM 8

יהוה, אֲדֹנֵינוּ, מָה־אַדִּיר שִׁמְךָ בְּכָל־הָאָרֶץ!
אֲשֶׁר תְּנָה הוֹדְךָ עַל־הַשָּׁמָיִם.
כִּי־אֶרְאֶה שָׁמֶיךָ, מַעֲשֵׂי אֶצְבְּעֹתֶיךָ;
יָרֵחַ וְכוֹכָבִים אֲשֶׁר כּוֹנָנְתָּה,
מָה־אֱנוֹשׁ כִּי־תִזְכְּרֶנּוּ,
וּבֶן־אָדָם כִּי תִפְקְדֶנּוּ?
וַתְּחַסְּרֵהוּ מְּעַט מֵאֱלֹהִים,
וְכָבוֹד וְהָדָר תְּעַטְּרֵהוּ!
תַּמְשִׁילֵהוּ בְּמַעֲשֵׂי יָדֶיךָ,
כֹּל שַׁתָּה תַחַת־רַגְלָיו:
צֹנֶה וַאֲלָפִים, כֻּלָּם, וְגַם בַּהֲמוֹת שָׂדָי, צִפּוֹר שָׁמַיִם, וּדְגֵי הַיָּם.
עֹבֵר אָרְחוֹת יַמִּים.
יהוה, אֲדֹנֵינוּ, מָה־אַדִּיר שִׁמְךָ בְּכָל־הָאָרֶץ!

Eternal One, our God, how glorious is Your name in all the earth!

You have stamped Your glory upon the heavens!

When I look at the heavens, the work of Your fingers;

the moon and the stars that You have established,

What are we, that You are mindful of us,

we human beings, that You care for us?

Yet You have made us little lower than the angels,

and crowned us with glory and honor!

You have appointed us to look after all that You have made,

You have placed all creation in our care:

Sheep and cattle, all of them; beasts and birds and fish,

and all who travel the ocean's paths.

Eternal One, our God, how glorious is Your name in all the earth!

❧

Divine presence in the human world:
a mystery within us; a mystery beyond us.

❧

You are with me in my prayer and my love, my doubt and my fear, in my longing to feel Your presence and do Your will. You are the still, clear voice within me.

When doubt troubles me, when anxiety makes me tremble and pain clouds the mind, I look inward.

Looking inward for an answer to my prayer, may I find You: finding courage, insight, and endurance; finding that which gives meaning and purpose to my journey.

בָּרוּךְ אַתָּה יי אֱלֹהֵינוּ מֶלֶךְ הָעוֹלָם, שֶׁנָּתַן מֵחָכְמָתוֹ לְבָשָׂר וָדָם.

We praise You, Eternal One, for You share Your wisdom with flesh and blood.

Psalms, Poems, and Readings

PSALMS, POEMS,

AND READINGS

From the Psalms

FROM PSALM 3

How many are my foes, O God,
How many rise up against me!
How many say of me
That You will not help me.
Oh, but You are the shield that covers me,
My glory who keeps my head high!
I cry out to You, the Infinite,
And from Your holy mountain's summit
Your answer comes.
I lie down and sleep,
and then I am awake,
Safe in Your hand,
And unafraid . . .
Eternal One, rise up;
Help me, O my God,
For You are the One
From whom help comes,
And Your blessing rests upon Your people.

FROM PSALM 4

When I call, be my answer, O God, my Champion.
In my times of trouble You have set me free:
Be gracious to me now, and hear my prayer.
Great ones of the world,
How long will you put me to shame?
How long will you love illusions and run after lies?
See how the Eternal One shows me marvelous love,
How the Eternal One hears my every prayer.
Tremble, then, and sin no more;
Look into your heart as you lie abed,
And hold your peace.
Let your offering be justice,
And trust in the Eternal One.
There are many who say,

263

Oh, that we could see some good,
But the light of Your presence, O God, has fled from us!
Yet you have put joy in my heart,
More than some have
From a rich crop of grain and wine.
Now I will lie down in peace, and sleep;
For you alone, Eternal One, make me live unafraid.

FROM PSALM 5

Give ear to my words, Eternal One,
Hear the whisper of my soul.
Listen to my cry for help,
My Sovereign God,
For to You alone do I pray.
Eternal One, hear my voice at daybreak;
At daybreak I plead with you,
and wait.
You are not a God who welcomes wickedness;
Evil cannot be Your guest.
The arrogant cannot look You in the face.
You despise all who do evil.
You make an end to liars;
Murderers and traitors sicken You.
As for me, in Your abundant loving kindness
Let me enter Your house,
Reverently to worship in Your holy temple.
As You are just, Eternal One, lead me,
Safe from those who lie in wait for me;
Make Your way straight for me.
They are not sincere—they are empty inside,
Their throat a gaping tomb, their talk so smooth!
Judge them, God: their own schemes make them fall;
Their many crimes drive them out, for they defy You.
But all who trust in You rejoice; they sing for ever.
You give them shelter; and all who love Your name
exult in You.
For You give Your blessing to the just;
You throw Your favor about them like a shield.

FROM PSALM 11

In the Eternal One I have found refuge.
Why then say to me:
'Flee to the hills like a bird;
see how the wicked have bent the bow,
fitting the arrow to the string,
to shoot in the dark at the upright.
When the foundations are destroyed,
what can the righteous do?'
Eternal One, You are in Your holy dwelling-place;
Eternal One, the skies are Your throne;
Your eyes look down upon the world,
You take our measure in a glance.
Eternal One, You weigh just and unjust,
You detest the lover of violence.
For You are righteous, Eternal One;
You love righteous deeds;
the upright shall behold Your face.

FROM PSALM 12

Help, O God, for the loyal have vanished;
good faith among Your people is gone.
Empty forms of speech pass among neighbors,
they speak with smooth lips and double hearts.
Make an end, O God, of such smooth lips,
such high-sounding words,
of those who say: 'Our tongue can win the day;
words are our friends; none can vanquish us.'
'Now,' says the Eternal One,
'I will bestir Myself
for the poor who are oppressed,
for the needy who groan.
I will grant them the help for which they plead.'
The words of the Eternal One are pure words,
silver from a furnace,
seven times refined.
Though the wicked walk about,
stepping high as though they owned the earth,

You will keep us, Eternal One,
preserving us from this base breed.

FROM PSALM 13

Must I still go unremembered?
How long will You turn Your face from me?
Each day my soul is torn,
my heart filled with grief: how long?
How long shall my enemy have the upper hand?
Look at me and answer, Eternal One my God;
give light to these eyes lest I sleep the sleep of death,
lest my enemy say: 'I have prevailed';
lest my foes rejoice to see my fall.
As for me, I trust in Your unfailing love;
my heart shall rejoice in Your deliverance.
I will sing to the Eternal One,
who has shown me such good!

FROM PSALM 36

Sin speaks to the wicked
deep in their hearts.
There is no fear of God
before their eyes.
They flatter themselves
that their hateful guilt
will never come to light.
Their words are cruel and false.
All wisdom and good are gone.
They lie awake plotting mischief.
The course they choose is not good,
they never tire of evil.
But Your love, O God,
is high as heaven,
Your faithfulness reaches to the skies.
Your righteousness is like the mighty mountains,
Your justice is like the great deep;
You help every human, every beast.
How precious is Your faithful love, O God!

Your children take refuge in the shadow of Your wings.
We feast on the riches of Your house;
we drink from the fountain of Your delights.
For with You is the fountain of life;
and by Your light shall we see light.
O continue to show Your love
to those who would know You,
and Your justice to the upright in heart.
Let the foot of pride not crush me,
nor let the hand of the wicked cast me out.

From Talmud and Midrash

1

May it be Your will, Eternal God,
that love and harmony, peace and friendship
may dwell among us.
Help us to look forward with confidence and hope.
Guide us in the world with good companions and good intentions.
When we rise up in the morning, may we find our hearts ready to
    revere You,
and may our deepest longings be fulfilled for our good.
And make Paradise our destination.

2

Eternal God, grant us long life,
a life of peace,
a life of good,
a life of blessing,
a life of prosperity,
a life of health,
a life guided by fear of sin,
a life lived without shame,
a life rich and honorable,
a life quickened by love of Torah and fear of Heaven,
a life in which our hearts' desires are fulfilled for our good.

3

May we find the world in our lifetime,
our completion in the World to Come,
and our hopes realized in those who follow us.
May our hearts meditate in understanding,
our mouths speak wisdom,
our tongues sing songs of jubilation.
May our eyes look straight before us,
afire with the light of Torah,
our faces shining with a heavenly light.
May our lips utter knowledge,

and our inward parts rejoice.
May our footsteps hasten towards the words
of the Ancient of Days.

Prayers and Meditations

1

The stars of heaven,
awesome in their majesty,
are not more wonderful
than the one who charts their courses.
The elements,
arrayed in perfection,
are not marvels greater
than the mind that beholds them.
This miracle, matter,
begets a wonder:
the body thinks,
insight comes from flesh;
the soul is born of dust
to build towers of hope,
opening within us
doors of lamentation and love.
For You have made us little less than divine,
and crowned us with glory and honor!
Glory and honor within us:
but every age has despised its endowment.
And yet, O God, we look with hope beyond the near horizon.
Beneath this trampled earth,
a seed of goodness will grow, we trust,
to be our tree of life.
Within and beyond us,
O God of life,
You are there.
You dwell wherever we let You in.
When we flee from You,
we flee from ourselves.
When we seek You,
we discover that we are not alone.

2

The gods we worship write their names on our faces, be sure of that,

And we will worship something—have no doubt of that either.

We may think our tribute is paid in secret in the dark recesses of the heart—but it will out.

That which dominates our imagination and our thoughts will determine our life and character.

Therefore it behooves to be careful what we are worshipping, for what we are worshipping we are becoming. . . .

3

We rejoice in the light of day, in the warmth of the sun.

We rejoice in the light of day.

In the quiet night, whose dark sky reveals worlds beyond the dark.

We rejoice in the peace of night.

In the earth and its hills and valleys, its fields of grain, its fruit and flowers.

We rejoice in the beauty of earth.

We rejoice in homes where we find shelter from the cold and storm.

We rejoice in the shelter of home.

In the love of fathers and mothers with whose blessing we have gone forth into the world.

We rejoice in the love of parents.

In the children who bless our homes, who are the promise of tomorrow.

We rejoice in our children.

In friends who stand by our side in sorrow and in joy, in triumph and defeat.

We rejoice, and will rejoice for evermore.

4

At break of day You wake us;
at end of day You give us rest;
morning, noon and night You bless us.

5

When I awaken to a world that seems bleak, I feel lonely and alone.

The Psalmist said: *'Show me Your light and Your truth; let them lead me, let them bring me to You.'* Be with me in ways I can understand: in a loved one's touch, the smile of a friend, the green world's grace. Help me to see them as Your love-letters, an earnest of Your care.

Show me Your light and Your truth; let them lead me, let them bring me to You.'

6

Let me hear You, God, when I hear my spirit soaring in prayer. May I sing because I love, not afraid to waste my sweetness upon the void, but reflecting in my soul's flight the universal God who sings through me.

7

God enthroned by Israel's praise, God my hope, my heart waits in silence for You alone. By day extend Your steadfast love, and at night I shall sing to You, a prayer to the God of my life. Praised be God my Help, who day by day upholds me.

8

O give thanks
that spring will always come
to make the heart leap,
that your winter ear remembers
a summer song,
and autumn colors return
to the jaded eye.

O make song
for lucid air of morning,
bright blood's beating,
life's flow deep and swift,
a kingdom of joy and awe
for us to dwell in.

O be glad,
for eye and tongue,
to see and taste
the common of our days.

9

Welcome alike the day and its labor, the night and its repose; throw yourself into the waters of life and swim bravely and without anxiety, for these waters are native to you; you were born to swim in them.

Accomplish what you can; endure what you must; understand what you may—and this do for yourself, but not only for yourself: do this for yourself and others.

In your prayer and your love, your doubt and your fear, seek out the still, clear voice within you.

Look inward for an answer to prayer. Find courage there, and endurance; find insight there, and the knowledge that you are part of the divine creation.

Know that love gives meaning and purpose to your journey. May such love be the fruit of your prayer.

10

O Holy One, I ran through the fields and gathered flowers of a thou-
sand colors—
And now I pour them out at Your feet.
Their beauty and their brightness shout for joy in Your presence.
You created the flowers of the field and made each one far more
lovely
than all that human skill could design.
Accept my joy along with theirs,

this field of blossoms at Your feet.
Holy One,
as the wind blows through these flowers
till they dance in the ecstasy of creation,
send Your Spirit to blow through my being
till I too bloom and dance with the fullness of Your life.

11

The garden is rich with diversity
With plants of a hundred families
In the space between the trees
With all the colors and fragrances.
Basil, mint and lavender,
God keep my remembrance pure;
Raspberry, apple, rose,
God fill my heart with love;
Dill, anise, tansy,
Holy winds blow in me;
Rhododendron, zinnia,
May my prayer be beautiful.
May my remembrance, O God,
be as incense to Thee
in the sacred grove of eternity
as I smell and remember
the ancient forests of earth.

12

Grant me the ability to be alone;
may it be my custom to go outdoors each day
among the trees and the grasses,
among all growing things,
there to be alone
and enter into prayer,
talking to the One
to whom I belong.
May all grasses, trees and plants
awake at my coming.

Send the power of their life into my prayer,
making whole my heart and my speech
through the life and spirit of growing things . . .

13

❧ *A meditation on the flight of prayer.*

For so have I seen a lark rising from his bed of grass and soaring upwards, and singing as he rises, and hopes to get to heaven, and climb above the clouds; but the poor bird was beaten back with the loud sighings of an eastern wind, and his motion made irregular and unconstant, descending more at every breath of the tempest than it could recover by the libration [fluttering] and frequent weighing of his wings, till the little creature was forced to sit down and pant, and stay till the storm was over; and then it made a prosperous flight, and did rise and sing, as if it had learned music and motion from an angel as he passed sometimes through the air about his ministries here below. . . .

14

In Prayer the lips ne'er act the winning part,
Without the sweet concurrence of the Heart.

Poems

1

Praised be the One whose word made this world be,
this world so small and strange,
where all things begin
in the middle of their growth,
and end there;
where all things hide
from the one who longs to understand them.
Here in space and time they hide
from their beginning in time
to their eternal end.

And praised be the One who keeps a covenant
with this world,
so strange and small,
where God's good is sown to the winds,
so that hope lifts even the least of us,
and even I find my spirit rising to redeem me.
And in my heart wells up this word:
Praised be the One whose word. . . .

2

Something is very gently,
invisibly, silently,
pulling at me—a thread
or net of threads
finer than cobweb and as
elastic. I haven't tried
the strength of it. No barbed hook
pierced and tore me. Was it
not long ago this thread
began to draw me? Or
way back? Was I
born with its knot about my
neck, a bridle? Not fear
but a stirring

276

of wonder makes me
catch my breath when I feel
the tug of it when I thought
it had loosened itself and gone.

3

❦ *In Jewish tradition, the Divine Presence (Shechinah) is feminine. And letters/numbers often point to hidden and ultimate truths.*

Mothering Presence
enfold me
unfold me
& walk with me.
& walk with me.

      I need to turn to You
      I need to walk with You
      I need to rest in You.

Beloved come to me
but not to win my wars.
Beloved come to me
but not to make my peace.
Come, O Loved One,
but not to build my house.

      If only You will walk with me
      If only You will be with me
      If only You will shelter me.

Maker of arithmetic
Weaver of number-worlds
Redeemer of equalities
Mother of odd/Sister of even
Creator of Aleph/Author of Bet:

      If only You will walk with me
      If only You will shelter me
      If only You will be with me.

Do not tell me no,
do not tell me,
no, do not tell me NO!
Do not say my life adds up to naught.

> If only You will shelter me
> If only You will be with me
> If only You will walk with me.

Nor say that two & two are always four
and must be so.
Nor say because our hearts must stop
that love must end.
Tell me YES!
that two and two need not make four,
for five & seven will often do,
for now and then again and now again
the sum I ask is life.

> If only You will walk with me
> If only You will be with me
> If only You will be . . .

I swear that one & one are three:
I see it always so
when lovers kiss
& friends embrace.
If only You will walk with me
If only You will be . . .
YES!
Although my heart is stone.
YES!
Because my heart is stone.

> I need to turn to You.
> I need to hope in You
> I need to turn to You
> I need to rest in You.

Mother present in all
Mother present in all presence
in all whom I am present to:
move me, move us;
move head, move hand
with the promise of Your word
with the Presence of Your life.
Move the heart in us,
that stranger in our midst,
and let it turn to flesh from stone.

        We need to turn to You
        We need to walk with You
        We need to rest in You.

So the garden planted,
garden planted in our wilderness
be safe from harm.
So the planted flowers bloom
though empires wither.
So You be our dwelling place
and we are free.

        If only You will be with us
        If only You will be . . .

4

Our God was to be a breath, and not a postcard
Of the sun setting over Niagara Falls:
"Wish you were here." Our God was first the breath
That raised a whirlwind in the desert dust,
The Wilderness of Sin. And then a word
Unspeakable, a stillness, and a standing stone
Set in the road; you would not raise a chisel
Upon that stone. Nothing but sky and sand
To purify a forbidden generation
Of Egypt's kitchens. In that wilderness
I've wandered for my forty years also,
Lifting mirages to break horizons, dreaming
Idolatries to alphabet the void,

Sending these postcards to the self at home:
Sunlight on pouring water; wish I were here.

5

God, You taunt me: 'Flee if you can!'
But I can't flee.
For when I turn away from You, angry and heartsick,
With a vow on my lips like a burning coal:
'I will not see You again'—

I can't do it.
And I turn back
And knock on Your door,
Tortured with longing.
As though You had sent me a love-letter.

6

Now, on the gleaming jewels of dew,
the splendor of the setting sun!
And now you come to me
bearing gifts.
I cannot remember picking flowers,
yet my hands are quite full!

7

Light breaks upon the heart, and
            on sea,
        on sky, on stone.
        Its falling is
great, beautiful and new.
            And now
        in silent song
        the angels glow,
            and
        you are blessed,
        addressed and known.

8

To be a Jew means always to run to God,
Even when you want to flee;
means you are ready right now to hear
—even if you are a skeptic—
the blare of messiah's horn.

To be a Jew means you never escape from God,
however much you may want to;
means you cannot stop your prayer
even when the prayers are done,
even when the 'evens' have been said.

9

Will you seek far off? You surely come back at last, in things
best known to you, finding the best, or as good as the best—
Happiness, knowledge, not in another place, but in this place—
not for another hour, but this hour.

10

I think continually of those who were truly great.
Who, from the womb, remembered the soul's history
Through endless corridors of light where the hours are suns,
Endless and singing. Whose lovely ambition
Was that their lips, still touched with fire,
Should tell of the spirit clothed head to foot in song.
And who hoarded from the spring branches
The desires falling across their bodies like blossoms.

What is precious is never to forget
The delight of the blood drawn from ageless springs
Breaking through rocks in worlds before our earth;
Never to deny its pleasure in the simple morning light,
Nor its grave evening demand for love;
Never to allow the traffic to smother
With noise and fog the flowering of the spirit.

Near the snow, near the sun, in the highest fields
See how these names are fêted by the waving grass,
And by the streamers of white cloud,

And whispers of wind in the listening sky;
The names of those who in their lives fought for life,
Who wore at their hearts the fire's center.
Born of the sun they traveled a short while towards the sun,
And left the vivid air signed with their honor.

11

O world, thou choosest not the better part.
It is not wisdom only to be wise,
And on the inward vision close the eyes,
But it is wisdom to believe the heart.

Our knowledge is a torch of smoky pine
That lights the pathway but one step ahead
Across a void of mystery and dread.
Bid, then, the tender light of faith to shine
By which alone the mortal heart is led
Unto the thinking of the thought divine.

12

. . . Into my heart's night
Along a narrow way
I groped; and lo! the light,
An infinite land of day.

13

A woman doesn't meet her God every day,
a man doesn't always feel his prayers,
not every hour is one of grace.
We fall, we fail,
to the end of our road.
We turn back only to lose our way yet again,
to wander in search of forgotten paths.

But God holding a candle
looks for all who wander, all who search.

14

    For I have learned
To look on nature, not as in the hour

Of thoughtless youth; but hearing oftentimes
The still, sad music of humanity,
Nor harsh nor grating, though of ample power
To chasten and subdue. And I have felt
A presence that disturbs me with the joy
Of elevated thoughts; a sense sublime
Of something far more deeply interfused,
Whose dwelling is the light of setting suns,
And the round ocean and the living air,
And the blue sky, and in the mind of man:
A motion and a spirit, that impels
All thinking things, all objects of all thought,
And rolls through all things. Therefore am I still
A lover of meadows and the woods,
And mountains; and of all that we behold
From this green earth; of all the mighty world
Of eye, and ear—both what they half create,
And what perceive; well pleased to recognize
In nature and the language of the sense
The anchor of my purest thoughts, the nurse,
The guide, the guardian of my heart, and soul
Of all my moral being.

15

A certain day became a presence to me;
there it was, confronting me—a sky, air, light:
a being. And before it started to descend
from the height of noon, it leaned over
and struck my shoulder as if with
the flat of a sword, granting me
honor and a task. The day's blow
rang out, metallic—or was it I, a bell awakened,
and what I heard was my whole self
saying and singing what it knew: *I can.*

16

There is joy
in all:
in the hair I brush each morning,

in the Cannon towel, newly washed,
that I rub my body with each morning,
in the chapel of eggs I cook
each morning,
in the outcry from the kettle
that heats my coffee
each morning,
in the spoon and the chair
that cry 'hello there, Anne'
each morning,
in the godhead of the table
that I set my silver, plate, cup upon
each morning.

All this is God,
right here in my pea-green house
each morning,
and I mean,
though often forget,
to give thanks,
to faint down by the kitchen table
in a prayer of rejoicing
as the holy birds at the kitchen window
peck into their marriage of seeds.

So while I think of it,
Let me paint a thank-you on my palm
for this God, this laughter of the morning,
lest it go unspoken.

The Joy that isn't shared, I've heard,
dies young.

17

Mont Blanc yet gleams on high;—the power is there,
The still and solemn power of many sights,
And many sounds, and much of life and death.
In the calm darkness of the moonless nights,
In the long glare of day, the snows descend
Upon that Mountain; none beholds them there,

Nor when the flakes burn in the sinking sun,
Or the star-beams dart through them:—Winds contend
Silently there, and heap the snow with breath
Rapid and strong, but silently! Its home
The voiceless lightning in these solitudes
Keeps innocently, and like vapor broods
Over the snow. The secret Strength of things
Which governs thought, and to the infinite dome
Of heaven is as a law, inhabits thee!
And what were thou, and earth, and stars, and sea,
If to the human mind's imaginings
Silence and solitude were vacancy?

18

I wonder if
anything is impossible
to a God
who can make
evergreen trees with black trunks
cast blue shadows
on white snow.

19

    Even today,
a man will suddenly pull up and pray.
He's not wrapped in Tallit,
No, he wears a knotted tie and polished shoes;
and he's not bowed down in a synagogue,
but standing in the middle of town at the depot.
Waiting for the next train,
he stands and prays *to whom it may concern:*
        I am. There is.

20

    And now we praise the weaver:
    weaving the word, this life,
    weaving it;
    weaving, weaving, weaving & weaving;
    shearing/spinning

shearing and spinning it
forth and back,
shearing, spinning, weaving
0 & dyeing the vivid hues in the colors of Why
& mending the faded fabric in the shades of Because . . .
a single simple song to you:
you are the silence & I the song
you you you the song are,
 and I, I am the silence
I/you/we are the
blue burst of dawn/ and the darkening dusk

21

Maker of all the living
every passing moment You create Your world anew:
withdraw Your gracious love an instant,
and all You've made would cease to be . . .
Instead, every passing moment finds You pouring out Your endless
    blessing,
and morning stars appear to sing their song of love to You,
the blazing sun comes forth to sing its song of light to You,
and angels voice their sacred chant to You,
and soul intone their psalms of thirst for You.
Once more the grasses carol their longing for You,
and birds chirp their joy in Your presence.
Trees shawled in leaves now sigh their prayer to You,
and springs softly bubble in adoration.
And still the oppressed bare their hearts to You, a Tallit their armour,
As their soul's pleading splits the heavens.
One ray only of Your light, and we are bathed in Your light!
One word only of Your words, and we rise to life renewed.
One hint only of Your eternal presence, and we are drenched in the
    dew of youth.
O God, You make all things new, ever and ever:
Take us, Your children, and make us new.
Breathe Your living spirit into us,
that we may start life afresh
with childhood's unbounded promise.

22

God of lonely hours,
God holy and awesome,
    who breathed my puzzled Jewish soul
        (so apparent, and so hidden)
    within me,
        and within me kindled the human light
    in all its colors;
God who made me an emblem
    for my age:
at dusk, dawn, noon
You grind me with desert stone, sand and with
sweet promise of grapes that will be wine,
    You lure me, and
hang me over the abyss of my own depths
    day after day —
Don't now disappear,
You who keep me whole:
Be with me.
Gather my blossoms falling at Your feet,
my honest thanks
    for Your love
    and being's wonder.

23

A prayer, that is said alone,
Starves, having no companion.
Great things ask for, when thou dost pray,
And those great are, which ne're decay.
Pray not for silver, rust eats this;
Ask not for gold, which metal is:
Nor yet for houses, which are here
But earth: such vowes nere reach Gods eare.

24

The prologues are over. It is a question, now,
Of final belief. So, say that final belief
Must be a fiction. It is time to choose.

25

All, all for immortality!
Love, like the light, silently wrapping all!
Nature's amelioration blessing all!
The blossoms, fruits of ages—orchards divine and certain;
Forms, objects, growths, humanities, to spiritual Images ripening.
Give me, O God, to sing that thought!
Give me—give him or her love, this quenchless faith
In Thy ensemble. Whatever else withheld, withhold not from us,
Belief in plan of Thee enclosed in Time and Space;
Health, peace, salvation Universal.
Is it a dream?
Nay, but the lack of it the dream,
And, failing it, life's lore and wealth a dream,
And all the world a dream.

26

Left alone under the heavens
sitting on a bench
I tell God about remembered friends
now gone without a word
and I tell God about the flowers I liked to smell,
I speak of broad fields.

Left alone under the heavens
—are there heavens still I wonder—
sitting on a bench
somewhere
I tell God about the heavens
though I can't say now where—or if— they might be:

Do I enfold them?
Do they enfold me?

27

Every evening, God, You take Your burnished goods from Your shop
        window
—Works of the Chariot, Tables of the Covenant, marvelous tales,
        radiant crosses and bells—

Putting them back inside their dark boxes You close the shutters and
    say:
'Not a single prophet came to buy!'

28

Your fate, God,
is now the fate
of trees and stones, of sun and moon,
whose believers left them
when they began to worship You.

But You must stay with us,
like the trees, at least, like the stones, at least,
like the sun the moon and the stars.

29

You,
whom we turn to
not knowing where,

You,
who are everywhere
yet not here,

You,
whom we question
without reply,

Please,
give us tomorrow's good
today.

30

Think not it was these colours, red and white,
Laid but on flesh that could affect me so,
But something else, which thought holds under lock
And hath no key of words to open it.
They are the smallest pieces of the mind
That pass the narrow organ of the voice;
The great remain behind in that vast orb
Of the apprehension, and are never born.

31

i thank you God for most this amazing
day:for the leaping greenly spirits of trees
and a blue true dream of sky;and for everything
which is natural which is infinite which is yes

(i who have died am alive again today,
and this is the sun's birthday;this is the birth
day of life and of love and wings:and of the gay
great happening illimitably earth)

how should tasting touching hearing seeing
breathing any—lifted from the no
of all nothing—human merely being
doubt unimaginable You?

(now the ears of my ears awake and
now the eyes of my eyes are opened)

32

My God,
teach me to bear
time's grace, that passes
without return.

Teach me to bear
the yoke of promises
too easy to say
and to renounce.

Teach me to bear
the pain of surrender
unsought,
and unforetold.

33

O God
give me strength to forget
evils over and done,
history's falls and fouls,
yesterday's frozen hope.

And give me strength to keep watch
for fair weather after a stormy day,
incense of flowers
and quiet waves.

Give me strength to wait and time to hope:
until the last day
strength to keep watch and rejoice
as doves are hatched and babes are born,
as flowers bud and blossom
and visions break out and grow.
Give me strength,
O God.

34

Where the mind is without fear and the head is held high;
Where knowledge is free;
Where the world has not been broken into fragments by narrow
    domestic walls;
Where words come from the depths of truth;
Where tireless striving stretches its arms towards perfection;
Where the clear stream of reason has not lost its way in the arid
    desert sands of dead habit;
Where the mind is led forward by You into ever-widening thought
    and action—
Into that heaven of freedom, my Maker, let my people awake.

35

For poor brides who were servant girls
Mother Sarah taps sparkling wine
from dark barrels and pitchers.
She who is destined to have a full pitcher,
to her, Mother Sarah carries it with both hands;
and she who is given only a small goblet
has Mother Sarah's tears that fall into it.
And to the street girls
dreaming of white wedding shoes,
Mother Sarah brings clear honey
on tiny trays

to their tired mouths.
To poor brides of noble birth,
ashamed to lay their trousseau of patches
under their mother-in-law's eye,
Mother Rebecca brings camels
heaped with white linen.
And when darkness spreads out around them
and all the camels kneel down to rest,
Mother Rebecca measures out ell after ell of linen
from the rings of her hand
to her golden bracelet.
For those whose eyes are weary
from gazing after every neighbourhood child
and whose hands are thin from longing
for a small soft body
and a cradle's rocking,
Mother Rachel brings healing leaves
from faraway mountains,
and comforts them with a kind word,
'at any hour God may open the closed womb.'
To those who weep at night on lonely beds
and have no one to bring their grief to,
murmuring to themselves with burnt lips,
to them Mother Leah comes softly
and covers their eyes with her pale hands.

36

Whenever two people begin
to write
Their lives' poem
On a single leaf,
Of hammered paper,
The angels sing,
Of course,
and the ends of the universe,
Bright with stars
Move somehow closer.
And even
In the deep of winter,

The earth fallen with snow,
Like a jewel, yes,
Shines in the sunlight,
So
Their joy together
Eternally
Becomes
God's smile.

37

Among the old men that you know,
There is one, unnamed, that broods
On all the rest, in heavy thought.

They are nothing, except in the universe
Of that single mind. He regards them
Outwardly and knows them inwardly,

The sole emperor of what they are,
Distant, yet close enough to wake
The chords above your bed to-night.

38

cutting greens
curling them around
i hold their bodies in obscene embrace
thinking of everything but kinship.
collards and kale
strain against each strange other
away from my kissmaking hand and
the iron bedpot.
the pot is black,
my hand,
and just for a minute
the greens roll black under the knife,
and the kitchen twists dark under the knife,
and i taste in my natural appetite
the bond of live things everywhere.

39

The road is so beautiful, says the lad.
The road is so hard, says the youth.
The road is so long, says the man.
    The old man sits on the roadside to rest.
Sunset colours his beard a reddish gold.
Grass gleams with evening dew.
A late bird sings unbidden . . .
    Will you remember how long it was, and its beauty?

40

Not because of victories
I sing,
having none,
but for the common sunshine,
the breeze,
the largesse of the spring.

Not for the victory.
but for the work done
as well as I was able;
not for a seat upon the dais
but at the common table.

41

Success is counted sweetest
By those who ne'er succeed.
To comprehend a nectar
Requires sorest need.

Not one of all the purple host
Who took the flag to-day
Can tell the definition,
So clear, of victory,

As he, defeated, dying,
On whose forbidden ear
The distant strains of triumph
Break, agonized and clear.

42

Hope is the thing with feathers
That perches in the soul,
And sings the tune without the words
And never stops at all,

And sweetest in the gale is heard;
And sore must be the storm
That could abash the little bird
That kept so many warm.

I've heard it in the chillest land,
And on the strangest sea;
Yet, never, in extremity,
It asked a crumb of me.

43

Who are happy?
Those who see a blossoming world
and give it their blessing.

Who are strong?
Those who restrain their grief
and teach it to smile.

44

Why put your trust in Time, which has no truth in it?
Alas, my task is so great and my day is so short!
We urge our neighbors not to sin, saying:
"Don't let your passions lead you astray."
But when we ourselves sin, we say:
"What can I do? What I am and what I do are in the hands of the
     One who made me."

45

Each of us has a name
given us by God,
and given us by our father and mother.

Each of us has a name
given us by the way we stand,

our way of smiling,
and the clothes we wear.

Each of us has a name
given us by the planets,
and by our neighbors.

Each of us has a name
given us by our sins,
and by our longing.

Each of us has a name
given us by our enemies
and by the ones we love.

Each of us has a name
given us by our feast days,
and by our craft.

Each of us has a name
given us by what do not see,
and by the way we die.

46

They are not gone from us. O no! they are
The inmost essence of each thing that is
Perfect for us; they flame in every star;
The trees are emerald with their presences.
They are not gone from us; they do not roam
The flaw and turmoil of the lower deep,
But now have made the whole wide world their home,
And in its loveliness themselves they steep.

They fail not ever; theirs is the diurn
Splendor of sunny hill and forest grave;
In every rainbow's glittering drop they burn;
They dazzle in the massed clouds' architrave;
They chant on every wind, and they return
In the long roll of any deep blue wave.

47

They alone are left me; they alone still faithful,
for now death can do no more to them.

At the bend of the road, at the close of day,
they gather around me silently, and walk by my side.

This is a bond nothing can ever loosen.
what I have lost: what I possess forever.

48

The garlands wither on your brow;
    Then boast no more your mighty deeds!
Upon Death's purple altar now
      See where the victor-victim bleeds.
        Your heads must come
        To the cold tomb:
Only the actions of the just
Smell sweet and blossom in the dust.

49

They list for me the things I may not know:
Whence came the world? Whose hand flung out the light
Of yonder stars? How could a God of Right
Ordain for earth an ebbless tide of woe?

Their word is right; I would not scorn their doubt
Who press their questions of the how and why.
But this I know: that from the star-strewn sky
There comes to me a peace that puts to rout

All brooding thoughts of dread, abiding death;
And, too, I know with every fragrant dawn
That Life is Lord, that, with the Winter gone,
There cometh Spring, a great reviving breath.

It is enough that Life means this to me.
What death shall bring, some sunny morn shall see.

50

It may be so with us, that in the dark
When we have done with time and wander space,
Some meeting of the blind may strike a spark,
And to death's empty mansion give a grace.
It may be that the loosened soul may find
Some new delight in living without limbs,
Bodiless joy of flesh-untrammeled mind,
Peace like a sky where starlit spirit swims.
It may be that the million cells of sense,
Loosed from their seventy years' adhesion, pass
Each to some joy of changed experience,
Weight in the earth or glory in the grass;
It may be that we cease; we cannot tell.
Even if we cease, life is a miracle.

51

Birth is a beginning
And death a destination.
And life is a journey:
From childhood to maturity
And youth to age;
From innocence to awareness
And ignorance to knowing;
From foolishness to discretion
And then, perhaps, to wisdom;
From weakness to strength
Or strength to weakness—
And, often, back again;
From health to sickness
And back, we pray, to health again;
From offense to forgiveness,
From loneliness to love,
From joy to gratitude,
From pain to compassion,
And grief to understanding—
From fear to faith;
From defeat to defeat to defeat—

Until, looking backward or ahead,
We see that victory lies
Not at some high place along the way,
But in having made the journey,
stage by stage,
A sacred pilgrimage.
Birth is a beginning
And death a destination.
And life is a journey,
A sacred pilgrimage—
To life everlasting.

52

It is a fearful thing
to love
what death can touch.

A fearful thing
to love,
hope, dream: to
be—

to be,
and, oh! to lose.

A thing for fools, this,
a holy thing,
a holy thing
to love.

For
your life has lived in me,
your laugh once lifted me,
your word was gift to me.

To remember this
brings painful joy.

'Tis a human thing, love,
a holy thing,
to love
what death has touched.

53

Apparently with no surprise
To any happy flower,
The frost beheads it at its play
In accidental power.

The blond assassin passes on,
The sun proceeds unmoved
To measure off another day
For an approving God.

54

> "Upon Israel and upon the Rabbis, and upon their disciples and upon
> all the disciples of their disciples, and upon all who the engage in the
> study of the Torah in this place and in every place, unto them and
> unto you be abundant peace, grace, lovingkindness, mercy, long life,
> ample sustenance and salvation, from their Father who is in Heaven.
> And say ye Amen."
>
> *[Kaddish deRabbanan, transl. by R. Travers Herford]*

Upon Israel and upon the rabbis
and upon the disciples and upon all the disciples of their disciples
and upon all who the study the Torah in this place and in every
    place,
to them and to you
peace;

Upon Israel and upon all who meet with unfriendly glances,
    sticks and stones and names—
on posters, in newspapers, or in books to last,
chalked on asphalt or in acid on glass,
shouted from a thousand thousand windows by radio;
who are pushed out of class-rooms and rushing trains,
whom the hundred hands of a mob strike,
and whom jailers strike with bunches of keys, with revolver butts;
to them and to you
in this place and in every place
safety;

Upon Israel and upon all who live
as the sparrows of the streets

under the cornices of the houses of others,
and as rabbits
in the fields of strangers
on the grace of the seasons
and what the gleaners leave in the corners;
you children of the wind—
birds
that feed on the tree of knowledge
in this place and in every place
to them and to you
a living;

Upon Israel
and upon their children and upon all the children of their children
in this place and in every place
to them and to you
life.

55

Merely to have survived is not an index of excellence.
Nor, given the way things go,
Even of low cunning.
Yet we have seen the wicked in great power,
And spreading himself like a green bay tree.
And the good as if they had never been;
Their voices are blown away on the winter wind.
And again we wander the wilderness
For our transgressions
Which are confessed in the daily papers.

Except the Lord of Hosts had left unto us
A very small remnant,
We should have been as Sodom,
We should have been like unto Gomorrah.
And to what purpose as the darkness closes about
And the child screams in the jellied fire,
Had best be our present concern,
Here, in this wilderness of comfort
In which we dwell.

Shall we now consider
The suspicious posture of our virtue,
The deformed consequences of our love,
The painful issues of our mildest acts?
Shall we ask,
Where is there one
Mad, poor and betrayed enough to find
Forgiveness for us, saying,
"None does offend,
None, I say,
None?"

56

Will there yet come days of forgiveness and grace,
When you will walk in the field as the innocent wayfarer walks?
And the soles of your feet caress the clover leaves:
Though stubble will sting you, sweet will be their stalks.
Or rain will overtake you, its thronging drops tapping
On your shoulder, your chest, your throat, your gentle head bowed,
And you walk in the wet field, the quiet in you expanding
Like light in the hem of a cloud.

And you will breathe the odor of furrow, breathing and quiet,
And you will see mirrored in the gold puddle the sun above,
And simple will be these things and life, permitted to touch,
Permitted, permitted to love.

Slowly you will walk in the field. Alone. Unscorched by flame
Of conflagrations on roads that bristled with horror and blood.
Again
You will be peaceful in heart, humble and bending
Like one of the grasses, like one of us.

57

> And he said: No longer shall your name be Jacob, but Israel;
> for you have contended with God and with human beings,
> and have prevailed.
>
> *(Genesis 32:28f)*

And so night after night, God, You come to me,
Not with favor, but to try my strength,

And as I prevail against You 'til morning—again I am alone,
A poor wayfarer, a stranger, limping on my thigh.

"You have contended with God and with human beings, and have
     prevailed"—
Wondrous One, is this is all the blessing You allotted me!
Alas, I know, I have prevailed against you all, overcome all things
but one. This one thing: myself—

Your blessing weighs heavily upon me, I cannot bear it,
Limping, alone, on all the world's roads.
Defeat me once at least and give me rest when morning comes,
The rest that all the vanquished know!

Night again. I am alone. Again God descends.
"Israel!" — Here I am, God, here I am.
Oh, why do you come to wrestle with me night after night,
And with dawn abandon me to limp along my way?

58

The ram came last of all. And Abraham didn't know that it came
to answer the boy's question[1]—that boy, first of his strength when
his day was on the wane.

The old man raised his head. Seeing that it was no dream and that
the angel stood there—the knife slipped from his hand.

The boy, released from his bonds, saw his father's back.

Isaac, as the story goes, was not sacrificed. He lived for many years,
saw what pleasure offered, until his eyesight dimmed.

But he bequeathed that hour to his offspring. They are born with a
knife in their hearts.

59

Bound hand and foot he lies
on the stony altar
and waits.

Eyes half shut
he looks at his father
and waits.

Father sees his eyes
and strokes his son's brow
and waits.

With old and trembling hands,
father picks up the knife
and waits.

From above a Voice cries: Stop!"
The hand freezes in air
and waits.

The veined throat dances
with the miracle of the test
and waits.

Father gathers up the son.
The altar is bare, now,
and waits.

Ensnared in thorns a lamb
looks at the hand with a knife
and waits.

60

'Where is the lamb for the burnt-offering?'

[Genesis 22]

Quite without poems
I've reached a shore where the words are thick,
So that thought cannot fly without losing its feathers.
Here the nettles catch my hair,
and slaughter is an afternoon's diversion, like prayer;
so that this saint slits my throat to spare another
whose greater worth escapes me.

I am quite without rhymes, equally short on reasons:
I feel the knife too keenly on my skin
and hear a cry. It may be
the lips from which the sound expired
were mine.
I cannot say for certain.

In this place, this time, are many sounds:
cries and the occasional scream;
one cannot locate one's own with that confident precision
that marks the lying witness.

I've reached a shore where dreams are dead.
Before me stands a dark wood, handle for this knife.
Your image holds me bound.
Quite without poems I cry out to you,
my whole desire and center of my screaming heart.
And even now,
as my blood slips off the shining blade,
your claim on me is love.

61

> "And though after my skin worms destroy this body, yet in
> my flesh shall I see God."
>
> *[Job 19:26]*

O the chimneys
On the ingeniously devised habitations of death
When Israel's body drifted as smoke
Through the air—
Was welcomed by a star, a chimney sweep,
A star that turned black
Or was it a ray of sun?

O the chimneys!
Freedom way for Jeremiah and Job's dust—
Who devised you and laid stone upon stone
The road for refugees of smoke?

O the habitations of death
Invitingly appointed
For the host who used to be a guest—
O your fingers
Laying the threshold
Like a knife between life and death—

O you chimneys
O you fingers
And Israel's body as smoke through the air!

62

The first ones to be destroyed were the children,
    orphans, abandoned upon the face of the earth,
they who were the best in the world,
the acme of grace on the dark earth!
From them, the bereaved of the world,
in a house of shelter we drew consolation;
Form the mournful faces, mute and dark,
we said the light of day will yet break upon us!

They, the children of Israel, were the first in doom and disaster,
most of them without father and mother,
were consumed by frost, starvation and lice;
holy messiahs sanctified in pain. . . .
Say then, how have these lambs sinned?
Why in days of doom were they the first victims of wickedness,
the first in the trap of evil!

The first were they detained for death;
the first into the wagons of slaughter,
they were thrown into the wagons, the huge wagons,
like heaps of refuse, like the ashes of the earth—
They killed them,
and they transported them,
exterminated them
without remnant or remembrance. . . .
The best of my children were all wiped out!
I woe unto me—
Doom and desolation!

63

But who emptied your shoes of sand
When you had to get up, to die?
The sand which Israel gathered,
Its nomad sand?
Burning Sinai sand,
Mingled with throats of nightingales,
Mingled with wings of butterflies,
Mingled with the hungry dust of serpents;

Mingled with all that fell from the wisdom of Solomon,
Mingled with what is bitter in the mystery of wormwood.
O you fingers
That emptied the deathly shoes of sand.
Tomorrow you will be dust
In the shoes of those to come.

64

We orphans
We lament to the world:
Our branch has been cut down
and thrown in the fire—
Kindling was made of our protectors—
We orphans lie stretched out on the fields of loneliness.
We orphans
We lament to the world:
At night our parents play hide and seek—
From behind the black folds of night
The faces gaze at us.
Their mouths speak:
Kindling we were in a woodcutter's hand—
But our eyes have become angel eyes
And regard you.
Through the black folds of night
They penetrate—
We orphans
We lament to the world:
Stones have become our playthings,
Stones have faces, father and mother faces
They wilt not like flowers, nor bite like beasts—
And burn not like tinder when tossed into the ovens—
We orphans we lament to the world:
World, why have you taken our soft mothers from us
And the fathers who say: My child, you are like me!
We orphans are like no one in this world any more!
O world
We accuse you!

65

Why the black answer of hate
to your existence, Israel?

You stranger
from a star one farther away
than the others.

Sold to this earth
that loneliness might be passed on.

Your origin entangled in weeds—
your stars bartered
for all that belongs to moths and worms,
and yet: fetched away from dreamfilled sandy shores of time
like moonwater into the distance.

In the others' choir
you always sang
one note lower
or one note higher—

you flung yourself into the blood of the evening sun
like one pain seeking the other.
Long is your shadow
and it has become late for you
Israel!

How far your way from the blessing
along the aeon of tears
to the bend of the road
where you turned to ashes

and your enemy with the smoke
of your burned body
engraved your mortal abandonment
on the brow of heaven!

O such a death!
When all helping angels
with bleeding wings
hung tattered
in the barbed wire of time!

Why the black answer of hate
to your existence
Israel?

66

Black milk of dawn we drink it at even
we drink it at noon and mornings we drink it at night
we drink and we drink
we are digging a grave in the skies there one lies uncrowded.
A man lives in the house he plays with the serpents he writes
he writes when the dark comes to Germany your golden hair
    Margarete
he writes it and steps from the house and the stars flash he
    whistles up his dogs
he whistles out his Jews let a grave be dug in the earth
he commands us now play for the dance.

Black milk of dawn we drink you at night
we drink you mornings and noon we drink you at even
we drink and we drink.

A man lives in the house he plays with the serpents he writes
he writes when the dark comes to Germany your golden hair
    Margarete
your ashen hair Shulamith we are digging a grave in the
skies there one lies uncrowded.
He calls stab deeper into the earth you there you others sing
    sing and play
he reaches for the iron in his belt he swings it his eyes are blue
stab deeper your spades you there you others play on for the dance.

Black milk of dawn we drink you at night
we drink you noon and mornings we drink you at even
    we drink and we drink.
A man lives in the house your golden hair Margerete
your ashen hair Shulamith he plays with the serpents.

He calls play sweeter of death death is a master from Germany
he calls stroke darker the violins then you will climb as smoke into
    the sky
then you will have a grave in the clouds there one lies uncrowded.

Black milk of dawn we drink you at night
we drink you at noon death is a master from Germany
we drink you at even and mornings we drink and we drink
death is a master from Germany his eye is blue
he hits you with a lead bullet his aim is true
A man lives in the house your golden hair Margerete
he sets his dogs upon us he gives us a grave in the sky
he plays with the serpents and dreams death is a master from
 Germany
your golden hair Margerete
your ashen hair Shulamith.

67

You called us
and trembling we armed ourselves
for a stony road, grown over with thorns.
Bodies aflame and blazing pyres
were our light on the way.
Stones whistled murder;
howls, screams of hate:
Above them all, we heard Your voice,
a voice they'd stilled a while—
but not forever.
Now out of the ovens
You cry out.
Now You whisper within us,
a secret terrible to reveal.
Too many answers to a riddle
too difficult to solve.
This people Israel:
our cries choked off by hangmen's ropes,
every road to safety blocked,
Every light of rescue darkened . . .
And yet above the noise of so many throats
thirsty for our blood,
we hear Your voice—
a voice they'd stilled a while
by their deeds:
But not forever.

68

We are not the silent!
The only silence is Yours.
Grant perfect rest
to the scream and the hope. For
we haven't many choices,
only the one prospect of reaching the fair
    at the end of it all, by filling
the Promised Cup with our spilt blood
for the soul to drink
and find strength to walk
a straight line
back
    to the world.

69

Yes, I did not plow, I did not sow,
I did not pray for the rain.
Suddenly, see now, my fields have sprouted
Sun-blessed grain in place of thorn.

Is it the aftergrowth, provender from of old,
Grains of delight harvested long ago?
They have remembered me in days of affliction,
Burst forth, growing in me by a secret way.

Burgeon, flourish, plains of wonder,
Burgeon, flourish, ripen in haste!
I remember the words of comfort:
Aftergrowth and aftergrowth shall you eat.

70

Working is another way of praying.
You plant in Israel the soul of a tree.
You plant in the desert the spirit of gardens.

        Praying is another way of singing.
        You plant in the tree the soul of lemons.
        You plant in the gardens the spirit of roses.

Singing is another way of loving.
You plant in the lemons the spirit of your son.
You plant in the roses the soul of your daughter.

> Loving is another way of living.
> You plant in your daughter the spirit of Israel.
> You plant in your son the soul of the desert.

71

I have not sung to you
or praised your name, my land,
for mighty deeds
and war's victories;
my hands have planted seedlings
by Jordan's quiet shore,
my feet have beaten paths
in lonely forests.
How poor, Mother, how very poor
your daughter's gift.
Only:
a shout of joy at the break of light,
a stifled sob for your pain.

72

If my days remaining on earth be few,
Let me know beauty.

Let the heat of battle sear the earth no more,
Let us live out our lives.

Let my people come back to its loved land.

Let me have a small house in a village
Hidden among the fields.

For I am weary:

My life has been a long flight
Along unmarked roads,
Unsheltered.

And let my windows be open to the world.

73

Would that I were a stone
like all the stones of Jerusalem;
and how blessed,
were my bones joined to the Wall!
Why should my body be spared more than
my soul, which endured
fire and water with my people?

Take me with the Jerusalem stone
and place me in the walls
and set me with plaster,
and out of the very walls my bones
will sing,
that pine to greet the messiah.

74

The earth grows still
The lurid sky slowly pales
Over smoking borders.
Heartsick but still alive
A people stands by
To greet the miracle
Second to none.
Readied, they wait beneath the moon,
Wrapped in awestruck joy,
Before the light.
And now
A girl and boy step out,
And slowly walk
Before the waiting nation.
In workday clothes and heavy shoes,
Dressed for battle still,
They climb in silence.
Their hands still show
The filth of the day's battle
And the night of fire.
Infinitely weary,
But vowing not to rest,

They wear their youth
Like dewdrops on the hair.
Silent the two approach
And stand unmoving.
No sign tells:
Do they live,
Or are they dead?
Through wondering tears,
The people asks:
Who are you?
And the silent two reply:
We are the silver platter
Upon which the Jewish State
Was served to you.
This said,
They fall in shadow
At the nation's feet.
In Israel's chronicles
Will the rest be told.

Readings for Reflection and Study

A New Year

The old year has died and the new year has scarcely begun. In this pause before the account is made of the past, and my life is judged for what it is, I ask for honesty, vision, and courage. Honesty to see myself as I am, vision to see myself as I should be, and the courage to change and realize myself.

Many obstacles block my return: my lack of trust, my anxieties and fears, and old habits of selfishness and greed. They divide me from my true nature, and deny me the contentment and peace You offer.

Your hand is open to every living being. At the smallest sign You come to meet us, for You are generous to forgive. On this day of repentance and return, stretch out Your hand to me, so that I may grasp it, and walk with me along the paths of love and duty into the harmony and peace that are waiting for me.

Resolution

There are many fine things which you mean to do some day, under what you think will be more favorable circumstances. But the only time that is surely yours is the present; hence this is the time to speak the word of appreciation and sympathy, to do the generous deed, to forgive the fault of a thoughtless friend, to sacrifice self a little more for others. Today is the day in which to express your noblest qualities of heart and mind, to do at least one worthy thing which you have long postponed, and to use your God-given abilities for the enrichment of some less fortunate fellow traveler. Today you can make your life significant and worthwhile. The present is yours to do with as you will.

God in life and in history

Philosophy can teach us only that God is plausible, but Jewish history shows us God in action—the freeing of the slaves, their decision to commit themselves to the Torah, the guidance in their building of a small, weak people into a nation that changed the face of the world, their strength in enduring tragedy and resisting brutalization and the faith and the energy involved in building Israel in the years following the Second World War. We experience the reality of God in our own lives, but we experience it vicariously as well when we examine the history of the Jewish people. No one who reads the story of our 3,000 years of tribulation and accomplishment can deny that God makes a difference in the world.

Spiritual reality

Belief in God is more than a simple acceptance of the idea that God exists. It involves a particular view of life, a belief that there is a spiritual quality in human life and in the universe—and a belief that this spiritual quality matters.

Two kinds of searching

. . . the admitted, conscious, whole-hearted searching for God in itself constitutes the finding of God. You see, there are two kinds of searching. There is firstly the searching for something that is lost, shall we say, a precious stone. Now the process of searching for the stone, and the act of finding the stone, are completely separated from one another in time. We can describe the very point at which the searching ended and the finding began. Now the search for God is not of that kind, and those who feel that the search for God must necessarily end in some kind of experience which will in effect be the finding, are generally sure to be disappointed.

There is another kind of searching. This kind may be likened to listening to a piece of music. Now it is true that the piece of music will have a final climax and resolution, and that will be our finding. But that climax, unlike the precious stone, is completely worthless without the musical moments that have preceded it. In fact we have begun to discover that climax as soon as we have heard the first note of the music, and the whole of the listening process not only leads up to the discovery, but is the discovery of the climax.

Religious experience

There are no easy ways, there are no simple solutions. What comes easy is not worth a straw. It is a tragic error to assume that the world

316

is flat, that our direction is horizontal. The way is always vertical. It is either up or down; we either climb or fall. Religious experience means struggle uphill.

How to see

As the hand held before the eye hides the tallest mountain, so this small earthly life hides from our gaze the vast radiance and mystery of which the world is full; and if you can take life's distractions from before your eyes, as one takes away one's hand, you will see the great radiance within the world.

The religious answer

Religion offers answers without obliterating the questions. They become blunted and will not attack you with the same ferocity. But without them the answer would dry up and wither away. To question is a great religious act; it helps you live great religious truth.

Holy and unholy

Even more frustrating than the fact that evil is real, mighty and tempting is the fact that it thrives so well in the disguise of the good, that it can draw its nutriment from the life of the holy. In this world, it seems, the holy and the unholy do not exist apart, but are mixed, interrelated and confounded. It is a world where idols may be rich in beauty, and where the worship of God may be tinged with wickedness.

Worship is not easy

In worshipping—as others have worshipped and others will worship—we transcend our smaller lives and feel ourselves part of a larger existence, illuminated by the light of eternity.

I say 'worship,' not 'prayer,' because to most people prayer means asking God for something. But worship means turning one's whole personality towards God and focussing on God with such intensity that one's thoughts are transformed into an attitude of love. It is unlikely this experience will happen right away. For worship, like other activities of the human spirit, grows in power with experience.

You may have thought it easy to worship. Religions tend to encourage this impression, by suggesting that worship simply involves reciting prayers sanctified by tradition. But although traditional prayers can serve as a means of worship—to express and stimulate it—they do not constitute it. Worship is a directing of the spirit towards God, so that through it there comes to the worshipper a personal awareness of God's presence.

The Presence of God in prayer

Why are we told to recite the verse "Eternal God, open my lips, and let my mouth declare Your praise" before our most sacred prayer? Like banks to a river, lips form the outer edges of human speech. We pray that God may release us from those limits, so that our mouths may declare God's endless praise.

As you begin your prayer, reciting the words: "Eternal God, open my lips and let my mouth declare Your praise," the Presence of God comes into you. Then it is the Presence herself who commands your voice; it is she who speaks the words through you. One who knows in faith that all this happens within him/her will be overcome with trembling and with awe.

The right attitude in prayer

It seems . . . that we use our prayers as a jargon, and like those who use holy and divine words for sorceries and magical effects; and that we count on their effect depending on the texture, sound, or sequence of the words, or on our bearing. For with our soul full of lust, untouched by repentance or by any fresh reconciliation with God, we go and offer words that memory lends to our tongue, and hope from them to derive expiation for our sins. There is nothing so easy, so gentle, and so favorable as the divine law; she calls us to herself, sinful and detestable as we are; she stretches out her arms to us and takes us to her bosom, no matter how vile, filthy, and besmirched we are now and are to be in the future. But still, in return, we must look on her in the right way. We must receive this pardon with thanksgiving, and, at least for that instant when we address ourselves to her, have a soul remorseful for its sins and at enmity with the passions that have driven us to offend her. Neither the gods nor good people, says Plato, accept the wicked person's present.

Our secret wishes

There are few who would dare place in evidence the secret requests they make of God.

A God to praise and rejoice in

Once l remember (I think l was about 4 year old, when) l thus reasoned with myself, sitting in a little Obscure Room in my Father's poor House. If there be a God, certainly He must be infinite in Goodness. And that l was prompted to, by a real Whispering Instinct of Nature. And if He be infinit in Goodness, and a Perfect Being in Wisdom and Love, certainly He must do most Glorious Things: and give us infinit Riches; how comes it to pass therefore that l am so poor? of so Scanty and Narrow a fortune, enjoying few and Obscure Comforts? l thought l could not believ Him a GOD to me, unless all His Power were Employed to Glorify me. l knew not then my Soul, or Body: nor did l think of the Heavens and the Earth, the Rivers and the Stars, that Sun or the Seas: all those were lost, and Absent from me. But when found them made out of Nothing for me, then l had a GOD indeed, whom l could Prais, and rejoyce in.

A form of life

Prayer is not a discourse. It is a form of life, the life with God. That is why it is not confined to the moment of verbal statement. The latter can only be the secondary expression of the relationship with God, an overflow from the encounter between the living God and the living person.

How to fulfill a commandment

Know that all the practices of worship, such as reading the Torah, prayer, and the performance of the other commandments, have only the end of training you to occupy yourself with God's commandments . . . rather than with matters pertaining to this world; you should act as if you were occupied with God, and not with that which is other than God. If, however, you pray merely by moving your lips while facing a wall, and at the same time think about your buying and selling; or if you read the Torah with your tongue while your heart is set upon the building of your habitation and do not consider what you read; and similarly in all cases in which you perform a commandment merely with your limbs—as if you were digging a hole in the ground or hewing wood in the forest—without reflecting either upon the meaning of that action or upon the One from whom the commandment proceeds or upon the end of the action, you should not think that you have achieved the end.

The ideal of freedom

The ideal of freedom is essential to Judaism. Its value is implicit in many of the laws, in the institution of the Sabbath, and it is expressly celebrated at Passover.

The Exodus is about a quest for freedom—the freedom to worship God. Yet in worshipping God we take on a responsibility. Indeed, Freedom and Responsibility are intimately related. Freedom is a necessary condition of responsibility; and the assumption of responsibility gives worth and meaning to freedom.

Carry your own lantern

A young disciple complained to his Rebbe: 'When I am studying Torah I feel filled with light and life, but as soon as I cease from study this feeling leaves me. What should I do?'

The Rebbe replied: 'You are like someone who walks through a forest on a dark night, accompanied by a companion who carries a lantern. Then their paths divide, and each must go on alone.

'Carry your own lantern, and you need not fear the darkness.'

Self and others

To begin with oneself, but not to end with oneself;
to start from oneself, but not to aim at oneself;
to comprehend oneself, but not to be preoccupied with oneself.

Interdependence

If you think you can live without others, you are mistaken, and you are even more mistaken if you think others cannot live without you.

The path to freedom

Darkness is not the road to light, dictatorship and paternalism are not the paths to freedom and independence, terror is no express train to the golden age.

Love is a decision

To love somebody is not just a strong feeling—it is a decision, it is a judgment, it is a promise. If love were only a feeling, there would be no basis for the promise to love each other for ever. A feeling may come and go. How can I judge that it will stay for ever, when my act does not involve judgment and decision?

A man's ethical will

Visit the sick and suffering. Be cheerful in their presence, but not excessively so. Respect the feelings of poor people by giving to them anonymously. Respond when someone asks you for help, and do not speak harshly. When a poor person eats with you, do not keep back your best food.

Keep far from wicked people and scandal-mongers. Do not . . . broadcast the faults and failings of your acquaintances.

Marry someone with whom you can share your life. Encourage your children to study God's teachings. Do not rejoice if things go badly for someone you dislike. If your enemy is hungry, provide food. Be careful not to cause pain to those who have lost their loved ones, and refrain from setting yourself up as both judge and jury against anyone.

Never storm into your house or cause those that live with you to be afraid of you. Rid your soul of anger, that inheritance of fools. Love wise people and strive to improve.

A woman's ethical will

I wanted, on the occasion of my farewell, to leave you, my dear children, instructions and rules for conduct. As all of you, however, are grown up, I shall limit myself to some general though important instructions.

Above all I admonish you to cherish virtue and fear God; otherwise you can neither achieve full happiness on earth nor find peace and reward in the world to come. Content yourself with your fate and fortune and accommodate your needs to your income, behave peacefully to everybody and among yourselves. Live, moreover, in concord and assist each other with advice and deeds.

You must hold together ever more closely and firmly. You need such closeness, and you will need it more than ever, once the sad event occurs—so much sadder for you than for me—your mother's being torn from you, and thus, as it were, the center disappearing from the circle.

Farewell, and accept the blessing of your always faithful mother.

Selections from Pirkei Avot

Chapter 1

SIMEON THE RIGHTEOUS was one of the [last] members of the Great
    Assembly. He would say:
The world stands on three things:
On Torah,
On worship,
On deeds of loving kindness.

ANTINGONUS OF SOCHO received [Torah] from Simeon the righteous.
    He would say:
Are you servants who serve in the hope of reward —
or servants who serve without thought of reward?
And let the fear[2] of Heaven be upon you.

YOSE BEN YO'EZER of Zareida and Yose ben Yochanan of Jerusalem
    received [Torah] from them. Yose ben Yo'ezer says:
Let your home be a meeting-place for the wise,
Sit in the dust of their feet,
And with thirst drink in their words.

Yose Ben Yochanan of Jerusalem says:
Let your house be opened wide.
Let the poor be members of your household.

JOSHUA BEN PERACHIA and Nitai the Arbelite received [Torah] from
    them. Joshua ben Perachiah says:
Find yourself a teacher.
Get yourself a friend.
And give everyone the benefit of the doubt.

HILLEL AND SHAMMAI received [Torah] from them.
Hillel says:
Be a disciple of Aaron,
Loving peace and pursuing peace,
Loving people and drawing them near to the Torah.

He would say:
A name made great is a name lost.
Who does not add, subtracts.
Who does not learn is self-destructive.
Who uses the crown passes away.

He would say:
If I am not for myself, who will be for me?
And if I am [only] for myself, what am I?
And if not now, when?

SHAMMAI SAYS:
Set aside a regular time for study.
Say little, do much.
Greet everyone with a cheerful countenance.

RABBAN SIMEON BEN GAMALIEL says:
    The world sustains itself by three things:
By truth,
by justice,
and by peace,
as it is said *[Zechariah 8:16]:* Execute the judgment of truth and
    peace in your communities.

Chapter 2

HILLEL SAYS:
Do not separate yourself from the community.
Do not be sure of yourself until the day you die.
Do not judge your friends until you are in their place.
Say nothing that cannot be understood³ [at once, hoping that] in
    the end it will be understood.
And do not say, 'When I have time I will study'— you may never have
    the time.

He would say:
A boor does not fear sin.
The ignorant cannot be pious.
The bashful cannot learn.
The hot-tempered cannot teach.
One too steeped in business cannot grow wise.
Where no one else rises to the occasion,⁴ you must make the effort.

RABBAN YOCHANAN BEN ZAKKAI SAID to them: What is a right path to take?

Rabbi Eliezer says: A good eye.[5]

Rabbi Joshua says: A good friend.

Rabbi Yose says: A good neighbor.

Rabbi Simeon says: Foresight.[6]

Rabbi Elazar says: A good heart.[7]

He said to them: I prefer the words of Elazar ben Arach, for his words include all of yours.

And he said to them: What is a wrong path to avoid?

Rabbi Eliezer says: A bad eye.[8]

Rabbi Joshua says: A bad friend.

Rabbi Yose says: A bad neighbor.

Rabbi Simeon says: A person who borrows and does not repay.

Rabbi Elazar says: A wicked heart.

He said to them: I prefer the words of Elazar ben Arach, for his words include all of yours.

THEY SAID three things [each].

Rabbi Eliezer says:

Let your friend's honor be as precious to you as your own.

Do not be easily angered.

Return[9] one day before you die.

Rabbi Joshua says:

The bad eye,

the Yetzer Hara,[10]

and hatred of others

drive one out of the world.[11]

Rabbi Yose says:

Let your friend's property be as precious to you as your own.

Discipline yourself to learn Torah, for it is not born within you.

And let your every deed be for the sake of Heaven.

Chapter 3

RABBI CHANINA BEN DOSA says:

When your fear of sin comes before your wisdom, your wisdom will endure. And when your wisdom comes before your fear of sin, your wisdom will not endure.

He would say: When your deeds are greater than your wisdom, your wisdom will endure. And when your wisdom is greater than your deeds, your wisdom will not endure.

RABBI AKIBA says:

Beloved is human kind, created in the Divine Image.

Love greater still made us aware that we were created in the Image of God, as it is said *[Genesis 9:6]*: God made human kind in the divine image.

Beloved are Israel, who are called children of the Omnipresent. Love greater still made them aware that they are called children of the Omnipresent, as it is said *[Deuteronomy 14:1]*: You are children of the Eternal One, your God.

Beloved are Israel, who have been given a precious instrument. Love greater still made them aware that they had been given that precious instrument with which the world was created,[12] as it is said *[Proverbs 4:2]*: I have given you a good doctrine, My Torah; do not forsake it.

All is foreseen, yet free choice is given.
The world is judged as good.[13]
And all depends on the balance of deeds.

RABBI ELAZAR BEN AZARIAH says:
Where there is no Torah, there is no right conduct;
where there is no right conduct, there is no Torah.
Where there is no wisdom, there is no reverence;
where there is no reverence, there is no wisdom.
Where there is no understanding, there is no knowledge;
where there is no knowledge, there is no understanding.
Where there is no meal, there is no Torah;
where there is no Torah, there is no meal.

Chapter 4

BEN ZOMA says:

Who are wise? Those who learn from every person, as it is said *[Psalm 119:99]*: From all my teachers I have gained understanding.

Who are strong? Those who control their own passions, as it is said *[Proverbs 16:32]*: Those slow to anger are better than the strong, and those who rule their spirits than one who takes a city.

Who are rich? Those who are happy with what they have, as it is said *[Psalm 128:2]*: When you eat what you have worked for, happy are you, fortunate your lot. (Happy are you—in this world; fortunate your lot—in the world-to-come.)

Who are honored? Those who honor others, as it is said *[I Samuel 2:30]*: For those who honor Me I will honor . . .

BEN AZZAI says:

Run to do a minor Mitzvah as [though it were] a major, and flee from transgression. For one good deed leads to another, and one transgression leads to another; and the reward of one good deed is another, while the punishment of one transgression is another.

He would say:

Despise no one, and regard nothing as impossible, for you will find no one whose hour does not come, and not a thing that does not have its place.

RABBI SIMEON says:
There are three crowns:
the crown of Torah,
the crown of priesthood,
and the crown of royalty,
but the crown of a good name is best of all.

RABBI YANNAI says:
We have in our hands neither the prosperity of the wicked nor the
    suffering of the righteous.

RABBI JACOB says:
This world is like an anteroom to the world-to-come. Prepare your-
    self in the anteroom, so that you may enter the banquet-hall.

He would say:
Better one hour of repentance and good deeds in this world than

all the life of the world-to-come,
and better one hour of bliss in the world-to-come than all the life
    of this world.

RABBI SIMEON BEN ELAZAR says:
Never try to pacify[14] your friend who is in the grip of rage,
nor attempt to console one whose loved one has just died,
nor raise a question about a vow[15] just made,
nor rush to see your friend who has just been disgraced.

ELISHA BEN ABUYAH[16] says:
Learning as a child: what is that like? Ink inscribed on new paper.
Learning in old age: what is that like? Ink inscribed on blotted
    paper.

RABBI YOSE BAR YUDAH of Kefar Habavli says:
A person who learns from the young is like one who eats unripe
grapes and drinks wine straight from the vat. A person who learns
from elders is like one who eats ripe grapes and drinks vintage wine.

RABBI says:
Don't look at the flask but at what's in it. There are new flasks full
of old wine, and old ones that don't even contain new wine.

Chapter 5

A CLOD[17] has seven traits and so does a sage:
The wise never speak before one whose wisdom is greater;[18]
they do not interrupt their companions;
they are not afraid to reply;[19]
they ask to the point and reply as they should;[20]
they speak of first things first and of last things last;
concerning something of which they have not heard they say,
    "I have not heard";
and they acknowledge the truth.[21]
The reverse is true of fools.

PEOPLE COME in four [basic] types. One says:
What's mine is mine and what's yours is yours: this is the average
    type. (But some say: This is the way of Sodom.[22])
What's mine is yours and what's yours is mine: simple-minded.

What's mine is yours and what's yours is yours: the best.
What's mine is mine and what's yours is mine: the worst.

THERE ARE four [basic] temperaments:
Quick to anger and quick to appease: its gain is cancelled by its
     loss.
Slow to anger and slow to appease: its loss is cancelled by its gain.
Slow to anger and quick to appease: the best.
Quick to anger and slow to appease: the worst.

STUDENTS COME in four [basic] types:
Quick to learn and quick to forget: their gain is cancelled by their
     loss.
Slow to learn and slow to forget: their loss is cancelled by their gain.
Quick to learn and slow to forget: a sage.
Slow to learn and quick to forget: a misfortune.

EVERY CONTROVERSY that is for the sake of Heaven will bear fruit. And
     one that is not for the sake of Heaven will not bear fruit.
What is a controversy for the sake of Heaven? That of Hillel and
     Shammai.
And one not for the sake of Heaven? That of Korach and his cabal.[23]

JUDAH BEN TEMA says:
Be bold as a leopard,
light as an eagle,
swift as a gazelle,
and strong as a lion
to do the will of your Divine Parent in Heaven.

He would say:
Five years old for [the study of] Scripture,
Ten for Mishnah,
Thirteen for the Mitzvot,
Fifteen for Talmud,
Eighteen for the Chuppah,[24]
Twenty to pursue,[25]
Thirty for vigor,
Forty for understanding,

Fifty for counsel,
Sixty for old age,
Seventy for whitened hair,
Eighty for strength,[26]
Ninety for bent back,
One hundred—one is as good as dead and passed away and faded
    from the world.

BEN BAG BAG[27] says:

Turn it[28] and turn it again, for everything is in it; reflect on it and
grow old and grey in it and do not move away from it, for there is
no better way than this.

NOTES

1. "Where is the lamb for the burnt-offering?" (Genesis 22).

2. The 'fear' of Heaven is not terror but awe or reverence, and that is expressed by us through ethical behavior.

3. Hertz suggests another possibility: "Divulge nothing that ought to be kept secret, on the plea that in the end all things are sure to become public knowledge."

4. Literally, "Where there are no men, you must strive to be one."

5. Or, 'A generous spirit.'

6. Cf. Tamid 32a: "Who is wise? One who foresees the consequences of things."

7. 'Good will.'

8. The 'bad eye' (עַיִן הָרַע, ayin hara) came in time to mean the 'evil eye.'

9. to God; i.e., 'repent.'

10. Translated in various ways: 'The Evil Impulse,' 'The Will to Evil,' 'The Evil Inclination.' The term derives ultimately from Genesis 8:21 (cf. Genesis 6:5), and sometimes, without the modifier, יֵצֶר, yetzer, means, simply, 'human nature.' See, e.g., Deuteronomy 31:21, Psalm 103:14. Its root, יצר, yatzar, means 'create, fashion, form.' Here, it may be rendered 'wrongful, illicit desires.' More often than not, in rabbinic literature, it is associated with sexual desire, though sometimes it is used to refer to our passional nature in a broader sense—in fact, to those things that drive us not only to destroy but also to create. The rabbis also utilize an opposite term in reference to energies which have their approval, namely, יצר הטוב, Yetzer Hatov, 'The Good Inclination,' etc.

11. I.e., "exclude one from human society."

12. The Midrash (Genesis Rabbah 1.1) pictures God as consulting the Torah (the 'precious instrument') and using it as the blueprint for the Creation.

13. I.e., we are given the benefit of the doubt. There is a presumption of innocence in the divine judgment, as there should be in human judgment.

14. Or, 'make amends with.'

15. Or, 'try to persuade him to annul a vow.'

16. 80–ca. 145 CE. He is included despite the fact that he was a notorious apostate.

17. Heb. גולם, golem, an unformed, incomplete being; unfinished matter; a fool.

18. Cf. Proverbs 18:13.

19. Or, "do not hasten to reply"; or, "are not at a loss for an answer."

20. I.e., 'pertinently'; the Heb. has the word הלכה—Halachah—'the law.'

21. I.e., they give up their own view when shown to be wrong.

22. See Ezekiel 16:49. The parenthetical view holds that, far from being the way of the average person, the first type follows the way of intense selfishness, denying all relation between people, leaving each shut away in radical aloneness. (Travers-Herford)

23. See Numbers 16–17.

24. I.e., marriage.

25. I.e., a livelihood. Or, according to Rashi, righteousness.

26. See Psalm 90:10.

27. B–G, the 2nd and 3rd letters of the Heb. alphabet. The Eng. equivalent would be: 'X' (Anonymous) Sometimes this saying is attributed to a proselyte—one of Hillel's disciples, perhaps. If so, the Heb. ב, ג B+G=H (2+3=5), and ה [H], is the letter added to Abram's name when he became Abraham, a sign of exaltation; and Abraham is the quintessential convert and the quintessential 'missionary.' This applies also to Ben Hei Hei in the next Mishnah.

28. I.e., the Torah.

Notes

Introduction

The purpose of the Notes is to identify the sources of the prayers, readings, and meditations contained in *Al M'zuzot Beitecha, On the Doorposts of Your House,* (the successor volume to *Shaarei Habayit, Gates of the House*) and to draw attention to, and explain, any textual changes that have been made as well as features of the translations which require special comment. Since much in this volume derives from *Shaarei Tefillah, Gates of Prayer* (C.C.A.R., 1975), the reader of these Notes will find that they contain many references to the Notes to *Gates of Prayer.* The Notes to the latter volume may be found in *Shaarei Binah, Gates of Understanding,* also published by the C.C.A.R., in cooperation with the Union of American Hebrew Congregations.

In addition to the prayers and readings which *Shaarei Habayit* has borrowed from *Shaarei Tefillah,* it owes to that volume (of which it had been intended originally to be a part) its basic design and English style. Other main sources of the present volume include *Service of the Heart* (edited by Rabbis John D. Rayner and Chaim Stern for the Union of Liberal and Progressive Synagogues, London, 1967) and *The Union Home Prayerbook* (C.C.A.R., 1951), which the earlier incarnation of this volume replaced. In addition, many items have been written specially for this volume by the Editor.

The Notes that follow owe much to Rabbi John D. Rayner, who compiled the Notes to *Service of the Heart,* and to Rabbi A. Stanley Dreyfus.

Chaim Stern

Abbreviations

Books of the Bible

N.B. The references are to the Hebrew (Masoretic) division into chapters and verses, as maintained in Jewish translations of the Bible; Christian translations differ slightly in this respect.

Deut.	Deuteronomy
Exod.	Exodus
Gen.	Genesis
Eccles.	Ecclesiastes
Hos.	Hosea
Isa.	Isaiah
Jer.	Jeremiah
Josh.	Joshua
Lev.	Leviticus
Neh.	Nehemiah
Num.	Numbers
Prov.	Proverbs
Ps., Pss.	Psalm, Psalms
Sam.	Samuel

Other Abbreviations

Abrahams	Dr. Israel Abrahams (1858-1925), *A Companion to the Authorized Daily Prayer Book*, Hermon Press, N.Y., 1966 (first published 1922).
ASD	Rabbi A. Stanley Dreyfus
B.	Babylonian Talmud
b.	ben (son of)
Baer	Seligman Baer: *Seder Avodat Yisrael*, Roedelheim, 1868, and often reprinted.
Ber.	Berachot (tractate of Mishnah, Tosefta, or Talmud)
C.	Century (Common Era, unless otherwise stated)
CCAR	Central Conference of American Rabbis
C.E.	Common Era
cf.	compare
CS	Rabbi Chaim Stern
Eng.	English
ed.	edited, edition, editor
e.g.	for example
f., ff.	following (one or two pages)
FOP	*Forms of Prayer* (Reform Synagogues of Great Britain, 1977)
GOH	*Gates of the House (Shaarei Habaayit)*, ed. by CS (1977)
GOP	*Gates of Prayer (Shaarei Tefillah)*, ed. by CS (1975)
Heb.	Hebrew
ibid.	in the same place
J.	'Jerusalem' Talmud
JE	*The Jewish Encyclopedia*, Funk and Wagnalls Company, N. Y. and London, 1901
JR	Rabbi John D. Rayner
loc.cit.	in the passage cited
M.	Mishnah
MV	Machzor Vitry
p., pp.	page, pages

pb	Prayerbook
R.	Rabbi, Rav
R.H.	Rosh Hashanah (tractate of Mishnah, Tosefta, or Talmud)
RSGB	Reform Synagogues of Great Britain (Publisher of FOP, etc.)
SB	Rabbi Sidney Brichto
Soferim	'Minor Tractate' Soferim
SOH	*Service of the Heart*, ed. by CS and JR (1967)
SPJH	*Services and Prayers for Jewish Homes* (ULPS, 1955 ed.)
SRA	*Seder Rav Amram Gaon*, ed. Daniel Goldschmidt, Hotza'at ha-Rav Kook, Jerusalem, 1971
trad.	tradition, traditional, traditionally
trsl.	translated by, translation, translator
ULPS	Union of Liberal and Progressive Synagogues (London)
UPB	*The Union Prayerbook for Jewish Worship*, Newly Revised, Part 1, 1940
v., vv.	verse, verses
vol.	volume
Y.K.	Yom Kippur (tractate of Mishnah, Tosefta or Talmud)

Prayers and Readings for Every Day

EVENING AND MORNING PRAYERS FOR CHILDREN

All the translations (except as otherwise indicated) are newly revised versions by CS of his translations in Gates of the House, which this volume supercedes.

Number	Page	
1	3	*Creator of day and night . . .* Freely adapted by CS from SOH, p. 389, where it was freely adapted from SPJH, p. 192. The beginning is based on the *Ma-ariv Aravim* (See GOP Notes No. 53), and the conclusion reflects, somewhat, a prayer already found in SRA, p. 6, which forms the sequel of the prayer beginning 'Master of all worlds' (See GOP Notes No. 493). Here revised by CS.
2	3	*Modeh ani l'fanecha . . .* The first three words of a prayer trad. recited upon arising: 'I give thanks to You, O living and eternal Sovereign, for having restored my soul to me in mercy: great is Your faithfulness.'
3	3	*Thank You, God . . .* New, by CS, influenced by SOH, p. 391. Here revised by CS.
4	4	*Hear, O Israel . . .* See GOP Notes No. 55.

EVENING AND MORNING PRAYERS FOR ADULTS

5	4	*God of the light . . .* New, by CS. Suggested by the trad. night prayer (see Birnbaum, *Daily Prayer Book*, pp. 777 and ff. The second paragraph alludes to Ps. 121:4. On the opening words, see No. 2. On *Hear, O Israel . . .*, see Notes to GOP, No. 55; *Into Your hands . . .* is trsl. rather freely from the last stanza of *Adon Olam* (See Notes to GOP, Notes to Songs, No.1). Here revised by CS.
6	5	*Praised be the Eternal God . . .* New, by CS. Based on a trad. morning prayer; see GOP, pp. 286f. On *Hear, O Israel . . .*, see Notes to GOP, No. 55.

BLESSINGS BEFORE EATING

7	7	See note 18.

THANKSGIVING FOR FOOD

           We praise You . . . from the earth. The blessing is based on Ps. 104:14, and is cited in M. Ber. 6.1. For other blessings related to food and drink, see Nos. 15 and 38. The trsl. is new, by CS.

           A Pilgrim Song . . . Ps. 126. The custom of chanting Ps. 126 before the *Birkat Hamazon* on Sabbaths and Festivals has been traced back to the year 1603 (Abrahams, p. 208).

          Let us praise God . . . The custom of thanking God after meals is very ancient (Cf. Josephus, *Wars of the Jews II;* 8.5, referring also to the blessing *before* meals; B. Sota 10a; B. Ber. 35a-b). The obligation to do so was derived from Deut. 8:10 (B. Ber. 48b). The text of the *Birkat Ha-mazon,* 'The Blessing after Meals,' consists of four benedictions. The introductory formula (here modified by CS) derives from M. Ber. 7.2; B. Ber. 45b; 49b–50a. All four benedictions are mentioned in B. Ber. 48b. Our version has benefitted from consultation with R. Norman Hirsh.

         Sovereign God . . . for all who live. B. Ber. 48b. Contains an allusion to Ps. 136:25. See, too, Ps. 145:15f. The trsl. is new, by CS.

         For this good earth . . . Quotes Deut. 8:10 (See B. Ber. 48b). Our version of this, the second benediction, is slightly abridged. The insertions for Chanukah and Purim are trad. See Notes to GOP, Nos. 78 and 79. The trsls. are new, by CS. The English is somewhat abridged. We change the trad. text in one phrase, replacing '. . . the covenant You have sealed in our flesh' with '. . . the covenant You have sealed in our hearts'.

         Eternal God, Source of our being . . . Our version of this benediction is slightly abridged, and our trsl. somewhat free. The benediction is mentioned in B. Ber. 49a. It includes both a Sabbath ('Eternal God, strengthen our resolve') and a Festival ('Our God . . . be mindful . . . .') insertion, both alluded to in B. Pesachim 105a. The Festival insertion comes from the Festival *Kedushat Hayom* (See GOP Notes Nos. 76 and 800). Here we add Yom Ha-atsma-ut to the insertions for the Day, and we include part of the final sentence of the 'Ya-aleh Veyavo,' omitted elsewhere. The Hebrew which underlies our English phrase, 'Your open and generous bounty,' contains the word 'overflowing,' while other versions of the Ashkenazi liturgy print, incorrectly, 'holy.'

         We praise You, divine Parent of Israel . . . A slightly abridged version of the last benediction of the Grace after Meals. This benediction is said to have been introduced at the end of the Bar Kochba revolt, 135 C.E. (B. Ber. 48b; B. Ta'anit 31a). Some parts of this benediction are, however, medieval. The phrase 'may divine and human grace and favor . . .' alludes to Prov. 3:4. We have added an insertion for Yom Ha-atsma-ut to the other insertions in this benediction. It is derived from the trad. *Yotser.* See GOP Notes Nos. 258 and 100. We have added a number of (optional) insertions to this benediction. The first four and the sixth derive from the Sefardi liturgy. The fifth is a composite, the first half coming from the Sefardi liturgy and the conclusion from SRA, p. 46. In the penultimate sentence we have added, in English 'and all the world' (see GOP Notes No. 83). The last sentence is Ps. 29:11, both alluded to in B. Pesachim 105a.

         Thanksgiving for Food (short form) . . . The *Birkat Hamazon* ('Thanksgiving after meals') was formerly much shorter than the present versions, and only grew longer in the course of time as additional passages were included. The trad. knows of a number of 'short forms' designed for particular purposes—for use by working men (B. Ber. 16a), mourners (SRA, p. 187), and for general use (Singer, *The Authorised*

Number	Page

Daily Prayer Book, 14th ed., London, 1929, p. 286). Our version is similar to but not identical with the latter one, which is based on one which first appeared in Venice in 1603, by R. Naftali b. David Zechariah Mendel.

16   24   *Thanksgiving for certain fruits and grains* . . . This is, in fact, substantially the short form devised by R. Naftali b. David Zechariah Mendel (first published in Venice, 1603), referred to in the preceding Note.

17   26   *Short thanksgiving for other foods* . . . B. Ber. 37, 44; J. Ber. 6.1.

BENEDICTIONS OF PRAISE AND THANKSGIVING

18   27   *We praise You, Eternal God, Sovereign of the universe* . . . "'The earth is God's, and all its fullness (Ps. 24:1),' but when consecrated by a benediction it becomes our privilege to enjoy it (R. Levi, in B. Ber. 36a)." We offer here a number of trad. benedictions in the light of that statement. The trad. benediction is distinguished by a formula which praises God and proclaims God's sovereignty (B. Ber. 40b), and which is a Rabbinic composition made up of Scriptural phrases: Ps. 119:12; Deut. 6:4; Jer. 10:10. A longer form of the benediction (adding *asher kidd'shanu b'mitzvotav, v'tzivanu*) is recited before the performance of a Mitzvah (e.g., kindling Sabbath lights); it adds these Scriptural allusions: Deut. 28:9; 26:19; 33:4. We omit some trad. benedictions, especially those that occur elsewhere with some regularity in the present PBs. The blessings before eating begin on page 7. The sources of our benedictions are: 'bread,' M. Ber. 6.1; 'wine,' *ibid.*; 'many kinds of food,' B. Ber. 36b; 'fruit of the tree,' M. Ber. 6.1; 'fruit of the earth,' *ibid.*; 'by whose word,' M. Ber. 6.3; 'for giving us life,' B. Pesachim 7b; 'Source of creation,' 'power and might;' 'the great sea,' M. Ber. 9.2; 'filled with beauty,' B. Ber. 54b; 'keep faith with us,' B. Ber. 59a; 'lovely trees,' B. Ber. 43b; 'You share Your wisdom,' B.Ber. 58a; 'You give of Your wisdom,' *ibid.* We have added, in this edition, a substantial number of trad. benedictions, also deriving mainly from B. Ber. Through these benedictions we are reminded of the beauty of the natural world, and of the human world, and of our obligation not to take for granted life and its experiences.

19   30   *To You . . . I offer* . . . The benediction of thanksgiving after recovery from illness or escape from danger is trad. recited after the completion of the Reading of the Torah and before the return of the Scroll to the Ark. It is partially cited in B. Ber. 54b. Our version of the benediction ('You bestow great goodness') is abridged. To the benediction and its response ('May the One who has been gracious . . .'), we add Ps. 116:17 and *Shehecheyanu* (See GOP Notes No. 661). Cf. Maimonides, Mishneh Torah, Hilchot Berachot 10.8.

20   30   *We praise You . . . the Source of all good.* M. Ber. 9.2.

NEW BENEDICTIONS

This section derives from a collection of original blessings for various occasions edited by Rabbis Norman Hirsh and Daniel Polish. The English of the first section ('New Benedictions of Praise') was written by Rabbi Norman Hirsh. All but one of the New Life Cycle Benedictions (later in the book) were written by Rabbis Sue Levi Elwell and Nurit Shein. Rabbi Hillel Cohn wrote the original version of the New Benedictions for the Fulfillment of Mitzvot. All the Bene-

dictions were written in English and then translated into Hebrew by Rabbis Robert Samuel, Nurit Shein and Stanley Chyet. The Hebrew and English were then revised by CS. CS thanks the members of the Chug Shabbat at Temple Beth El of Northern Westchester for their helpful comments and suggestions with regard to these benedictions.

Shabbat and Festivals

WELCOMING SHABBAT

Number   Page

cept of the parental blessing plays an important part already in the Bible (e.g., Gen. 27 and 48f.), as a regular practice on the eve of the Sabbath and of Festivals it is first attested in an ethical treatise *(Brautspiegel)* of the year 1602 (David Philipson in JE, Vol. III, p. 243). There is, however, a reference to the custom in Soferim 18.5. Our first passage is from SOH, p. 401, which adapted it from SPJH, p. 13. Our second is trad. (See Gen. 48:20). Our third passage is Num. 6:24ff.; cf. GOP Notes No. 843; its trsl. is new, by JR and Rabbi Charles Middleburgh.

36   40   *Six days shall you labor* . . . New, by CS. Based on UPB, p. 93 (cf. SOH, p. 401). The quotation is Exod. 20:9f. Here and elsewhere, we note that grape juice may replace wine.

37   41   *Now the whole universe* . . . Gen 2:1ff. Trad. recited before the *Kiddush* only at home. See GOP Notes No. 214.

38   41   *We praise You* . . . *the fruit of the vine.* The benediction to be said before drinking wine [or, as already suggested, grape juice] (M. Ber. 6.1). Wine is a symbol of joy (cf. Ps. 104:15); and since the Sabbath is a day of joy (cf. Isa. 58:13), wine became associated especially with the Sabbath. Thus the commandment: the Sabbath day and sanctify it' (Exod. 20:8), was taken by the Rabbis to mean 'Remember it over wine' (B. Pesachim 106a). So originated the ritual of the *Kiddush,* which is short for *Kiddush Hayom,* 'the Sanctification of the Day.' It consists of the blessing over the wine, followed by a prayer giving thanks for the Sabbath and proclaiming its sanctity. The Mishnah (e.g., M. Ber. 8.1) testifies to its antiquity. It was and is essentially a *home* rite, preceding the evening meal; but the practice of reciting *Kiddush* also in the synagogue (originally for the benefit of travellers who might eat and sleep there) began already in Talmudic times (B. Pesachim 101a). Rav Amram quotes his predecessor, Natronai Gaon, to the effect that 'they make *Kiddush* in the synagogues even when no travellers are present who eat there' (SRA, p. 65). Today this is the general practice.

39   41   *We praise You* . . . *for the holiness of Shabbat.* See preceding Note. The essential themes of this prayer are stipulated in B. Pesachim 117b. The full text, practically as now, appears in SRA, p. 66.

40   42   *We praise You* . . . *from the earth.* See No. 8.

41   43   *For Shabbat Morning* . . . See Notes to GOP, No. 1150.

SONGS FOR SHABBAT

42   45   *Songs for Shabbat* . . . See Notes to GOP, Notes to Songs, Nos. 8, 7, 17, 20, 22, 43, 39, 10, 12, and 11.

HAVDALAH

The word Havdalah *means separation, and especially between the holy and the commonplace (or, as others put it, the profane). The ceremony is known from the time of the Mishnah (M. Ber. 8.5–6). According to the Mishnah, the* Havdalah *began as a home rite; hence the wine, which was part of the afternoon meal on the Sabbath; similarly, the kindling of lights was natural at the end of Shabbat, when no light could be kindled. And it was the custom to bring glowing coals topped with spices into the room at the close of meals. However, the Talmud (B. Ber. 33a) explains* Havdalah *as originally a synagogue rite. The kindling of light at the end of the Sabbath (and therefore on the eve of the first day of the week), in this view, commemorates the light that was created on the first day of creation, and the spices symbolize the 'higher soul' that dwelt with Adam (and that dwells with his descendants) throughout the Sabbath (see B. Pesachim 53b; Gen. Rabbah 12, and Abrahams, pp. 182f.).*

FOR THE NEW MOON

WELCOMING YOM TOV

Number	Page	

69 66 *This festival teaches that . . . Adapted from SOH, pp. 406f., where it is new, by SB.*

70 67 *Now the whole universe . . . Gen. 2.1ff. See No. 37.*

71 68 *We praise You . . . sacred to Israel.* The custom of reciting *Kiddush* over a cup of wine on the eve of Festivals, as on Sabbath eve (See No. 38), was well established in the days of the Talmud (cf. B. Pesachim 105a). The prescribed text is partly cited in Soferim 19.3 and is found fully (almost as now) in SRA, p. 173.

72 68 *We praise You . . . this season.* See GOP Notes No. 661.

73 68 *We praise You . . . in the Sukkah.* Cited in B. Sukkah 46a. Alludes to Lev. 23:42.

74 69 *We praise You . . . from the earth.* See No. 8.

75 70 *For Yom Tov morning . . .* See GOP Notes No. 1152.

BUILDING A SUKKAH

76 73 *Who may abide . . .* See GOP Note No. 292. The trsl. of Ps. 15:1–3, 4b–5. is new, by CS. The ritual for building a Sukkah was an innovation of GOH.

77 73 *Eternal God . . .* New, by CS. It refers to a prayer trad. recited in the Sukkah deriving from a compendium of mystical prayers called *Shaarei Zion* by Nathan b. Moses Hannover, Prague, 1662. See Singer, *op. cit.,* p. 232.

78 74 *We praise You . . . building a Sukkah.* New, by CS, in GOH.

79 74 *We praise You . . . this season.* See Notes to GOP, No. 661.

WELCOMING GUESTS IN THE SUKKAH

80 75 *Eternal One, our God . . .* Adapted by CS (and revised for this volume) from the prayer by Nathan b. Moses cited in No. 77.

81 75 *Abraham, exalted guest . . .* By Isaac Luria (1534–1572; known as the holy Ari, 'Lion,' Luria was the leading Safed Kabbalist). To the seven male 'guests' of the trad. passage, we have added seven equivalent female guests. On each day, all are 'invited,' but a different pair receives the first invitation and serves, as it were, as the leader.

82 78 *I take Lulav and Etrog . . .* Based on a meditation in *Shaarei Zion* (See No. 77). *We praise You . . . the Lulav.* See GOP Note No. 847.

HAVDALAH FOR A FESTVAL

83 79 *We praise You . . . fruit of the vine.* See Notes to GOP, No. 1000.

84 79 *We thank You . . .* See Notes to GOP, No. 1008.

85 79 *We praise You . . . the commonplace from the holy.* See Notes to GOP, No. 1009.

WELCOMING ROSH HASHANAH

86 80 *Happy are those . . .* See No. 29.

87 80 *Fountain of life . . .* New, by CS. It alludes to Ps. 43:3.

88 80 *We praise You . . . the Festival lights.* See No. 63.

89 81 *May God bless you . . .* See No. 65.

90 82 *The observance of Rosh Hashanah . . .* Adapted by CS from *Gates of Repentance* (ULPS, London, 1973), where it is new, by CS. It introduces the *Kiddush,* 'Sanctification.' *Kiddush* is essentially a domestic rite, preceding the meal on the eve of Rosh Hashanah, though the practice of reciting it also in the Synagogue, preceding the *Aleinu* (See

Notes to GOP, No. 978) is ancient (cf. No. 38). It is, however, not essential that it be recited in the Synagogue, and some authorities have actually opposed it on that ground that *Kiddush* should be recited only where one eats. It follows, however, that the recitation of *Kiddush* in the home is regarded by the tradition as mandatory. *Now the whole universe . . .* Gen. 2:1ff. See No. 37. *We praise You . . .* See No. 38. *Eternal God . . . sacred to Israel.* The R.H. *Kiddush* is largely identical with the version for other Festivals that is already mentioned in the Talmud (B. Pesachim 105a). The earliest reference specifically to the R.H. version is Soferim 19.4. Our text is virtually the trad. one, omitting two words that are trad. inserted when R.H. coincides with Shabbat. *We praise You . . . this season.* See GOP Notes No. 661. *We praise You . . . from the earth.* See No.8. *We praise You . . . fruit of the tree.* See No. 18. The custom of eating sweet things on R.H. eve, as a 'good omen,' goes back to Gaonic times (See H. Schauss, *The Jewish Festivals*, p. 158 and Note 167). According to MV, the Jews of France used to eat red apples. The custom of eating sweet apples with honey is first mentioned in Sefer Maharil (a compendium of laws and customs by R. Jacob Moellin, who lived in the Rhineland, 1365–1427), p. 38a. Cf. also Neh. 8:10. *Our God . . .* Also first cited in Sefer Maharil, *loc. cit.*

For Rosh Hashanah Morning . . . Our version of the R.H. morning *Kiddush* is slightly more full than the trad. one, to whose content we add Num. 10:10. The other (and trad.) Scriptural vv. are Exod. 31:16f. and Ps. 81:4f. *We praise You . . . fruit of the vine.* See No. 38. *We praise You . . . from the earth.* See No. 8.

KINDLING THE YOM KIPPUR LIGHTS

Happy are those . . . See No. 29.
The holiest day . . . Adapted from *Gate of Repentance* (ULPS, London, 1973, p. 428), where it is new, by JR.
We praise You . . . Day of Atonement. The custom of lighting a candle on Y.K. eve is already mentioned in the Mishnah (Pesachim 4.4). The text of our blessing is rendered by R. Moses Isserles in his gloss to Shulchan Aruch, Orach Chayim 610.1. *We praise You . . . this season.* See GOP Notes No. 661.
May God bless you . . . See No. 35 (last ten lines).

HAVDALAH FOR ROSH HASHANAH AND YOM KIPPUR

Behold, God is my Help . . . See Notes to GOP, No. 999.
We praise You . . . fruit of the vine. See Notes to GOP, No. 1000.
We praise You . . . all the world's spices. See Notes to GOP, No. 1001.
We praise You . . . of fire. See Notes to GOP, No. 1002.
We praise You . . . the commonplace from the holy. See Notes to GOP, No. 1005.
You teach us to distinguish . . . See Notes to GOP, No. 1006.

THANKSGIVING DAY

Creative Source of all being . . . Adapted by CS (and here revised) from a prayer in the *Union Home Prayerbook*, pp. 29f. *We praise You . . . from the earth.* See No. 8.

Number Page

CHANUKAH

103	95	*The lights of Chanukah* . . . See Notes to GOP, No. 1019.
104	95	*Blessed is the match* . . . See Notes to GOP, No. 675.
105	95	*Zion hears and is glad* . . . Ps. 97:8.
106	95	*The light of our faith . . . Let the lights we kindle* . . . See Notes to GOP, No. 1023. Here revised by CS.
107	96	*We praise You . . . the Chanukah lights.* Cited in B. Shabbat 23a.
108	96	*We praise You . . . You showed wonders* . . . See Notes to GOP, No. 1025 It seems appropriate to include our mothers.
109	96	*We praise You . . . this season.* See Notes to GOP, No. 1026.
110	97	*The people who walked in darkness* . . . See Notes to GOP, No. 1027. However, we replace the last verse of the series with Isa. 2:5.
111	98	*We kindle these lights* . . . See Notes to GOP, No. 1028.
112	99	*Chanukah Songs* . . . See Notes to GOP, Notes to Songs, Nos. 55, 56, 57, and 58. The Heb. text of *Maoz Tzur* is as amended by J.H. Hertz in his PB.

PURIM

113	102	*We come before You* . . . This was new, by CS, in GOH, but reference to it was inadvertantly omitted in the Notes to that volume. Here revised and abridged. *We praise You . . . from the earth.* See No. 8.

The Path of Life

BEGINNINGS

NEW LIFE-CYCLE BENEDICTIONS

See the introduction to New Benedictions above.

114	105	*Menarche blessing* . . . New, by Sue Levi Elwell and Nurit Shein and revised by CS. *I praise You . . . this season of my life.* See GOP Notes No. 661.
115	105	*At the onset* . . . New, by Rabbi Elyse Goldstein and revised by CS. *I praise You . . . for making me a woman.* Modelled after the trad. morning blessing, in which males thank God for not having been made women, while women give thanks for having been made according to God's will. Ours is a positive formulation, also used in other pbs. On these benedictions as a whole, see Notes to GOP, No. 490.
116	105	*On having had confirmation of a pregnancy* . . . New, by Sue Levi Elwell and Nurit Shein and revised by CS.
117	106	*Upon a miscarriage* . . . New, by Sue Levi Elwell and Nurit Shein and revised by CS. It quotes Ps. 130:1, Isa. 1:30.
118	106	*Upon giving birth* . . . New, by Sue Levi Elwell and Nurit Shein and revised by CS. It quotes Prov. 23:25. *We praise You* . . . See GOP Notes No. 661.
119	106	*Upon breast feeding* . . . New, by Sue Levi Elwell and Nurit Shein and revised by CS.
120	107	*Upon experiencing any profound change* . . . New, by Sue Levi Elwell and Nurit Shein and revised by CS.

ON LEARNING OF A PREGNANCY

121   107   *We stand humbled* . . . New here. Adapted by CS from a prayer by Rabbi Sandy Eisenberg Sasso, in an unpublished manuscript ed. by Rabbi Barton Lee, *Rabbi's Manual*, Vol. 2. *We praise You . . . this day.* See Notes to GOP, No. 1026.

DURING PREGNANCY

122   108   *God of all generations* . . . Adapted by CS in GOH from a prayer in the *Union Home Prayerbook*, p. 50, and further revised for this volume. In GOH this was called 'On Behalf of a Woman in Childbirth.'

BY A COUPLE WHO FEAR THEY MAY BE INFERTILE

123   108   *Our God* . . . Adapted by CS from a prayer adapted from Mark Mahler, in an unpublished manuscript ed. by Rabbi Barton Lee, *Rabbi's Manual*, Vol. 2.

BY THOSE SEEKING TO ADOPT A CHILD

124   108   *God of mercy* . . . New here. Adapted by CS from a prayer adapted from Mark Mahler, in an unpublished manuscript ed. by Rabbi Barton Lee, *Rabbi's Manual*, Vol. 2.

ON THE BIRTH OR ADOPTION OF A CHILD

125   109   *Source of all life* . . . Freely adapted by CS from two prayers in the *Union Home Prayerbook*, pp. 52f., and here revised from GOH by CS. *We praise You* . . . See GOP Notes No. 661. *How small you are* . . . New here. Adapted by CS from a prayer by Rabbi Sandy Eisenberg Sasso, in an unpublished manuscript ed. by Rabbi Barton Lee, *Rabbi's Manual*, Vol. 2. *Sovereign God of the universe* . . . M. Ber. 9:2. See No. 18.

ON THE BIRTH OR ADOPTION OF A GRANDCHILD

126   110   *We are thankful* . . . New, by CS, and here slightly revised from GOH by CS. Suggested by a prayer in SPJH, pp 198f. *We praise You* . . . See GOP Notes No. 661.

ON BRINGING A NEW CHILD HOME

127   110   *How lovely are your tents* . . . New here. Adapted by CS from a prayer by Rabbi Sandy Eisenberg Sasso, in an unpublished manuscript ed. by Rabbi Barton Lee, *Rabbi's Manual*, Vol. 2. The opening passage is Num. 24:5. The closing quotation is adapted (Heb. & Eng.) from the last benediction of the morning T'filah.

THE COVENANT OF MILAH

128   112   *Blessed be the child* . . . From Ps. 118:26. The opening words of the circumcision service since the 14th C.

129   112   *The rite of circumcision* . . . Partly adapted by CS from 1952 *Rabbi's Manual*, CCAR, p. 9, and incorporating Gen.17:9, 12a; Gen.17:1, and an allusion to Deut. 30:6. Here revised from GOH by CS .

130   112   *Eternal One, You established a testimony* . . . Ps. 78:5–6a. *You are for*

Number	Page	

ever mindful . . . Ps. 105:8ff. (The trsls. of both of the preceding passages are slightly adapted.) *Give thanks to the Eternal One* . . . Ps. 118:1

131	113	*We praise You* . . . *Mitzvah of circumcision.* Mentioned already in Tosefta Ber. 6.7, a source dating from the time of the Mishnah (2nd–3rd C.)
132	113	*We praise You* . . . *Covenant of Abraham.* See preceding Note.
133	113	*We praise You* . . . *fruit of the vine.* Its use in this service is mentioned already in SRA, p.179, and doubtless is much earlier. Cf. No. 38.
134	114	*Our God and God of our mothers and fathers* . . . Attested since the 14th C. Cf. Baer, p. 583. Here the trsl. is revised from GOH.
135	114	*May the One who blessed* . . . From 1952 *Rabbi's Manual,* CCAR, p. 12. The trsl. is influenced by the latter and by SOH, pp. 430f., and is here revised from GOH.
136	114	*May God bless you* . . . Num. 6.24ff. Cf. ST Notes No. 843. The trsl. is new, by JR and R. Charles Middleburgh.
137	115	*We give thanks* . . . Freely adapted by CS from 1952 *Rabbi's Manual,* CCAR, pp. 12f., and here revised from GOH.

THE COVENANT OF LIFE

In accordance with the principle of the equality of the sexes, for which Reform Judaism has long stood, we offered in GOH a ceremony prepared by CS, entitled 'The Covenant of Life' as the feminine equivalent of The Covenant of Milah, above. It is here revised by CS.

138	116	*Blessed be the child* . . . Ps. 118:28, adapted. Cf. No. 128.
139	116	*Reverence for life* . . . New, by CS, quoting Deut. 30:19.
140	116	*The Mitzvah is a lamp* . . . Prov. 6:23a. *We praise You* . . . Based on a prayer cited in B. Ber. 60b. Cf. SOH, p. 112, GOP, p. 151.
141	116	*Joyfully I bring* . . . New, by CS. *We praise You* . . . *the Covenant of Life.* New, by CS, already in GOH.
142	117	*I, the Eternal One, have called you* . . . Isa. 42:6, slightly adapted.
143	117	*Joyfully I bring* . . . New, by CS. *We praise You* . . . *to sanctify our life.* New, by CS.
144	117	*We praise You* . . . *this season.* See GOP Notes No. 661.
145	117	*This is the day* . . . Ps. 118:24. The use of this and the preceding passage in the present context was suggested for GOH by Michael Isaacson.
146	117	*This is the covenant* . . . Jer. 31:32f. *Give thanks to the Eternal One* . . . Ps. 118:1. Cf. No. 130.
147	118	*We praise You* . . . *fruit of the vine.* See No. 38. Cf. No. 133.
148	118	*Our God and God of our mothers and fathers* . . . See No. 134. Here we have changed the masculine references to the feminine.
149	119	*May the One who blessed* . . . See No. 135. Here we have changed the masculine references to the feminine.
150	119	*May God bless you* . . . See No. 136.
151	119	*We give thanks* . . . See No. 137. Here we have changed the masculine references to the feminine.

FOR THE NAMING OF A CHILD

| 152 | 120 | *God and Creator* . . . Very slightly adapted from SOH, p. 432, where it is adapted from 1952 *Rabbi's Manual,* CCAR, p. 14, and SPJH, p. 151. |

The custom of having such a service of thanksgiving after childbirth has been known since the 15th C.; cf. Abrahams, p.223. The underlying idea can be traced back to Lev.12:6ff. and I Sam. 1:24. On the naming of a child, see H. Schauss, *The Lifetime of a Jew*, pp. 12f., 27ff., 43f., 51ff. Trad. a boy is named at his circumcision, and a girl on the first or fourth Sabbath after birth. In Reform congregations both girls and boys (even though the boy was previously named at his *B'rit Milah*, and the girl at her *B'rit ha-Chayim*) are named and blessed in the synagogue shortly after birth. If desired, the ceremony may be conducted in the home.

153   120   *We praise You . . . Your love and kindness . . .* The present version of this benediction differs from the trad. text; for that text (and a correspondingly different trsl.) see No. 19.

154   120   *We praise You . . . this season.* See GOP Notes No. 661.

155   121   *May the One who blessed . . .* Adapted by CS from SOH, pp. 434f., where it is adapted from 1952 *Rabbi's Manual*, CCAR, p. 14. Here further adapted by the inclusion of the Matriarchs and the provision of separate texts for girls and boys. It is a somewhat condensed version of the Hebrew that precedes it.

156   121   *O God, for the gift . . .* Adapted by CS from SOH, p. 433, where it is adapted from SPJH, pp. 150f.

157   122   *Friends, may you dedicate . . .* Based on a passage by James Hunt and Paul Killinger in *Great Occasions*, ed. by Carl Seaburg (Beacon Press, Boston), 1968, p. 32.

158   122   *Now, in the presence of loved ones . . .* New, by CS.

159   122   *May God bless you . . .* See No. 136.

160   122   *We praise You . . . fruit of the vine.* See No. 38.

AT A BIRTHDAY CELEBRATION

161   123   *God of days and years . . .* Slightly adapted by CS from a prayer in the *Union Home Prayerbook*, p. 31. *We praise You . . . the fruit of the vine.* See No. 38. *We praise You . . . this season.* See Notes to GOP, No. 661. *We praise You . . . many kinds of food.* B. Ber. 36b. See No. 18.

AT THE BEGINNING OF A CHILD'S RELIGIOUS EDUCATION

162   124   *Let these words . . .* Adapted by CS from a prayer in the *Union Home Prayerbook*, pp. 55f. The quotation is from Deut. 6:6f. Here CS has further revised the text and has added the benediction *We praise You . . . to love Torah.*

AT BAR MITZVAH, BAT MITZVAH, OR CONFIRMATION

163   125   *And all your children . . .* Adapted by CS from a prayer in the *Union Home Prayerbook*, pp. 57f. The quotation is from Isa. 54:13. Here CS has further revised the text. *We praise You . . . this season.* See Notes to GOP, No. 661.

BY A BAR MITZVAH OR A BAT MITZVAH

164   126   *O God of Israel . . .* New here, by CS. *We praise You . . . this season.* See Notes to GOP, No. 661.

Number   Page

MENSTRUATION

165   126   *Holy One, as the circle of my life* . . . New here, by CS. Cf. 'Prayer for the New Month,' by Rabbi Vicki Hollander, in *Four Centuries of Women's Spirituality*, ed. by Ellen M. Umansky and Diane Ashton, Beacon Press, Boston, 1992, p. 319. The passage itself is based on the trad. prayer for the New Month. See Notes to GOP, No. 763. *I praise You . . . for making me a woman.* Modelled after the trad. morning blessing, in which males thank God for *not* having been made women, while women give thanks for having been made according to God's will. Ours is a positive formulation, also used in other pbs. On these benedictions as a whole, see Notes to GOP, No. 490.

ON ENTERING COLLEGE

166   127   *By Your grace* . . . New, by CS, here revised by CS from GOH. On the opening quotation, see GOP Notes No. 63. The final sentence alludes to Ps. 119:103.

MARRIAGE PRAYERS

IN CONTEMPLATION OF MARRIAGE

167   128   *I have agreed to enter* . . . New, by CS, here revised by CS from GOP. Based in part on two prayers in the *Union Home Prayerbook*, pp. 45f.

BEFORE THE WEDDING

168   129   *In mercy* . . . New, by CS, here revised by CS from GOP. In addition to its primary use, this prayer might be offered especially by those who, their first marriage having failed, are about to remarry.

ON THE MARRIAGE OF A SON OR DAUGHTER

169   129   *How can I give thanks enough* . . . New, by CS, here substantially revised by CS from GOP. Based on two prayers in the *Union Home Prayerbook*, pp. 47–50.

WEDDING SERVICE

The inclusion of the wedding service is an innovation of the present volume. These benedictions are cited in the Talmud, B. Ketubot 7–8. The Hebrew word for the wedding service is Kiddushin, *'sanctification.' The* Chuppah, *originally a litter in which the bride was conveyed to the site of the service (the home of the groom), is now symbolic of the home the couple will establish. The reading of the wedding contract, the* Ketubah, *during the service, trad. in most Jewish rites, dates from Mediæval times.*

170   130   *Blessed are you* . . . Ps. 118:26. This is one of several biblical vv. that begin the trad. wedding service. Others are Pss. 95:6, 100:2.

171   130   *May the One* . . . Anon. The second word of the first three lines are in alphabetical order, emphasized here by larger initial letters.

Number	Page	

172   130   *Do you . . .* The requirement of consent to marriage may be traced back to Gen. 24, especially vv. 57f.

173   130   *We praise You . . . this season.* See Notes to GOP, No. 661. This benediction is not trad. in the wedding service, but some may wish to use it.

174   131   *We praise You . . . the fruit of the vine.* See No. 38.

175   131   *We praise You . . . You sanctify our life.* A revision by CS of the *Birkat Erusin*, the trad. benediction which ends the ancient betrothal service. This was later incorporated into the wedding service. Its presence here is an innovation, earlier Reform wedding rituals having omitted it.

176   131   *Set me as a seal . . .* An optional passage from Song of Songs 8:6.

177   131   *I betroth you . . .* An optional passage from Hosea 2:21–22a.

178   132   *By this ring . . .* B. Kiddushin 5a (partial citation). The full text of the ring formula is post-Talmudic, as the wedding ring was not used in Talmudic times (See Abrahams, pp. 215f.). In our practice the man and the woman each gives a ring to the other; hence the double ring formula.

179   132   *We praise You . . . marriage-canopy.* The concluding eulogy of Birkat Erusin. See No. 175. Here we use it as the conclusion of the ring ritual.

180   132   *We praise You . . . the fruit of the vine.* See No. 38. This is the first of the trad. Seven [Wedding] Benedictions (*Sheva B'rachot*). The seven benedictions are Talmudic. See Ketubot 8a. The 2nd, 3rd and 4th benedictions refer to the creation story in Genesis, and are here trsl. somewhat freely. The 5th refers to the restoration of our people to Zion, alluding to Isa. 62:5; our text treats it as an accomplished fact. The 6th refers again to Genesis, this time with a reference to the Garden of Eden. The 7th benediction quotes Jer. 33:10f. Our trsl. adds a universal note by inserting a reference to 'earth's four corners'.

181   134   *May God bless you . . .* See No. 136.

182   134   *Alternative benedictions . . .* Here we provide a set of alternative Eng. benedictions, by CS, and place the wine blessing last instead of first.

FRAGRANCE: A WEDDING CUSTOM

183   135   *How precious . . .* Ps. 36:8f.

184   135   *Life's pleasures . . .* Adapted by CS from a passage in an unpublished ms. by Rabbi Barton Lee, *Rabbi's Manual*, Vol. 2, which includes this Sephardic wedding custom.

185   135   *We praise You . . . fragrance.* This is one of the benedictions referred to in Note No. 18.

ANNIVERSARY PRAYERS

186   136   *I am my beloved's . . .* New, by CS, here revised by him from GOH. Based on a prayer in the *Union Home Prayerbook*, p. 32. The quotation is from Song of Songs 2:16, slightly adapted.

187   136   *In the fullness . . .* Slightly adapted by CS from a prayer in the *Union Home Prayerbook*, pp. 32f. For this volume we have included a version of this prayer which may be used when someone other than the couple is asked to bless them. *We give thanks . . . this season.* See GOP Notes No. 661.

Number   Page

OTHER PERSONAL OCCASIONS

CONSECRATION OF A HOUSE

188   138   *In the spirit of our Jewish faith* ... SOH, p. 425, where it comes, slightly adapted, from SPJII, p. 143. The practice of consecrating a new house may have existed already in Biblical times; see Deut. 20:5. According to the Mishnah (M. Ber. 9.3) a person who builds a new house says the *Shehechyanu* (GOP Notes No. 661). The Palestinian Talmud (J. Ber. 9.4) mentions a benediction, similar to the trad. one, to be recited when affixing a *Mezuzah*. Both ideas are combined in our service

189   138   *Hear, O Israel* ... See GOP Notes No. 55. Included here, following SOH (although it does not trad. belong to this ceremony) because it stresses the duty to 'speak of them in your home,' and because it alludes to the *Mezuzah*.

190   139   *Our homes have always been the dwelling place* ... Freely adapted by CS from 1952 *Rabbi's Manual*, CCAR, pp. 50f. The quotation is an adaptation of M. Avot 3.3. On the benediction, see No. 8.

191   139   *We praise You ... fruit of the vine.* See No. 38.

192   139   *The Torah has been our life* ... New, by CS in GOH (Cf. 1952 *Rabbi's Manual*, CCAR, p. 52). On the benediction, see GOP Notes No. 93.

193   140   *Who may abide* ... Ps. 15:1–3, 4b–5. See No. 88. The trsl. is new, by CS.

194   141   *This ancient symbol* ... Adapted by CS for GOH from SOH, p. 426, where it is adapted from 1952 *Rabbi's Manual*, CCAR, pp. 52f. On the benediction itself, see No. 188. The word *Mezuzah* means 'doorpost,' but it has come mainly to signify the scroll containing Deut. 6:4–9; 11:13-21 which is placed in a cylindrical case. The word *Shaddai*, 'Almighty' is inscribed on the back of the scroll, so that it can be seen through an aperture in the case, or it is inscribed on the case itself. *Shaddai* is, in its present use, sometimes interpreted as an acronym for *Shomeir Dal'tot Yisrael*, 'Guardian of the doors (i. e., dwellings) of Israel.' According to Maimonides (Mishneh Torah, Hilchot Mezuzah 6.13), the sole purpose of the *Mezuzah* is to serve as a reminder of the unity of God.

194A   141   *We praise You ... this season.* See GOP Notes No. 661.

195   142   *Unless the Eternal One* ... Ps. 127:1a.

196   142   *In this awareness* ... Slightly adapted in GOH (and here slightly revised) from SOH, p. 428, where it was adapted from A. Minda, *The Sanctuary of the Home*, pp. 7f, and from SPJH, p. 143. The quotations are Num. 24:5 and Ps. 121:8.

BEFORE A JOURNEY

197   143   *The Eternal One shall guard* ... Freely adapted by CS from a prayer in the *Union Home Prayerbook*, p. 41. The quotations are Pss. 121:7; 139:8ff. The concluding paragraph includes an allusion to Ps. 119:105. The concluding eulogy ('We praise You ... Protector of wayfarers.') is new, by CS.

UPON ARRIVING IN ISRAEL

198   143   *On this soil* ... New, by CS. It echoes the Declaration of Independence of the State of Israel, and quotes Isa. 2:3b. *I rejoiced* ... Ps. 122:21–3, 5–9. Verse 3 is repeated to take advantage of the difference in empha-

sis derived from the two trsls. of that verse. Love of Zion, manifested (among other things) in pilgrimages, has been a feature of Jewish life since early times.

ON BEGINNING A NEW ENTERPRISE

199   145   *Unless the Eternal One* . . . Adapted by CS for GOH from a prayer in the *Union Home Prayerbook,* pp. 43f., and here substantially revised by CS. The quotation is from Ps. 127:1a.

AT A TIME OF ACHIEVEMENT

200   145   *I have aspired* . . . Adapted by CS for GOH from the *Union Home Prayerbook,* pp. 188f., 131, and here substantially revised by CS. *God, give me hills . . . to climb them.* From a poem, *Hills,* by Arthur Guiterman.

AT A TIME OF DISAPPOINTMENT

201   146   *My high hopes* . . . New, by CS in GOH, and here substantially revised by CS. It is based on two prayers in the *Union Home Prayerbook,* pp. 102, 184. It quotes Deut. 31:6, Ps. 46:1.

AT A TIME OF ANXIETY

202   146   *Eternal God* . . . New, by CS, for this volume. It quotes Ps. 84:5 and Isa. 41:10.

WHEN OUR BURDENS SEEM TOO HEAVY

203   147   *I come to You* . . . New, by CS for this volume. It quotes Isa. 40:31.

AFTER A TRAUMA

This ritual is new in the present volume, by CS, but was inspired by a number of rituals that have been published in recent years, including the one mentioned in Note 204, and a proposed 'Mikveh Ceremony of Purification after Rape', in an unpublished manuscript ed. by Rabbi Barton Lee, Rabbi's Manual, Vol. 2. *It should be noted, however, that the actual content of the ritual here depends only slightly on other sources.*

204   148   *Just and holy God* . . . Slightly adapted by CS from *Healing—More or Less,* by Jim Cotter, Cairns Publications, Sheffield (England), 1990, p. 92. It is there an adaptation of a ritual devised by Bernice Broggio and Teresa Parker.

205   148   *You are in need* . . . New, by CS. Cf. Cotter, *ibid.*

206   148   *I have been wounded* . . . New, by CS.

207   148   *The God who has implanted* . . . New, by CS. This is followed by Jeremiah 17:14.

208   148   *The God who created* . . . New, by CS, followed by Psalm 27:1.

209   149   *May the God* . . . New, by CS, followed by Psalm 16:11.

210   149   *When we are born* . . . New, by CS. It includes Ezekiel 16:4a, 4–5b, 6b–7a.

211   149   *I have grown* . . . New, by CS. It includes Ezekiel 16:8b,d–9. Ezekiel there

describes God as midwife to Israel, bringing it into life and doing for the infant people what a midwife does for a newborn infant.

212   149   *God is not far off . . .* New, by CS. It includes Lamentations 3:22–24
213   150   *As I know . . .* New, by CS. It includes Pss. 42:3, 131:2.
214   150   *We praise You . . . healing waters.* Trad. upon entering a Mikveh.

ON LIFE WITH OTHERS

215   151   *Loving God . . .* New, by CS in GOH, and revised by him for this volume. It is based on two prayers in the *Union Home Prayerbook*, pp. 139, 157f.

UPON RETIREMENT

216   151   *As I look back . . .* New, by CS, in GOH, and revised by him for this volume. Based on a meditation by Morris Lazaron in UPB II, pp. 215ff. In the 2nd paragraph, the conclusion ('. . . the spirit of wisdom . . . reverence for life.') is adapted from Isa. 11:2. The Isa. passage is utilized in a prayer trad. recited during the Torah Ritual on Sabbaths and Festivals, deriving from *Shaarei Zion* (see No. 77).

SIMCHAT CHOCHMAH

217   152   *River of light . . .* New, by Rabbi Donna Berman, revised by CS, Cantor Dr. Edward Graham, and Rabbi H. Leonard Poller. On the concluding benediction, see No. 18. The ritual called 'Simchat Chochmah', wherein one marks a significant birthday such as the sixtieth, has been developing in recent times particularly among women. We offer this prayer, which might be included in such a ritual. Not in GOH.

ILLNESS AND RECOVERY

Some of these prayers are adapted by CS and ASD from a series issued on cards by the CCAR, 1963. For the concluding eulogy, see GOP Notes No. 67. The section entitled 'In Chronic Illness or Disability' is new for this volume, by CS. Prayers for the sick go back to the Bible (e.g. Moses' prayer for Miriam, Num. 12:13). The Talmud has prayers for the sick: B. Nedarim 39b; and the weekday T'fillah includes a prayer for healing. See Notes to GOP, No. 67. Some of the Psalms are prayers by the sick. The cycle of prayers in chronic illness or disability is an innovation of this volume.

218   153   *In sickness I turn to You . . .* Card No. 8. Here revised by CS.
219   153   *My God and God of all generations . . .* Card No. 14. Here slightly revised by CS. The quotation is Ps.118:17.
220   154   *Sunday . . . There are many . . .* Ps. 4:7; *Light that makes . . .* Sir Thomas Browne; *What is it . . .* New, by CS; *I praise You . . .* Based on a prayer cited in B. Ber. 60b. Cf. SOH, p. 112; GOP, p. 151.
221   154   *Monday . . . Why do You stand . . .* Psalm 10:1; *You know how much . . .* New, by CS, alluding to Ps. 51:12; *I praise you . . . to the weary.* See Notes to GOP, No. 490.
222   155   *Tuesday . . . Be gracious . . .* Ps. 6:3a, 4; *Let these words . . . a loving spirit.* New, by CS, quoting from a poem by H.W. Longfellow, 'The Reaper and the Flowers'; *I praise You . . . who hearken to prayer.* The

concluding eulogy of the 12th Intermediate Benediction of the T'fillah in GOP. See Notes to GOP, No. 74.

223   155   *Wednesday . . . Many are my heart's distresses . . .* Ps. 25:4, 17; *May I not think . . . out of it.* New, by CS, quoting a well known saying by Helen Keller. *I praise you . . . to the weary.* See Notes to GOP, No. 490.

224   156   *Thursday . . . Lead me in Your truth . . .* Ps. 25:5; *The times . . . pain or joy.* New, by CS, mainly quoting a passage by Janet Harrison. *I praise You . . . of all good.* M. Berachot 9:2. Cf. Note No. 18.

225   156   *Friday . . . Now I will lie down . . .* Ps. 4:9; *As the week turns . . .* New, by CS, quoting Ps. 71:14 and two lines from a poem, *From House to House*, by Christina Rossetti; *I praise You . . . who hearken to prayer.* See No. 202.

226   157   *Shabbat . . . Hear me . . .* Ps. 30:11f.; *On Shabbat I see . . .* New, by CS, quoting a passage by Francis Bacon; *I praise You . . . of all good.* See No. 204.

227   158   *Loving God, the healing power . . .* Card No. 21. Here substantially revised by CS.

228   158   *For health of body and spirit . . .* Card No. 20. Here substantially revised by CS.

229   159   *O God, help me . . .* Card No. 25. Here slightly revised by CS.

230   159   *I thank all . . .* Card No. 26. Here slightly revised by CS.

231   159   *We are grateful . . .* Card No. 1. Here substantially revised by CS.

THE VALLEY OF THE SHADOW

IN CONTEMPLATION OF DEATH

The custom of confession on a death-bed is ancient; see B. Shabbat 32a. And cf. Josh. 7:19. The trad. form, which we do not follow here in its entirety, is probably post-Talmudic in origin.

232   160   *Everlasting God . . .* Adapted by CS in GOH from SOH pp. 440f., where it is new, by SB, based on the trad. prayer. Here revised by CS. The quotations are: the last couplet (in a rather free trsl.) of the *Adon Olam* (See Notes to GOP, Notes to Songs, No. 1); an expansion of Exod. 15:18; the response to the *Shema* (GOP Notes No. 55); I Kings 18:39; Deut. 6:4 (See GOH Notes No. 55).

ON HEARING OF A DEATH

233   161   *We praise You . . . the righteous Judge.* M.Ber 9.2. See No. 18 *We praise You . . . eternal life.* We follow the most recent ed. of the CCAR *Rabbi's Manual* and provide an alternative to the benediction said trad. after [hearing of] a death. The words 'You have implanted within us eternal life' are used elsewhere in some Reform liturgies, including UPB, and derive from the benediction after the reading of the Torah.

AFTER A STILLBIRTH OR UPON THE DEATH OF A YOUNG CHILD

234   162   *Out of the depths . . .* Ps. 130:1. *We looked for joy . . .* New, by CS. *How our laughter . . .* New, by CS, quoting Job 11:16. *A woman lost her*

Number   Page

child . . . Anon., from an Eastern source—perhaps Sufi. *Out of the depths* . . . Ps. 130:1. This prayer is an innovation of the present volume.

UPON TERMINATING A PREGNANCY

235   163   *Mother of all life* . . . New, by Rabbi Donna Berman, revised by Cantor Dr. Edward Graham and Rabbi H. Leonard Poller. Not in GOH, this prayer is written to be recited by a woman.

READINGS FROM SCRIPTURE AT A TIME OF BEREAVEMENT

236   163   *I have set You* . . . The 1st of 14 biblical passages, some of which will be read at a funeral service, and whose inclusion here is an innovation of the present volume. All the trsls. are new, by CS. The passages are: Psalm 16:8–11; Ps. 1:1–3; Pss. 144:3f., 90:5f., 3; Ps. 36:8–10; Ps. 90:1b–6, 9b–10, 12, 14–17; Ps. 15: 1–3, 4b–5; Isa. 40:6–8; Ps. 23; Job 28:1f., 12, 28, Ps. 119:2; Ps. 121; Prov. 31: 10, 20, 25f., 28 (adapted)–31; Eccles. 3:1–7; Ps. 112:1–9; Ps. 139:7–11, 14, 23.

ON RETURNING HOME AFTER A FUNERAL

237   176   *Out of the depths* . . . New, by CS, in GOH, and revised by him here. It begins by quoting Ps.130:1b–2a.

238   176   *Your word, O God* . . . Ps.119:105. *Your light, O God* . . . Prov. 20:27. On the concluding eulogy, see No. 20.

THE OTHER DAYS OF MOURNING

The prayers and meditations provided here are an innovation of this volume, and are new, by CS. With Nos. 237–238 and No. 240, they make available readings for the entire seven days of Shiv'ah, the trad. mourning period.

239   177   *The second day* . . . *For everything* . . . Eccles. 3:1f., 4, 6a. *You once brought wholeness* . . . New, by CS. *The third day* . . . Eccles. 1:4, 7a. *You have gone, now* . . . New, by CS, quoting a passage by Anon. *The fourth day* . . . Jer. 31:13b. *At this hour* . . . New, by CS. *The fifth day* . . . Eccles. 7:1. *We come into this world* . . . New, by CS. The quotation is a Persian proverb. *The sixth day* . . . *For silver* . . . Prov. 17:3. *Creator of the universe* . . . Slightly adapted from SOH, p. 366.

AT THE END OF THE MOURNING PERIOD

240   180   *Your sun* . . . Isa. 60:20. *God of spirit and flesh* . . . New, by CS, in GOH, and here slightly revised by him.

CONSECRATION OF A MEMORIAL

It is customary to consecrate a memorial at the end of the year of mourning, although, if desired, it may be done after thirty days; the custom varies. It may, indeed, be postponed beyond the year, if the family so desires.

241   181   *Eternal One, our God* . . . Ps. 8:2, 4ff., 10.

Number	Page	
242	182	*Praise the Eternal One, O my soul* . . . Ps. 103:1f., 4, 6, 8, 10f., 14–19, 21f. Some of the verses are adapted.
243	183	*A woman of valor* . . . See No. 35.
244	184	*Who may abide* . . . Ps. 15:1–3, 4b–5. See No. 76.
245	185	*Happy is the man* . . . Ps. 112: 1–4, 7b–8a, 9. Ours is a somewhat free trsl., though based on the *Revised Standard Version* of the Bible. This alphabetical acrostic extols the ideal man in terms similar to those of the passage from Prov. 31, which extols the ideal woman. See No. 35.
246	186	*Eternal God, You are my shepherd* . . . Ps. 23. See GOP Notes No. 886. Here the trsl. is new, by CS.
247	187	*I lift up my eyes* . . . Ps. 121 Cf. GOP Notes No. 887. Here the trsl. is new, by CS.
248	188	*On behalf of our family* . . . Adapted from 1952 *Rabbi's Manual*, CCAR, p. 96. Here we provide two slightly different forms of the dedicatory sentence.
249	188	*God of infinite love* . . . Adapted from 1952 *Rabbi's Manual*, CCAR, p. 96. The second paragraph was freely adapted by ASD, and is here very slightly revised by CS.
250	189	*To You, O Source of peace* . . . Adapted in GOH from *Rabbi's Manual*, CCAR, p. 97. The second paragraph is here revised by CS.
251	190	*Yitgadal Veyitkadash* . . . See GOP Notes No. 997. The trsl. is new, by JR for New SOH (in preparation).
252	191	*God full of compassion* . . . See GOP Notes No. 895. The trsl. is here revised by CS.

FOR A YAHRZEIT

253	192	*At this moment* . . . Adapted by CS in GOH and here very slightly revised by him, from a prayer in the *Union Home Prayerbook*, pp. 37f. The quotation is from Prov. 20:27.

AT THE GRAVE OF A LOVED ONE

254	193	*God of all generations* . . . New, by CS, with allusions to several Psalm verses.
255	193	*To this sacred spot I come* . . . New, by CS in GOH and here slightly revised by him. Based in part on a series of prayers in the *Union Home Prayerbook*, pp. 80-89, and especially pp. 87f.

Weekday Services

AFTERNOON SERVICE

256	197	*Happy are those* . . . See Notes to GOP, No. 187. To the services that appeared in GOP we have added here the introductory portion of the afternoon service. The trsl. here is as revised by CS in *Gates of Prayer for Shabbat and Weekdays*, CCAR, 1994.

EVENING SERVICE

All the English in this service is revised, by CS, except as otherwise noted.

257	202	*And after the fire* . . . See Notes to GOP, No. 178. Here revised by CS. The quotation from I Kings 19:12 is newly added.
258	202	*Praise the One* . . . See Notes to GOP, No. 52.

MORNING SERVICE

All the English in this service is revised, by CS.

AT A HOUSE OF MOURNING

All the English in this section is revised, by CS.

ALEINU

All the English in this section is revised, by CS.

MEDITATIONS FOR MOURNERS

All the English in this section is trsl. by CS.

Number   Page

PRIVATE WEEKDAY PRAYERS

This section is new; it does not appear in GOH. It was created by CS and borrows liberally from portions of the weekday morning service in New SOH (in preparation). The trsls. are new.

328   245   *Sunday . . . In the beginning . . .* Gen. 1:1-5; *Yours is the earth . . .* Ps. 24:1-6; *Heaven and earth . . .* See Notes to GOP, No. 145; *We praise You . . . and its light.* The concluding eulogy of 'Yotzer'. See Notes to GOP, No. 100.

329   247   *Monday . . . And God said . . .* Gen. 1:6–8; *Praise the Eternal One . . .* Ps. 104:1–2, 3b–4, 24, 33; *Love lights our way . . .* New, by CS; *Loving God . . .* See Notes to GOP, No. 146. Here slightly adapted by CS; *We praise You . . . to serve You.* The concluding eulogy of 'Ahavah Rabbah'. See Notes to GOP, No. 101.

330   248   *Tuesday . . . And God said . . .* Gen. 1:9–13; *Those who came before . . .* New, by CS; *Sing to God . . .* Ps. 33: 3–6, 9, 20–22; *You are the notes . . .* from a poem by Rumi, trsl. by Robert Bly, in *The Enlightened Heart*, ed. by Stephen Mitchell, Harper & Row, Publishers, New York, 1989, p. 58; *Let me hear You . . .* From GOP, p. 232, where it was new, by CS, and here slightly adapted by CS. See Notes to GOP, No. 392; *We praise You . . .* One of the 'Blessings in Praise of Life and its Creator,' See No. 18.

331   251   *Wednesday . . . And God said . . .* Gen. 1:14–19; *Halleluyah . . .* Ps. 148:1–13; *Of all that God has shown me . . .* Mechtild of Magdeburg, in Mitchell, *op. cit.* (See preceding Note), trsl. by Jane Hirshfield; *The slant of winter light . . .* New, by CS; *We praise You . . .* One of the 'Blessings in Praise of Life and its Creator,' See No. 18.

332   254   *Thursday . . . And God said . . .* Gen. 1:20–23; *Halleluyah . . .* Ps. 146; *The life so short . . .* from *The Parliament of Birds*, by Geoffrey Chaucer; *O God, how can I know You . . .* See Notes to GOP, No. 298. Here adapted by CS; *We praise You . . .* One of the 'Blessings in Praise of Life and its Creator,' See No. 18.

333   257   *Friday . . . And God said . . .* Gen. 1:24–28a, 31; *Eternal One . . .* Ps. 8: 2, 4–10; *Divine presence . . .* New, by CS; *You are with me . . .* See Notes to GOP, No. 250, here adapted by CS; *We praise You . . .* One of the 'Blessings in Praise of Life and its Creator,' See No. 18.

Psalms, Poems, and Readings

FROM THE PSALMS

These Psalms are trsl. by CS.

334   263   *How many . . .* Ps. 3:2–7a, 8a, 9. In a number of instances we trsl. 3rd person Heb. by 2nd person Eng. This results in a somewhat more 'normal' Eng. style, and it enables us, in these instances, to avoid the unnecessary use of the masculine pronoun.

335   263   *When I call . . .* Ps. 4:2–9. In v. 7, we trsl. נסה as 'fled,' in agreement with the *New English Bible*. Others have 'lift up,' presumably from נסא.

336   264   *Give ear . . .* Ps. 5:2–13. In v. 7, we render the 3rd person Heb. by 2nd person Eng., to make it conform to the rest of the Psalm. See No. 334.

337   265   *In the Eternal One . . .* Ps. 11 (with the superscription omitted). Several 3rd person Heb. words are trsl. in the 2nd person. See No. 302.

NOTES

FROM TALMUD AND MIDRASH

This section is new; it does not appear in GOH.

PRAYERS AND MEDITATIONS

This section is new; it does not appear in GOH.

Number	Page	
357	275	*In Prayer* . . . Robert Herrick, 'The Heart', from *His Noble Numbers*, 1647. Suggested by Cantor Dr. Edward Graham.

POEMS

358	276	*Praised be the One* . . . By Avraham Eliyahu Kaplan (1890–1924, Russia- Germany), in *Beran Yachad*, ed. A.M. Haberman, Jerusalem, Mosad Harav Kuk, 5705, p. 209. A somewhat free trsl. by CS in GOH.
359	276	*Something is very gently* . . . By Denise Levertov (Goodman), 'The Thread' (New Directions, Publishers, 1958, 1961).
360	277	*Mothering Presence* . . . From *Gates of Forgiveness*, CCAR, 1980, pp. 31ff., where it was new, by CS. Here it replaces an earlier version by CS, in GOH pp. 222f. ('Lord, we will never ask . . . ').
361	279	*Our God was to be* . . . By Howard Nemerov, in *Gates of Forgiveness*, CCAR, 1980, pp. 33f. See that volume's Notes, No. 57.
362	280	*God, You taunt me* . . . Adapted by CS from a poem by Uri Zvi Greenberg in *Gates of Forgiveness*, CCAR, 1980, p. 30. See that volume's Notes, No. 54.
363	280	*Now, on the gleaming jewels* . . . Anon.
364	280	*Light breaks* . . . New, by CS.
365	281	*To be a Jew means* . . . A poem by Aaron Zeitlin, in *The Penguin Book of Modern Yiddish Verse*, ed. by I. Howe, R.R. Wisse, and K. Shmeruk, 1987, pp. 539f. Trsl. by CS.
366	281	*Will you seek far off* . . . By Walt Whitman. See GOH, p. 231 for a longer passage of this poem.
367	281	*I think continually* . . . By Stephen Spender, in `Poems' (Random House, Inc., 1934).
368	282	*O World* . . . By George Santayana.
369	282	*. . . Into my heart's night* . . . By Rumi, in *From Darkness to Light*, ed. by Victor Gollancz, p. 29. Richard Clay & Co., 1956, abridged ed., 1964.
370	282	*A woman doesn't meet* . . . By Shifra Alon, in *Ha-avodah She-balev*, the prayerbook of the Israel Reform Movement (Jerusalem 5742, 1981–82). Trsl. by CS.
371	282	*For I have learned* . . . By William Wordsworth, from *Lines Composed a Few Miles Above Tintern Abbey* . . . *July 13, 1798* (ll. 88–111).
372	283	*A certain day* . . . Denise Levertov, *The Book of Hours*, Book I, Poem 1, Stanza 1, 'Variations on a Theme by Rilke,' in *Cries of the Spirit*, ed. by Marylin Sewell (Beacon Press, Boston, 1991)
373	283	*There is a joy* . . . Anne Sexton, *Welcome Morning*, in *Cries of the Spirit*, ed. by Marylin Sewell (Beacon Press, Boston, 1991)
374	284	*Mont Blanc yet gleams* . . . By Percy Bysshe Shelley, from *Mont Blanc: Lines Written in the Vale of Chamouni*.
375	285	*I wonder if* . . . Anon.
376	285	*Even today* . . . By Yitzchak Lamdan, in *Ha-avodah She-balev* (See No. 370). Trsl. by CS.
377	285	*And now we praise* . . . New, by CS.
378	286	*Maker of all the living* . . . By Hillel Zeitlin. Trsl. by CS. The Hebrew is in the *Reconstructionist Sabbath Prayerbook*, pp. 352ff. Zeitlin (1871–1942, Russia) was a writer, thinker, and mystic, who died on the way to Treblinka. Cf. *Gate of Repentance*, ULPS, London, 1973.
379	287	*God of lonely hours* . . . By Yehudah Karni, in *Ha-avodah She-balev* (See No. 370). Trsl. by CS.
380	287	*A prayer, that is said* . . . 'Prayer,' by Robert Herrick from *His Noble Numbers* (1647). Suggested by Cantor Dr. Edward Graham.
381	287	*The prologues* . . . By Wallace Stevens, from *Asides on the Oboe*, in *Poems* (Vintage Books/Random House, N.Y., 1947). Suggested by Can-

Number	Page	
		ture—An Anthology, ed. by A. Chapman, p. 319. Mentor, 1974. Here abridged.
412	301	*Merely to have survived* . . . By Anthony Hecht, in *The Hard Hours* (Antheneum, N.Y., 1968), pp. 45f.
413	302	*Will there yet come* . . . By Leah Goldberg; Lithuania–Palestine/Israel), trsl. by R.F. Mintz, in *Modern Hebrew Poetry*, p. 248.
414	302	*And so night after night* . . . 'Israel,' by Yitzchak Lamdan (1900–1955, Russia–Palestine/Israel). Trsl. by CS but influenced by the trsl. by R.F. Mintz, in *Modern Hebrew Poetry, op. cit.*, p. 136.
415	303	*The ram came last of all* . . . By Hayim Gouri, in *The Penguin Book of Hebrew Verse*, ed. by T. Carmi, p. 346. the trsl. is very slightly revised by CS.
416	303	*Bound hand and foot* . . . By Halper Leivick, in *The Penguin Book of Modern Yiddish Verse*, ed. by I. Howe, R.R. Wisse, and K. Shmeruk, 1987, pp. 321f. The trsl. by Robert Friend is here revised by CS.
417	304	*Quite without poems* . . . By CS. The superscription is Gen. 22:7.
418	305	*O the Chimneys* . . . By Nelly Sachs (See GOP Notes No. 918). She begins by quoting Job 19:26, in the trsl. of the Authorised (King James) Version of the Bible. The JPS trsl. renders this difficult v. as follows: 'And when after my skin this [dust] is destroyed, then without my flesh shall I see God.'
419	306	*The first ones* . . . By Yitzchak Katzenelson.
420	306	*But who emptied* . . . By Nelly Sachs, *op. cit.*, p. 9.
421	307	*We orphans* . . . By Nelly Sachs, *ibid.*, pp. 29f.
422	308	*Why the black answer of hate* . . . By Nelly Sachs, *ibid.*, pp. 65f.
423	309	*Black milk of dawn* . . . 'Death Fugue,' by Paul Celan (1920-1970, Russia–France). Trsl. by Albert Friedlander, in *Pointer* (quarterly journal of the ULPS), Vol. VII, No. 1.
424	310	*You called us* . . . 'Voice,' by Yitzchak Ogen, in *Beran Yachad* (See No. 352), p. 219. The somewhat free trsl. by CS in GOH is here revised by CS.
425	311	*We are not the silent* . . . By Abba Kovner, in *Ha-avodah She-balev* (See No. 364). Trsl. by CS.
426	311	*Yes, I did not plow* . . . By Rachel [Bluwstein], in trsl. by R.F. Mintz, in *Modern Hebrew Poetry*, p. 112. The trsl. is somewhat revised here by CS.
427	311	*Working is another way of praying* . . . From a poem entitled *Song For Dov Shamir*, by Dannie Abse (contemporary, Great Britain).
428	312	*I have not sung to you* . . . By Rachel [Bluwstein], in *Ha-avodah She-balev* (See No. 364). Trsl. by CS.
429	312	*If my days remaining* . . . By Sh. Shalom (Galicia–Palestine/Israel), 'Night Prayer,' in *Beran Yachad* (See No. 352), p. 217. Trsl. CS.
430	313	*Would that I were* . . . From a poem by Yehuda Karni (Russia–Palestine/Israel, 1884–1948), adapted by CS from a trsl. by I. Halevy-Levin. From *Yerushalayim*, Tel Aviv, 1944.
431	313	*The earth grows still* . . . By Nathan Alterman (Poland–Palestine/Israel). Trsl. by CS.

Number   Page

READINGS FOR REFLECTION AND STUDY

This section is new; it does not appear in GOH.

432   315   *The old year has died* . . . Adapted by CS from a passage in FOP, p. 250.

433   315   *There are many fine things* . . . By Grenville Kleiser, in *A Treasury of Comfort*, ed. by Sidney Greenberg, Hartmore House, 1974, p. 172.

434   315   *Philosophy can teach us* . . . By Harold S. Kushner, *When Children ask About God*, Reconstructionist Press.

435   316   *Belief in God* . . . By Israel I. Mattuck, *The Spirit of the Jew*, in Day of Atonement Sermon 1936, from 'Extracts from Dated Sermons' by IIM.

436   316   *. . .the admitted, conscious, whole-hearted searching* . . . Rabbi David Goldstein, London, Kol Nidre Sermon 1965.

437   316   *There are no easy ways* . . . 'On Prayer,' by Abraham J. Heschel, in J.J. Petuchowski, *Understanding Jewish Prayer*, KTAV Publishing House, Inc., 1972, p. 81.

438   317   *As the hand* . . . Adapted by CS from a saying by Rabbi Nachman of Bratzlav. See Notes to GOP, No. 619.

439   317   *Religion offers answers* . . . By Shmuel Sperber, in FOP, p. 387.

440   317   *Even more frustrating* . . . By Abraham J. Heschel, in *God in Search of Man*, Farrar, Strauss & Giroux, 1955, p. 372.

441   317   *In worshipping* . . . By Israel I. Mattuck, *The Light of Eternity; The Way of Faith*, in Day of Atonement Sermon, from 'Extracts from Dated Sermons' by IIM.

442   318   *Why are we told* . . . From *Your Word is Fire*, ed. by Arthur Green and Barry W. Holtz, pp. 60f.

443   318   *It seems . . . that we use our prayers* . . . Michel de Montaigne, *Essays*, 'Of Prayers', in *The Complete Works of Montaigne*, trsl. by Donald Frame, Stanford University Press, 1957, p. 236.

444   319   *There are few* . . . *Ibid.*

445   319   *Once I remember* . . . Thomas Traherne, in *Centuries of Meditations*, 'The Third Century,' No. 16. Suggested by Cantor Dr. Edward Graham. We preserve his spelling.

446   319   *Prayer is not a discourse* . . . By Jacques Ellul, *Prayer and Modern Man*, p. 58. Suggested by Cantor Dr. Edward Graham.

447   319   *Know that all the practices* . . . Moses Maimonides, in *The Guide of the Perplexed*, trsl. with an Introduction and Notes by Shlomo Pines, pp. 622f., The University of Chicago Press, 1963.

448   320   *The ideal of freedom* . . . By Israel I Mattuck, *The Problem of Freedom*, in First Day of Passover Sermon, from 'Extracts from Dated Sermons' by IIM.

449   320   *A young disciple* . . . Chasidic tale rewritten by CS from a version in *A Year of Grace*, ed. by Victor Gollancz, p. 395.

450   320   *To begin* . . . FOP, p. 118. Attributed there to Martin Buber.

451   320   *If you think* . . . *Ibid.*, p. 392. Rewritten by CS.

452   320   *Darkness is not the road* . . . *Ibid.*, p. 390. By Hayyim Greenberg.

453   321   *To love somebody* . . . From *The Art of Loving*, by Erich Fromm. Harper & Row, Inc., 1974. Also in *Gates of Forgiveness*, p. 14.

454   321   *Visit the sick and suffering* . . . A 're-translation' of a passage by Eliezer ben Isaac, 1050, quoted in Hertz, *A Book of Jewish Thoughts*, p. 7. Here slightly adapted and abridged.

455   321   *I wanted* . . . By Fanny Wolf, in *Written out of History*, by Sandra Henry and Emily Taitz, Biblio Press, NY, 1983.

Number   Page

SELECTIONS FROM PIRKEI AVOT

This section is new; it does not appear in GOH. The translations and notes are new, by CS. For a somewhat different selection and translation, see GOP, pp. 16–28.

456	323	*Chapter 1* . . . The selections are 1:2, 3, 4, 5, 6, 12, 13, 14, 15, 18.
457	324	*Chapter 2* . . . The selections are 2:5, 6, 13, 14, 15, 16, 17.
458	325	*Chapter 3* . . . The selections are 3:11, 18, 19, 21.
459	326	*Chapter 4* . . . The selections are 4:1, 2, 3, 17, 19, 21, 22, 23, 25, 26, 27.
460	328	*Chapter 5* . . . The selections are 5:9, 12, 13, 14, 19, 22, 23, 24.

Scriptural Readings

No.   Page

461   366   *A Table of Scriptural Readings* . . . We follow UPB and others in providing a suggested Scriptural lectionary of Torah and Haftarah Readings, for the entire year. Our lectionary is new, compiled by ASD, based on the trad. one, here revised by CS. UPB was prepared by Kaufmann Kohler, that in the third edition by Solomon B. Freehof.

A Table of Scriptural Readings

The readings given in this table for the fifty-four sidrot into which the Torah is divided, and for the corresponding haftarot, are those prescribed by tradition, and are in bold print. Occasionally the Sefardi rite differs from the Ashkenazi in the choice of haftarah. In those instances the Sefardi reading is given in parentheses. Alternative readings are suggested for the haftarot and for several sidrot, and some readings are suggested for more than one occasion.

On Shabbat afternoon, and Monday and Thursday mornings, the first parasha of the sidra for the coming Shabbat is read. The parasha is indicated in the table by italics.

In some years several or all of the following sidrot are combined: Vayakheil-Pikudei, Tazria-Metsora, Acharei-Kedoshim, Behar-Bechukotai, Chukat-Balak, Matot-Masei, Nitsavim-Vayeilech. When this occurs, read the haftarah assigned to the second sidra, except that when Nitsavim-Vayeilech are joined, Isaiah 61:10-63:9 (the haftarah for Nitsavim) is the traditional reading.

The readings given for the holidays are in accordance with the practice of the Reform synagogue.

For those congregations which conduct daily services, readings have been suggested for the intermediate days od Sukkot and Pesach, as well as for Chanukah, Purim, and Tish'a be-Av.

In the traditional synagogue, appropriate selections from two Sifrei Torah are read on holidays and special Sabbaths, and, on rare occasions, selections from three are read. Some of these selections have been indicated in the Table. Choice may be made from the regular weekly portion, from the special reading or readings for the day, or excerpts from all may be read.

Reform Jews throughout the world observe Pesach and Sukkot for seven days, and Shavuot and Sh'mini Atzeret- Simchat Torah for one day. This is also the practice in traditional congregations in Israel. Traditional Jews in the Diaspora add an extra day to these festivals. When, in the Diaspora, the eighth day of Pesach or the second day of Shavuot falls on Shabbat, Reform congregations read the sidra assigned to the following week in the standard religious calendars. However, in order to preserve uniformity in the reading of the Torah throughout the entire community, it is suggested that on these occasions, the sidra be spread over two weeks, one portion to be read while traditional congregations are observing the festival, and another portion to be read the following Shabbat.

	TORAH	HAFTARAH
בראשית	**Genesis 1:1–6:8**	**Isaiah 42:5–43:11 (*Sef:* 42:5–21)**
	Genesis 1:1–13	
	Genesis 1:1–8, 26–9;	II Samuel 11:1–12:7
	2:1–3	I Kings 21:1–20
	Genesis 3:1–24	Isaiah 40:25–31
		Isaiah 42:5–12, 16
	Genesis 4:1–16	Psalm 8:2, 4–9
		Psalm 139:1–2, 7–18
נח	**Genesis 6:9–11:32**	**Isaiah 54:1–55:5 (*Sef.:* 54:1–10)**
	Genesis 6:9–22	
	Genesis 6:9–7:1	Isaiah 14:12–20
	Genesis 8:6–22	Isaiah 54:1–10
	Genesis 11:1–9	Jeremiah 31:27–36
		Zephaniah 3:9–15, 20
לך לך	**Genesis 12:1–17:27**	**Isaiah 40:27–41:16**
	Genesis 12:1–13	
	Genesis 12:1–9	Joshua 24:1–11, 14, 24
	Genesis 13:1–15	Isaiah 40:27–31; 41:8–10
	Genesis 17:1–14	Isaiah 51:1–8
	Genesis 17:15–22	Isaiah 66:7–13
		Joel 2:21–3:2
		Psalm 105:1–10
וירא	**Genesis 18:1–22:24**	**II Kings 4:1–37 (*Sef.:* 4:1–23)**
	Genesis 18:1–14	
	Genesis 18:1–14	Isaiah 1:10–18
	Genesis 18:16–33	Ezekiel 18: 1–5, 7–9, 21–23
	Genesis 21:1–21	Micah 6:1–8
	Genesis 22:1–18	Psalm 111:1–10
		Job 5:17–26

Traditional readings are in bold.
Weekday readings are in italic.
Alternative readings are in roman.

*Readings from outside the sidra have an asterisk.

(Sefardic readings are in parentheses.)

	TORAH	HAFTARAH
חיי שרה	**Genesis 23:1–25:18**	**I Kings 1:1–31**
	Genesis 23:1–16	
	Genesis 23:1–19	Jeremiah 32:1–2, 6–16, 24–27, 42–44
	Genesis 24:29–49, 57–8	Psalm 15:1–5
		Psalm 45:1–5, 14b–18
		Psalm 112:1–4, 7–9
		Proverbs 31:10–12., 20, 25–26, 28–31
תולדות	**Genesis 25:19–28:9**	**Malachi 1:1–2:7**
	Genesis 25:19–26:5	
	Genesis 25:19–34	Psalm 5:2–13
	Genesis 27:1–22	Psalm 12:2–9
	Genesis 27:30–45	Psalm 119:1–15, 133
		Proverbs 4:1–6, 10–19. 23–27
ויצא	**Genesis 28:10–32:3**	**Hosea 12:13–14:10** (*Sef.:* **11:7–12:12**)
	Genesis 28:10–22	
	Genesis 28:10–22	I Kings 19:1–12
	Genesis 29:1–20	Jeremiah 31:1–9
		Psalm 62:1–9
		Psalm 63:1–9
		Psalm 139:1–2, 7–18
		Proverbs 2:1–9
		Ruth 4:9–17
וישלח	**Genesis 32:4–36:43**	**Hosea 11:7–12:22** (*Sef.:* **Obadiah 1:1–21**)
	Genesis 32:4–13	
	Genesis 32:4–14, 21–2	Isaiah 35:1–7
	Genesis 32:23–32	Isaiah 44:1–8, 21–23
	Genesis 33:1–17	Isaiah 55:1–3, 10–13
		Jeremiah 10:1–16
		Jeremiah 31:10–20
		Psalm 37:1–11

	TORAH	HAFTARAH
וישב	**Genesis 37:1–40:23**	**Amos 2:6–3:8**
	Genesis 37:1–11	
	Genesis 37:1–11	I Kings 3:5–15
	Genesis 37:12–36	Amos 2:6–3:2
		Psalm 27:1–14
		Psalm 34:1–3, 12–19
מקץ	**Genesis 41:1–44:17**	**Kings 3:15–4:1**
	Genesis 41:1–14	
	Genesis 41:1–16 (17–36)	I Kings 3:15–28
	Genesis 41:(1–16) 17–36	Psalm 67:2–8
	Genesis 41:33–49	Proverbs 9:1–6, 13–18; 10:4
	Genesis 42:1–24	
ויגש	**Genesis 44:18–47:27**	**Ezekiel 37:15–28**
	Genesis 44:18–30	
	Genesis 44:18–34	Ezekiel 37:15–28
	Genesis 45:1–15	Amos 8:4–11
	Genesis 47:13–26	Psalm 72:1–8, 12–14, 17–19
		Psalm 72:1–8, 12–14, 18–19
ויחי	**Genesis 47:28–50:26**	**I Kings 2:1–12**
	Genesis 47:28–48:9	
	Genesis 48:8–21	Psalm 71:1–9, 14–23
	Genesis 50:15–26	Job 5:17–27
		Ecclesiastes 11:9–12:7, 13–14
		I Chronicles 28:1–10
שמות	**Exodus 1:1–6:8**	**Isaiah 27:6–28:13; 29:22–23** **(*Sef.*: Jeremiah 1:1–2:3)**
	Exodus 1:1–17	
	Exodus 1:1–14	I Samuel 1:1–28
	Exodus 2:11–25	I Samuel 3:1–4:1a
	Exodus 3:1–15	Isaiah 6:1–10; 9:1
		Jeremiah 23:1–8
		Joel 2:21–3:2

	TORAH	HAFTARAH
וארא	**Exodus 6:2–9:35**	**Ezekiel 28:25–29:21**
	Exodus 6:2–13	
	Exodus 6:2–13	Isaiah 42:5–12, 16
	Exodus 6:28–7:13	Isaiah 52:1–10
		Jeremiah 1:1–10
		Ezekiel 29:1–9
		Ezekiel 31:1–12
בא	**Exodus 10:1–13:16**	**Jeremiah 46:13–28**
	Exodus 10:1–11	
	Exodus 10:1–11	Isaiah 19:19–25
	Exodus 13:3–10	Jeremiah 46:13–28a
	Deuteronomy 6:20–25*	Psalm 105:16–45
		Ezra 6:16–22
בשלח	**Exodus 13:17–17:16**	**Judges 4:4–5:31 (Sef.: 5:1–31)**
	Exodus 13:17–14:8	
	Exodus 13:17–14:4	Joshua 3:9–4:3, 20–24
	Exodus 14:5–15	Isaiah 43:1–12
		Isaiah 63:7–14
		Psalm 106:1–12
		Psalm 124:1–8
יתרו	**Exodus 18:1–20:23**	**Isaiah 6:1–7:6; 9:5–6 (*Sef.:* 6:1–13)**
	Exodus 18:1–12	
	Exodus 18:13–24	I Kings 3:3–15
	Exodus 19:1–11, 16–19	Isaiah 42:1–4; 45:22–24; 48:17–19
	Exodus 20:1–14	Jeremiah 7:1–11, 17–23
		Jeremiah 31:23–36
		Psalm 19:1–15
משפטים	**Exodus 21:1–24:18**	**Jeremiah 34:8–22; 33:25–26**
	Exodus 21:19	
	Exodus 22:20–26;	Joshua 24:1–2a, 13–17, 19–28
	23:1–3	Jeremiah 17:5–14
	Exodus 23:4–16	Amos 5:4–8, 10–15
	Exodus 24:1–18	Habakkuk 2:9–20

	TORAH	HAFTARAH
תרומה	**Exodus 25:1–27:19**	**I Kings 5:26–6:13**
	Exodus 25:1–16	
	Exodus 25:1–9	I Kings 8:22–43
	Deuteronomy 8:11–18*	Zechariah 8:7–13, 16–17
		Psalms 24:1–6; 1:1–3
		I Chronicles 22:1–13
תצוה	**Exodus 27:20–30:10**	**Ezekiel 43:10–27**
	Exodus 27:20–28:12	
	Exodus 27:20–28:5	Joshua 24:1–28
	Deuteronomy 4:9–13*	I Kings 18:20–39
	Exodus 32:1–14*	Isaiah 61:1–11
		Isaiah 65:17–66:2
		Psalm 19:1–15
		Psalm 43:1–5
כי תשא	**Exodus 30:11–34:35**	**I Kings 18:1–39**
	Exodus 30:11–22	
	Exodus 33:12–23	Isaiah 40:15–31
	Exodus 34:1–10	Jeremiah 31:31–36
		Psalm 42:1–12
		Psalms 63:1–8; 139:7–12, 23–24
		Psalm 81:1–11
ויקהל	**Exodus 35:4–9, 20–29**	**I Kings 7:40–50 (*Sef.:* 7:13–26)**
	Exodus 35:1–20	
	Exodus 35:4–9, 20–29	Psalm 106:1–12, 48
	Deuteronomy 11:1–9,	Psalm 146:1–10
	18–21*	I Chronicles 29:1–3, 9–19
פקודי	**Exodus 40:1–8, 33–38**	**I Kings 7:51–8:21 (*Sef.:* 7:40–50)**
	Exodus 38:21–39:1	
	Exodus 40:1–8, 33–38	I Kings 8:10–30
	Deuteronomy 4:10–20*	Isaiah 66:1–5, 22–23
		Daniel 3:1–9, 12–30
		II Chronicles 5:1–14

	TORAH	HAFTARAH
ויקרא	**Leviticus 1:1–5:26**	**Isaiah 43:21–44:23**
	Leviticus 1:1–13	
	Leviticus 5:17–26	Isaiah 1:10–20, 27
	Deuteronomy 4:1–9*	Isaiah 33:13–16
		Amos 5:16–25
		Psalm 50: 1–23
צו	**Leviticus 6:1–8:36**	**Jeremiah 7.21–8.3; 9.22–23**
	Leviticus 6:1–11	
	Leviticus 8:1–13	Isaiah 42:1–12
	Deuteronomy 10:12–20*	Jeremiah 7:21–28; 8:7–9; 9:22–23
		Hosea 6:1–6
		Malachi 1:6–14; 2:10
		Malachi 3:1–4, 22–24a
שמיני	**Leviticus 9:1–11:47**	**II Samuel 6:1–7:17 (*Sef.*: 6:1–19)**
	Leviticus 9:1–16	
	Leviticus 10:1–11	Isaiah 28:1–13; 29:22–24
	Leviticus 11:1–8, 44–47	Isaiah 61:1–4, 8–11
		Psalm 39:2–11, 13–14
		Psalm 51:1–6, 8–19
		Psalm 73:1–28
		Proverbs 6:12–23
		Daniel 1:1–21
תזריע	**Leviticus 12:1–13:59**	**II Kings 4:42–5.19**
	Leviticus 12:1–13:5	
	Leviticus 19:23–37*	Jeremiah 22:1–9, 13–16
	Deuteronomy 12:28–13:5*	Job 2:1–10
מצרע	**Leviticus 14:1–15:33**	**II Kings 7:3–20**
	Leviticus 14:1–12	
	Deuteronomy 26:12–19*	Joel 1:10–11, 19–20; 2:12–13, 25–27
		Psalm 103:1–2, 4, 6, 8, 10–11, 14–19, 21–22
		Proverbs 10:11–19

TORAH	HAFTARAH
	Job 31:5–8, 13–17, 19–20, 24–25, 29–34, 38–40
אחרי מות **Leviticus 16:1–18:30**	**Ezekiel 22:1–19 (*Sef.:* 22:1–16)**
Leviticus 16:1–17	
Leviticus 16:7–10, 20–4, 29–34	Isaiah 58:1–14
	Isaiah 59:1–16
	Ezekiel 22:23–30; 36:22–28
קדושים **Leviticus 19:1–20:27**	**Amos 9:7–15 (*Sef.:* Ezekiel 20:2–20)**
Leviticus 19:1–14	
Leviticus 19:1–4, 9–18	Isaiah 1:10–20, 27
	Jeremiah 22:1–9, 13–16
	Zechariah 7:4–10; 8:16–19
	Psalm 15:1–5
אמר **Leviticus 21:1–24:23**	**Ezekiel 44:15–31**
Leviticus 21:1–15	
Leviticus 22:31–23:3; 24:1–9	Isaiah 56:1–7
	Psalm 27:1–4, 7–14
Leviticus 23:4–10, 15–16, 21–28, 31–32	Psalm 42:2–12
	Psalm 108:2–7
	Nehemiah 8:1–4a, 5–18
בהר **Leviticus 25:1–26:2**	**Jeremiah 32:6–27**
Leviticus 25:1–13	
Leviticus 25:1–10	Jeremiah 31:1–13
Leviticus 25:19–28, 35–42	Jeremiah 34:8–17; Isaiah 42:5–7
	Nehemiah 5:1–13
בחקתי **Leviticus 26:1–6, 9–13**	**Jeremiah 16:19–17:4**
Leviticus 26:3–13	
Leviticus 26:1–6, 9–13	Isaiah 11:1–9
Deuteronomy 12:28–13:5*	Jeremiah16:19–17:4
	Jeremiah 23:13–29
	Micah 4:1–5
	Psalm 46:2–10, 12

	TORAH	HAFTARAH
במדבר	**Numbers 1:1–4:20**	**Hosea 2:1–22**
	Numbers 1:1–19	
	Numbers 1:1–19	Isaiah 48:1–13
	Deuteronomy 5:29–6.9*	Isaiah 56:8–57:2
		Psalm 107:1–16, 35–43
		Proverbs 6:16–23
נשא	**Numbers 4:21–7:89**	**Judges 13:2–25**
	Numbers 4:21–33	
	Numbers 5:5–10; 6:22–27	Judges 16:4–21
	Numbers 6:1–8, 13–15	Jeremiah 35:1–14, 18–19
		Psalm 4:2–9, 15:1–5
		Psalm 67:1–8
		Ezra 3:8–13
בהעלתך	**Numbers 8:1–12:16**	**Zechariah 2:14–4:7**
	Numbers 8:1–14	
	Numbers 9:15–23;	Jeremiah 3:14–18; 4.1–2
	10:29–34	Joel 2:21–3:2
	Numbers 11:16–17,	Psalm 68:1–11, 33–36
	21–30	Psalm 77:12–21
		Psalm 81:1–11
		II Chronicles 5:1–14
שלח לך	**Numbers 13:1–15:41**	**Joshua 2:1–24**
	Numbers 13:1–20	
	Numbers 13:1–3, 21–33	Joshua 14:6–14
	Numbers 14:1–9	Ezekiel 20:1–22
		Psalm 106:1–3, 24–26, 47–48
קרח	**Numbers 16:1–18:32**	**I Samuel 11:14–12:22**
	Numbers 16:1–13	
	Numbers 16:1–11	Judges 9:1–21
	Numbers 16:12–22	I Samuel 11:14–12:8, 19–25
		I Kings 12:1–14, 16
		Isaiah 57:7–21

	TORAH	HAFTARAH
חקת	**Numbers 19:1–22:1**	**Judges 11:1–33**
	Numbers 19:1–17	
	Numbers 20:1, 14–21	Ezekiel 36:1–2, 5–12
	Numbers 20:1, 22–29	Ezekiel 36:24–28, 33–36
		Psalm 42:1–12
		Psalm 73:1–3, 13–28
		Psalm 78:1–7, 12–24
בלק	**Numbers 22:2–25:9**	**Micah 5:6–6:8**
	Numbers 22:2–12	
	Numbers 22:2–12	Joshua 24:1–14
	Numbers 22:21–35	Isaiah 54:11–17
		Micah 5:9–12; 6:1–8
		Habakkuk 3:8–19
פינחס	**Numbers 25:10–30:1**	**I Kings 18:46–19:21**
	Numbers 25:10–26:4	
	Numbers 27:12–23	Joshua 17: 1–6
	Numbers 14:11–20b	Joshua 22:11–34
		Joshua 23:1–8, 11–14
		Ezekiel 20:1–14, 41–42
מטות	**Numbers 30:2–32:42**	**Jeremiah 1:1–2:3**
	Numbers 30:2–17	
	Numbers 32:1–2, 4–20,	Joshua 22:1–10
	22–4	Joshua 22:11–34
	Deuteronomy 17:14–20*	I Samuel 8:1–22
מסעי	**Numbers 33:1–36:13**	**Jeremiah 2:4–28; 3:4; 4:1–2**
		(Sef.: 2:4–28; 4:1–2)
	Numbers 33:1–10	
	Numbers 35:9–15, 22–29	Joshua 20:1–9
	Deuteronomy 20:1–9*	Jeremiah 2:4–19; 4:1–2
		Jeremiah 33:4–11
		Psalm 3:1–7, 9
		Psalm 5:2–13

	TORAH	HAFTARAH
דברים	**Deuteronomy 1:1–3:22**	Isaiah 1:1–27
	Deuteronomy 1:1–11	
	Deuteronomy 1:1, 6–18	Isaiah 1:1–18, 26–7
		Amos 2:1–12; 3:1–2
		Lamentations 3:19–41
ואתחנן	**Deuteronomy 3:23–7:11**	Isaiah 40:1–26
	Deuteronomy 3:23–4:8	
	Deuteronomy 5:1–3, 6–18	Isaiah 40:1–11
		Jeremiah 7:1–11, 17–23
עקב	**Deut. 7:12–11:25**	Isaiah 49:14–51:3
	Deuteronomy 7:12–21	
	Deuteronomy 8:1–11	Isaiah 42:1–12
	Deuteronomy 11:1–9,	Zechariah 8:7–13, 16–17
	18–21	Psalm 106:1–13, 19–23, 48
	Deuteronomy 10:12–20	
ראה	**Deut. 11:26–16:17**	Isaiah 54:11–55:5
	Deuteronomy 11:26–12:10	
	Deut. 12:28–13:5	Joshua 8:30–35
		I Kings 22:1–14
		Isaiah 11:1–9
		Jeremiah 23:13–29
		Psalm 15:1–5
		Psalm 24: 1–10
שפטים	**Deut. 16:18–21:9**	Isaiah 51:12–52:12
	Deuteronomy 16:18–17:3	
	Deuteronomy 17:14–20	I Samuel 8:1–22
	Deuteronomy 21:1–9	Isaiah 26:1–9
		Ezekiel 34:1–31
		Psalm 1:1–6

	TORAH	HAFTARAH
כי תצא	**Deut. 21:10–25:19**	**Isaiah 54:1–10**
	Deuteronomy 21:10–21	
	Deuteronomy 22:1–8	Isaiah 5:1–16
	Deuteronomy 24:10–22	Psalms 33:1–5, 16–17; 34:12–16, 18–19
		Proverbs 28.1–14
		Proverbs 30:1–8
כי תבוא	**Deuteronomy 26:1–29:8**	**Isaiah 60:1–22**
	Deuteronomy 26:1–15	
	Deuteronomy 26:1–11	Joshua 4:1–24
	Deuteronomy 26:16–27:8	Isaiah 35:1–10
		Isaiah 49:1–6
נצבים	**Deut. 29:9–30:20**	**Isaiah 61:10–63:9**
	Deuteronomy 29:9–28	
	Deut. 29:9–14; 30:11–20	Joshua 24:1–11, 14–17, 22
		Isaiah 51:1–6, 11
		Jeremiah 31:27–36
וילך	**Deuteronomy 31:1–30**	**Isaiah 55:6–56:8**
	Deuteronomy 31:1–3	
	Deuteronomy 31:1–13	Isaiah 55:6–13; 56.6–8
		Joel 2:15–19a, 21–27
האזינו	**Deuteronomy 32:1–52**	**II Samuel 22:1–51**
	Deuteronomy 32:1–12	
	Deuteronomy 32:1–12	Isaiah 62:1–7
	Deuteronomy 32:44–52	Isaiah 65:8–10, 16–25
		Psalm 78:1–38
וזאת הברכה	**Deut. 33:1–34:12**	**Joshua 1:1–18 (*Sef.:* 1:1–9)**
	Deuteronomy 33:1–7	
	Deuteronomy 34:1–12	Joshua 1:1–17
		Isaiah 52:7–10, 13–15

ॐ

TORAH	HAFTARAH

Shabbat Shuvah

	Weekly Portion	Hosea 14:2–10; Micah 7:18–20,
		Joel 2:15–27
		(*Sef.:* Hosea 14:2–10; Micah 7:18–20)

Sukkot

1st day	Leviticus 23:33–44	Zechariah 14:6–9, 16–21
		Isaiah 32:1–8, 14–20
		Isaiah 35:1–10

2nd day	Leviticus 23:39–44	

3rd day (if Shabbat)

	Exodus 33:12–34:26	Ezekiel 38:18–39:7
	Deuteronomy 8:1–10	Nehemiah 8:13–18
		Ecclesiastes 11:9–12:14

3rd day (if weekday)

	Exodus 23:14–17	

4th day	Exodus 34:21–24	

5th day (if Shabbat)

	Exodus 33:12–34:26	Ezekiel 38:18–39:7
	Deuteronomy 8:1–10	Nehemiah 8:13–18
		Ecclesiastes 11:9–12:14

5th day (if weekday)

	Deuteronomy 16:13–17	

6th day (if Shabbat)

	Exodus 33:12–34:26	Ezekiel 38:18–39:7
	Deuteronomy 8:1–10	Nehemiah 8:13–18
		Ecclesiastes 11:9–12:14

6th day (if weekday)

	Deuteronomy 31:9–13	

7th day	Deuteronomy 11:10–15	

N O T E : *The Book of Ecclesiastes is read on the Shabbat during Sukkot.*

Atzeret-Simchat Torah

	Deuteronomy 34:1–12;	Joshua 1:1–18 (*Sef.:* 1:1–9)
	Genesis 1:1–8,	Isaiah 42:5–12, 16; Psalm 8:2, 4–9
	26–29; 2:1–3	

TORAH	HAFTARAH

Chanukah

1st day	Numbers 6:22–7:17	
2nd day	Numbers 7:18–29	
3rd day	Numbers 7:24–35	
4th day	Numbers 7:30–41	
5th day	Numbers 7:36–47	
6th day	Numbers 7:42–53	
7th day	Numbers 7:48–59	
8th day	Numbers 7:54–8:4	

1st Shabbat during Chanukah

Weekly Portion	Zechariah 4:1–6a, 10b–14, 6b
	Psalm 119:97–111

2nd Shabbat during Chanukah

Weekly Portion	I Kings 7:40–50
	I Kings 8:54–66
	Isaiah 12:1–6

NOTE: *The first day of Tevet falls on the sixth or seventh day of Chanukah. The special reading for Rosh Chodesh may be added to that for Chanukah or substituted for it. If Rosh Chodesh and Shabbat coincide, three Sifrei Torah may be taken from the Ark. A selection from the regular weekly portion is read first, the Rosh Chodesh passage second, and third, the day's portion from Numbers.*

Shabbat Sh'kalim

Weekly portion	II Kings 12:5–16 (*Sef.*: 11:17–12:17)
Exodus 30:11–16	

Shabbat Zachor

Weekly Portion	Esther 7:1–10; 8:15–17
Deuteronomy 25:17–18	Esther 9:20–24, 26–28

Purim

Exodus 17:8–16	

NOTE: *The Book of Esther is read on Purim.*

Shabbat Parah

Weekly Portion	Ezekiel 36:22–36
Numbers 19:1–9	

Shabbat Hachodesh

Weekly Portion and	Ezekiel 45:16–25
Exodus 12:1–20	Isaiah 66:1–5, 22–23

TORAH	HAFTARAH

Shabbat Hagadol

    Weekly Portion — Malachi 3:4–5, 13–20, 22–24

Pesach

1st day   Exodus 12:3–42; 13:3–10   Isaiah 43:1–8, 10–15
     Isaiah 43:1–15

2nd day   Exodus 13:14–16

3rd day (if Shabbat)
     Exodus 33:12–34:26   Ezekiel 37:1–14
     Exodus 34.1–8   Songs 2:8–17; 8:6–7
     Leviticus 23:1–8

3rd day (if weekday)
     Exodus 23:14–17

4th day   Exodus 34:18–23

5th day (if Shabbat)
     Exodus 33:12–34:26   Ezekiel 37:1–14
     Exodus 34.1–8   Songs 2:8–17; 8:6–7
     Leviticus 23:1–8

5th day (if weekday)
     Deuteronomy 16:13–17

6th day (if Shabbat)
     Exodus 33:12–34:26   Ezekiel 37:1–14
     Exodus 34.1–8   Songs 2:8–17; 8:6–7
     Leviticus 23:1–8

6th day (if weekday)
     Leviticus 23:1–8

7th day   Exodus 14:30–15:21   II Samuel 22:1–51
     Isaiah 11:1–6, 9

NOTE: *The Song of Songs is read on the Shabbat during Pesach.*

Yom Hashoah

     Deuteronomy 4:30–40   II Samuel 1:17–27
     Psalm 11:1–7
     Psalm 12:2–7, 9, 8
     Psalm 13:2–6

SCRIPTURAL READINGS

TORAH	HAFTARAH

Yom Ha-atzma-ut

Deuteronomy 8:1–18	Isaiah 60:1–9, 15
Deuteronomy 11:8–21	Isaiah 10:32–11:12
Deuteronomy 30:1–16	Isaiah 65:17–25

Shavuot

Exodus 19:1–8; 20:1–14	Isaiah 42:1–12

NOTE: *The Book of Ruth is read on Shavuot.*

Tish'a b'Av

Morning	Deuteronomy 4:25–41	Jeremiah 8:13–9:23
Afternoon	Ex. 32:11–14; 34:1–10	Isaiah 55:6–56:8
		(*Sef.:* Hosea 14:2–10, Micah 7:18–20)

NOTE: *The Book of Lamentations is read on Tish'a b'Av.*

Rosh Chodesh

Weekday	Numbers 28:11–15

Shabbat and Rosh Chodesh

Weekly portion	Isaiah 66:1–24
	Isaiah 66:1–13, 23

Shabbat when Rosh Chodesh is next day

Weekly portion	I Samuel 20:18–42

NOTE: *In the traditional calendar, when a month has thirty days, the thirtieth day and the first day of the new month are observed as Rosh Chodesh. It is suggested that, in the Reform Synagogue, Rosh Chodesh should be observed on the first day of the new month.*

Acknowledgments

The Editor thanks Rabbis Donna Berman and H. Leonard Poller (current Chairman of the Liturgy Committee), and Cantor Edward Graham, whose assistance in the preparation of this volume was unstinting and invaluable. These, along with the Editor, formed a small committee that discussed the Editor's work and improved it. Rabbi Elliot Stevens was, as always, efficient, helpful, and encouraging. Rabbi Joseph B. Glaser was, once again, concerned and helpful. Rabbi Adam Fisher's comments and suggestions were especially full and useful. The title was suggested by Rabbi Ned Soltz. Rabbis Elyse Goldstein, Walter Jacob, and Michael Signer also made helpful suggestions.

❧ *The following is reprinted from* Gates of the House, *1977*

The Central Conference of American Rabbis is grateful to all who helped shape the contents of this volume. Many suggestions were received during the course of its preparation; each was carefully considered, and many were accepted.

The Conference is especially indebted to a number of individuals. Rabbi Chaim Stern served as Editor of *Gates of the House.* He prepared the carious drafts, compiling and shaping their contents, translating the Hebrew, writing many new prayers, and adapting many others. He wishes to record his special gratitude to Rabbi A. Stanley Dreyfus (Chairman of the Liturgy Committee), who was his indispensable co-worker. At all times Rabbi Dreyfus was the source of valuable comments and suggestions. In the latter stages of this volume's preparation, they were partners in the work of preparing the manuscript for publication.

The Conference wishes to thank Rabbi Harvey J. Fields and Dr. Edward Graham (who served on the Liturgy Committee as delegate from the American Conference of Cantors) for their help. Rabbi Robert I. Kahn, who served as Chairman of the Liturgy Committee until 1973, contributed leadership, energy, and devotion to the work which led to the creation of this prayerbook. Rabbi Malcolm Stern served as Secretary of the Committee and as a most helpful advisor. Rabbi James R. Michaels assisted the Editor and Rabbi Dreyfus with the proofreading in the early stages of the work. Rabbi Elliot Stevens was most helpful in a number of matters related to preparation of the volume for publication. Rabbi Joseph B. Glaser was always available for counsel and assistance. All these have earned the gratitude of the Conference.

In addition to those named in *Shaarei Tefillah*, pp. xvi–xvii, the Committee and Conference thank the following persons, whose suggestions were helpful to the Editor: Rabbis Elyse Goldstein, Philip Horowitz, Peter Knobel, Robert Levine, Simeon J. Maslin, W. Gunther Plaut, and Bernard Taylor; Mr. Michael Isaacson. The present volume owes much to two previous works: *Service of the Heart* (Union of Liberal and Progressive Synagogues, London, 1967, edited by John Rayner and Chaim Stern), especially to the section entitled 'Supplements for Home and Synagogue'; and the *Union Home Prayerbook* (Central Conference of American Rabbis, 1951).

Every effort has been made to ascertain the owners of copyrights for the selections used in this volume, and to obtain permission to reprint copyrighted passages. For the use of the passages indicated, the Central Conference of American Rabbis expresses its gratitude to those whose names appear below. The Conference will be pleased, in subsequent editions, to correct any inadvertent errors or omissions that may be pointed out.

ATHENEUM PUBLISHERS: From *The Hard Hours*, by Anthony Hecht. Copyright © 1967 by Anthony E. Hecht. Reprinted by permission of Atheneum Publishers.

BEACON PRESS: From *Great Occasions*, ed. by Carl Seaburg, and from *Cries of the Spirit*, ed. by Marylin Sewell.

BIBLIO PRESS: from *Written out of History*, by Sandra Henry and Emily Taitz.

CAMBRIDGE UNIVERSITY PRESS: From *The New English Bible*. Copyright © The Delegates of the Oxford University Press and the Syndics of the Cambridge University Press 1961, 1970. Reprinted by permission.

COLLINS PUBLISHERS, LTD.: From *Ardours and Endurance*, by Robert Nichols, 1917.

FARRAR, STRAUSS & GIROUX, INC.: From *O The Chimneys*, by Nelly Sachs, Copyright, 1967, poems on pp. 3, 9, 29–30, 61, 65–66, and from *God in Search of Man*, by Abraham J. Heschel.

HARCOURT BRACE JOVANOVICH, INC.: 'i thank you god.' Copyright, 1950, by e.e. cummings. Reprinted from his volume, *Complete Poems 1913–1962*, by permission of Harcourt Brace Jovanovich, Inc.

HARPER AND ROW PUBLISHERS: From *The Enlightened Heart*, ed. by Stephen Mitchell; from *Earth Prayers from Around the World*, ed. by Elizabeth Roberts and Elias Amidon; and from *The Art of Loving*, by Erich Fromm.

HARTMORE HOUSE: From *A Treasury of Comfort*, ed. by Sidney Greenberg.

THE JEWISH PUBLICATION SOCIETY OF AMERICA: From *The Torah* and *Psalms* for occasional use of the translation.

JEWISH RECONSTRUCTIONIST FOUNDATION, INC.: From *The Reconstructionist Sabbath Prayerbook*, and from *When Children Ask About God*, by Harold Kushner.

KTAV PUBLISHING HOUSE, INC.: From J.J. Petuchowski, ed., *Understanding Jewish Prayer*, 1972.

LITTLE, BROWN AND COMPANY: From *The Complete Poems of Emily Dickinson*, ed. by Thomas H. Johnson.

MACMILLAN PUBLISHING CO. INC.: From *Poems*, by John Masefield. Copyright 1916 by John Masefield, renewed 1944 by John Masefield; Reprinted by permission of Macmillan Publishing Co. Inc.

MENTOR BOOKS, N.Y.: From *Jewish-American Literture: An Anthology*, ed. by A. Chapman.

THE MOVEMENT FOR PROGRESSIVE JUDAISM IN ISRAEL: From *Ha-avodah she-balev (The Service of the Heart)*.

THE NATIONAL COUNCIL OF CHURCHES: *Revised Standard Version of the Bible*, for occasional use of the translation.

NEW DIRECTIONS PUBLISHING CORPORATION: Denise Levertov, *The Jacob's Ladder*. Copyright 1961 by Denise Levertov Goodman, and Charles Reznikoff, *By the Waters of Manhattan*. Copyright 1951 by Charles Reznikoff. Both selections are reprinted by permission of New Directions Publishing Corporation and the San Francisco Review.

OXFORD UNIVERSITY PRESS: From *A Book of Jewish Thoughts*, selected and arranged by J.H. Hertz.

PAULIST PRESS: From *Your Word is Fire*, ed. by Arthur Green and Barry W. Holtz.

PENGUIN BOOKS: From *The Penguin Book of Modern Jewish Verse*, ed. by I. Howe, R.R. Wisse, and K. Shmeruk.

RANDOM HOUSE, INC.: 'I think continually of those ...' is reprinted from *Selected Poems* by Stephen Spender, by permission of Random House, Inc., 1934, and from *Poems*, by Wallace Stevens (Vintage Books).

RICHARD CLAY AND COMPANY LIMITED: From *From Darkness to Light*, ed. by Victor Gollancz.

THE SEABURY PRESS: From *Prayer and Modern Man*, by Jacques Ellul, trsl. by Edward Hoplein.

THOMAS Y. CROWELL COMPANY, N.Y.: From *Poems from the Hebrew*, selected by Robert Mezey. Copyright 1973 by the editor. Hebrew copyright by ACUM, Ltd. of Tel Aviv.

THE UNIVERSITY OF CALIFORNIA PRESS: From *Modern Hebrew Poetry*, selected and translated by Ruth Finer Mintz, Copyright © 1966. Originally published by the

ACKNOWLEDGMENTS

University of California Press; reprinted by permission of The Regents of the University of California.

THE UNIVERSITY OF CHICAGO PRESS: From *The Next Room of the Dream: Poems and Two Plays*. Copyright 1962 by Howard Nemerov, and from *The Guide of the Perplexed*, trsl. with an Introduction and Notes by Shlomo Pines, © Copyright 1963 by The University of Chicago Press.

THE STANFORD UNIVERSITY PRESS: From *The Complete Works of Montaigne*, trsl. by Donald Frame, © Copyright 1948, 1957, by the Trustees of Leland Stanford University.

THE VIKING PRESS/PENGUIN BOOKS: From *The Penguin Book of Modern Jewish Verse*, ed. by I. Howe, R.R. Wisse, and K. Shmeruk, and from *The Penguin Book of Hebrew Verse*, ed. and trsl. by T. Carmi.